MERCHANTS AND THE MILITARY IN EIGHTEENTH-CENTURY BRITAIN: BRITISH ARMY CONTRACTS AND DOMESTIC SUPPLY, 1739–1763

In memory of my mother and father

MERCHANTS AND THE MILITARY IN EIGHTEENTH-CENTURY BRITAIN: BRITISH ARMY CONTRACTS AND DOMESTIC SUPPLY, 1739–1763

BY

Gordon E. Bannerman

LONDON
PICKERING & CHATTO
2008

Published by Pickering & Chatto (Publishers) Limited
21 Bloomsbury Way, London WC1A 2TH

2252 Ridge Road, Brookfield, Vermont 05036-9704, USA

www.pickeringchatto.com

All rights reserved.
No part of this publication may be reproduced,
stored in a retrieval system, or transmitted in any form or by any means,
electronic, mechanical, photocopying, recording, or otherwise
without prior permission of the publisher.

© Pickering & Chatto 2008
© Gordon E. Bannerman 2008

BRITISH LIBRARY CATALOGUING IN PUBLICATION DATA

Bannerman, Gordon
Merchants and the military in eighteenth-century Britain: British Army contracts and domestic supply, 1739-1763
1. Great Britain. Army – Procurement – History – 18th century 2. Great Britain. Army – Supplies and stores – History – 18th century 3. Great Britain. Army – Equipment – History – 18th century 4. Military-industrial complex – Great Britain – History – 18th century
I. Title
355.6'212'0941'09033

ISBN-13: 9781851969371

This publication is printed on acid-free paper that conforms to the American National Standard for the Permanence of Paper for Printed Library Materials.

Typeset by Pickering & Chatto (Publishers) Limited
Printed in the United Kingdom at Athenaeum Press Ltd., Gateshead, Tyne & Wear

CONTENTS

Acknowledgements	vi
List of Abbreviations	vii
List of Tables	ix
Note on Dates	x
Introduction	1
1 The Supply System of the British Army from the Seventeenth Century	7
2 The Growth of Army Contracting	23
3 Procedures and Patronage	41
4 Administration of Encampment Contracts in England, 1740–62	59
5 Performance of Encampment Contracts	73
6 A Domestic Contractor: John Willan	89
7 Domestic Supply and Contracting in Scotland, 1746–62	103
8 Profit and Wealth	121
Conclusion	139
Appendix A: Sample of Army Contractors in Britain	151
Appendix B: The Legacy	157
Appendix C: The Business Life of Contractors	159
Appendix D: Property-Holding	161
Notes	163
Works Cited	235
Index	255

ACKNOWLEDGEMENTS

I wish to thank the Trustees of the Paul Woodhouse Scholarship Fund, in particular Peter Willan, whose funds made the thesis on which this book is based possible. I also wish to thank the School of Humanities, King's College London, for financial assistance towards research outside London. The British Library of Political and Economic Science, an outstanding research library, provided a wealth of invaluable material. The staff at the National Archives, British Library, Bank of England archives, Guildhall library, Westminster City archives, and King's College library provided material with courtesy and efficiency. Outside London, the North Yorkshire, East Suffolk, and Essex County Record Offices, the Manuscripts Department of Nottingham University Library, National Archives of Scotland, and the National Library of Scotland were particularly helpful.

I was privileged to receive expert advice, encouragement and supervision from Professor David McLean of King's College London. Professor Anthony Howe and Dr Cheryl Schonhardt-Bailey were always willing to offer advice and encouragement. I will not forget their kindness and generosity. I wish to thank Professor Stephen Conway and Professor John Childs of Leeds University for their helpful advice and constructive criticism. I also wish to thank Professor Miles Taylor for his encouragement and enthusiasm, and Professor McLean and Professor Andrew Porter of King's College London for presenting me with the opportunity to undertake the research project. I wish to express my warm thanks to my sisters Audrey and Dorothy for their help over the years and, most importantly, to Samantha for being there.

I wish to thank the Duke of Buccleuch for permission to consult the Townshend papers from the Buccleuch muniments in the National Archives of Scotland, and Mr Peter Willan for permitting use of material in the Willan family archive.

LIST OF ABBREVIATIONS

British Library, London

BL, Add. MS: Additional Manuscripts [Newcastle Papers unless stated]

National Archives (PRO), London

PRO, Adm.: Admiralty papers
PRO, AO 1: Audit Office declared accounts
PRO, AO 17: Comptrollers of Army Accounts minutes
PRO, C: Chancery proceedings
PRO 30/8/: Chatham papers
PRO, T 1: Treasury papers
PRO, T 27: Treasury out-letters
PRO, T 29: Treasury minutes
PRO, SP: State papers
PRO, WO 1: War Office in-letters
PRO, WO 4: War Office out-letters
PRO, PROB: Probate wills and registers

Other collections

RA Cumberland: Duke of Cumberland papers, Royal Archive, Windsor
NeC: Newcastle Papers, (Clumber), Manuscripts Department, Nottingham University Library
NLS MS: National Library of Scotland Manuscripts
NAS: National Archives of Scotland
WFA: Willan Family Archive
ZA: Zetland Archive, North Yorkshire County Record Office

Printed Sources

CTB: Calendar of Treasury Books
CTBP: Calendar of Treasury Books and Papers
CTP: Calendar of Treasury Papers
GM: Gentleman's Magazine
HCJ: House of Commons Journals
HMC: Historical Manuscripts Commission
LG: London Gazette
ODNB: Oxford Dictionary of National Biography
Cobbett, *PHE*: William Cobbett, *Parliamentary History of England*
Hansard, *PD*: Hansard, *Parliamentary Debates*
PP: Parliamentary Papers
JCTP: Journals of the Commissioners for Trade and Plantations
JSAHR: Journal of the Society for Army Historical Research

LIST OF TABLES

1.1	Army Expenditure 1738–63: Select Years	7
1.2	Supply Granted, 1747–60	14
1.3	Distribution of Taxation, 1756–63	19
5.1	Approximate Number of Troops in 1756 Encampments	77
5.2	Payment for Encampment Contracts, 1756–62	87
5.3	Total Supplies to Encampments, 1756–62	88
5.4	Prices for Encampment Articles	88
5.5	Volume of Encampment Articles, 1756–62	88
5.6	Total Weight of Encampment Articles, 1756–62	88
6.1	Sums Received for 1759 Encampment Contract	94
6.2	Approximate Costs of 1759 Encampment Contract	95
6.3	Division of Contract for Artillery Horses, 1760–2	97
7.1	Forces in Great Britain, 1742–8	107
A.1	Age at First Contract and on Entering Parliament	151
A.2	Age Groups at First Contract and on Entering Parliament	151
A.3	Duration of Parliamentary Career	153
A.4	Location of Seats by County	154
A.5	Constituencies of Contractors	154
C.1	Contractors and Chartered Companies	159

Except where directly relevant, sums of money have been rounded off, with shillings and pence deleted.

NOTE ON DATES

Dates given are those on correspondence; that is, letters from Continental Europe before 1752 are dated eleven days earlier than those from Britain. Years are treated as beginning on 1 January, not 25 March.

INTRODUCTION

Modern scholarship has convincingly portrayed the extent to which eighteenth-century British governments presided over a newly created 'fiscal military state'. Incorporating the ability of government to harness private capital and credit for state purposes, this conceptual framework has become firmly embedded in eighteenth-century historiography.[1] As the 'fiscal military state' evolved, indeed existed in order to finance war, it is remarkable that military contracting, an area in a sense at the nexus of the fiscal military structure, has received little scholarly attention. This is particularly notable since military victories were largely a question of money rather than men.[2] In the eighteenth century, British military success was not achieved by force of arms alone but was underpinned by sophisticated administrative, financial and economic organization.[3] This organization encompassed an efficient military supply system. The limited parameters of eighteenth-century government meant that the complexity of supplying a large army was assuaged by contracting out supply to private enterprise. In effect, the state used financial power to purchase expertise in economic organization. This privatization of supply was not new but by the mid-eighteenth century was more extensive than any previous period.[4]

The resources at the disposal of contractors were thus a central component of the war-making capacity of the state.[5] Whilst a number of historians working in different fields have acknowledged the importance of contractors in these terms, such scholarly diversity is indicative of the variability of historical analysis of contractors, as well as the somewhat contingent nature of contracting.[6] It is perhaps fitting that as perhaps the greatest 'middlemen' of the eighteenth century the economic functions of contractors have contributed towards their historiographical status. The multiple capacities and separate spheres of activity in which contractors were engaged have led to analytical compartmentalization. For political historians, contract allocation and the connections of elite contractors represent a component of the politics of patronage and place. Indeed, historical comment upon contractors has been overwhelmingly concerned with rooting out abuses from the body politic, or in defining contractors as clients of the aristocratic political elite.[7] Allusions to 'Old Corruption' are common whenever contractors are cited in such works, arising from Namier's observation that contracts were the 'places' of merchants'.[8] Amongst military historians, there is a tendency to discuss contracting when logistical dilemmas imposed restrictions on strategic decisions and military operations, and the strategic constraints that provisioning armies imposed on military campaigns has been fully acknowledged.[9] Whilst it has been asserted that the logistics of supply 'dwarfed all other factors in making late seventeenth century armies lethargic in movement and unimaginative in strategy', most studies of this nature focus on either the difficulties of particular campaigns or economic and administrative developments over a long period, and in several countries.[10]

In political and strategic studies, British army contractors are subject to varying degrees of criticism. In some cases, this is justified; in others, it is not. Political partisanship and deeply-rooted preconceptions are fundamental problems of historical scholarship relative to contractors. Yet there were sectors of military supply, particularly domestic contracts for encampments and horses, where most contractors were not Members of Parliament and where patronage in contract allocation was, if not negligible, far less important. The relative neglect of these sectors has arisen from an exaggerated linkage between political connection and contract allocation. Whilst such connections cannot be ignored it is incorrect to assume that the entire system of contracting for the British army was informed by this relationship.[11] Similarly, whilst strategic studies form the basis for examining the evolution of military supply, it is impossible to assess the economic activities of contractors, the resources at their disposal, and the type of men they were, without narrowing the analysis.

In examining British army contractors between 1739 and 1763 it is therefore appropriate to address the aforementioned historiographical imbalance by concentrating largely but not exclusively on previously neglected sectors. The supply of basic necessities such as bread, forage, fuel and horses were particularly vital, for they directly affected the operational efficiency of the army on a daily basis. Despite or perhaps because of the multi-faceted nature of contracting, only relatively recently have attempts been made to examine these sectors.[12] These studies have demonstrated the difficulties that could beset the actual performance of contracts, whilst also implicitly indicating that contractors in this sector were from a different social milieu from elite financiers and London merchants. The latter groups dominated financial and victualling contracts for colonial garrisons. Higher social status should not be equated with economic or military importance, for contractors supplying troops in field and camps were equally if not more important to military effectiveness. Despite a divergence in economic function and social status, all contractors possessed many similar attributes, notably reserves of capital and credit allied to business experience and expertise. Together, these qualities constituted an impressive reservoir of commercial ability at the service of government. Whilst the absence of wartime requisitioning in Britain has been interpreted as resulting in the state competing with the private sector for resources, state employment of contractors effectively utilized private sector expertise.[13] War in the eighteenth century saw the state become 'the largest single actor in the economy'.[14] With supply operations conducted on an unprecedented scale, contractors operated on a scale far in excess of the normal demands of a largely localized agrarian and proto-industrial economy. This factor alone justifies examination of contracting as a central component of state economic organization. Encompassing the War of Austrian Succession, Jacobite Rebellion, and Seven Years' War, the period 1739–63 witnessed a substantial increase in the number of contracts. Heightened military demands necessitated expansive supply operations and a higher degree of administrative organization and cooperation. Consequently, this period not only demonstrates the economic capability and capacity of contractors, but is also noteworthy for significant developments in the administrative apparatus governing military supply. Not for the first or last time, war was a forcing house for change.

A sectoral approach to contracting is necessary, for analysis of all sectors of the armed forces would be beyond the scope of a single scholar. Nevertheless, such an approach can only be useful when assessed against a wider examination of military contracts. Thus, whilst this study predominantly concerns contracts for 'non-military' material such as bread, forage, fuel and horses, as opposed to 'military' materiel, other types of contract will be considered.[15] This is necessary in order to provide the basis of contextual and comparative analysis, for there were various sectors in the military supply system, and personnel, procedures and practices differed in each sector. Broadly speaking, there were differences in economic organization between contracts for military materiel and those for provisions. Whilst the latter were dominated by merchants and tradesmen, the former were the preserve of nascent industrialists.[16]

Whilst the core of the book is concerned with the economic and administrative organization surrounding domestic military supply, in order to provide the context for analysis of domestic contracting, the first three chapters examine the historical background of the military supply system. In detailing the complex and somewhat disorganized evolution of military supply from the seventeenth century to the mid-eighteenth century, the introductory chapter indicates that contractors represented something of a coordinating element within a complex multi-agency supply system. Financial, logistical, strategic and constitutional issues all impacted on and influenced the nature of supply, and assessment of each factor forms the basis for the detailed discussion in Chapter 2 into why contracting emerged as the most rational and effective supply method in the eighteenth century. Whilst long-term factors continued to influence the contours of the eighteenth-century supply system, more immediate factors account for the growth of contracting. Most obviously, Britain's emergence as a major commercial and imperial power in the international state system, and her involvement in two major conflicts in the mid-eighteenth century formed the basis for deployment of a large military force. Short-term practical considerations such as government inexperience, allied to the successful performance of European and colonial contracts recommended contracting as a reliable supply method. Reliability was of some importance amidst the extensive warfare of the mid-eighteenth century, with the period 1739–48 particularly important in terms of administrative experience and continuity of personnel. The extent to which contractors provided much-needed state infrastructure indicates the complexity and scale of global military activity, whilst the successful performance of most contracts, in the face of great difficulties, demonstrates that the system attained a high degree of efficiency.

The administrative organization, procedures of awarding contracts and terms and conditions under which foreign victualling and remittance contracts were performed are the subjects of Chapter 3. An assessment is made as to how far Treasury contract administration was a component of 'Old Corruption'. Particular emphasis is given to mercantile portfolios and the extent to which contractors were qualified to perform contracts. This factor appears at least equally important as patronage in determining personnel. Whilst patronage clearly informed contract allocation in this sector, competition was not excluded, and patronage did not equate with inefficiency or unsuitability. Although not wholly successful, the Treasury's adoption of stringent terms and conditions as a means to curb expenditure and eliminate fraud and collusion indicates that contracts were never viewed as a form of outdoor relief to political friends.

Chapter 4 addresses similar issues relative to contracts for the army in field or camp, whilst examining the wider administrative organization of English encampments between 1740 and 1762. In this sector, marked differences in administrative organization and personnel are notable, with patronage less important and a more explicit concern for economy apparent. Continuity in personnel and a heightened degree of administrative experience are notable features of this sector in the mid-eighteenth century. Chapter 5 continues examination of this sector by assessing contract performance, with particular reference to English encampments during the Seven Years' War. In examining products supplied and the timing of deliveries and distribution, it is readily apparent that these contracts required a higher degree of management than foreign victualling or remittance contracts. The success of government and contractors in meeting unprecedented demands reveals a degree of administrative innovation and business expertise rather than extensive experience, for as the account of encampments before 1756 demonstrates, this was a rather unfamiliar form of supply in

Britain. Overall administrative and economic competence is apparent from the rarity of supply failure, and the reasonable cost of contracts.

Chapter 6 continues analysis of encampment supply with a case study of the contractor John Willan, whose activities demonstrate the lucrative nature of government contracting, whilst also indicating that much of his success was based on hard work, business expertise, and the assumption of considerable responsibility. As a contractor outside Parliament, Willan can to some degree be viewed as representative of a type of contractor who rarely features in historical works, but whose activities were of fundamental importance in military supply. These themes also permeate Chapter 7, which examines military supply in Scotland between 1745 and 1762. The military experience of Scotland in this period was very different to that of England, and justifies separate examination. The unique circumstances of the 1745 Rebellion imparted a distinctive colouring to the Scottish supply system in the following years. Loyalty to the Hanoverian dynasty was a more overt factor in determining contracting personnel. Moreover, distance from London, and ignorance of Scottish conditions, led to considerable decentralization and allowed military commanders to assume an important role in conducting or supervising supply operations. Despite these differences, the effectiveness of the supply system under the pressure of unprecedented domestic military mobilization was a feature common to both countries.

Chapter 8 returns to a broader theme, by examining the relationship between contracting, profitability, wealth creation and social mobility in the eighteenth century. There are several reasons to justify shifting the analysis towards these issues. Firstly, such examination, by assessing all types of contractors, illustrates the broad differences between sectors, and assesses the comparative importance of contracts towards wealth creation. Secondly, the relationship between contracting and wealth creation was controversial in the eighteenth century, and recent scholarly interest in identifying the sources and nature of wealth creation in Britain make such an examination particularly pertinent. A prevalent historical assumption exists which posits possession of contracts as an assured and rapid route towards vast riches. Whilst accepting that contracts were profitable, this chapter argues that a simple equation between mere possession of contracts and vast riches is untenable. There are very simple reasons for this. For most contractors, contracting represented only one form of economic activity in a wider mercantile portfolio. Moreover, in performing contracts, an array of factors including economic volition, risk, and good fortune all affected levels of profitability.

The concluding chapter contains an overall assessment of contracting in the mid-eighteenth century, and argues that although it was not always the most economical mode of supply there were few viable alternatives. The concerns of government did not in any case relate simply to cost, but encompassed reliability and efficiency. The successful formula for achieving these objectives encompassed mercantile expertise, sound finance, and reasonable profitability. Greater reliance on contractors reflected the inability of the state's administrative apparatus to keep pace with the burgeoning size of armies. Although the cost of alternative supply methods is impossible to assess in terms of military efficiency, the disasters of the Commissariat in Ireland at the end of the seventeenth century and in Germany during the Seven Years' War, indicate it may have been high. There were of course supply failures under contract but variability in contract performance was an inherent and inevitable feature of a system reliant on thousands of people performing separate tasks.

The fundamental requirement of an effective military force is that it does not starve. This rarely happened to the British army. Despite administrative deficiencies emanating from inexperience, shortages of qualified personnel, and supply difficulties arising from the sheer weight of demands imposed on contractors, the mid-eighteenth century supply system functioned remarkably well. The privatization of military supply meant the personal and business attributes of contractors were fundamentally important in determining the efficiency of the system. Remarkably, their contribution has been little acknowledged. This is almost certainly a consequence of the tension arising from performing contracts in the national interest whilst making private profit, and a pervasive, though largely misguided, suspicion of the rapacious sacrifice of the former for the latter. Effectively an unofficial adjunct of the eighteenth-century army, contractors made a significant contribution towards British military organization, and upon this much military success depended.

1 THE SUPPLY SYSTEM OF THE BRITISH ARMY FROM THE SEVENTEENTH CENTURY

The mid-eighteenth century was a period of extensive British military activity.[1] From 1739 several conflicts emerged and coalesced[2] to form the basis, except for an uneasy truce between 1748 and 1754, of Anglo-Spanish, and particularly Anglo-French conflict until 1763. The increase in military expenditure during this period (Table 1.1) is particularly notable since Britain fought no major wars in the period 1713–39.

[Table 1.1: Army Expenditure, 1738–63: Select Years[3]]

Year	Expenditure
1738	£845,944
1739	£1,066,284
1740	£1,417,874
1741	£1,775,854
1742	£2,522,716
1743	£2,878,411
1744	£3,226,675
1745	£2,790,226
1754	£1,070,731
1755	£1,399,391
1756	£2,395,716
1757	£3,210,227
1758	£4,585,589
1759	£5,743,536
1760	£8,249,276
1761	£9,922,959
1762	£8,780,601
1763	£4,067,118

Larger armies and a lengthy period of conflict were essential prerequisites towards the employment of contractors.[4] As wars occasioned an augmentation of military forces 'merchants and contractors have always been introduced into the army when war has been declared'.[5] That it was contractors rather than state officials who conducted supply operations requires explanation. From the late seventeenth century, escalating military and financial demands induced European states accustomed to small armies and limited warfare to turn towards contractors to resolve supply problems and logistical dilemmas.[6] In Europe, state officials and military officers assumed a larger role in military supply, although 'military enterprisers', officers raising armies under contract, were in decline by the eighteenth century. State assumption of these responsibilities led to officers diversifying in supplying accoutrements such as clothes and horses.[7] In Britain, there was no such official involvement in supply. Whilst this may have owed something to associations with Continental absolutism it appears more likely to have arisen from the intermittent existence of the army. As early as the sixteenth century, 'spasmodic demand' has been noted as an inhibiting factor towards the formation of a supply corps.[8] Directives against officers and troops selling provisions were issued in the seventeenth and eighteenth centuries, and a state supply organization (Commissariat), employing commissaries, salaried officers managing procurement, was not a consistent feature of British military organization.[9] Constitutional restrictions may have reinforced the absence of official organization and in this sense affected the evolution and contours of the supply system. Whilst the cause of this lacuna is open to debate, the result appears sufficiently clear. The eighteenth-century British state was ill-equipped to meet escalating military demands through their own supply organizations because these simply did not exist.

The absence of supply organization and concomitant reliance on contractors was not unique to Britain. France and Austria also employed contractors, thus indicating the inability of eighteenth-century states to provide an administrative framework capable of meeting the requirements of larger armies.[10] That private enterprise should perform such essential work is somewhat remarkable. It was not that the state failed to recognize the enhanced role it had to play commensurate with a quantitative shift in military demands. For example, the formation of a long-term credit structure, the centralization of government fiscal policy, and greater efficiency in raising revenue and collecting taxation were largely responses towards meeting higher levels of military expenditure. The sophisticated financial apparatus of government did not extend to military administration, where a bewildering array of departments and private individuals were involved in military supply.[11] The irrationality of the eighteenth-century supply system, when considered alongside the modernized fiscal structure, illustrates the limitations of the organizational abilities and reforming instincts of the 'fiscal military state'. Private individuals had a role to play within the fiscal military structure, and army contracts were an area where such individual expertise was exercised.[12]

From the late sixteenth century, technological progress and a revolution in strategic thought led to larger armies, notably in the early eighteenth century.[13] Larger armies impacted on Anglo-French dynastic and commercial conflict to extend warfare from European theatres to a global stage.[14] In discussing recruitment in 1761, Lord Barrington illustrated how far this development had gone:

Both are liable to great difficulties and objections; but where 150,000 British subjects wear Red Coats either on Shoar or aboard the fleet, (tho' the great Duke of Marlborough thought 70,000 the utmost we could raise) no means of recruiting them should pass without due consideration.[15]

It was the type as well as the scale of warfare that facilitated greater opportunities for contractors. Armies were deployed according to strategic thought which emphasized the importance of avoiding battle until a clear and perceptible advantage was obtained. Siege warfare rather than battles predominated, with even the Duke of Marlborough fighting only four battles compared with conducting thirty sieges.[16] Translated into military operations, the emergence of this strategic thought, alongside enhanced firepower and military capability has often been termed a 'Military Revolution'. Although precise dating is impossible, by the late seventeenth century contemporaries appeared aware of a transformation in the nature of warfare.[17] In 1677, Roger Boyle in *A Treatise on the Art of War* claimed 'Battells do not now decide national quarrels ... For we make war more like foxes, than like lyons; and you will have twenty sieges for one battell'.[18]

A revolution in arms production and development underpinned and facilitated this transformation. In battle, the strategic uses of firepower replaced headlong charges and hand-to-hand combat.[19] Contemporaries recognized that a more static form of warfare conducted by a larger number of troops, resulting in longer campaigns and greater expense, tested the economic condition and resources of combatant nations as much as the fighting qualities of men or leadership qualities of officers. These factors were linked, for inability to concentrate a sufficiently large number of troops to gain decisive victories meant prolonged hostilities and greater expense, which in turn raised acute logistical problems.[20] In earlier centuries, three supply methods have been identified: government victualling, private contracting and living off the country.[21] Throughout Europe, the latter method was most common, with armies living off the produce of surrounding areas by foraging (gathering hay for horses), or by imposing contributions on localities.[22] Lest the areas in question became quickly exhausted, sutlers 'not exactly under contract nor exactly independent traders', followed the army and sold their wares.[23] Such supply methods were recognized in the bureaucratic structure of English military administration, where during the Elizabethan period a 'Forage Master' supervised foraging parties.[24] An element of state compulsion existed, through the Crown's feudal rights of purveyance and preemption, that is, the privilege of obtaining supplies and transport for the Royal Household at prices below market rates.[25] Neither the abandonment of these feudal rights at the Restoration nor parliamentary control of the army led to systematic state involvement in military provisioning.[26] Nevertheless, whilst a degree of demilitarization occurred after 1660, England's heightened capacity for military and fiscal mobilization was an important legacy of the Cromwellian period.[27] Logistical difficulties in organizing supply on an extensive scale were readily apparent in provisioning the New Model Army. During the Naseby campaign, local procurement alone proved insufficient, and sutlers supplied the deficiency.[28] Although such informal methods were apposite for a period of small armies and short, highly mobile campaigns, they survived into the eighteenth century, although even in earlier centuries they were not always practical or reliable.[29] Generally, problems arose when armies remained stationary, for it was easier to provision armies that were encountering fresh sources of supply as they marched.[30] During the Civil War, centralized organization became necessary, with contracts made by a central body of six members of Parliament, and commissaries appointed to provide victuals, ammunition, draught horses and horse provisions.[31]

If the size and mobility of armies impacted on supply methods, inhospitable country also posed considerable problems. In the seventeenth century, Oliver Cromwell successfully provisioned troops in Ireland and Scotland by adopting methods suitable to prevailing conditions. With an insufficient quantity of local supplies, procurement from a wider geographical area was necessary. Cromwell therefore planned troop movements near the sea or navigable rivers, where English and Dutch supplies were landed.[32] When the Scottish campaign moved inland, General Monck simply provided troops with biscuit and cheese in knapsacks with additional quantities on packhorses. Alongside strategically placed garrisons, this method enabled an army of 6,000 to travel 1,600 kilometres.[33] The necessity for a degree of foresight and planning, however rudimentary, was readily appreciated, even when supplying a small army in inhospitable territory. These methods were suitable for a 'horde army' embarking on particular operations with limited objectives, and necessarily bore a makeshift character.[34] Neither the number of troops nor scale of operations demanded a more formal supply. When informal methods and short-term expedients sufficed, there was no need for contractors, far less a regular supply corps.

State planning of military provisioning was most apparent in France, where, building on the ideas of Cardinal Richelieu, Michel le Tellier and his son, the Marquis de Louvois, planned location of magazines stocked with non-perishable supplies at no more than one day's marching distance. Formal contracts replaced the 'multitude of ad hoc agreements' previously governing supply and the employment of official intendants alongside contractors represented a necessary intensification of state planning.[35] Le Tellier linked subsistence with military effectiveness, for 'to secure the livelihood of the soldier is to secure victory for the king'.[36] Magazine construction aimed at countering the devastation of local areas that often accompanied an army's presence. Establishing magazines was a supplement, not a substitute, to living off the land. With the prevailing military thought identifying the capture of towns and territory, and subsequently denial of subsistence to the enemy, as equally important to that of winning battles, it could not be otherwise.[37] Supply considerations, always important in strategic calculations, assumed heightened importance with magazine establishment contributing both towards secure subsistence of troops and prolongation of war.[38]

Despite the temporary centralization of supply during the Civil War, in Britain the idea of supply on an army-wide basis did not fully emerge until later in the century. The martial interests and knowledge of William III inaugurated a revolution in military supply. Amidst disastrous shortages and official peculation during the Irish campaign, the King abolished the Commissariat, and henceforth relied on wealthy Portuguese Jews as private contractors.[39] Possessing their first contract under William III in 1672, as Jews they enjoyed the privilege of being treated as neutrals by both French and Dutch. Their European mercantile experience, connections, and financial credit were exceptional, and men of equivalent experience and knowledge were not to be found in Britain. From William's expedition to England, through campaigns in Ireland and Europe, it was these 'Court Jews' who supplied bread, wagons and forage to the British army.[40] These items were always, because the most basic, necessary and extensive, the most problematic to supply.

In employing contractors, the King aimed for reliability within the supply system. It was fundamental to accountability that contractors, unlike commissaries, were only paid upon satisfactory performance. Moreover, with contracts made at set rates the approximate cost was known in advance. As salaried officers, commissaries procured supplies, and charged government in their accounts. Unless particularly conscientious, they had no incentive to curb expenditure. Commissaries were particularly important in military emergencies, when supply had to be established quickly on a local basis, such as Scotland in 1715 and 1745, or where the size of the army demanded extensive supply organization, such as Germany during the Seven Years' War.[41] The greater involvement of contractors within the supply system did not therefore mean commissaries were unnecessary, but their functions were redefined. Where no contracts were made, commissaries retained their position in supply management, but where contractors procured supplies, commissaries acted as a check in ensuring due performance of contracts.[42] As government officials, commissaries could not act as contractors, and were prohibited from profiting from the sale of provisions. The government stance towards military and civilian officials' involvement in managing procurement was simple:

> The Officer is a Trustee for the Public; as such, he is bound to husband the Public Money committed to his Charge with as much frugality as if it were his own; what he saves, or what he gains, he saves and gains not for himself, but for the Public.[43]

High salaries were paid to commissaries in order to bolster their trustworthiness.[44] By mid-century, the separate functions of contractors and commissaries were fairly well delineated, and government proved assiduous in ensuring a strict demarcation of duties was observed.[45] During the War of Spanish Succession the absence of a commissarial structure precluded the possibility of directing supply operations from Britain.[46] Deemed unnecessary in wartime, there was little prospect of a supply corps being established in peacetime. In abolishing the Commissariat, the King had taken a significant step towards determining the centrality of contractors within the eighteenth century supply system.[47]

The employment of contractors, whilst entailing the assumption of considerable responsibility, introduced a high degree of accountability. Although traditional methods of local procurement possessed strategic and military value in denying subsistence to the enemy, reliance on informal methods was increasingly untenable amidst the extensive warfare of the eighteenth century. Events such as the suppression of the 1715 Jacobite Rebellion were temporary campaigns with limited objectives. Local cooperation and procurement alongside traditional features of plundering, seizures and contributions characterized such campaigns.[48] Large-scale warfare was different, for there were campaigning seasons, larger armies and, above all time to organize supply.[49] For campaigning armies or garrisoned troops too numerous to live off local produce, contracts appeared a safer option.

Larger armies and higher military expenditure caused financial problems for Britain. In 1711 army debts amounted to £400,000, and although by 1717 the debt was reduced to £205,800, over one-tenth was owed to one contractor for bread and wagons.[50] With £569,000 expended on bread, wagons and forage between 1706 and 1713, basic necessities consumed a large proportion of the debt.[51] The worst case of indebtedness saw a contractor owed £126,000 in 1715 for forage supplied in 1711/12, but debts owing to contractors were a familiar feature of the system.[52] The burgeoning cost of war and 'Dutch finance' provoked much contemporary comment:

> I see nothing else in the modern way of making war, but that the side, which can hold out longest, will end it with most advantage ... If you will count upon sacrificing so much blood and treasure, the rest is all a regular, established method, which cannot fail.[53]

Although City 'monied men' were a target for Jonathan Swift's Tory invective, there was implicit acceptance that a higher degree of governmental organization was necessary, however deplorable, to meet the demands of modern warfare.[54] The importance of credit in sustaining the state's capacity to wage war constituted 'a tremendous relief' to governments in financial difficulties and facilitated the continuation of military operations.[55] In 1697, temporary inability to make payments jeopardized the entire credit structure, and required immediate payments to restore confidence.[56] Underpinning the provision of credit was confidence in the financial rectitude of the British state. For government, the quid pro quo in securing credit was payment of high rates in order to induce merchants to undertake business. Government made allowances for delays in payment, either with interest-bearing victualling bills as in the navy, or other financial devices.[57] The relationship between contract prices and delays in payment operated across all government departments connected with the armed forces. Requesting funds from the Treasury, the Ordnance Board indicated the importance of payment to contractors in reducing costs, for 'if we are not able to pay them 3 Months of their Arrear, we may with reason expect they will advance their Prices, which we have hitherto reduced as low as possible on a presumption we should not generally be more than 6 Months at a time indebted to them'.[58] A credit-based system required contractors capable of withstanding delays in payment, but credit amongst merchants could relieve difficulties. Naval suppliers often financed contracts by borrowing, and then assigned navy bills to lenders. With borrowing obviating delays in payment, small suppliers were not discouraged in performing contracts.[59] Various schemes aimed to remove the uncertain timing of repayment in order to allow government to negotiate better contract terms.[60] This was implicit recognition that such delays raised costs, whilst Treasury rejection of claims for interest on the basis of delays indicated tacit acceptance that contractors factored this into prices.[61] Whilst this method made contracts more expensive, it was effectively the price of utilizing the credit facilities of contractors for state purposes.[62]

Escalating military expenditure heightened the importance of credit. Constitutionally, the army was subject to parliamentary control and parliaments dominated by landowners were reluctant to embrace a large military establishment. In controlling military finance, the House of Commons could 'make or break armies at will'.[63] The Commons closely scrutinized annual army estimates whilst much larger, less detailed naval estimates passed with few dissenting voices.[64] Nevertheless, large majorities almost always attended army estimates, although amidst Whig divisions in 1717 the majority was only four votes.[65] Remarkably, the strict scrutiny of military expenditure was accompanied by acceptance of 'extraordinary expenditure', that is, expenditure incurred in the previous year exceeding the estimates voted by Parliament. The army was allowed the liberty to overspend and have the shortfall voted retrospectively. To many this appeared antithetical to the strict scrutiny of expenditure, even a defiance of parliamentary authority.[66] In 1729:

> Mr. Poltney took exception to that for services incurred not provided for by Parliament, as if it was now become an annual demand, and that the services should be mentioned before ... but answered by Secretary at War ... that it was impossible to

foresee some services the year before, and so a demand would happen in that case, and so it dropped.[67]

Presentation of military estimates and establishments was an overt demonstration of parliamentary control. However, governments were well-attuned to the concerns of country gentlemen and presented low estimates safe in the knowledge extraordinary expenditure would be voted in the following year.[68] An acute observer noted:

> It is worth observing that it has been the constant Policy of Government to contract the Estimated Expence of the Army, & to leave a Variety of Charges, not unforeseen or accidental, but fixed & regular, to be brought in with the Extraordinaries, by which the Publick, who have no Opportunity of knowing the Truth of the Matter, are deceived with respect to the real Expence of the Army, & the Ho. of Commons are in some Measure obliged to pay for Services already performed.[69]

Both views possessed some truth. Some services, national emergencies such as the outbreak of rebellions, clearly could not be foreseen. Nevertheless, between 1756 and 1762 amidst the most extensive war waged by Britain, a sufficiently clear indication that vast expenditure would be required, the disparity between parliamentary estimates and sums required assumed massive proportions.

[Table 1.2: Supply Granted, 1747–60[70]]

1748	£10,620,186
1749	£5,125,736
1750	£4,334,323
1751	£2,904,751
1752	£4,150,000
1753	£2,422,911
1754	£2,544,348
1755	£4,241,004
1756	£7,077,065
1757	£8,410,822
1758	£11,041,848
1759	£13,108,555
1760	£15,852,706

Between 21 November 1761 and 13 May 1762, sums of £1,353,662 and £958,384 were voted for extraordinary expenditure.[71] Between 1748 and 1754, annual average extraordinary expenditure, after deducting remaining payments of wartime accounts, amounted to £25,430. Such was the impact of war.[72] There were areas where expenditure could be foreseen, but where there was deliberate omission. Government reluctance to inflate military estimates played a part in this process, but constitutional restrictions, prohibiting the Secretary at War from presenting a realistic assessment of military expenditure, when precluded from including essential items such as transport, appears more significant.[73] Extraordinary expenditure existed to absorb all excess military expenditure not included in the estimates. The proper course for payment of unforeseen

regimental expenditure was by Contingent Bills. Although a sum for 'Contingencies' was included in the estimates, it was usually much lower than the final cost.[74] These expenses related to marching regiments who received allowances for carriage of ammunition, fire and candle, and officers' horses lost in service. The Secretary at War examined claims, and issued warrants for payment after thorough examination.[75]

Votes of Credit were another example of insufficient parliamentary funding.[76] This was money Parliament promised to set aside at its next session for the purpose of funding loans.[77] The amount and its application had to be specified, yet the regularity of Votes of Credit during the Seven Years' War indicates Parliament's acquiescence towards vast military expenditure.[78] Nevertheless, care was taken that the propriety of parliamentary authority was respected. Having received £1,000,000 by Vote of Credit in 1757 'to enable HM to defray Extraordinary Expenses of War', Lord Hardwicke advised the Duke of Newcastle the money could be applied to provisions for the Army of Observation. Although this army was not engaged in hostilities, Hardwicke considered extraordinary expenses incorporated 'all Incidents & Contingencies relative to that War'.[79] Similarly, issuing public money for defending Portugal could not occur until Parliament authorized expenditure for that purpose.[80] This was resolved by application for Vote of Credit 'to enter into such Engagements as the Situation of any of his Majesty's Allies may render expedient for his & their common Interest'.[81] Such a wide construction allowed parliamentary authority to be obtained for unprecedented sums, for extraordinary expenditure was frequently as high as the estimates.[82] In this unusual way, Parliament theoretically retained control of expenditure and held in reserve the power to withhold supply. Yet this never happened, and extraordinary expenditure remained a 'fathomless gulf of unappropriated expenditure'.[83]

Although military estimates were deliberately kept low, drastic demobilization after 1713 and a long period of peace until 1739 minimized the disparity between estimates and actual expenditure.[84] Whilst the 1715 Jacobite Rebellion produced a temporary increase, sharp reductions followed. Dramatic fluctuation between large wartime expenditure and drastic peacetime retrenchment was the familiar pattern of eighteenth-century military expenditure, but reductions were generally never so drastic as to reduce expenditure to pre-war levels.[85] This pattern of expenditure reflected the guiding principles of Walpolean foreign policy, of maintaining peace and relying on naval defence.[86] Inevitably, when hostilities threatened, rapid and extensive mobilization from a very low base was required. Nevertheless, military mobilization was viewed as a temporary expedient designed for reduction as soon as possible after cessation of hostilities. The expense of paying, feeding and accommodating a large army was frowned on, particularly when large sums were expended on the navy, the 'senior service' of the British military establishment.[87] To a large degree, geography dictated that the navy was viewed as the logical, natural, and permanent defence force.[88]

The practical question of cost was important, but no less so was the prejudice firmly enshrined within the Constitution against a standing army. Article VI of the 1689 Bill of Rights stipulated there was to be no peacetime army in England without parliamentary consent. From 1689, troop numbers, finance and military regulations were voted by Parliament in the annual Mutiny Acts. Strictly speaking, as the monarch's 'Guards and Garrisons' were the only troops authorized on the British military establishment, no peacetime army existed. Whilst providing a constitutional basis for weakening the army, no one seriously suggested Britain could completely dispense with a professional army.[89] In fact, parliamentary control appears to have made the concept of a standing army more acceptable.[90] Yet in 1730 the Speaker reminded the Commons that 'An occasional army is alone to be maintained in these realms. Know of no army that belongs to this country'.[91] The more overt militarization of the mid-eighteenth century and the emergence of the Duke of Cumberland as a strong military and political figure again raised fears of military despotism and military government.[92] Although somewhat hackneyed rhetoric, these sentiments continued to pervade debates concerning army augmentations, whilst Parliamentary authority ensured it was not merely rhetoric nor solely applied to the army.[93]

Underpinned by fear of a despotic monarch, the 1699 Disbanding Act (10 Wm III cap I) fixed the establishments of England and Ireland at 7,000 and 12,000 troops respectively.[94] Even after the huge augmentations of the mid-eighteenth century, the Attorney General considered that the Act remained in force, with Parliament remaining the sole authority permitting army augmentations.[95] Legislative sanction was therefore given to fixing the military establishment within safe boundaries and many military augmentations were tenaciously contested.[96] Parliamentary authority produced several damaging effects. With no Ministry of War there was a lack of central direction with separate bodies from the King to the Master General of the Ordnance involved in military affairs.[97] Supply was similarly affected. The singular nature of the army's supply organization is readily apparent on comparison with the navy, where the diverse needs of a large permanent establishment prompted a high degree of administrative and technical organization and a range of administrative bodies managing personnel and supply. The Navy Board, Victualling Office, and Sick and Wounded Office all operated under the Admiralty in separate spheres of authority with precise demarcation of functions and responsibilities. Although the Treasury regulated the funds issued to the navy they questioned neither its allocation nor the level of expenditure.[98] Procedural regularity was established in supply matters and considerable autonomy exercised in making contracts.[99] Administrative infrastructure was necessary for an organization whose peacetime existence was recognized to be of equal importance as during wartime.

On the face of things, the army appears not to have suffered from any administrative deficit. A multiplicity of offices and overlapping jurisdictions, variously explained as a consequence of historical accident or deliberate design underpinned by fear of military despotism, characterized military supply.[100] The War Office, Ordnance Board, and Treasury were all involved in administering men, materiel and victuals. Although demarcation of responsibility and authority was less clearly defined than naval administration, the division of responsibilities appears to have been generally understood. The responsibility of providing weaponry, gunpowder and artillery horses, alongside administering and maintaining barracks at home and abroad belonged to the Ordnance Board.[101] As with naval offices, specialization led to considerable autonomy. The Ordnance presented separate estimates of expenditure and made their own contracts through their Principal Officers.[102] As the repository of statistical, technical and financial information relating to the army, the War Office was effectively the coordinating centre of military administration, and its head, the Secretary at War, the 'chief officer of the military administration'.[103] The War Office conveyed orders and regulations from the King, Commander-in-Chief, and Secretaries of State to regimental officers whilst maintaining constant correspondence with government departments on military affairs. The Secretary at War accounted for items of expenditure to the Treasury and presented military estimates to Parliament.[104] The Secretary at War, rarely a senior political figure or of Cabinet rank, was subordinate to the Secretaries of State, who in consultation with senior military officers and the King decided on troop movement and strategy.[105] Nevertheless, familiarity with military administration made the Secretary of War much sought after in the practical execution of policy.[106] Possessing the most accurate information relating to military establishments and troop numbers, the War Office was frequently consulted by the Treasury when contracts were pending.[107] The War Office was involved in supervising supply at regimental level, although their responsibility for medical supplies was disputed and the legitimacy of their issuing directives to other departments was frequently a source of conflict.[108] Contracts for 'non-military' supplies, encompassing the most essential articles of money, bread, forage and fuel were the responsibility of the Treasury.[109] Control of these contracts appears to have arisen from the Treasury Board's financial authority, and the requirement of immediate payment for procuring provisions and supplying pay.[110] Wartime mobilization heightened demands for 'non-military' supplies and led to the Treasury assuming a more active role in military supply.[111]

It would be misleading to examine military administration purely in terms of government departments for divided responsibility did not stop here. A strong commander-in-chief wielded considerable influence in all military matters, including supply. Such authority was not inherent in the position but dependent on personal and political status. As Captain General, Cumberland's dominance of military affairs led to a diminution of War Office authority and initiative, but his successor John Ligonier possessed far less authority.[112] Lower rank officers were also involved in supply. The personal, proprietary nature of the eighteenth-century army meant it was as much a collection of regiments as a unified force.[113] In supply terms, this was particularly notable. Colonels appointed agents to their regiments who administered regimental funds received from the Pay Office. Colonels provided clothing for their regiments by deductions from the pay of each man, known as 'off reckonings', and as these were paid for the number of troops voted rather than those actually in service, they could profit from the differential.[114] On the Colonel's behalf, agents made contracts with clothiers or secured contracts themselves.[115] Colonels were also responsible for providing 'camp necessaries', with agents acting in the same capacity, on receiving directions from the War Office.[116]

Supply on a regimental basis illustrates the decentralized nature of the supply system but there were also many areas where considerable responsibility devolved on commanding officers in particular localities. This particularly applied to transport. As the army did not possess a transport corps, local hiring was necessary.[117] Before receiving local aid, it was necessary to obtain the permission of civil magistrates who required directions by War Office warrants. All arrangements with local suppliers were subject to the supervision of local constables.[118] Whilst local contractors or those hired by the Ordnance Board provided transport abroad, within Britain local impressment of transport and billeting of troops in public houses were provided under the Mutiny Act.[119] Even in the bloody battle against smuggling, the army was subject to the jurisdiction of civil magistrates and Customs Commissioners.[120] For troop movement within Britain, local impressment continued during the Seven Years' War, although contractors provided wagons for artillery trains and conveyance of bread and forage to camps.[121]

A similar local dimension, indicating the makeshift character of military organization was operative in accommodation arrangements. When the army was not encamped, troops were housed at inns and public houses where they paid regulated rates for provisions.[122] In 1757 the Mutiny Act widened local liability by empowering magistrates to quarter troops in the houses of retail wine-sellers.[123] The mass of petitions from innholders and victuallers in areas where troops were regularly quartered expressing weary exasperation at the number of men and horses imposed on them indicates that local quartering was considered a heavy and unjust burden.[124] Extensive barrack construction did not begin until the 1790s, and many problems of earlier wars were repeated later in the century.[125] That these basic though essential requirements were supplied in this way was symptomatic of a fundamental distrust of permanent military organization.[126]

Inevitably, higher military expenditure posed revenue problems.[127] Several European governments, including Britain, reformed the bureaucratic machinery of government in an attempt to match revenue with expenditure.[128] Table 3 illustrates the expansion of the tax base through higher customs duties and wider application of Excise duties. In this way, military expenditure was financed without raising the Land Tax to unacceptable levels.[129]

[Table 1.3: Distribution of Taxation, 1756–63 (£ millions)[130]]

Years	Customs	Excise	Land & Assessed Taxes	Total
1756	£1.699 (25.3%)	£3.649 (54.3%)	£1.375 (20.4%)	£6.723
1757	£1.872 (25.9%)	£3.303 (45.8%)	£2.043 (28.3%)	£7.218
1758	£1.918 (25.5%)	£3.477 (46.1%)	£2.139 (28.4%)	£7.534
1759	£1.830 (23.9%)	£3.615 (47.2%)	£2.216 (28.9%)	£7.661
1760	£2.113 (24.2%)	£4.218 (48.3%)	£2.407 (27.5%)	£8.738
1761	£2.191 (24%)	£4.671 (51.3%)	£2.253 (24.7%)	£9.115
1762	£1.824 (20.2%)	£4.816 (53.4%)	£2.386 (26.4%)	£9.026
1763	£2.283 (24.4%)	£4.793 (51.2%)	£2.288 (24.4%)	£9.364

Even with a formidable array of taxes recourse was had to loans, effectively deferred taxation, for they were repaid by taxes earmarked by Parliament.[131] State control of public finance was bolstered by the end of tax farming in the late seventeenth century, and efficient tax collection and an increasing number of indirect taxes to service the debt contributed towards investor confidence in the security of government loans.[132] In the period 1739–48, loans amounted to £24,620,000, but the corresponding figure for 1756–63 was £50,600,000.[133] A higher proportion of expenditure was borne by borrowing during the Seven Years' War than any previous conflict, and from the Seven Years' War to the wars with Revolutionary France, military expenditure and debt servicing never accounted for less than 90 per cent of net wartime expenditure.[134]

To 'Country' patriots, such activity represented an unpatriotic exploitation of national distress. Horace Walpole famously informed Horace Mann how 'merchants thrive by taxes, which ruin everybody else'.[135] The wartime profiteering of cosmopolitan financiers, 'sucking on the vitals of the nation', had long been, and continued to be resented:

> Pray consider, upon the foot you now are [sic], you certainly ruin those that have only land to depend on, to enrich Dutch, Jews, French and other foreigners, scoundrel stock-jobbers and tally-jobbers, who have been sucking our vitals for many years.[136]

Three elements contributed towards the unpopularity of those involved in government finance. Firstly, the participation of a considerable foreign element in loans and remittances inflamed patriotic opinion.[137] Secondly, the political connections of these men were more prominent and widely known than other contractors. Thirdly, loans and remittances were perceived to be most lucrative when the nation was making wartime sacrifices. Nevertheless, alongside such 'Country' views, there emerged an increasingly pragmatic view that the 'fiscal military state' was, by protecting English liberties against despotic foreign states, a necessary evil.[138] This outlook explains the acceptance rather than approval of parliament to increasing military expenditure, the emergence of a large bureaucracy, a wider tax base, and fortunes made by financiers. In financing military expenditure by an equitable, efficient expansion of the tax base, the state's ability to tax its citizens enhanced military capability.[139] The efficient collection of Excise and the successful floating of loans indicate public and private elements within the fiscal military structure, whilst administrative innovation in the navy and in customs and excise merely underline the naval and financial basis of the national security policy of the English state.[140] Whilst fiscal reform enhanced the war-making capacity of the state, there was no equivalent reform of military administration. Colonels maintained their privileged financial position whilst the notable lack of central organization meant the complexity of military supply and the labyrinthine nature of regimental finance continued into the nineteenth century.[141] Alongside the highly successful fiscal structure, this ramshackle administration appeared a standing affront to advocates of institutional rationalization and modernization.

The continuing impost on the country, supply on a regimental basis, and the respective responsibilities of the Ordnance, War Office and Treasury reflect the unusual administration of military supply, accurately described as derived from a curious admixture of official and unofficial sources.[142] Starving the army of permanent resources and forcing supply from a variety of ad hoc sources may have been viable in earlier periods with smaller armies. It was clearly inappropriate in an age of large standing armies. The mid-eighteenth century was the point when this immature administrative structure met the pressing need for efficient organization of large-scale provisioning. Informal supply methods remained useful and even necessary in emergencies, but were increasingly untenable as a primary mode of supply. It was recognized that the 'growth of an effective bureaucracy was an essential pre-requisite for the creation, control and supply of larger and better equipped armies', but reform of military organization was more notable in Europe than in Britain.[143] The modernity of the British state was underpinned by fiscal rather than military reforms. There was no desire, for financial and constitutional reasons, to establish a permanent supply organization. Translated into supply terms the effect was simple. With sutlers and local suppliers incapable of supplying a heavily concentrated domestic army and a widely dispersed army overseas, the employment of contractors was implicit recognition that the old methods would not suffice and that a higher degree of supply organization was required.[144] Nevertheless, there was a long way to go before permanent military supply organizations would be acceptable. In the interim, this meant greater reliance on contractors as a coordinating element within the supply system. Whilst this could be characterized as a typically British way of muddling through, there was clearly a rationale to such methods. Contractors possessed the expertise and resources to supply large armies, and with profit as an incentive, their employment was rational as well as necessary.

Contractors should therefore be viewed as an important element enhancing the military capability of the eighteenth century British state. The historical shift in emphasis from corrupt practices and pluralism associated with the Excise to the effects of efficient collection indicate the dangers of selective argument and a whiggish preoccupation with 'Old Corruption'.[145] A similar emphasis is applicable to contracting, where patronage, nepotism and abuses are noted as characteristic features. Whilst these elements clearly existed, the wider importance of contracting lay in meeting the heightened demands arising from British military activity and imperial expansion, and, it can be tentatively suggested, contributing towards British military success in the mid-eighteenth century.

This then was the political, fiscal and military context within which army contracting assumed greater importance. That these developments were to some degree obscured by the period of peace between 1713 and 1739 indicates, naturally enough, that a period of sustained warfare was necessary before the extent of government reliance on contractors became fully apparent. Large armies and heightened military activity raised supply difficulties for all states. In this sense, Britain was not unique. Yet whilst subject to similar logistical pressures as other states, Britain was distinctive in several ways. Most notably, this unmilitaristic nation found itself organizing an extensive and diverse military supply system.[146] It was the anti-militarism of the British state that fundamentally determined that contractors would profit from war, for the absence of state supply organizations left a large gap not only in providing provisions but also in planning and coordinating supply and providing supply infrastructure. Constitutional and financial constraints meant the state alone could not fulfil these functions. A fusion between constitutional status, financial necessity, and the need to resolve logistical dilemmas underpinned the shift towards contracting as a central component of the eighteenth-century supply system.

2 THE GROWTH OF ARMY CONTRACTING

In the eighteenth century no single factor made contracting the most viable or attractive supply method. At different times, different imperatives, pressures, and considerations assumed preponderance. Larger armies, global conflict and British territorial expansion to areas where traditional supply methods were inadequate were fundamentally important in this process. Equally, credit was important in easing the strain on state finances in the face of unprecedented military expenditure. A factor of some importance was governmental inexperience in acting as provider of goods. More positive were several successful examples of supply by contract in Europe and the colonies, with the War of Spanish Succession particularly influential.[1] Nevertheless, the latter type of supply only became operational with the existence of a large, concentrated army. This was not to be the case again until 1740. In the interim, developments in the supply of colonial garrisons indicated a tendency towards formal contracting.

Despite Britain's acquisition of North American and Mediterranean garrisons by the Treaty of Utrecht, only a small number of garrisoned troops were deployed. The largest garrisons, Gibraltar and Minorca, consisted of 2,500 and 1,500 men respectively in 1713, with small independent companies in the 'Plantations' of New York, Bermuda, Jamaica, Nova Scotia, and Newfoundland. Before the official cession of these garrisons, an informal system operated whereby military commanders made contracts locally, or the navy's Victualling Office supplied provisions. The former was unsatisfactory, for it was dependent on whether military officers could competently procure supplies of the requisite quality and quantity. Continual representations of shortages at Gibraltar indicated their inability to do so.[2] Warfare obstructed regular deliveries but towards the end of hostilities the Treasury sought to regularize supply, with the Victualling Office temporarily assuming responsibility.[3] The latter body recommended contracts, but although proposals were received, no contracts were made.[4] Facing continual problems, the Treasury eventually accepted Victualling Office recommendations relating to terms and conditions of victualling contracts. Proposals were made on the price of rations of one man per week. Additional regulations concerned quantity, quality, contract duration, and storehouses.[5] In the following years these recommendations formed the basis of the standard formula for receiving proposals and in determining terms and conditions.[6] Considering the exposed position of Gibraltar, an absence of adjacent sources of supply, and the intermittently hostile relationship with Spain, shipping a full range of provisions from Britain was prudent, for even after the peace of 1748 stipulated the garrison was to have access to neighbouring territories, this was not always adhered to.[7]

Minorca was easier to supply locally, and not subject to the prevarication and delays that blighted Gibraltar. In 1712, proposals were received and the Treasury appointed a Surveyor 'To settle a Method whereby the Garrison may be best served with Provisions'.[8] With plentiful harvests and secure trade and navigation, it was unnecessary to supply all provisions from Britain, although a contract for salted meat was concluded.[9] This pattern continued throughout the century, with bread and other provisions procured locally by the resident commissary.[10] Local conditions largely determined supply methods. Perilous conditions in North America prompted the Treasury to request the Victualling Office to supply garrisons at Annapolis Royal and Placentia.[11] Despite supplying these garrisons during 1713–15, the Victualling Office was dissatisfied with the arrangement, claiming a £157,000 debt for provisions supplied since 1710.[12] Troops endured hardships, partly through lack of planning but also by the actions of local inhabitants removing stock and cattle. Facing an area of low cultivation, officers argued that contracts should be made in Britain.[13] The Victualling Office continued supplying these garrisons until 1719, when the Commissary of Stores briefly assumed supply, purchasing provisions by drawing Bills of Exchange on the Paymaster.[14] A contract for a specific quantity of provisions at fixed rates was eventually made in 1721.[15] The continual representations of the Victualling Office that they were not responsible for supplying garrisons but only acted under particular direction indicated an administrative deficit in accountability and responsibility arising from an absence of clearly designated supply functions. The Victualling Office was responsible for provisioning troops on board ships but not in garrisons.[16] Later in the eighteenth century, whilst they remained an important provider of troops in recently captured territories, or in meeting sudden emergencies, in both cases this was viewed as a temporary expedient until contracts were concluded.[17]

Variable supply methods indicate that contracts were made when local supply arrangements broke down, but the shift towards garrison contracts in the period 1713–39 indicates an acceptance that contracts offered a higher degree of certainty in provisioning troops. This was a significant development. In making contracts at set rates, government avoided paying the inflated prices that commonly accompanied a military presence. There was a greater guarantee of an adequate supply of provisions, for it was not in the contractor's interest to default on the contract. Although shipping supplies risked capture at sea, naval protection provided a degree of security. Consistent with the mercantilist Navigation Laws, contracts stipulated purchase of provisions in Britain or the colonies and transportation in British ships, which enjoyed exemption from embargoes on provisions for foreign ports.[18] More positively, greater control could be exercised over nutritional quality. The variability in quality, quantity, and prices in diverging climates and economies made local supply potentially hazardous, and contracts a relatively safe and frequently cheap option. The parliamentary committee reviewing the army in 1746 adjudged price variability near garrisons as sufficient justification for continuing supply by contract.[19] In 1746, estimates for provisions in the Plantations, Gibraltar and Minorca amounted to £51,778; by 1760, Parliament voted, excluding Minorca, £141,609.[20] Warfare impacted on expenditure, but steady growth owing much to the intermittent Spanish threat to Gibraltar, occurred before 1739. By 1734–5 those provisioned numbered between 3,500 and 4,000, with the contractor receiving over £29,000 p.a.[21] Gibraltar contract expenditure increased from £184,782 between 20 December 1725 and 27 July 1731 to £206,245 between February 1734 and 13 July 1740.[22] Nevertheless, the necessity for contracts was always constrained by the continuation of peace.

The outbreak of war in 1739 occasioned a discernible shift towards contracting, in which the acquisition of colonial garrisons played a part. Contracting became the regular mode of victualling troops in North America.[23] The largest contract, for the captured Louisbourg garrison saw numbers victualled increase from 3,600 to 5,200.[24] Smaller contracts, for garrisons at New Providence, Placentia, Annapolis Royal and Canso and settlements at Georgia and Rattan, were more typical.[25] Procurement difficulties, emanating from the remoteness of garrisons led to a proliferation of contracts. At Rattan, the contractor supplied settlers with provisions for a year until food could be successfully cultivated.[26] Climate was also important. Cold winters meant coals and wood were necessary for firing. The Treasury accepted the contractor's proposals to supply these articles annually thus eliminating the risk to vessels belonging to the garrison.[27] Towards the end of the war, the Treasury directed 'for the future, when any Contract shall be made for the Victuallg of any Garrison, an Authentick Copy thereof be sent to the Governr'.[28] This directive indicates the relative novelty of supplying garrisons under contract, and the need to regularize procedures. A further indication of this shift occurred in 1751, with the Articles of War prohibiting officers, soldiers and sutlers from bringing provisions for which contracts had been made into garrisons, thus bolstering contractors' exclusive supply.[29] By 1764, garrison contracts were so common that Charles Jenkinson informed Governor Johnston he would receive a copy of the victualling contract from the contractors' agent, and that this was always done.[30] Away from the colonial sphere, contracting for field armies re-emerged with British involvement in the Low Countries between 1742 and 1748.[31] European campaigns in the mid-eighteenth century, as earlier in the century, meant the employment of European contractors. The impracticality in terms of resources and cost of shipping vast amounts of bulky items such as forage and flour had been amply demonstrated. By mid-century, the required shipping tonnage made 'Direct Supply' even less viable.[32] In both wars however, contractors were required to export from Britain an equivalent amount of grain to that used for making bread, although the clause was dropped in years of scarcity.[33]

Acting on the precedent of the last war, contracts for bread and wagons were made by the Treasury, whilst military commanders were empowered to make forage contracts abroad.[34] Commanding officers could also make bread and wagons contracts but all contracts were subject to Treasury approval, revision or rejection.[35] In Germany during the Seven Years' War the Treasury, fearing officers would agree to expensive contracts, reiterated that contracts must only be temporary until they assessed their propriety.[36] Indeed, the Duke of Marlborough was censured for 'extremely unreasonable' contracts he had made.[37] This mode of proceeding was a sensible precaution, for this was a particular problem with campaigning armies amidst wider concerns that officers exercise care in incurring expenditure.[38]

Treasury control meant contractors required a representative to act on their behalf. These representatives, styled 'Merchant-Attorneys', attended the Treasury, presented proposals, and generally administered the contract in London. Alexander Hume acted in this capacity for Nicholas Carpentier, and earlier for his own brother Abraham.[39] Hume received instructions and proposals directly from Carpentier, thus sparing military commanders any involvement in the process. By 1746, the Earl of Rothes informed Harrington that he made no contracts as Carpentier informed him they were being made in London.[40] There were many positive reasons for employing foreigners. Familiarity with and knowledge of the country were obviously important in supplying a campaigning army. A mobile army could not be provisioned from a fixed point and it was occasionally necessary, because of an absence of windmills, to transport flour for storage.[41] The successful conduct of such operations required topographical and geographical knowledge few British merchants possessed. In negotiating with sub-contractors, officials and peasants it was obviously advantageous if one could speak the native language.[42] In the case of Abraham Hume, the exception proves the rule, for although British he was experienced in foreign business and fluent in foreign languages.[43] His foreign mercantile activities were so extensive that for many years he does not appear to have possessed a permanent London residence.[44] Linguistic ability allied to geographical knowledge made it difficult for British merchants to act in the capacity of Pierre Nottet as 'Entrepreneur des

Fourages' in establishing magazines throughout the Low Countries.[45] Contemporaries viewed the use of foreign merchants as sensible, for:

> Countries used to employ great Armies on the Continent, furnish people qualified for all the functions thereto appertaining. Our wars in Flanders required little skill, and produced little knowledge in that way.[46]

Before making the Flanders bread contract in 1742, the Treasury consulted similar contracts from 1704 and 1712 and asked the contractor what advance payment he expected.[47] For a generation accustomed to peace making these contracts was an unfamiliar task, and even the Secretary of War admitted he did not know how much forage money each regiment was entitled to.[48] If 'neither fighting units nor administrative departments were prepared' for war, experience was not wholly lacking.[49] Senior military officers possessed valuable experience of military administration, with Sir Philip Honywood, the Earl of Stair, John Ligonier, Sir John Cope and John Huske all veterans of the War of Spanish Succession.[50]

Establishing the supply method was the first problem but there remained the problem of procurement. A shortage of dry forage around Ghent, Oudenarde and Bruges prompted Humphrey Bland to advise John Carteret to delay embarking the British cavalry otherwise it would be necessary to put the horses to grass and canton the cavalry near Ghent. Another problem arose with local magistrates representing they had insufficient stable room.[51] Forage continued problematic, with complaints from contractors and States providing forage but remaining unpaid, leading Stair to consider such discouragement 'might come to be of very dangerous Consequence'.[52] Stair himself placed the Allied Army in danger of starvation with his march up the Main in 1743. The advance of a 60,000 strong French army from the Rhine cut off supplies at Hanau, and attempts to procure local supplies failed dismally. Earlier, George II pertinently inquired how the army was to be supplied crossing the Rhine, and in opposing Stair's abortive march on Paris supply issues were foremost in Ligonier's mind.[53]

Shortages led to plundering, prompting Court resolutions attempting to suppress 'all Violences, Excesses, Disorders, Outrages and Robberys'.[54] For many, the causes of such excesses, such as the lack of supply organization and the alleged partiality towards Hanoverian troops were of more consequence.[55] Whilst the King's presence was considered beneficial towards supply organization, the German problem persisted.[56] Decisions concerning camp formation and location were made without consulting English officers, with the result that 'the Forage masters & Bread Contractors know nothing where we are going'.[57] A symptom of this lack of co-ordination was the absence of magazines. Despite representations that magazines should be constructed and commissaries appointed, little was done.[58] The failure of British troops to take the field in 1742 aborted the bread contract, but more widely a general stagnation in supply occurred, with continual delays in forming magazines the most serious symptom.[59] Widely attributed for the inaction of British troops, the Duke of Newcastle attributed this stagnation as a consequence of Carteret's apprehension and irresolution in countenancing the army crossing the Rhine.[60]

Early in the war, Britain heeded the representations of the States General that foraging the country would ruin the kingdom.[61] The resulting increase in costs was passed on to the Treasury. In 1743 the wagon contractor was obliged to accept dry forage at 'exorbitant rates' for 800 horses rather than procuring it in the country.[62] The expense incurred led to heated debates in Parliament in March–April 1744 on presentation of extraordinary expenditure for 1742–3 amounting to over £524,023, of which wagons, bread and forage accounted for almost £220,000.[63] Following severe criticism orders were issued to begin foraging the country on the basis that with British troops in Flanders to defend the country 'so that it is but just that the Inhabitants should contribute to their maintenance'.[64] A higher degree of organization was apparent in procuring forage, and greater emphasis placed on the positive attributes of contracting:

> ... when things are done by Contract, You then know the whole expence ... whereas there is never any end of those wch. are done at the expence of the Publick, by charging more than what they really pay for it ... Men of fortune will always take care not to engage themselves in undertakings where they have not, morally speaking, some certainty of being handsomely rewarded for the indefatiguable [sic] pains they must give themselves in affairs of this nature, & consequently the prices they will ask, will exceed those of necessitious [sic] people, but at the same time the General will be sure wth. them, that the Army will be regularly & well supplied, as much as the nature of the War will allow of.[65]

In urging the convergence of the self-interest of contractors with the needs of government, contracts were viewed as mutually advantageous arrangements underpinning successful supply operations. From 1744, systematic recommendations concerning magazines were implemented, with military commanders empowered to make contracts for magazine construction.[66] Uncertainty over impending military action led to stockpiling of forage in widely dispersed magazines.[67] Yet the occasions when supply became perilous merely illustrated the danger in failing to make contracts:

> We meet with the Greatest Difficultys In Providing forage. Mr Carpentier not Being Bound By any Contract makes difficultys which makes me extreamly uneasy ... I find By Experience that nothing But Great Gains makes that sort of People act.[68]

Such adverse comments should not detract from the point that contracts appeared necessary to enforce accountability and ensure reliability.

Contracts for wagons to transport bread, baggage, and sick men were particularly problematic in the Low Countries, where impressment was not permitted. In 1742, the contractor was forced to hire wagons of an unsuitable size, which the owners would not permit to leave the country.[69] Hiring was unreliable and expensive, and in subsequent years extensive contracts aimed at precluding it, but miscalculations occurred and hiring remained necessary.[70] Wagon capacity varied but a capacity of 200–250 6lb loaves of bread, between 1,200 and 1,500lb, appears to have been normal. Wagon capacity for carrying forage depended on the tightness of bales. However, it was recognized that an impractical number would be required to transport forage by land to widely dispersed magazines. River transport would, it was hoped, obviate such an operation, with General George Wade warning that 'Wheele Carriage is a great Imcumberance to an Army'.[71] Nevertheless, in 1747, with the southern mouth of the Scheldt inaccessible, all forage was transported overland. Those under contract proved insufficient, and the Commissary General, Abraham Hume, recommended further funds for hiring.[72] In making the contract for 1748, the Duke of Cumberland attempted to remove this uncertainty by contracting at a cheaper rate for 500 rather than 300 wagons.[73]

Despite Cumberland receiving plaudits for reducing the expense of forage in the latter years of the war, costs remained high. Criticism was made of sums of £353,000 and £80,000 extraordinary expenditure paid in the final two years of the war.[74] Further complaints related to Cumberland issuing warrants amounting to £325,000 on his sole authority without requisite information such as dates, number of rations supplied, or even the names of suppliers. This was criticized as 'one of the highest strains of complaisance that ever was paid either to English General, or English King'.[75] With Hume and Lawrence Dundas, ex-contractors now employed as commissaries, government aimed at using their knowledge to prevent exorbitant demands.[76] Yet, although civilian officials assumed greater involvement in examining proposals and assessing accounts later in the war, a rigorous system of accounting does not appear to have been established earlier.[77] Symptomatic of such laxity was Dundas's recommendation after examining a contractor's account that no warrants should be issued as the contractor had received too much money.[78]

There were areas where supply by contract was not the preferred method. Wood and straw were procured by specified commissaries, and many supply tasks devolved upon regimental officers. Quartermasters remained important in organizing foraging and in notifying commissaries and contractors of regimental requirements.[79] At the beginning of the war, a Commissary General of Provisions and a Deputy were appointed for British troops, and a commissary for States General troops.[80] Only a small number of commissaries were employed inspecting magazines. One was employed throughout the war, whilst another was promoted to this position after December 1747. Many appointments were replacements rather than the creation of new positions.[81] This even applied to the Commissary General. Hume returned home by the end of March 1748 and Dundas, although designated a 'Deputy', performed his functions.[82] The nascent commissarial structure appears to have been insufficient in ensuring adequate supervision, particularly of forage magazines, for in 1747, Hume unsuccessfully argued for a deputy commissary resident at each magazine.[83] Not until 1756 was this advice heeded, and the end of hostilities in 1748 brought a swift dismantling of the supply organization.[84]

Despite administrative and logistical problems, contractors were crucial to the war effort. Mercantile confidence in Britain's financial stability and integrity was vital, with Britain far better equipped than other European states to organize supply. Austrian mobilization against Prussia was hampered by insufficient credit to engage merchants to agree to contracts for horses, wagons and forage. They were permitted to take part of British magazines at cost price from contractors.[85] The relationship between financial health and military efficiency was starkly illustrated in the case of Austria, whose pitiful financial condition was such that it was unlikely they could continue the war without Britain. Henry Pelham pertinently asked 'can that Court furnish an Army without Subsidies, who have not been able to furnish a complete one Even with the vast sums we have paid 'em?'.[86] With inefficient, unreliable, and insolvent Allies, Britain shouldered the financial burden of the war. Contracts were not always the cheapest supply method but amidst difficulties attending traditional supply methods, they appeared the least unreliable.

Post-war demobilization and the return of colonial garrisons led to a significant reduction in army contracts, although victualling contracts were made for the Nova Scotia settlement.[87] Countering uncertainty continued to be important, but cost could also be a factor, for there were areas where expensive local supplies meant government lacked a cheaper alternative. For example, in 1751 the Ordnance Board conveyed a request from garrison employees at Newfoundland for inclusion within the victualling contract on account of exorbitant local prices.[88] In such cases, contracts represented the best bargain to be had. Indeed, suspicions arose when contracts were demonstrably cheap. For Admiral Vernon, the maxim 'that best is best cheap' was nonsense, 'for they that contract at an under price must sell you a bad commodity'.[89] Military officers could perhaps afford to adopt this stance. For politicians cost entered the equation. Pelham opposed a commission for a commissary in Scotland in 1747 as cheaper forage could often be obtained without issuing a commission.[90] Similarly, in 1759, the commanding officer in Scotland opposed contracts on account of the 'extraordinary Expense', particularly as there were 'plentiful markets' locally.[91]

During the Seven Years' War, this was something of an exceptional response. Facing the problem of supplying troops under variable conditions in different theatres of war, the continued absence of a supply corps and the inadequacy of traditional supply methods meant there were few alternatives to contracting. The experience of the previous war was valuable, with many contractors and commissaries continuing in a similar capacity.[92] Although the lack of experienced personnel remained problematic, the number of administrative staff, including positions hitherto unknown, increased significantly.[93] Expansion was necessary to meet the global demands of the Seven Years' War. The enhanced scope of the conflict meant sheer numbers accentuated the shift towards contracting. In North America, troops in British pay supplied under contract steadily increased. In 1756, contracts were made for 12,000 men, but by 1759 totalled 35,000.[94] At the end of 1758, contractors were directed to supply 20,000 Provincial troops; by March 1760 these troops numbered 51,142.[95] The capture of Louisbourg and Guadeloupe added a further 6,700.[96] The expense of this worldwide commitment was one where 'non-military' supplies assumed huge importance. Between 1755 and 1761, of £7,943,009 North American expenditure, only £2,306,776 was allocated to troops' pay. The remainder met food and transport requirements. Similarly, expenditure for African garrisons for 1759–61 amounted to £206,859, with only £69,974 allocated to pay, and £136,885 extraordinary expenditure exclusive of transport and ordnance charges.[97]

Europe remained a major theatre of war. At the beginning of the British military presence in Germany, the Treasury specifically mentioned foreigners as most likely to supply bread and wagons. The subsequent involvement of Jewish merchants illustrated the accuracy of this prediction.[98] The necessity of employing British men familiar with the country who could speak German, as 'Mr. Hume did the last war' was recognized, but problematic, for few men were suitably qualified.[99] The Treasury initially insisted on awarding contracts to men with experience of the country, but a failed attempt to 'seek out for persons of credit & character to make proposals' led to advertisement, and a relaxation of the insistence on foreign experience.[100] The foreign element in supplying the army in Germany was vital, for insufficient knowledge or linguistic shortcomings could result in improvident bargains or the use of untrustworthy and unreliable sub-contractors.[101] The terms in which Lawrence Dundas preferred to employ a foreigner rather than a fellow Scot reflected these concerns:

> But Sir, from all these difficultys, from your want of the Language & a Stranger to the Country & Customs of the Generals I find it more and more necessary to send Faber to take the direction of serving General Inhofs Corps.[102]

Logistical problems, notably an absence of good roads and navigable rivers, combined with poor harvests to inflate costs. The expense of the previous war proved to be an inadequate guide. In 1759, it was estimated £1,177,485 would be necessary for the 1760 German campaign. By April 1759, £100,000 per month was requested, rising to £150,000 in May 1760.[103] Between 1 January and 17 April 1761, £1,384,798 was remitted to Germany, computing at £4,000,000 per annum. Contemporaries correctly viewed such expenditure as unprecedented.[104] The disparity between resources and objectives permeated all discussion of military expenditure. Some argued that the extensive military effort Britain had undertaken contributed heavily to the regrettable but unavoidable expense.[105] The army in Germany alone, consisting of 60,000 horses and 100,000 men, consumed upwards of sixty-six tons of oats and nearly ninety tons of bread every day.[106] Others viewed the inflated claims of commissaries and contractors as symptomatic of a breakdown in supply organization. Lord George Sackville stated that compared with Queen Anne's wars, fewer troops were abroad but the cost of the war was higher, a situation he attributed to 'a want of economy in the managers of the German war'.[107]

A failure to fully comprehend logistical difficulties led to bewilderment at the vast expenditure incurred, with Newcastle wondering how countries with larger armies supplied them cheaper.[108] Britain's commitment to expensive foreign subsidies and extensive military operations, alongside unpropitious supply conditions appear to have been the answer. Between 1755 and November 1763 an estimated £12,499,016, approximately 55 per cent of total military expenditure of £22,640,421 in Germany was paid for 'extraordinary expenditure' of wagons, bread, and forage.[109] Amidst this vast expenditure there was an appreciation of how integral and expensive contracts were to the functioning of the army. Noting a plan for reducing American forces, Newcastle pointedly referred to the cost of supplying the army.[110] Barrington reiterated the prospective saving when victualling American Provincial troops was ended but such planning was wishful thinking, for the war dragged on, and the integral role of contractors encompassed not only supplying provisions but in financing the war effort.[111]

Contractors financed war by extending credit facilities to government, either as loan subscribers, or in performing contracts. Many did both. Whilst loan allocations embraced the foremost financiers in Britain, including those not possessing contracts, most contractors were involved. City financiers had long combined government loans with remittance contracts.[112] Financial contractors acted as underwriters by subscribing for a sum before allocating portions to customers including nominees of politicians.[113] Other contractors can be found in these lists.[114] For the 1757 loan, those possessing contracts at the time or in the following years, together with family connections, accounted for £408,900. This was much lower than later years. Eight contractors for the 1760 loan subscribed £3,320,000, whilst the same number was allocated £3,720,000 in 1761. For the 1762 loan, eleven men were allocated £3,420,000.[115] Investor confidence did not falter, with the result that the National Debt increased from £72,289,673 in January 1755 to £130,606,586 at the end of 1762, an increase of £58,316,913, including £2,050,053 interest. Since 1759 the increase was £32,240,000 principal and £1,417,850 interest.[116] Newcastle considered the £8 million loan of 1760 'a work, which never was attempted before, & I believe will now astonish all Europe'.[117] Although recognizing loan terms could be high, considerable emphasis was given to the certainty of securing funds.[118] Throughout the war, Newcastle consistently argued that money must be raised through the financial elite of the City of London.[119]

The ability of the British government to tap vast resources of wealth was equalled only by the ability of contractors to withstand delays in payment. During the Seven Years' War it was recognized that with repayment so long postponed, the interest on victualling bills could not be reduced.[120] The linkage between credit and military activity was portrayed rather baldly in the assertion that contractors must be paid 'or Services will not be answered and a 'Total Stop' may be put to the present operations'.[121] Demands consistently outran supplies. In 1759 demands stood at £1,202,751 whilst only £150,000 remained in the Exchequer. £716,656 extraordinary expenditure incurred in 1759 was paid out of supplies voted for 1760.[122] In 1762, £7,098,845 was paid for services incurred in 1761, and £6,986,232 for services of 1762 paid from supplies voted for 1763.[123] The credit mechanism of contracting assumed more importance as expenditure exceeded payments from current revenue. Despite the financial strain imposed on government, the continued application and performance of contracts is a striking demonstration of continued confidence in the financial stability of the British state.[124]

Quantitatively, contractors assumed greater prominence during the mid-century wars, but how efficient were they? The difficulties facing contractors must be factored into any assessment of performance based on regularity, quantity and quality. Another mitigating factor is the responsibility of the state, sub-contractors and agents for contract performance. That there were supply failures is indisputable. Between 1713 and 1739 supply problems largely emanated from deficiencies in administrative organization, and the failure of government to provide necessary infrastructure. If not inevitable this was understandable given the long distances involved and inexperience in administering colonial possessions.[125] Problems began immediately. An absence of clearly designated functions between government departments, and a delay in making contracts resulted in late deliveries of meat at Gibraltar in 1715. The contractor complained he did not begin killing until April when it was 'somewhat too hot'.[126] This was a legitimate complaint. For preservation reasons, carcass butchers of Newgate and Leadenhall slaughtered far more animals in winter.[127] The delay, caused by Treasury procrastination and Victualling Office complacency was avoidable, and the latter body should have been well aware of the seasonal nature of such supplies.[128]

The presence of commissaries at garrisons also created problems, with complaints and allegations of late and insufficient deliveries, which were found to emanate from jealousy over contract allocation.[129] Nevertheless, throughout the 1720s the garrison was regularly supplied, despite a testing troop augmentation from 1,500 to 6,000.[130] Despite initial problems, the contract was efficiently performed with minimal difficulties.[131] Insufficient state infrastructure proved problematic. Garrison contracts stipulated the Crown would provide sufficient storehouses for provisions.[132] This was particularly important for those garrisons inaccessible for part of the year, where winter provisions were shipped in summer months. Storehouses were either hired, although this was expensive, or constructed by the Ordnance Board.[133] Another clause stipulated that at least six months' provisions must be stored at all times. A large storage area was therefore required, for in auditing accounts government did examine whether this had been complied with.[134] Where storehouses were inadequate, contractors themselves often provided them. At Gibraltar, storehouses were almost a constant problem. In 1717, provisions were moved to the church after storehouses were bombed.[135] By the 1730s inadequate capacity and a dilapidated condition led to the contractor building an extension.[136] He also assumed responsibility for building a coal yard and undertook improvements to wharves and landing areas.[137]

If provisions were not properly stored, the risk of spoliation increased.[138] Problems of insufficient capacity could easily arise from any augmentation, as this inevitably meant delivery of a larger volume of provisions, which in turn required a larger storage area. This problem was seldom anticipated, and the government's response to continuing complaints was languid. In 1747, after continual representations from the contractor of insufficient storage the Treasury eventually informed the Ordnance three months after the original complaint was made.[139] The Treasury did however indicate their wish to be promptly informed of any complaints concerning non-delivery.[140] Another potential problem was the calculation that had to be made in order to provide a sufficient amount of provisions. Despite the contractor for Rattan accepting responsibility for failing to punctually supply provisions, a deficiency met by the Victualling Office, he claimed payments owing for provisions supplied to Ordnance staff not included within the contract.[141] This was a legitimate point, for consumption by all garrison residents, including those not included within the contract could undermine calculations of the required volume of provisions. The potential for shortages was enhanced by privateer activity. One effect of the seizure of provision ships was an application from the Gibraltar contractor to supply Irish instead of English provisions.[142] The effective use of convoys and cruisers after

1743 reduced the number of merchant ships lost to privateers, and there was no major crisis in delivering provisions during the war.[143] Bad weather could also disrupt deliveries, as witnessed in 1741 when a ship destined for Georgia was stranded and then plundered.[144]

Remittance contracts also demanded a degree of organization and cooperation, not only between contractors and government but also between contractors' agents and deputy paymasters. In garrisons and on expeditions the Paymaster of the Forces issued subsistence money via remittance contractors to deputy paymasters who distributed money to regimental paymasters. At home, regimental agents and paymasters handled subsistence money.[145] The involvement of agents increased the likelihood of problems. The remitters for Jamaica discharged agents who refused to supply supplementary forces arriving under William Blakeney, as agreed under contract.[146] Many problems related to procurement of suitable currency. Areas such as Scotland where the credit structure was relatively undeveloped required specie from England, although in 1750 the Royal Bank of Scotland assumed responsibility for issuing subsistence and contingency money.[147]

In the period 1739–48 supply problems mainly arose from insufficient planning or difficult conditions. Sheer distance imposed difficulties in maintaining quality and quantity most notably from danger of seizure, bad weather or unavoidable accidents. These factors constitute a formidable array of variables that could adversely affect contract performance. When shortages occurred it was natural to blame the contractors. Although accountable to government in these terms, contractors did not fully control contract performance. Government had a role to play in providing necessary infrastructure such as storehouses and convoys. Agents and sub-contractors were vitally important and their shortcomings reflected badly on contractors who were held ultimately responsible. Between the wars, although only minor problems arose in the delivery of supplies, there were straws in the wind of problems that would emerge with renewed force in later years.[148] The Gibraltar contractors found it impossible to provide six months' provisions from Britain, and their request to provide provisions from Ireland was temporarily agreed to.[149] In 1757, a bad harvest and high prices led the government to permit contractors to export foreign corn and Irish beef. The contractors argued this would not only be cheaper but would benefit the poor in Britain by not exacerbating shortages.[150] A relaxation in terms was acceptable when the benefits of doing so were readily apparent.

A degree of flexibility was also necessary in supplying money to Nova Scotia garrisons. With communication impossible between November and March, the remittance terms whereby six months' advance payment to remitters was maintained by payments at bimonthly intervals was inadequate when money could not be regularly delivered.[151] A solution was found in directing the Deputy Paymaster at Halifax to apply to Governors of Halifax and Nova Scotia to issue warrants for conveying and transporting the subsistence in specie to distant garrisons.[152] The timing of advance payments continued to be vitally important, for money sent to North America could take four or five months to arrive. Facing rising demands on their credit, contractors reminded the Treasury that six months' subsistence and pay should always be in hand.[153] Remitters pointed out that as it took time to procure bullion, and as demands on their credit could be severe, regular supplies of money were necessary.[154] During the Seven Years' War, with Deputy Paymasters in North America attending troops at greater distances, there was an increasing risk of seizure.[155] To counter the danger, escorts were provided and an additional Deputy Paymaster appointed.[156] To some degree, this replicated the system before money left Britain, with government providing troop detachments to guard wagons belonging to remitters.[157] Whilst it was rare for the army to suffer from lack of subsistence, one spectacular failure occurred when John Bristow, the Gibraltar remitter, went bankrupt.[158] This was an exceptional occasion, and one that could not have been anticipated from the contractor's previous credit status. It did however illustrate that contractors were not immune from the financial irresponsibility of others, whether from unpaid loans or the failure of financial houses negotiating Bills of Exchange.[159]

As the Seven Years' War encompassed supply needs that were more extensive and covered a geographically wider area a higher incidence of supply failure was perhaps to be expected. Yet, facing only one naval power, and with efficient convoy coordination, it was rare for contractors to fail completely. Nevertheless, some old problems remained. In 1757, Gibraltar storehouses required strengthening to accommodate a larger volume of provisions.[160] The commanding officer earlier reported the ruinous condition of all military buildings, and similar representations were made from Minorca.[161] Delivery of correct quantities required efficient communication. With contracts made on War Office estimates of troop numbers, accurate estimates were obviously vital particularly when advance notice was required to order provisions as early as November to ensure delivery by May or June. The Treasury cautioned Governors to prepare to supply deficiencies arising from late arrival of provision ships.[162] When it was impossible to procure accurate information on troop numbers in the forthcoming year, the Treasury erred on the side of surplus rather than risk shortages.[163] This tendency towards providing surplus provisions was compounded in North America where a change of contractors raised fears of shortages and induced an overcautious approach to such a degree that contractors feared they would not be reimbursed for provisions remaining when the contract ended.[164] A lack of departmental communication led to Quebec receiving from Treasury contractors and the Victualling Office ten times the annual consumption of garrison provisions.[165] Victualling Office supplies were sent as a safeguard against non-arrival of provisions.[166] Although such a problem if regularly enacted could prove expensive, such confusion was not very common, and was preferable to non-delivery.

Difficulties concerning troop augmentations could be surmounted by proper communication.[167] Reports from Gibraltar of insufficient provisions in 1756 appear to have partly arisen from additional regiments from Britain and the alarming number of troops arriving from Minorca after its capture.[168] The 1756 estimates listed 3,260 troops (four regiments) for Gibraltar, but by 1757, 6,520 (eight regiments) were resident. During 1756, as many as 9,812 men were victualled during September and October but by November the numbers had fallen to 5,512. With the contract made for 3,000 troops, it was inevitable there would be a period when consumption appeared to proceed at a faster rate than deliveries.[169] At West African garrisons, the numbers victualled steadily increased. At Senegal, troop numbers increased from 412 in December 1758 to 1,078 in July 1759, whilst at Goree there were 400 troops in May 1758, but 628 by October 1758.[170] The augmentations do not appear to have had a deleterious effect on supply, despite an unfounded scare over shortages.[171] Nevertheless, in ordering provisions to be immediately sent without waiting for convoy the Treasury was responding to the contractor's claim that this was a source of delay.[172] Supply problems emanated from seizure of ships and difficulties landing provisions. The Governor at Goree accepted supply difficulties were not attributable to contractors but emanated from losses at sea.[173] With insufficient knowledge of how to combat the tropical climate, the type and quality of provisions was problematic. Barrington approved Hospital Board advice regarding consumption of sub-acid fruits and fresh provisions, and avoidance of the intense heat of the sun.[174] The main complaint, a problem elsewhere and the cause of much sickness and death, was the absence of fresh meat.[175] Continuing representations of the need for fresh provisions indicates that the problem remained unresolved.[176]

With multiple difficulties in supplying provisions overseas, food quality was extremely variable. Supplying a wide variety of provisions meant contractors used more sub-contractors and agents and more ancillary staff such as coopers and packers. Conditions aboard ship could also deleteriously affect quality. In this respect it is significant that it was rare for quality of provisions to be problematic in Europe. The longer the supply chain the greater the possibility of supply failure. With the best intentions, quality could be adversely affected by a number of factors. Yet it was occasionally suspected that poor quality provisions were deliberately provided, and claims that old and new provisions were blended together hinted at an intention to defraud.[177] Although government paid compensation for provisions damaged as a result of insufficient storehouses or enemy seizure, contractors were liable for provisions damaged in most other ways.[178] This guaranteed an interest in the safe delivery of good quality provisions. Contractors were responsible for provisions condemned on account of being kept too long or from packaging faults. The latter assumed various forms, from inadequate temperature control to rodent or insect infestation. Contractors usually sought to deny liability by pointing to factors such as the length of time goods were in transit.[179] Such disputes indicate it was sensible for the Comptrollers of Army Accounts to reiterate that payment should only be made for provisions actually issued to troops. The essential concomitant in preventing disputes was systematic sampling and inspection of provisions upon delivery.[180] In North America, the Commissary of Stores and deputies inspected provisions at Albany before transportation to their final destination. Centrally located storehouses were established at Albany, Halifax and New York, and there appears to have been strict examination.[181] In enforcing accountability, rigorous examination aimed at obviating disputes. Such complaints were made in North America during the earlier war, thus indicating a lack of official vigilance, but were rarely heard between 1756 and 1762.[182]

Although contracts assumed greater importance within the eighteenth-century supply system, the intermittent evolution and diverse demands of military supply led to a system with no body of permanent officials. Nevertheless, there was sufficient inherited knowledge arising from precedent, alongside notions of commercial propriety, to ensure there was a degree of clarity and guidance as to how contracts should be performed. By the mid-eighteenth century improvements in mercantile organization, financial credit, and transportation meant merchants were capable of conducting operations on an extensive scale. Yet these factors cannot be viewed as causes for the growth in contracting for their impact only became operative once a decision was made to employ contractors. In this sense, logistical and financial factors, the demand side of military supply, appear most important.

With the emergence of larger armies the conduct of expensive and extensive military operations could be achieved by utilizing the credit facilities of contractors. The quid pro quo was profitability; otherwise there was little incentive for men to perform contracts. Patriotism seldom outweighed self-interest. Nevertheless, it was never in the contractor's interest to perform a contract badly. In uniting the self-interest of the contractor with the interest of the state a greater degree of certainty in supply matters was achieved. The background upon which these factors operated was that of an ill-defined supply structure with little official organization beyond that provided by contractors themselves. In these terms, contractors enhanced the war-making capacity of the state, which despite 'an enhanced administrative structure ... which enabled the bureaucracy to transport, arm, clothe and feed larger and larger numbers', required considerable private mercantile activity.[183] Competent performance, in terms of regularity, quantity and quality, represent a considerable achievement given the difficulties often encountered. Not only was supply failure fairly uncommon, but many, though not all problems emanated from factors outside contractors' control.[184] The ideal contract for government was one where troops were punctually supplied with the correct quantity of high quality goods at a reasonable price. Significantly, most criticism of contracts concerned not performance but the methods of awarding them and their cost. The validity of this criticism can be determined by examining the administration of contracts by the Treasury.

3 PROCEDURES AND PATRONAGE

An increasing number of contracts necessitated a higher degree of administrative organization, and by examining the procedures of awarding contracts, and terms and conditions governing their performance, an evaluation can be made as to how the system operated at different levels or to assess whether there was anything approximating to a system. Such examination illustrates how contract procedures contained an inherent, but intentional, bias towards wealthy men. Procedures were carefully calculated to find suitable contractors whose economic activities closely approximated to the contractual work required, whilst equally importantly, eliminating unsuitable applicants. The ability to manage extensive supply operations was an essential prerequisite for all contractors, whether financier, merchant, or agricultural wholesaler. Diverse military demands encompassed a variety of business interests. For each type of contract, there were a group of men whose experience in relevant business sectors made them particularly well-equipped to undertake contracts. This close approximation between business experience and contractual services indicates the Treasury's success in identifying men whose abilities could be used for state purposes.

The marked procedural differences between different types of contract indicate the extent to which patronage permeated contract allocation. The most pertinent evidence relates to how far contracts were 'open' in terms of competitive tendering and advertisement. Variable procedures illustrate the limits to which a 'system' can be said to have existed. Whereas terms and conditions tended towards uniformity, contract allocation was only partially guided by regulatory standards and clear, comprehensive procedures. In the eighteenth-century, there was no single method of awarding contracts consistently applied by all government departments. Whilst this clearly facilitated the operation of patronage, an examination of procedures and personnel across a range of contracts indicates variability in type and incidence.[1] The profile of mid-eighteenth century contractors was influenced by a variety of factors. Contractors were never only contractors but men possessing extensive and frequently diverse commercial experience. Geographical factors, type of military presence and attendant nature of supply all influenced the profile of contracting personnel.

In the absence of selection procedures based on impersonal examination and formal qualifications, patronage was important but not all-encompassing and seldom the only reason in appointing contractors.[2]

As contracts involved considerable work, responsibility and risk, business experience and competence were always fundamentally important. The close approximation between contractors' business interests and their contracts indicates that another dimension should be considered in explaining the composition of contracting personnel. Often converging with patronage, but always distinct, mercantile ability and experience were required to manage extensive supply operations. As an area of economic activity, contracting called forth dynamic elements in British commercial life.[3] The implications of this argument impact on contract administration, and the extent to which government sacrificed the public interest for the sake of patronage. More widely, such evidence challenges the connection between contracts and 'Old Corruption'. Yet, whilst methods of awarding contracts can be justified in terms of mercantile expertise, and Treasury administration reveals a concern for economy, irregularities remained. One of the graver defects of the system was the absence of clear guidelines relating to the propriety of official involvement in contracts.

Army contracts made at the Treasury can be divided into three types: money remittances, victualling contracts for troops abroad, and encampment contracts within Britain.[4] Despite differences in how these contracts were awarded, in each case the adopted procedures aimed to ensure suitable men obtained contracts they were best capable of performing. An examination of the first two types of contract provides a suitable context for the discussion on domestic contracting that follows.

That contracts for remitting money were amongst the most lucrative contracts was a reflection of the need to ensure troops throughout the world were regularly paid. Remittances concerned the use of financial services, for although government supplied subsistence money, contractors used their financial connections to remit money into local currencies for distribution to troops. The Treasury employed remitters on the basis that exchange was a problem that could only be met by employing men possessing financial connections in places where money was remitted. Remittance by Bills of Exchange necessitated the presence of correspondents in foreign financial houses, and the system relied on remitters possessing credit facilities where troops were located, as balances held in foreign houses could be used in a way that would not destabilize foreign exchanges.[5] The international credit structure was also safer. Bills of Exchange were not payable at sight, thus eliminating the danger of theft, whilst conveyance of specie was inconvenient, hazardous, and expensive.[6]

Remittance contracts were usually made for one year with six or twelve months' termination notice. Bonds were submitted as security.[7] Proposals could encompass payment by commission or a fixed rate for every pound sterling remitted.[8] Commission was less attractive as it linked profitability to the precise sums incurred. Charges for correspondents in foreign financial houses, and carriage, freight and insurance for conveying specie were also payable.[9] The financial connections and credit facilities of remitters were therefore of paramount importance. City of London 'monied men' dominated remittances throughout the eighteenth-century, and by mid-century an exclusive inner 'ring' of financiers dominated remittances and government loans.[10] An application from Peter Burrell to assume his late father's contracts indicates the qualifications required:

> My Correspondence at Lisbon gives me the same opportunities my Father had & my own fortune & Character in Life a full security to the public: But if that is not thought sufficient I can get the most unexceptionable Collateral in my own family.[11]

Although unsuccessful, Burrell correctly alluded to family antecedents, foreign connections and independent wealth. Connections with the great Chartered Companies was also advantageous as indicative of possession of the aforementioned qualities. Where dates are known, of eighteen contractors possessing Directorships of Chartered Companies, thirteen held them prior to their possessing contracts.[12] Despite the linkage between patronage, loans and contracts, the importance of regularly paying troops is often overlooked. This in itself may indicate the efficiency of the system. Contemporaries were well aware of its importance, for, as Marlborough reminded Newcastle of the 'terrible Consequences of an Army wanting Pay; which must cause infinite Marauding, & want of Discipline; as no Arguments or Authority can persuade Men to starve'.[13]

Procedural arrangements for remittances reflected the Treasury's confidence in the credit of City financiers. By mid-century it was accepted procedure to approach prospective remitters when contracts were pending.[14] The vast sums required precluded all but elite financiers. The latter would not risk participation if the prospective profits were uncertain, and alongside foreign investment in government funds, their participation indicates confidence in the financial rectitude of the British government.[15] Earlier in the century, remittances attracted intense competition amongst City financiers. Amongst the most prominent was Henry Furnese, remitter to Portugal, the Low Countries and Germany from 1705 until 1710. Favoured by the Whigs, he did not survive their fall from power.[16] Partisanship in allocating remittances was not always so transparent. Competition existed before and after Furnese's period of dominance. There were six proposals submitted in 1701, thirty-five between 1705 and 1710, including eighteen in 1706, and the Treasury encouraged rival proposals in 1711 and 1713.[17] The King's involvement in allocating remittances was a notable feature.[18] The competitive nature of the procedure meant the proposed terms were often decisive. At times the procedure could be very open, with newspaper advertisement stipulating the delivery of sealed proposals.[19] By 1730 this 'open' method had disappeared, with the Treasury directing the Paymaster of the Forces to receive proposals from Joseph Eyles for remittances to Gibraltar, Minorca 'or any other foreign service'.[20] Advertisement and competition succumbed to recommendation, and hereafter remittances became inextricably linked to Walpolean patronage, with contracts consistently awarded to the same group of men.

Controversy over remittances formed a component of the campaign against Sir Robert Walpole in 1742, when he faced accusations of making a contract for Jamaica at an inflated rate, thus making a 'bad bargain for the public'.[21] The remittance rate and procedural irregularities in making the contract were questioned. It was revealed that Walpole had informed Peter Burrell on a Commons stairway of the pending contract. Shortly afterwards the prospective contractors submitted proposals, which were accepted on the day they were received at the Treasury.[22] Walpole was censured for managing the contract to favour the contractors, for although not usually advertised the method of private approaches was more open than Walpole's actions. The absence of competition was highlighted by merchants before the Secret Committee.[23] Despite the revelation that two government officials possessed a share of the contract no criticism was made of this practice.[24] Moreover, although Walpole was accused of possessing 'sole direction' of the contract, Treasury minutes reveal two other Lords present when the proposals were read.[25] Both issues deserved closer attention. The latter indicated it was incorrect to consider Walpole had sole direction, whilst the former raised awkward questions over the propriety of government officials' involvement in contracts.

Despite the clearly orchestrated campaign against Walpole, the contract appears to have been hastily made at an injudicious rate, with the profit estimated at £12 8s. per £100 remitted.[26] Evidence produced indicated bills drawn from Jamaica in previous months for navy and ordnance services were drawn at £140 to £100. As Governor and Sub-Governor of the South Sea Company the contractors would have been fully aware of exchange conditions for the Company had resident agents at Jamaica.[27] Earlier, in 1740 the same contractors secured remittance and victualling contracts for Gibraltar and Minorca.[28] The involvement of the South Sea Company in events surrounding the outbreak of war in 1739 did not affect their loyalty to Walpole. Opposition to the Convention of Pardo encompassed a wide range of mercantile interests and institutions, but despite Company and City opposition to the £68,000 payment to the Spanish government, both men voted for it in the Commons.[29] A similar case arose in 1743 when Henry Pelham was attacked for a contract made with John Gore. The difference between the exchange rate and the rate paid by the contractor for every pound sterling remitted handed Gore a profit of 7½ stivers for every pound sterling. In the face of a favourable exchange rate this was subsequently lowered, but rejection of a lower rival bid led to parliamentary criticism. Pelham defended the contract on the basis of the contractors' experience and the need to remit money quickly.[30] Despite disarming his critics, suspicions remained that remittances were a scene of jobbery and favouritism.[31]

The involvement of many remitters in government loans indicates a close relationship, signified by the City's response to Pelham's resignation in 1746: 'If no Pelham, no money'.[32] Within governing circles the need for a good relationship with City financiers, harnessing financial expertise to the needs of state, was widely appreciated. Yet, government was far from being dictated to in awarding contracts.[33] There is little evidence that financiers received contracts on condition they vote with government. The reverse appears to have applied: they received contracts having previously voted for government.[34] Of twenty-nine contractors in Parliament during the mid-century wars, eighteen were MPs before possessing contracts. Most were financial contractors and administration loyalists.[35] Nevertheless, any deviation from loyalty could result in the loss of contracts as Sir George Colebrooke later discovered. Personal loyalty to Newcastle placed him in difficulties. In 1763, he absented himself from voting on the peace preliminaries, which he explained as 'having unliquidated accounts with Government to a great amount I did not think it prudent to act'. This 'mean neutrality' only heightened Henry Fox's anger.[36] This however, was an exceptional occasion emanating from the disruptive circumstances of Newcastle's retirement from office.

The relative absence of mercantile competition for remittances led to criticism which paralleled that of closed loan subscriptions.[37] Three principal reasons were given for the closed procedure.[38] Firstly, too few people were equal to the undertaking for advertisement to have any effect. Secondly, businessmen following public affairs would be aware of pending remittances.[39] Thirdly, advance warning introduced the danger of a combination of dealers in Bills of Exchange.[40] These were all weighty considerations and to a large degree justified the adopted procedure. Nevertheless, remittances were seldom so extensive that they could accommodate all those seeking a share.[41] Restrictive procedures facilitated favouritism and patronage, and as the inner ring of remitters under the Pelhams suggests, led to exclusivity and accommodation of certain contractors.[42] Although this did not necessarily translate into making bad bargains, upon awarding German remittances, Chancellor of the Exchequer, Henry Legge, was insistent they should be awarded according to cost, without favour or affection.[43] That this needed to be stated so baldly was an indication of the importance of 'favour' and 'affection', although cost was clearly a consideration in awarding this contract.[44] Whilst the absence of open competition raised suspicions that remittances were an area where monopoly and patronage operated, the nature of financial contracts meant some justification existed for this mode of proceeding.[45]

In the immediate post-Utrecht period, no clearly defined procedure existed for awarding victualling contracts for colonial garrisons. The unfamiliarity of the task facing the Treasury in supplying Gibraltar led to consultation of the 1664 contract for Tangier.[46] In 1712 and 1714, following the advice of the Victualling Commissioners, the Treasury placed advertisements in the *London Gazette*, prompting eight proposals.[47] The formula for receiving proposals was for contractors to stipulate a price for provisions for one man per week. With a degree of product variation this allowance remained remarkably consistent throughout the century. At its most extensive, provisions supplied included bread, beef, pork, beer, cheese, peas, oatmeal, butter, and spirits.[48] Yet, whilst the formula remained consistent, the competitive element in Treasury victualling contracts became less direct.

Predominantly involved in supplying naval stations or providing 'sea provisions' for ships, the Victualling Office sought contractors supplying a specific amount of provisions for a specific number of men for a specific time. Their method of awarding contracts was to advertise for tenders in the *Gazette* and at the Royal Exchange.[49] Other branches of the navy's supply organization such as the Sick and Wounded Office also advertised.[50] Conversely, after the aforementioned Gibraltar contract the Treasury rarely advertised, preferring instead to privately approach merchants.[51] For example, in 1750 William Baker was informed he would be notified of any pending North American contracts. Seven months later he was thus informed and his proposals accepted.[52] Whilst this method effectively restricted competition it was justified on the basis that advertisement was superfluous when merchants knowledgeable of political and military affairs would be aware of pending contracts. This was probably true. When the Gibraltar contractor died in July 1733, only two weeks passed before proposals were received from prospective contractors.[53]

Although restrictive, several examples relating to victualling contracts testify to the survival of competition without advertisement.[54] Reallocation of North American contracts in 1760 led to attempts to inculcate competition. On receiving several proposals, the Treasury requested further inquiries 'whether any other persons of great Substance will propose better terms'.[55] It was noted no other proposals had been received for the Nova Scotia contract of 1760, thus indicating some prior notice.[56] A similar sentiment relative to Gibraltar in 1752 may have been a device to reduce prices, for the original applicants received the contract but only after considerable bargaining, and with the proviso that they purchase provisions in Britain.[57] Thus, whilst the method of awarding contracts was irregular, or more accurately informal, it did not preclude a competitive element or a concern with economy.[58] Nevertheless, such a system was likely to incur criticism. In February 1757, Newcastle was 'severely abused' in Parliament over the North American contract of 1756. This debate, the only one of its kind during the war, concerned one contract and was not the prelude to an attack on contracting generally, although country gentlemen viewed it as symptomatic of a wider malaise.[59] Copies of all North American contracts and related correspondence were presented, before the Commons decided the contract 'prudent and necessary'.[60] This was only accomplished after a strident defence of procedure and terms, alongside a clear demonstration that haste in making the contract resulted from an urgent appeal from Lord Loudoun who advised against advertisement.[61] Despite the successful outcome the threat of a parliamentary inquiry was taken seriously.[62]

Before mid-century, political patronage does not appear to have been the prime determinant in allocating victualling contracts. Thomas Missing, contractor for Gibraltar, Minorca, and North America, an MP from 1722 to 1727, was awarded contracts years before and continued in them years afterwards. In 1734 his contracts were divided between Thomas Revell for Georgia and Gibraltar, and Matthew Woodford for American garrisons.[63] Woodford, a Southampton merchant, despite connections with Hans Stanley and Newcastle, was not an MP.[64] Revell's appointment appears justifiable from his experience as a Victualling Commissioner and Victualling Office agent at Gibraltar.[65] In awarding these contracts, there is no evidence of advertisement or competitive tendering.[66] The contracts were made after Missing's death, and with contract stipulations that six months' provisions must be stored at all times and six months' termination notice given there was no urgency to secure a new contractor on account of want of provisions.[67] There was therefore an opportunity to promote competition, and the proposals received in 1715, and the numerous applications made for Victualling Office contracts indicate advertisement would have done so. Nevertheless, procedural restrictions appear to have arisen almost inadvertently, from haste or convenience rather than from a conscious design to restrict competition.[68] Unlike the Victualling Office, for whom it was their raison d'être, contract negotiations were not the Treasury's main business, as the terse entries announcing new contractors indicate. In 1719 the Treasury advised the Gibraltar contractor to immediately apply for American garrison contracts. This appears to have arisen from the urgent need to supply the garrison rather than a desire to bestow contracts on particular contractors.[69] Victualling contracts continued to be awarded by private approaches.[70] Only upon exceptional occasions was this method departed from. Compared to competitive tendering, this method appears less explicitly aimed at driving down prices. Yet, there were positive elements of this method, not least the opportunity it presented to utilize mercantile specialization.[71]

Private approaches meant a bias towards the mercantile community of London, by far the largest in Britain in numbers, wealth, and diversity of business interests.[72] Foreign visitors and contemporary chroniclers consistently promoted the virtues, vigour, and global interests of London merchants.[73] Possessing capital, credit, and the ability to undertake expansive operations, London merchants were well-placed to perform contracts. Commercial ability was supplemented by geographical advantages, for even if contracts were advertised at the Treasury or Royal Exchange, London-based men possessed early notification. Treasury responsibility for army contracts meant that unlike the ordnance and navy, the contracts were made solely in London.[74] Although provincial merchants may have been sufficiently creditworthy and respectable, location restricted opportunities. For all contracts, it was desirable that prospective contractors were men of known character and substance, or at least could have their credentials checked. This was much easier for London merchants, for even if provincial merchants were acquainted with pending contracts, proposals had to be made in a matter of weeks, after applicants assessed their capability to perform the contract. This involved costing materials, planning deliveries from sub-contractors, making contingency plans to employ staff, and finally submitting proposals. It was then advisable to attend the Treasury when proposals were considered. Wealth and geography therefore conspired against provincial merchants.[75] However, they were not completely excluded, for sub-contracting was always necessary, and many contractors had provincial origins.[76] Nevertheless, in managing contracts as named contractors, London merchants held almost total sway between 1739 and 1763.

Many 'national' mercantile communities existed within London, a national dimension that was replicated in contracting personnel. By mid-century, with the Jewish element somewhat displaced, a number of Anglicized Huguenots assumed importance in financial contracts.[77] Despite Ireland's strategic importance for procuring and shipping supplies Arnold Nesbitt was the only major Irish contractor, and he served a mercantile apprenticeship and conducted most of his business in London.[78] During the mid-century wars, Scots were prominent in domestic and Continental military supply. However, with the exception of Adam Drummond who began a contract in 1764, no Scots held remittances or victualling contracts.[79] Despite attempts to associate Scots with anti-patriotic elements such as foreign loan merchants the majority of loan subscribers and contractors were English.[80] Thus, no significant national bias existed in the profile of contracting personnel but the metropolitan bias is clear. Only two English provincial merchants held garrison contracts, both dating from the 1730s before London merchants assumed dominance of victualling contracts.[81] In 1741, London merchants replaced the Cork-based contractor providing salt beef to Minorca.[82] New North American contracts were awarded to London merchants in the 1740s, and in 1752 a partnership of London merchants were awarded the Gibraltar victualling contract.[83] Patronage partly accounts for this shift, but underpinning the capability of London merchants was their access to a wide range of provisions carried from provincial towns to London.[84] Regional specialization in products such as cheese and butter meant provincial merchants shared in the benefits of contracting.[85]

By mid-century, the London merchant-contractor was a familiar figure. In 1764 an applicant for the Minorca contract was disappointed to hear the Treasury would make a contract with London merchants as this had always been done.[86] This dominance had another dimension, for by 1756 only seven garrison contractors were not MPs, including three partners of contractor MPs.[87] Five contractors entering Parliament towards the end of the 1740s was a significant accretion, for only five sat in the 1741 Parliament.[88] Nevertheless, there remained contractors outside Parliament. The partnership of John Thomlinson and John Hanbury held American remittances between 1745 and 1764, although they eventually shared the contract with Colebrooke and Nesbitt.[89] Newcastle admitted the latter partnership, in an apparently simple act of patronage in response to a direct request.[90] Nevertheless, the original contractors continued in the contract, and Colebrooke and Nesbitt, both long established in banking, possessed the requisite experience and credit for such operations.[91] Foreign victuallers and remitters shared many similar attributes. In many cases they were in fact the same men. Despite a shift amongst merchants towards financial rather than purely mercantile concerns in the mid-eighteenth century, in relation to contracts this process was frequently reversed.[92] Men predominantly concerned in finance frequently performed victualling contracts, thus indicating the importance of experience, connections and locality specialization over sectoral mercantile organization.[93] Merchants would not consider performing a contract if they possessed no experience of the part of the world concerned. Geographical expertise led to fluidity of personnel and adaptability in performing contracts. Chauncy Townsend held North American victualling and fuel contracts but also supplied the navy with masts.[94] Similarly, John Henniker combined mast contracts with victualling and remittance contracts at Florida.[95] The ability to operate in separate spheres and engage in multiple capacities emanated from geographical rather than sectoral expertise. Eighteenth-century mercantile enterprise was well-suited towards these needs, for in mercantile activity 'locality tended to prevail over specialization by objects'.[96]

Long established trading links often led to a high degree of organization and cooperation. Merchants trading to Portugal were particularly well-organized and often acted together.[97] For example, John Bristow concerned himself only in Iberian and West Indian contracts, often in partnership with Peter Burrell senior. Both families were long connected with this area.[98] Such business experience indicates that political considerations do not sufficiently explain contract allocation.[99] Instances of mercantile specialization by locality can be multiplied, and it was clearly an important consideration in contract allocation. Merchants were conscious of the value of specialization. Townsend informed Newcastle he was closely connected 'with the most considerable persons of New England'.[100] Extensive geographical specialization is also apparent from the extensive American contracts held by Sir William Baker.[101] He and Townsend possessed long experience, being amongst those with unsatisfied bills from James Oglethorpe's Georgia campaign.[102] Knowledge of the country was vital, for it was not always possible to rely on agents and correspondents. Baker's contract stipulated that one of the contractors personally supervise operations.[103] Christopher Kilby, having earlier supplied shoes to the army in America, and connected with the influential de Lanceys, crossed the Atlantic.[104] Baker and Kilby were also both involved in the Nova Scotia settlement where Kilby was Agent and Receiver.[105] Personal supervision by contractors appears however to have been rather exceptional. Delegation to agents, clerks, packers and brokers was entirely consistent with other areas of mercantile activity.[106] Beyond providing credit, the daily involvement of contractors in many cases was perhaps little more than general supervision and communication with agents and Treasury.

A number of contractors operated in diverse areas. The activities of Samuel Touchet encompassed African victualling contracts, German remittances, and distribution of naval prizes.[107] Anthony Bacon's contracts included victualling garrisons in Africa and the Isle of Man, and cannon manufacture.[108] These men were redolent of merchant adventurers, with an extensive range of activities incorporating cotton manufacture, arms production and the slave trade. Although exceptional, such diversity was consistent with the most notable characteristic of all contractors. This was the extent to which their business interests approximated with their contracts. Moreover, it is unsurprising that most remittance and victualling contracts were performed by partnerships. Despite diminishing profits, partnerships augmented capital, and reduced the risk of potentially catastrophic losses.[109] The close relationship that existed between contractors indicates the operation of contradictory forces in this age of mercantile capitalism. Individualism was promoted but tempered by the practical association required by mercantile operations.[110]

Irregular methods of appointing contractors did not therefore mean unsuitable men were appointed or that a concern for economy was lacking. However, there were exceptions. As Paymaster of the Forces, Walpole appointed the Purveyor at Chelsea Hospital, a position from which he dominated the Hospital's victualling contracts, and sold Hospital victualling bills to Walpole at a 5 per cent discount.[111] Years later Henry Fox appointed the Purveyor in exactly the same way, thus illustrating the legitimacy of influence and patronage that permeated eighteenth-century government. In this case, a right of nomination resided in the Paymaster as Hospital Treasurer.[112] Fox also ensured that his political ally, the regimental agent John Calcraft, obtained the contract providing coals for Gibraltar.[113] Yet Calcraft only administered the contract; he did not receive the profits of it. Accounts between the two men for 1760–2 record a payment of £80 from Fox to Calcraft for 'two years allowance'. The estimated annual profit from the contract was £400.[114] In opposing the Court in 1763 Calcraft lost the contract but was unperturbed as 'The Contract Mr Fox and his family had the Profit of so to me 'tis no loss'.[115] In instructions issued to Calcraft, Fox corroborates this evidence.[116] Despite the rapacious reputation of those involved, it appears unlikely this was an isolated occurrence. Unlike government positions incompatible with a seat in the Commons by successive Place Bills and secretly held 'in trust' for Members, no prohibition existed against politicians possessing contracts.[117] There was therefore no need for secrecy. No one appears to have known that Fox received the profits, and he chose not to disclose this information. This appears to indicate recognition that it was morally, if not legally, wrong for politicians to profit from contracts.[118] That it was Calcraft and not Fox who was identified with the contract illustrates an important point about contracts generally: much was hidden from public view.[119] The almost incidental details that emerged from government inquiries of official involvement in contracts appear to indicate a widespread phenomenon but the extent of official and political profiteering will never be fully known. It appears likely much evidence has been destroyed, lost, or never existed. Approaching a prospective contractor in 1742, Walpole allegedly stated 'I don't ask you to let any body in, for the Contract is yours', a comment which suggests it was common practice for contractors to admit others at the request of politicians.[120]

There was therefore some justification for suspicions of jobbery arising from closed procedures. Earlier in the century Committees of Public Accounts attacked Walpole and Marlborough for irregularities in making contracts and corruption in profiting from them. Both cases demonstrated a casual attitude towards perquisites.[121] Whilst Marlborough's case, involving differing interpretations of the customary usage of the army was complex, the case involving Walpole was simple, with Walpole and four others, two government officials and two military officers, appearing to have received payments from contractors.[122] The Treasury attempted to suppress such practices and informed the Victualling Commissioners that clerks and officials should not be interested in contracts or solicit them on behalf of others. Nevertheless, further abuses emerged, of officials and officers receiving payments.[123] A resolution followed:

> That for any Commissioner, or other Person intrusted by her Majesty in making Contracts for Publick Services, to be a Partner in such Contract, or to reserve a Share for any other Person, is an high Breach of Trust, and a notorious Corruption.[124]

Owing to 'An Act for the Queen's most gracious, general, and free pardon, relating to Publick Money', the Commons proceeded no further with the question, and no sanction remained against government officials participating in government contracts. Treasury directives and Commons resolutions pointed towards recognition of a problem for which it was not difficult to discover evidence. The power to scrutinize accounts, underpinned by political will or partisanship was all that were required for a substantial substratum of improper influence and pecuniary gain to emerge.[125] The central importance of influence, personal relationships and customary usage in politics and the army clearly sat uneasily alongside such notions of public probity.[126] The political elements of many such cases in this period meant contracts were almost incidental to the motivations of those making allegations.[127] Significantly, no attempt was made to establish regulatory guidelines regarding official involvement in contracts. Permeated by influence and patronage, contracts were an area where accusations of improper influence were easily made.

After the turmoil of the last years of Queen Anne a higher degree of administrative stringency in contract terms and conditions was discernible, and by the mid-eighteenth century there was greater emphasis given to the responsible expenditure of public money. On all occasions of awarding a contract, proposals were sent to the Comptrollers of Army Accounts for examination and possible revision.[128] Established in 1703 by Letters Patent, the Comptrollers maintained accounts of the issue and usage of Exchequer funds to the Paymaster General. The Comptrollers were also to 'inspect the Prices of all Contracts whatever' relating to the armed forces.[129] In examining contractors' accounts, government possessed an array of specialist administrative bodies and personnel.[130] Full payment was made only after a rigorous and laborious audit, with authentic certificates detailing delivery and issue of provisions. Although characterized as lengthy, leisurely, and unsuited to wartime expediencies, as a means of enforcing economy such a procedure often resulted in disallowed claims.[131]

Alongside those holding public office, contractors were required to provide sureties.[132] They served a dual purpose, instilling confidence in competent performance whilst providing financial recompense in the event of fraud. Formalized by economists as the 'Principal-Agent Problem', wherein employers induce employees to act in a way beneficial to their employers, forfeiture of bonds illustrates the limits to which the Treasury was willing to trust contractors.[133] £10,000 was demanded of the Gibraltar contractors in 1733 and 1752 but the amount was not fixed and depended on the extent of the contract.[134] Although the Treasury emphasized 'the Character of the person contracting is a Consideration no less essential to be regarded than the cheapness of the Contract' financial solvency was an essential component of 'Character'.[135] Advance payments were dependent on the same factors as sureties. Nominally, advances were given to facilitate delivery of six months' provisions, the amount stipulated in garrison contracts that must be permanently stored as a precaution against enemy attack or siege, thus necessitating regular deliveries.[136] Advances were undoubtedly important in facilitating bulk purchase and reducing costs, particularly important for garrison contracts where contractors dealt with a large number of suppliers. At Gibraltar, with six months' provisions required for 3,000 men, or 3,600 troops at Cape Breton, £10,000 was paid.[137] At 5½d. per man per day, the payment owing to the contractor for six months' provisions was £15,097 10s.[138] For smaller contracts such as the 456 men at Rattan, only £1,000 was paid, despite the contractor's obligation to supply twelve months' provisions in just over two months.[139] At 6d. per man per day, the annual payment to the contractor was £4,161. Providing twelve months' provisions meant considerable outlay which, whilst allowing for profits, exceeded £1,000. As advances represented a fraction of the sums necessary to purchase a large amount of provisions the importance of credit is readily apparent. Moreover, the advance was not paid as a lump sum. Half was usually paid after the contract was signed, with the remainder paid when certificates were received authenticating delivery.[140] The higher proportion of cost price of provisions given for larger contracts is notable and it appears the larger the number of troops victualled, the larger proportional sum government was prepared to advance.

Once sureties were provided, advances given and the contract signed, deliveries could begin. Payment was made upon the Treasury receiving signed victualling lists from the resident commissary or garrison commander detailing provisions issued, accompanied by a report from the Comptrollers.[141] Most contracts stipulated payments would be monthly, bimonthly or quarterly.[142] This meant government was frequently indebted to contractors although occasionally the opposite applied.[143] The efficient transmission of lists to London lent a degree of uncertainty over the timing of payment. The absence of the Deputy Commissary of Stores at Gibraltar delayed payments, as victualling lists remained unsigned.[144] Only men possessing considerable credit could withstand the delays that at times punctuated this process. Together with sureties and initial outlay on provisions, these factors effectively limited the number of men capable of conducting business under these conditions.

Terms and conditions provide a further demonstration of the Treasury's bargaining power. There was a difficult balance to strike between securing garrison supplies for a reasonable duration whilst leaving open the possibility of reducing costs. Contracts were usually made for a year with six months' notice thereafter. This time-frame ensured the supply of eighteen months' provisions, whilst allowing sufficient time to assess costs and adjust terms. The advantage for contractors was that such a period allowed reasonable profit. The power of renewal was a weapon government employed to reduce costs. Serving a termination notice did not preclude the incumbent contractor from submitting new proposals. Nevertheless, when enacted it was viewed as a declaration of intent either that the contractor had incurred the Treasury's displeasure or that they intended to cut costs.[145] Although additional allowances were made for wartime price rises this was predicated on the understanding prices would be reduced when either peace returned, prices fell or any other eventuality where the Treasury decided a reduction necessary. During the war of 1739–48, contract prices were reduced when a period of scarcity of wheat and beef was relieved.[146] With government often late in paying extra allowances after hostilities began it was not always possible to secure an immediate return to pre-war prices when hostilities ceased.[147] Prices were unlikely to fall immediately, and if the contract were properly performed up to twelve months' provisions purchased during a period of high prices would be stored.[148] Although delaying a return to pre-war prices, the Treasury displayed vigilance in ensuring this reduction occurred.[149]

Victualling contracts were carefully constructed to ensure government did not pay for unnecessary services. In performing a government service contractors were allowed certain privileges, such as freedom from customs duties, and indemnification for provisions supplied during the contract but subsequently unwanted. Compensation for losses resulting from enemy action or unavoidable accidents and a waste allowance were also permitted.[150] The Treasury was extremely careful regarding these payments and required solid proof that the loss had occurred before accepting liability.[151] Accidents such as loss of provisions at sea, where no government official was present, required bills of lading and sworn oaths to be submitted.[152]

Insurance was an area where the Treasury attempted to be parsimonious. Whilst it was often alleged that insurance made merchants less careful of their cargoes, the great risks attending wartime shipping were recognized. Losses such as that suffered by Chauncy Townsend reveal remarkable inconsistency towards insurance. Whilst the Comptrollers alluded to the high cost of insurance and recommended convoys for all victualling contractors, Townsend argued an insurance allowance should be given upon production of authenticated certificates.[153] Whilst Revell at Gibraltar claimed 10 per cent insurance, Townsend possessed none. In peacetime, government paid a 1½ per cent allowance but privateer activity in wartime fuelled rising insurance rates.[154] In 1741 the Treasury gave 4 per cent with or without convoy but in 1744 sanctioned a trial of 10 per cent for the duration of hostilities.[155] For safe conveyance of provisions, the Treasury advocated convoys. Contractors were obliged to contact the Treasury at least three weeks before their intended departure, allowing the Admiralty time to make convoy arrangements.[156] The right of contractors to a convoy was regularly stated; the right to an insurance allowance was not.[157] The condition 'with convoy' often halved the insurance premium.[158] Contractors were occasionally allowed to proceed without convoy, but the insurance allowances given were often inadequate.[159] Although reluctantly accepting its necessity, at the end of hostilities the Treasury unambiguously indicated their wish to terminate the 'great allowance' made for insurance.[160]

Problems over insurance re-emerged during the Seven Years' War and recourse was had to Treasury minute books to consult the policy of the earlier war.[161] The peacetime contract for Gibraltar specified insurance of 1 per cent but stipulated the use of convoys in wartime.[162] Wartime insurance rates were impossible to predict in peacetime but during the war, as contractors discovered, for payment of the current premium, authentic certificates were required.[163] The Treasury preferred victuallers to use convoys for insurance raised the cost of contracts.[164] An example of this stance was the Treasury's acceptance of proposals for victualling North America provided contractors paid insurance.[165] Convoys were potentially restrictive in making deliveries dependent on availability. Spithead was the usual departure point, but for contractors loading provisions at Cork, Dublin, Exeter and London this was an inconvenient diversion, and with contractors often bound by charter parties to wait for convoys, late arrival of pre-arranged escorts increased demurrage charges.[166] Alternatively, for ships chartered to sail directly from loading ports, contractors argued Spithead convoys were contrary to charter parties and insurance policies.[167] There was also the question of resources, for although the Admiralty always sought to be cooperative, it was not always possible to meet every demand:

> That their Lordships observe, these Two Ships are not to Sail together, but at different Times, and from different Places, and that it is impossible to provide Convoy for every single Ship that demands them.[168]

A coherent convoy policy did however emerge during the war. In 1758, the contractors for Gibraltar were directed not to send any provisions without convoy.[169] In February 1759, agreement was reached with North American contractors, with convoys sailing twice a year in March and September, with departure times circulated in advance.[170] Occasionally, provisions were so urgently required that contractors were permitted to sail without convoy.[171] The Treasury considered convoys as a device to save money on insurance, as well as an effectual defence against privateers and attempts to defraud insurance companies.[172] The enforcement of a coherent convoy policy, by offering a greater guarantee of safe delivery, minimized losses and cut costs, although this did not stem complaints of demurrage charges incurred by delays.[173] Nevertheless, convoy organization was much more effective than during the war of 1739–48.[174]

Despite the care taken over terms and conditions and examination of accounts, the Treasury was not completely successful at preventing fraud and collusion. Whilst the Earl of Hardwicke related to Newcastle that an autocrat such as Frederick II could ensure honesty by hanging offenders, Britain relied on commercial morality and financial inducement.[175] Alongside terms designed to ensure trustworthiness in personnel, contracts had to be sufficiently profitable firstly to reward contractors for the trouble and difficulty of performing them, and secondly to minimize fraud. If contractors were making a better profit than in their normal course of mercantile business it would be foolish to jeopardize this by illicit gain. The difficulty was to counter temptation when opportunities for illegal gain existed, for a system dependent on officials policing each other could never be free from collusion. Although the extent of collusive practices is impossible to determine, for the simple reason that successful collusion went undetected, it was widely believed to be pervasive, particularly for the British army campaigning abroad during both mid-century wars.[176] An effective way to reduce the likelihood of collusion was to increase the level of supervision, effectively widening the circle of accountability. For example, the clause in contracts stipulating that condemnation of provisions required the approval of two of three appointed inspectors, two of whom were appointed by the commanding officer, appears to have been successful. Signed certificates assigning the reason for condemnation had to be returned to London before payment was made.[177] The Comptrollers warned failure to specify was 'very irregular and would leave room for great abuses'.[178] The relative rarity of frauds of this nature may have emanated from heightened accountability. The absence of accountability and adequate supervision, allied to delegation of authority into unsuitable channels, facilitated extensive fraud in Germany.[179] William Pitt's accusation of Treasury mismanagement, although politically motivated, had some basis, but appears to have emanated from inexperience rather than wilful neglect. Conscious of recent parliamentary criticism, Newcastle earlier warned Pitt of the danger of being imposed on by contractors.[180] As Sir George Colebrooke related, in supplying money and provisions, Newcastle felt particularly accountable to Pitt, for 'Mr. Pitt threatened the Duke that if at any time a want of either should be found, He would impeach him in the Ensuing Session'.[181]

When the Earl of Bute established an investigation into Treasury management of the Commissariat, Newcastle was anxious 'insinuations and reflections' would be made, although most critics, including Pitt's supporters, directed the blame towards those whose 'particular province' was examination of accounts.[182] This was realistic, for the extent to which the Treasury could exert control was constrained by distance, time, and knowledge of local conditions and prices. The inadvertent discovery of a forage contract made in Germany at 9d. per ration, when the Treasury had made one for 6d., a difference of £70,000, was symptomatic of the difficulties, for a furious Newcastle admitted the Treasury discovered this discrepancy 'by meer Accident'.[183] The Treasury did attempt to be vigilant towards price movements and unwarranted costs. Noting contractors charged more for freight than stipulated under contract, the Treasury accepted the contractors' explanation that as the price of oats rose and the price of freight fell, they deemed it more responsible to charge the difference to freight. Yet they cautioned the contractors to inform them of any similar movement in future.[184] Close supervision of costs in concert with contract terms was admirable but official probity was not necessarily replicated further down the chain of authority. The conditions under which contracts were performed, distance, delegation of authority, and the government's inability to impose a higher degree of supervision were areas where a certain regulatory deficiency existed. Yet as the century progressed, regulations were tightened up alongside a closer scrutiny of accounts. Whilst these measures could not completely remove abuses, they amounted to a higher degree of administrative supervision and official accountability.

Although procedures, terms and conditions governing Treasury contracts varied considerably, some general observations are possible. Most obviously, there existed a contract 'system' only in very broad terms, by contract terms and conditions which bore some common features. The method of awarding contracts was neither entirely 'open' with competitive tendering and rival proposals, nor entirely 'closed'. It could be argued that the Treasury, if intent on reducing costs, should have adopted more open procedures. The allocation of victualling contracts is particularly difficult to defend for it cannot be defended on the basis there were too few capable persons. The scale of encampment contracts, discussed in the next chapter, exceeded many victualling contracts. If these could be advertised with successful results, why not garrison contracts? Yet in practical terms, the adopted method narrowed rather than precluded competition. The relatively short duration of contracts in itself promoted conscientiousness in performance, as well as indicating that the Treasury remained firmly in control of allocation. The power of renewal, as an opportunity to review performance and cost inserted accountability into the system. The Treasury's determination to avoid unnecessary expense indicates that, once awarded, a concern for economy did exist.

Treasury success in aligning business interests with contracts is particularly notable. Despite procedural differences, for all contracts the ability of contractors was always fundamentally important.[185] Patronage was tempered by the need to find capable men, and recommendation was seldom sufficient to secure a contract. Nevertheless, whether secured through sureties or from Treasury knowledge of candidates it was important that 'character references' were given. Indeed, more consideration appears to have been given to the quality of contracting personnel than to many government offices and departments.[186] That most financial and victualling contracts were awarded to merchants who were also members of parliament was of course more than a happy coincidence, but contract allocation was underpinned as much by the need to find suitably qualified men as by the desire to bestow patronage.

The pecuniary interest surrounding the relationship between government and contractors led to suspicion, seldom supported by firm evidence, of financial irregularity and 'sharp practice'. Typically, the embargo imposed on exporting provisions from Ireland in 1740 was suspected to be a measure aimed at enriching contractors, although the main purpose appears to have been a sensible strategic decision aimed at denying subsistence to the enemy.[187] Abuses appear less extensive than many believed. Several high-profile cases cannot be held as representative of an entire system. Examples of impropriety and the obloquy that fell on those involved indicate that official probity and responsible expenditure of public money were guiding principles for many of the governing elite. Although fraud was not completely eliminated, this did not emanate from a lack of political will, but from administrative deficiencies, most apparent in the Commissariat. Such problems also emerged during military emergencies when supply organization was hastily established. When time permitted, and the army did not become too large, the supply system operated efficiently. In these terms, methods of awarding remittance and victualling contracts were largely vindicated. Yet whilst the system possessed a clear rationale, such methods were not applied to contracts for troop encampments in England.

4 ADMINISTRATION OF ENCAMPMENT CONTRACTS IN ENGLAND, 1740–62

Despite their importance towards efficient military organization and the strategic use of troops, domestic encampments represent a hitherto neglected area of British military administration.[1] Their importance was not confined to military considerations, for as the visit of three Cherokee chiefs in 1762 demonstrated, encampments represented a symbolic display of British military power and prestige:

> During their stay in England, of about two months, they were invited to the tables of several of the nobility, and were shewn by a gentleman, appointed for that purpose, the tower, the camps, and every thing else that could serve to inspire them with proper ideas of the power and grandeur of the nation.[2]

In England, encampments were formed in 1740, 1741, and every summer from 1756 to 1762. In the latter period, regularity combined with unprecedented scale meant considerable organization was required to conduct efficient supply operations. As government possessed little experience of encampment administration, and with few experienced men in this sector, this was particularly problematic. Nevertheless, a collaborative effort between government and contractors blending administrative competence and economic expertise ensured domestic encampment supply was one of the least problematic areas of military contracting during this period. Encampment contracts differed from other Treasury contracts inasmuch as merit and business competence were unambiguously the most important factors in contract allocation. Differences in awarding contracts, alongside a variation in contracting personnel, illustrate the complex nature of the supply structure and further undermine the association between government contracts and 'Old Corruption'.

The method of awarding English encampment contracts was by competitive tender following newspaper advertisement, an identical method to that of the Victualling Office.[3] A deadline was set for receiving proposals and a day designated for reading proposals and awarding the contract.[4] This procedure was adhered to whenever camps were formed, and except for 1756, remained unchanged throughout the Seven Years' War.[5] Behind this procedural divergence the Treasury was conscious these contracts were qualitatively different from foreign garrison contracts. Although all contractors possessed some degree of sectoral and geographical expertise, the expertise of garrison contractors was previously demonstrated in geographical terms. For domestic encampment contractors, there was a closer identification with sectoral expertise, with many close to sources of supply or possessing greater knowledge relative to procurement. The nature of supply, in terms of products supplied and timing of deliveries necessitated this divergence in personnel. Three or six months' provisions could not simply be purchased, loaded, and shipped to destinations where agents supervised distribution. Troop dispersal meant supply operations were conducted on entirely different terms. Whereas garrisons were fixed, field armies were mobile, and required contractors to be continually aware of military movements. Even camps, although fixed, could easily be moved and in any case there were rarely ever only one or two camps. The Treasury therefore sought men who could provide products across a wide geographical area. It was necessary for contractors to possess a competent knowledge of surrounding counties, and managerial qualities were required to coordinate procurement and ensure punctual delivery and distribution. These requirements induced the Treasury to adopt a different procedure in awarding contracts, although it was again characterized by a desire to procure suitably qualified men. Although encampment contractors shared many similar attributes with remitters and victuallers such as creditworthiness and capacity to undertake extensive economic operations, a clear divergence in economic status and function existed.

The articles supplied for encampment contracts constituted the basic requirements of the army. Financial frugality dictated that the Treasury would contract for only the most basic items. The full range of articles supplied were bread, wagons for delivering bread, wood as fuel for boiling soldier's kettles, and straw for bedding.[6] Troops purchased other provisions including beef and beer from sutlers resident at camps. No more than one general sutler per regiment and one petty sutler per company were permitted to encamp.[7] The allowance of 'ammunition bread' per soldier was a 6lb loaf delivered every four days.[8] Contractors built ovens and employed bakers at rented buildings near encampments. On the evening before a delivery, sergeants informed Quartermasters of the quantity of bread each company or regiment required on the following day.[9] The Quartermasters then supervised distribution, and were obliged to keep accurate accounts of all products distributed to troops.[10]

Unless they specified before entering camp that they would purchase their own bread, troops were not permitted to purchase bread other than from the contractor.[11] Straw was delivered weekly. A truss of 36lbs was provided for five men per week. In camps, five men shared a tent, and supply was computed according to this formula. Wood was similarly computed at 105lbs per week for five men, or 3lbs per man per day.[12] The number of wagons and horses depended on the extent of the services required. Wagons were used for delivering bread and transporting sick men to hospital. Any other usage required the authorization of the commanding officer.[13] Wagons had to be covered with 'tilts' and equipped with drivers, strong harness, and a variety of tools including chain or rope, draghook, spade and hatchet. Spare wagons and wheels and a 'Betty' for raising wagons were also required. Horses had to be at least four years old, and contractors were required to replace those killed or disabled, although compensation was paid for horses killed and wagons destroyed by enemy action.[14] Forage for horses belonging to officers, staff, and cavalry regiments was supplied in rations of 15lbs of hay and 8lbs of oats. Contractors purchased forage for their horses from the King's magazines.[15] It was generally understood forage was only supplied under contract for encampments, and was not usually permitted to regiments in garrisons or quarters.[16] In England, the Treasury provided a forage allowance of 200 days, with the amount of rations issued dependent on rank.[17] In Scotland, 100 days was usual, although 200 days was allowed in 1760.[18]

In submitting proposals applicants were expected to indicate the price of articles and the camps they proposed to supply. Within this framework of competitive tendering, the Treasury assessed proposals on price but also in relation to convenience. One proposal might be lower in one article but more expensive in others. The Treasury did not divide the contract to correspond with the lowest bidder in each article but computed the price of all articles together, and pending sureties, awarded the contract to the lowest bidder.[19] The convenience of dealing with one contractor for all articles was, except in 1760, maintained between 1756 and 1762. This was where encampment contracts diverged from Victualling Office practice, for throughout the eighteenth century the latter body employed one contractor to supply all articles abroad but used separate contractors for single articles at home.[20] Early in the war, Ligonier argued that practical difficulties made it desirable that bread and wagons should not be provided separately.[21] There appears no practical reason why other supplies could not have been provided separately. In 1760 the Treasury diverged from their usual practice, in deciding that as John Martyr's bread proposal was lower, they would divide the contract.[22] Why they chose to do so for this year alone is something of a mystery, although that it was easily accomplished suggests that the convenience of dealing with a single contractor may have been dearly bought.

Proposals were not only limited by article but by camp, with many proposals offering to supply all articles to selected camps. Given the preference for a single contractor these proposals were unlikely to succeed. That proposals continued to be made in these terms suggests many applicants were unaware of the Treasury's preference for a single contractor. For example, in 1760 the competition was reduced to the two proposals made for all the required articles.[23] Comprehensive proposals, offering all articles to all camps stood a far better chance of success. Although separate contracts for separate products may have been cheaper, it may have been less secure, in heightening the possibility of supply failure. Employing a single contractor can also be justified in cost terms. Every contract made with a government department required payment of fees, later reimbursed by government, to public officials. Fees were payable for copies of contracts, for warrants from the Treasury, Pipe Office and Remembrancer, and to the Auditors for settling accounts. An increase in the number of contractors meant an increase in the amount of fees payable by the Treasury.[24]

Experience was also important. Richard Oswald's 'diligent execution of his Contract for supplying Bread & Wagons' in 1756 enhanced his future prospects.[25] Compared to other Treasury contracts political influence was less important. Whilst Oswald received several recommendations, notably for contracts in Germany in 1758, such recommendations although useful, do not appear to have been decisive.[26] Experience and recommendation could be important but only when allied to cheapness. There would have been little point in competitive tendering had it been otherwise. Competitive tendering could however be manipulated. In 1758, fearing a lower bid would emerge from advertisement Oswald used an acquaintance to present very low proposals. The latter were accepted but on pretence the bidder revised his proposals in a way the Treasury found unacceptable and Oswald's proposals were accepted as the next lowest bid.[27] This was exactly the outcome Oswald planned. Although illustrating how the system could be manipulated there was no guarantee of success. It was a calculated risk that paid off. That such a scheme was enacted is testimony that advertisement promoted competition.[28]

The number of proposals received each year appears to indicate that the Treasury's aim of encouraging competition to lower prices was largely achieved. The precise number of proposals in 1756 is unclear, although several proposals were read before referral to the Secretary at War and Commissary General of Stores and Provisions.[29] That competition existed is apparent from Barrington's recommendation of Oswald's proposals as cheapest for bread and forage, for although his price for wagons was not cheaper than others he offered to pay more for forage for his wagon horses.[30] For the remainder of the war there was significant competition; 1757 and 1762 were particularly competitive with nine proposals each, six proposals were made in 1759 and 1761, and five in 1758. The least competitive year was 1760, with only four proposals.[31] As with remittance and victualling contracts a similar emphasis was placed on financial solvency. Sureties perhaps assumed more importance for these contracts, for it was unlikely that the Treasury were personally acquainted with many applicants.[32] This also applied to foreigners.[33] Sureties appear to have been fixed at double the advance payment. The latter sum aimed to enable the contractor to begin work and was based upon estimating the number of troops and the duration of camps.[34] A sum was allowed for every man provided under contract.[35] For example, in 1756 the Treasury based their calculations on 25,000 troops for six months. On this basis, Oswald received an advance of £21,065 for bread and wagons contracts, whilst providing sureties for £42,130.[36] An advance of £10,465 was given for ninety-one days service for wagons, and £10,600 for bread.[37] The advance for the forage contract was £17,800, slightly over half the £35,000 bond.[38] The principle that the scale of operations determined the amount of advance payments and securities continued throughout the war, with smaller contracts receiving commensurately smaller advances of £5,000 or £6,000.[39] The Treasury did not concern itself with computation of advance payments but requested this information from the War Office and Commissary General of Stores.[40]

Advance payments facilitated bulk purchase, an essential component of profitability, but encampment contractors required a modicum of wealth and credit.[41] The securities demanded were a device to test financial solvency. It was important that contractors possessed reserves of capital or credit for, as with victualling contracts, payment could be long delayed. However, unlike victualling contracts, payment was not made for the precise amount of provisions issued in a specific period but on account with sums of £3,000 or £5,000 issued during the course of the contract.[42] When the contract was completed the balance was assessed by scrutiny of the contractors' claims, examination of signed lists from commissaries at magazines detailing amounts supplied, musters of horses, and information from officers relative to any disputed points or special circumstances. Although payments were regularly made contractors were usually owed money.[43] A lengthy inspection of accounts was conducted by the Commissary General of Stores, Comptrollers of Army Accounts, and Auditors, before the Exchequer declared accounts. The earliest settlement was approximately nine months but was more often over a year.[44] In an extreme but notable case, Oswald's 1758 contract was not declared at the Exchequer until 1813, twenty-nine years after his death.[45]

The personnel applying for and performing encampment contracts were significantly different from other Treasury contracts. The most striking feature was the absence of the hitherto ubiquitous London merchant. Remittance and foreign victualling contractors displayed little interest in encampment contracts.[46] In the 1740s it was British rather than London-based merchants who were notably absent. Bread contractors to English encampments of 1740 and 1741 were London-based Jewish-Portuguese merchants.[47] By the Seven Years' War, the domestic supply activities of this mercantile ethnic group had declined, but they were very active during the earlier war, most notably as bread contractors. When the Treasury advertised the bread contract for British troops in the Low Countries in 1742, four of the nine proposals received were from Portuguese merchants whilst a fifth was an Anglo-Portuguese partnership.[48] Military commanders also recommended Jewish-Portuguese merchants.[49] Close relations existed between this mercantile community and merchants in the Low Countries.[50] By mid-century these merchants, although operating on a smaller scale than the great contractors of Marlborough's era, possessed considerable prestige and wealth. In 1743, Francos, de Costas and Perieras joined the City elite in presenting a Loyal Address against the 'Popish Pretender'.[51]

In 1740, Thames Valley mealmen, millers, bakers and corn chandlers submitted an interesting joint proposal.[52] This area, particularly Kingston, was an important embarkation point for meal and malt loaded on barges for London with local wholesalers concerned in this trade engaged in multiple capacities.[53] Yet the scale of operations proved beyond their means and the proposal was withdrawn when they failed to find sufficient millers to grind the large amount of corn required.[54] For such men, sub-contracting was more consistent with their economic function and status. To act as the named contractor required the possession of great credit facilities and the assumption of considerable responsibility and risk.[55] The extensive nature of encampment contracts refutes insufficient profitability as an explanation for the absence of remittance and victualling contractors. The victualling contractors for Gibraltar, generally considered the most lucrative contract, received £263,505 between 19 December 1757 and 30 June 1763. The approximate annual sum, £47,910, divided between three partners, totals £15,970 for each partner per year.[56] Only in two years between 1756 and 1762, did the encampment contractor receive less. Whilst these figures do not reveal the rate of profit, it is difficult to see profitability as an explanation for the lack of mercantile interest. In terms of products supplied, there was a difference between garrison and encampment contractors, although most garrison contractors supplied bread or wheat. It was not beneath the dignity of London merchants to supply such products. Nevertheless, shipment of products was usually where the involvement of these merchants began and ended. It appears more likely that encampment supply, as a form of grass roots contracting, meant involvement in sectors that London merchants were unlikely to be familiar with, whilst demanding distributive skills they were unlikely to possess.

Although patronage was of secondary importance in encampment contracts, it was not entirely absent. Where it operated it tended to be for small, localized contracts with military men, such as wood and straw contracts made with Major-General Holmes for Isle of Wight camps in 1758, or emanated from a position on the military establishment, such as the Barrack Master in Scotland.[57] Although awarded partly on the basis of local knowledge and proprietary right, both men were MPs, and from Whig families where government patronage was expected and received.[58] Those performing English encampment contracts can be divided into two groups. One consisted of Scottish merchants with some experience of this sector. The second were agricultural wholesalers and large farmers based in and around London. None were Members of Parliament, and in the latter group, sectoral specialization in domestic agriculture was particularly notable. Although Richard Oswald held the contracts in the period 1756–8, there was a different contractor each year for 1759–62. Of the six men named as encampment contractors, two, Oswald and Archibald Fraser, were Scottish merchants. Oswald was a man of undoubted mercantile ability who later supplied troops in Germany as commissary and contractor.[59] In the former capacity, the Duke of Brunswick famously related how England sent him 'commissaries fit to be generals, and generals not fit to be commissaries'.[60] Active in foreign commerce, Oswald possessed business interests not dissimilar to remittance and victualling contractors, although he did not perform any contracts of this nature. Despite being the named contractor, Oswald worked in partnership with Lawrence Dundas, and Robert Haldane, an East India Company Captain. All were part of an extensive network of Scottish merchants in London.[61] Dundas obtained experience as contractor and commissary in Scotland and Flanders (1746–8), and possessed influential military connections.[62] Fraser, the contractor in 1760, was employed by Dundas in Germany in 1759 as a favour to the regimental agent George Ross, and was described by Dundas as a 'Mad young boy'.[63] Fraser was a son of the infamous Lord Lovat executed in 1747, half-brother to the remarkable Simon Fraser, and married to the sister of the fourth Duke of Argyll. Aged around ten at his father's death, he attended Glasgow College and a London academy before becoming a merchant.[64] His mother's emphasis on her son's loyalty to 'his majesty and present happy establishment' was part of a successful campaign to remove the stain of family Jacobitism.[65]

The Scottish element in English encampment contracts was not a consequence of favouritism, but emanated partly from experience, in which, for Oswald and Fraser, the association with Dundas appears crucial. Moreover, the clannishness of Scottish merchants in London as a defensive strategy against suspected Jacobitism was well-tailored towards contracting, where partnerships were common.[66] Nevertheless, collaboration between Oswald, Dundas and Haldane for the 1756 encampment contract dissolved when Haldane was bought out of the partnership in 1757. In 1758, Oswald secured the contract, and dropped Dundas, although his continued use of Dundas's equipment caused a rift between them.[67] Both succeeded, separately, to contracts in Germany in 1759.[68] Despite these disputes, in the wider context of the limited opportunities available in Scotland, and as a means of career advancement, such partnerships were clearly beneficial. As encampment contracts demanded familiarity with the southern counties, those with knowledge of agriculture in these areas possessed an advantage. Close to sources of supply, they were well-placed to organize procurement and distribution. John Willan, the contractor in 1759, was a wholesale farmer and horse dealer, possessing land and connections in many southern counties.[69] Samuel Tewkesbury, the contractor in 1762, was a Winchester farmer who leased land for encampments throughout the war.[70] The contractors in 1761, John Boghurst and John Martyr, were yeomen farmers from Kent. Martyr described himself thus, and the amount of land he held corresponds to this description, with thirty-five acres in Yalding parish and sixty acres in East Peckham. Martyr was still submitting applications for encampment contracts between 1779 and 1781.[71]

Terms and conditions of encampment contracts offer further evidence of the Treasury's concern with economy. Of all contracts, encampment contracts were of the most imprecise duration. It was known that troops were required in camp from approximately June until they moved to winter quarters, but contracts never gave an exact termination date. Realistically, troops could not remain encamped long after October. Inclement weather threatened sickness, and with most camps formed to counter a threatened invasion, that was unlikely in winter months, camps lost their raison d'être.[72] No duration was set for supplying bread, but there was usually a stipulated period for wagons. Facing the threat of invasion in 1756, the Treasury contracted for wagons for six months, but in the less panic stricken year of 1757, fifty days was deemed sufficient.[73] Contractors were expected to receive directions from the Commander-in-Chief or Commissary General as to camp location, the quantity of deliveries required and any other relevant information.[74] Whereas storehouses were provided for garrisons, it was the contractor's responsibility to establish storehouses and magazines for encampments. The Treasury made an allowance for rentals incurred under this head. In the first encampment of the war the contractor pointed out the Treasury's failure to include such a clause. With encampments fairly uncommon in Britain in the first half of the eighteenth century, such an omission was understandable.[75]

To facilitate ease of delivery, magazines were always located close to camps, with storehouses, granaries and bakeries rented from landowners and farmers.[76] Contractors were required to provide agents and staff at magazines to coordinate delivery and distribution, alongside state officials and officers. A clerk was to attend at the head of each brigade of the Artillery Train and at Headquarters to assist deliveries and take receipts from the Quartermaster. Compensation was paid if magazines were plundered, destroyed by fire, or taken by the enemy, if reported within twenty days. Contractors also provided guards for magazines.[77] Payment for these services was in effect an indemnification by government to contractors for providing supply infrastructure. Similar conditions pertained to wagons inasmuch as contractors were required to provide the personnel and materiel to make wagons fully operational. Conductors, drivers, smiths, harness makers, wheelwrights, and of course horses, were provided. Musters were taken to ensure the required number of wagons and horses were provided.[78]

Payment was met by stoppages from troops' pay and government subsidies. Government paid the entire cost of wagons, wood and straw, but partly subsidized forage and bread. Government met only a fraction of the cost of bread, such as 1*d.* of a 6*d.* loaf, or ½*d.* of a 5½*d.* loaf.[79] A higher ratio was paid for forage, from 5*d.*of the 11*d.* charged in 1756 to 2¼*d.*, 2½*d.*, and 4*d.* of the 10¼*d.*, 10½*d.*, and 12*d.* charged in 1759, 1760 and 1762.[80] The penalties included in encampment contracts reflected a desire to avoid unnecessary expense. Short weight bread and forage rejected as of poor quality were paid for by contractors. Government possessed little immediate sanction against late or irregular deliveries although this was never a problem during the war. It may possibly have been problematic to change contractors during the course of a contract, although given the short notice required it could have been done. Unsatisfactory performance did however place the contractor at a disadvantage when the next contract was pending, and this appears to have contributed towards ensuring contractors were conscientious.

The administrative organization necessary for planning encampment supply began as early as February 1756.[81] By March, Lawrence Dundas and Robert Haldane were engaged in purchasing hay, oats, clover and ryegrass, with at least six agents in the vicinity of projected camps at Chatham, Dorking, Ryegate, Petersfield, Dorchester, Winchester, Salisbury and Blandford. They were also shipping oats from Lynn, Norfolk.[82] Working in partnership with Oswald, they were strategically well-placed to obtain the contract. In preparing proposals Dundas argued that as it would take time to procure the number of horses required, and as prices would probably rise in the interim, the contract should be awarded quickly.[83] Before making a contract, the Treasury began employing administrative staff. Consistent with his practical control of military affairs between the Jacobite Rebellion and his disgrace in 1757, Cumberland was active in planning supply.[84] The Secretary at War suggested the appointment of a Commissary General of Stores, Provisions and Forage to supervise the entire system of provisioning. Highly valued for his expertise and knowledge, having acted in a similar capacity during the Jacobite Rebellion, Cumberland suggested Abraham Hume, whose employment began on 13 March.[85] Hume's responsibilities encompassed assessment of contract prices and accounts, and ensuring provisions of the requisite quantity and quality were provided. The position utilized his expertise in this area, which was immediately apparent. The Treasury sought advice from the Secretary at War as to the usual price of wagons. Finding no information in the office books, and possessing no personal knowledge, he referred the matter to Hume.[86] Hume's appointment was the catalyst for the emergence of a bureaucratic structure of camp administration. Recognizing the lack of experienced personnel Cumberland suggested that Hume recommend his own assistants. Hume recommended employment of two deputies, paid at one guinea per day with an inclusive allowance for horses, to implement his instructions. They were to visit and examine the condition of magazines, check the veracity of receipts, and ensure the due performance of contracts. Hume also recommended the appointment of an under deputy at each magazine recording all forage entering the magazine. In a separate ledger the amount of forage remaining would be recorded. Weekly reports were to be made of the amount delivered and removed.[87] With magazine returns sent to the Commissary General, the Commander-in-Chief would constantly be informed of the state of supplies.

Hume accepted that the responsibility attached to these positions made it imperative that those employed were honest and capable.[88] With Cumberland's approval, the Treasury accepted his proposals. In accepting the salaries proposed by Hume, Barrington realistically accepted the temptations these positions offered:

> The Service cannot be so well regulated as by having a proper Number of Persons Employed under the Commissary General, who may be a Cheque and Controul over the Contractors ... As the People to be Employed must have great Trust reposed in them, their Salaries ought to be such as will induce proper and sufficient Persons to accept these Employments.[89]

This meant men whose wealth, respectability, and sensibility protected them from the temptation to falsify returns for pecuniary gain. Hume's recommendations were quickly implemented, with most staff appointed on 28 April.[90] Two deputy commissaries were employed at one guinea each per day. Under-Deputies, paid 7s. 6d. per day, were employed at eight separate magazines. These salaries amounted to £8 17s. per day or £3,239 2s. per annum. Travelling allowances of Under-Deputies increased costs, and Hume indicated more staff would be required should further magazines be established.[91] From 1757, and for the remainder of the war, only one deputy commissary was employed, and the salaries of Under-Deputies were reduced to 6s. per day at Hume's recommendation.[92] Fewer Under-Deputies were employed after 1756, with six employed in 1757, four in 1758, five in 1759, seven in 1760, five in 1761 and four in 1762. The five deputies employed in 1759 continued through the winter of 1759 and the camps of 1760, with two added in June, before their employment was terminated in October 1760.[93]

In 1756, the administrative structure was further strengthened by the appointment of William Godfrey, recommended by Hume as 'very capable' for this 'necessary Service' as commissary for firing and straw.[94] With wood and straw not supplied under contract, Godfrey's responsibilities consisted of managing procurement and distribution of these articles. A head clerk and assistant supervised distribution at each magazine. By the nature of its functions, the supply organization employed men on the land gathering wood and straw.[95] As less responsibility was attached to these positions than that of commissaries located at magazines, salaries were lower. Having served during the Jacobite Rebellion, Godfrey attempted to secure £2 per day but Cumberland allowed him only £1 11s. 6d.[96] One of his relatives appears to have been employed as one of two deputy commissaries at 10s. per day each. Eight under-commissaries were employed at 5s. per day, with two others paid 2s. 6d. per day. The total cost of the establishment was £4 15s. per day.[97] The nepotism went unchecked, thus indicating that 'interest' operated at many levels of official appointments.[98] Nevertheless, Barrington robustly defended the reduced salaries:

> It is true that in the Rebellion Godfreys [sic] was allow'd 3£ a day, but there seems to have been no consideration of Oeconomy at that Juncture in the War Office.[99]

When requesting employment, Godfrey casually mentioned his former salary, whilst asserting his willingness 'to take for this Service what may be judged Adequate to the trouble'.[100] It was one thing to be modest before securing an appointment but Godfrey underestimated the emphasis on economy at the War Office.[101] With encampment supply entailing significant administrative expansion, in terms of staff employed by state officials and contractors, economy was a major concern.[102] Staff expenditure rose from £29,893 in 1756 to £47,060 in 1757, with new appointments on the military establishment including ancient offices such as Harbinger, Provost Marshal, and Wagon Master General.[103]

It was necessary to equip troops for camp life with canteens, kettles, tents and assorted camp equipage. These articles were the responsibility of colonels who employed regimental agents to negotiate contracts with suppliers, with payment from regimental funds of bat and baggage money. Under the special circumstances of 1756–7, blankets were issued to Hessian troops continuing in winter encampments.[104] The most successful supplier of camp equipment was John Trotter, from 1754 described as an 'Upholder' in Thrift Street, Soho. Catalogues at his shop detailing horses for sale indicate that Trotter possessed a well-known business.[105] Trotter's contracting career spanned the Seven Years' War and the American Revolution and he was considered an honest and reliable purveyor of quality products.[106] During the Seven Years' War, Trotter supplied tents, marquees, knapsacks, and gaiters. These products were not bound by geographical constraints, and Trotter was able to supply regiments in North America, Germany and Britain.[107]

Completing the admixture of encampment supply personnel was the position of Superintendent and Keeper of Magazines, a position created in January 1757 as a consequence of surplus supplies remaining from 1756. The necessity for the position reflected the difficulties assessing supply and demand emanating from the uncertain duration of camps and fluctuating numbers of troops. Accountable to the Treasury, his responsibilities began after encampments dispersed, when he was required to remove surplus forage to selected magazines under his supervision. Surplus supplies were sold if requested by the Commander-in-Chief.[108] The administrative costs of the position were high. The salary was 10s. per day, with 1s. 6d. each for a maximum of two labourers at each magazine. A guard was stationed at each magazine, whose duties included turning forage and keeping it clean. Many expenses, mainly concerned with transportation such as metage and wharfage, were allowed. A waste allowance of 4 per cent on delivered forage, and 3½ per cent on that remaining in magazines after twelve months was also given.[109] The position allowed government to contract for considerably lower amounts of forage in 1758 and 1761. No forage contract was necessary in 1757, when it was estimated that purchase of only 76,296 rations of hay and 26,166 rations of oats was necessary to supplement an accumulated surplus of 690,516 rations from 1756.[110] The utility of the position was immediately apparent when forage was supplied from the Superintendent's magazines to the Hessian winter encampment of 1756–7.[111] In July 1758 local Excise Collectors, receiving 5 per cent of all sales, sold off surplus magazine rations, consisting of 238,068 rations of hay and 144,052 rations of oats.[112] The position of Superintendent was revived in 1760, following the surplus of 420,000 forage rations remaining from 1759. In June 1761, orders were given to sell the remaining quantities.[113] The Treasury gained experience as the war developed, and with a closer approximation between supplies required and delivered, no Superintendent was necessary after 1761.

This administrative structure, with a carefully graded hierarchy, aimed at accountability at all levels. The official management of the supply of straw and wood, and the creation of the position of Superintendent illustrate the expansion of state activity as a necessary accompaniment to the employment of contractors in managing encampment supply. The cooperation of local state officials supplemented positions directly concerned with encampments. For payment of troops, Excise Collectors and Land Tax Receivers were instructed to supply Regimental Paymasters with cash for bills drawn on regimental agents.[114] This followed a complaint that a Regimental Paymaster paid poundage to a Land Tax Receiver for cash on a drawn bill. The use of local officials obviated the expense of providing a Deputy Paymaster at each camp.[115] Although recognizing the necessity for what amounted to the administrative organization of a supply corps, there were times when the professionalism of officials such as Hume sat uneasily alongside the gentle amateurism of aristocratic government. Treasury concern for economy conflicted with the necessity of employing sufficient administrative staff, and the reduction of Hume's salary appears to have been the cause of his request to resign in 1758. The refusal of Dundas to present his accounts occasioned the request, with Hume stating he could not 'with Honour receive the pay of an Employment wch. I am not permitted to perform in its' Several Branches'.[116] Hume also claimed that government did not appreciate the importance of his position, and indicated this was a particularly British problem:

> The Commissary General ought to be put on a respectable foot in [the] Army, as Intendants & Commissary Generals are, in the service of Foreign Nations: where the Importance of this Charge is better known and more considered than here.[117]

Although Newcastle allowed Hume £3 per day, the Pitt-Devonshire Treasury reduced the salary to £2 until 31 December 1756 and £1 in periods when there were no encampments.[118] Once camps were re-established the rate was again raised.[119] Hume argued that as Parliament voted his salary, the Treasury could not reduce it.[120] He appears to have gained his point, as he remained in place during the war.

Despite Britain's apparent lack of experience in preparing and organizing encampments such a view can easily be deceptive. Although few governmental personnel possessed experience of encampments, the experience of military officers appears to have been particularly valuable.[121] The role of military personnel in camps was fully delineated in military textbooks, and many officers drew upon the experience of earlier wars. As temporary summer affairs, there was in any case time to organize and consider administrative measures. Nevertheless, with an unprecedented scale of organization required, the appointment of supply personnel, whether as state officials or contractors represented only one step in resolving supply difficulties. The efficiency of supply organization remained to be tested under the pressure of wartime conditions.

5 PERFORMANCE OF ENCAMPMENT CONTRACTS

The organization of domestic military supply between 1739 and 1763, encompassing the War of Austrian Succession, Jacobite Rebellion and Seven Years' War was punctuated by the periodic revival of the threat of French invasion. Although the navy was expected to repel any invasion, a concentrated military force was necessary in the event of a breach of the wooden walls.[1] The invasion threat also determined troop location, for the threat towards Scotland and Ireland was more intermittent than that posed towards English southern counties. Consequently, English encampments were more frequent and contained a far larger number of troops, although the threat of simultaneous invasion of different parts of the British Isles meant the Celtic fringe could not be neglected.[2] Encampments resolved the problem, at least during summer months, of accommodating a large army. With a larger number of troops mobilized in England, and fewer barracks than Scotland or Ireland, this was a very pressing problem. Castles, the medieval defences against foreign invasion, were long neglected although a few housed French prisoners during the Seven Years' War.[3] Encampments could also provide a suitable environment for military training and practical value in assembling troops for Continental embarkations.[4] Yet these factors were generally subsidiary, for the main reason in forming camps was to counter the invasion threat.[5]

The contrast between England and the Celtic fringe in troop accommodation diminished later in the century amidst more overt militarization. In the mid-eighteenth century, the difference was significant, reflecting a divergence in historical experience and differing sentiments and values held towards the military. It also impacted on the nature of military provisioning. During winter months, wide troop dispersal made centralized supply methods and extensive contracts unnecessary. Yet with English encampments representing the largest concentrated military force in Britain, supply could not be left to the vagaries of local suppliers. Owing to the sheer number of troops, encampments constituted an important part of the war effort. To the civilian population, they were less objectionable than impositions on local communities, and more acceptable than barracks.[6] Extensive geographical distribution of camps during the Seven

Years' War meant planning supply operations posed problems not dissimilar to that of supplying isolated Scottish forts. However, in England there were better roads, greater agricultural productivity, and merchants and traders were better equipped than their Scottish counterparts to conduct extensive supply operations. In the context of military contracting, encampment supply is particularly notable inasmuch as management of extensive economic operations was not confined to wealthy merchants, but encompassed agricultural wholesalers, farmers and horse dealers. Agricultural and mercantile expertise is apparent in the organizational ability of contractors to surmount potentially problematic operations of procurement and distribution to widely dispersed camps. Government also deserves credit, for although historians have correctly pointed to the deleterious effect of imprecise demarcations within military administration, encampment supply offers an example of an intelligent use of available resources and personnel. Mistakes were made, but lessons learnt, and continuity in administrative framework ensured military and economic operations ran smoothly for the duration of the war.

Encampments in England were an important element of the war effort during the Seven Years' War. It was not always thus. Earlier, encampments were used for largely different purposes. Under Charles II and James II, annual training camps, 'Camps of Instruction' concerned with inculcating appropriate levels of military training, exercise and discipline were established, notably at Blackheath and Putney Heath. A camp containing approximately 14,000 men was established at Hounslow in May 1686, and camps continued to be held until 1688.[7] After the Glorious Revolution, this nascent attempt at military improvement fell into desuetude.[8] It was not until 1756 that encampments assumed a more active military function and became a regular feature of British military organization. Camps obviated difficulties arising from accommodating a large army at public houses, and from the opposition to barracks. The latter appears a more apposite mode of accommodation, but in 1697 barrack accommodation in England was estimated as sufficient for only 5,000 infantry troops. A century later, Britain possessed barrack capacity of 68,628 men, with 53,852 troops resident in 1797.[9] British society became somewhat reconciled to militarization during the French Revolutionary wars, but the powerful association made between barracks and absolutism was only slowly surmounted, and even those supportive of more overt military organization were attentive towards prevailing prejudices.[10] Opponents of barracks argued they promoted a military unity dangerous to state security and that military seclusion would make people insensible to the size of the army. It was therefore better to continue the burden on local communities.[11] Barrack building was of a piecemeal nature in England, and fewer barracks and the great distance between them meant that, unlike Scotland, a Barrack Master was unnecessary, although individual barrack masters were appointed.[12] Despite recognition that quartering troops was a major inconvenience to publicans, lively opposition to barracks remained.[13]

Amidst the progressive reduction of the British army between 1713 and 1739, there were, unlike France or Germany, no peacetime camps for military training.[14] The Jacobite scare of 1722 led to a display of military force, with encampments at Hounslow Heath and extensive troop gatherings at Hyde Park and Salisbury Plain.[15] For officers, the failure of rebellion to materialize and consequent lack of military activity proved frustrating and costly.[16] Not until 1740 when the threat of invasion re-emerged, were encampments again necessary to supplement the presence of the Fleet in home waters.[17] In meeting the supply demands of encampments, the mode of contracting during the War of Spanish Succession, described as 'one gigantic contract supplemented in all other matters by a multitude of petty contractors and sutlers' was a useful precedent.[18] Camps formed at Hounslow Heath, Newbury and Windsor in 1740 and Colchester in 1741 were supplied in this manner, with bread provided under contract, and commissaries procuring forage, wood and straw.[19] The Lords Justices accepted Wade's advice in organizing supply of provisions, whilst delegating responsibility for the bread contract to the Secretary at War.[20] Containing far more troops than the largest foreign garrison, the camps were not negligible affairs, with 13,981 troops in the three camps of 1740 and nearly 12,000 troops at Colchester in 1741.[21] Nevertheless, as temporary affairs, and with only bread provided under contract, the sums paid to contractors, £2,818 in 1740 and £1,167 in 1741 were rather small.[22] After 1741, the necessity for domestic camps largely subsided. In 1742, despite scepticism over proposed British military activity in the Low Countries, which was 'likely to end in another Pacific Camp at Colchester', 16,000 British troops embarked for the Continent.[23] Despite an invasion threat in 1744, and an intermittent threat of French intervention before, during and after the outbreak of the 1745 Jacobite Rebellion, neither led to large or lengthy encampments.[24] A chronic shortage of troops heightened panic but Britain remained free from foreign invasion.[25] The concentration of forces to crush the Rebellion resulted in temporary camps in London accommodating troops from an eighteen-mile radius.[26] In the context of military emergencies, the military value of encampments was valued by the Duke of Richmond, in his argument that 'there is no forming from a Cantonement, whereas tis done instantly from a Camp'.[27] Despite residual fears of foreign intervention and rebellion after Culloden, defeat of the Rebels had removed any threat of invasion.[28]

The requisite conditions for the formation of camps re-emerged early in 1756, with the discovery of French plans to invade Britain and Minorca, with the latter reportedly perceived as 'no difficult Undertaking'.[29] On 23 March, the King reported French designs to the Commons, prompting a higher degree of domestic military mobilization.[30] Augmentation of the army had begun in

1755, with ten new foot regiments consisting of 1,014 men per regiment.[31] By 1756 there were 65,403 troops in Britain, including eight battalions of Hessians consisting of 6,744 men and twelve battalions of Hanoverians, numbering 8,845 troops in British pay.[32] The intermittent existence and temporary, makeshift character of the army was perhaps best symbolized by employing foreign troops to ease recruitment pressures, whilst enabling Britain to raise an army comparable with Continental powers.[33] Camps were necessary to accommodate such a large army but could not be immediately established, so local quartering in public houses, barns, and stables proved necessary.[34] In May 1756, the War Office ordered Excise Commissioners to conduct a survey of available beds and stable room in southern counties. The survey aimed at providing troops 'may be more commodiously Quartered, and the Subjects bear a more equal proportion of that Burthen'.[35] The War Office was simultaneously reassuring localities grumbling at troop quartering that this was a temporary expedient until encampment. Amidst extensive mobilization, precautions were also taken to protect Jersey and Guernsey, with 900 troops embarking from Portsmouth with horses, tents and baggage in June 1756.[36]

The presence of German troops exacerbated tensions, and made it desirable to establish encampments as quickly and for as long as possible.[37] Local hostility and tension were most apparent in the refusal of innkeepers to accommodate German troops after encampments dispersed, leading to their continued encampment during the winter of 1756–7. The commissary for wood and straw, with wagons provided by the contractor, organized construction of cordwood huts accommodating sixty men each.[38] In this context, encampments not only obviated making unacceptable demands on localities but also relieved the tension of a fragile civil-military relationship.[39] In 1758, compensation was paid to innkeepers and victuallers in the counties most affected by quartering troops.[40] Camp location was predicated on an assessment of areas most vulnerable to invasion. During the period 1756–62, sixteen sites in the counties of southern England were selected, constituting an 'anti-invasion chain'.[41] In deciding on the precise ground for an encampment, the main considerations, aside from security from enemy attack, were accessibility to a plentiful supply of water and wood for cooking.[42] A large expanse of ground was necessary for performing exercises and marching. Once the Commander-in-Chief specified areas, it was the Quartermaster's responsibility to select suitable land, before negotiating terms and rates with owners.[43] Previously engaged in military reconnaissance of parts of England most exposed to invasion, David Watson was appointed Quartermaster-General in June 1756.[44]

Government paid owners for damage caused by troops, although this could prove expensive. At the Hessian encampment at Winchester, only £70 of expenses of £516 was paid for rental; the remainder was for damage caused to crops and land.[45] At Barham Downs in 1757, extensive damage included hedges torn down to provide turf huts, and land damaged by Artillery exercises.[46] Attempts to minimize damage by issuing orders against cutting wood or breaking hedges and standing corn failed to eliminate the problem.[47] Although suitable areas were usually found, numerous problems could arise from camp situation, climate, or lack of planning by the military authorities.[48] The relative novelty of encampments is apparent from entries in a soldier's diary:

> All our Camp Equipage was serv'd out, the tents Number'd & the men tented 5 Men too Each tent ... we had Orders to March with our tents etc to the Common where we pitch'd our tents and struck them by Beat of Drum to learn the men Camp Duty, this being the first Camp I had ever seen.[49]

During the war there were adequate opportunities to become acquainted with encampments. There were four camps in 1756, seven in 1757, two in 1758, seven in 1759, six in 1760, and four apiece in 1761 and 1762. Essex, Kent, Surrey and Hampshire were the counties where most encampments were located, although further west encampments were established in Wiltshire and Dorsetshire. Only Chatham was held annually between 1756 and 1762, although Warley Common, Sandheath and Winchester were held annually between 1759 and 1762.[50]

[Table 5.1: Approximate Number of Troops in 1756 Encampments[51]]

Dragoons (two regiments)	762
Foot (six battalions)	6,246
Hessians (eight regiments)	6,744
Hanoverians (twelve regiments)	8,845
Five Regiments at Chatham	3,350
Total	25,947

The number of encamped troops in 1756 was never exceeded during the remainder of the war. Alongside the return of Hessians and Hanoverians, troops embarkations to Germany, Africa and Asia depleted regiments, resulting in a declining number of troops available for encampment.[52] Nevertheless, troop numbers remained sufficiently large to make supply operations and the volume of provisions supplied notably impressive. The volume of bread and forage required assumed massive proportions. In 1756, 994,754 6lb loaves and 1,059,707 forage rations were supplied. In absolute terms these figures are impressive, but coordination of transportation and distribution necessary for delivering these articles multiplied the logistical difficulties, with 5,968,524lbs of bread and 24,373,261lbs of forage transported in 200 bread wagons, which in turn required 200 conductors and 800 horses.[53] The baking of bread offers some indication of the scale of operations. The English Field Bakery in Germany employed 200 bakers with portable iron ovens baking eighty 6lb loaves at a time. This was less than the 120 baked in stone ovens but iron ovens baked faster and were more economical.[54] Iron ovens used less fuel and less baking time meant less weight loss, meaning less flour was required to ensure 6lb loaves were produced. Although the use of iron ovens increased productivity baking in either type of oven was very labour intensive.[55]

The extensive resources required for encampments could destabilize local economies, for contracts were made between April and July, generally months when grain was in shortest supply. Contractors purchasing supplies in the vicinity of camps exacerbated shortages.[56] At Chelmsford in 1756, in anticipation of a proposed camp, Oswald ordered his agent to purchase forage locally. His extensive purchasing caused a shortage of hay, and led to local innkeepers and publicans requesting release of a quantity of the amount purchased, which Cumberland ordered.[57] With the number of troops supplied in 1756 exceeding the population of most English cities there was always a danger of exacerbating shortages.[58] This episode was indicative not only of the zeal with which Oswald performed the contract but also official overreaction. Cumberland was instrumental in initially ordering provisions, and his calculations proved wildly inaccurate.[59] Cumberland directed that wheat and rye meal sufficient for 40,000 British and 23,000 German troops should be provided at four magazines, whilst also ordering 1,120,000 complete forage rations. Owing to late encampments, a regulation that the contractor must supply his own forage for his horses, and with only two regiments of dragoons encamped, magazine consumption was well below official estimates. Surplus forage, including 100,000 rations in Essex magazines, remained when encampments dispersed.[60] These problems largely emanated from inexperience and can perhaps be excused, for erring on the side of surplus rather than risking shortages appears a safer option.[61] To alleviate distress, the Treasury directed that a portion of the surplus wheat should be sold to the Salisbury and Dorchester poor.[62] In the eighteenth century such activity, 'a customary response of the authorities to dearth', was accompanied by legislative measures.[63] A grain embargo that lasted three years was imposed, and importation of Irish provisions was permitted.[64] Owing to poor harvests, scarcity and high prices characterized encampment supply in 1756 and 1757.[65] Troops employed in suppressing food riots appear to have evinced considerable sympathy towards the poor.[66] Dearth combined with the establishment of camps raised understandable fears in localities of further price rises.[67]

From 1757, there was some variation in the products supplied. The separate commissariat providing wood and straw was discontinued, and henceforth these articles were provided under contract. Orders were given to sell the remaining quantities, with the contractor receiving preference.[68] This appears a sensible and economical change. With wages inflating costs and the accumulation of a surplus, employing a contractor was cheaper. Making a contract at fixed rates avoided price fluctuations arising from market knowledge that the government was in the market as a buyer. This was particularly relevant given the seasonal regularity of encampments. The large amount of forage remaining from 1756 meant no forage contract was necessary in 1757, the only year when this occurred.[69] Wagons were deemed unnecessary in 1758, 1761 and 1762.[70]

Whilst the encampments of 1757 and 1758 were on a smaller scale than in 1756, high prices undermined potential economies. After the passive camps of 1756, the following two years saw camp formation integrally linked with offensive operations. There were six camps in 1757, but most military activity centred on the Isle of Wight as an embarkation point for attacks on the French coast. Much time and resources were expended in transportation, with sixty-six of the 100 bread wagons used at the Isle of Wight, Salisbury and Dorchester, with the contractor disassembling wagons before they were put aboard ship.[71] The military campaigns of 1757 led to many smaller encampments, often for only one night such as Wimbledon Common, established for troops marching from Blackheath to Portsmouth, or as temporary stopovers, such as Clapham Common, where troops destined for Chatham awaited embarkation of troops from that camp.[72] Troops encamped at Amersham for only fifteen days before dispersal. Orders were given to sell the remaining wood, forage, straw and meal.[73] A similar situation pertained in 1758, when sixteen regiments were reported as resident at the Isle of Wight. Although five camps were reportedly planned, the only substantial encampments occurred at Chatham and the Isle of Wight.[74] With troops regularly embarking for Germany, many small temporary encampments were necessary for marching troops.[75] With better harvests, the Treasury attempted to reduce contract prices commensurate with reduced market prices. In 1759, the supplier of wood and straw at the Isle of Wight received a request to lower prices.[76] Yet the re-emergence of the threat of French invasion meant encampment supply of 1759 bore some similarities to that of 1756. Although prices were lower than previous years, extensive supply operations in a larger number of camps raised costs. With the passing of the invasion threat, emergency measures were relaxed. At Dover, provisions acquired in case of siege were forgotten about, and a sale recommended before they spoiled.[77] This episode was symptomatic of measures and expenditure accompanying military emergencies, but the aftermath saw a renewed emphasis on economy.

After 1756, troops available for encampment within Britain declined. By July 1757, of 39,066 troops in South Britain, only 16,271 were unassigned for any service abroad or domestic garrison duty. After considerable recruitment, troops available for encampment rose to 26,953 in May 1759 and in 1760 fluctuated between 34,212 in January, 23,037 in February, and 29,549 in April.[78] In 1759, with invasion a possibility, no troops were sent to Germany from Britain but by 1760 the effect of augmentations for service abroad was beginning to be felt.[79] The militia made their first appearance in camps in 1759, and after 1760, comprised the majority of encamped troops.[80] In performing domestic military duties of guarding prisoners and manning garrisons the militia facilitated the conduct of overseas operations.[81] At a Conference concerning German augmentations, it was resolved:

> That some of the best Regiments of Militia should be Encamp'd with some of the Regular Troops, To make the Face of an Army at Home.[82]

Maintaining adequate forces for domestic defence, whilst conducting extensive overseas military operations was a constant dilemma. Even with a large number of militia troops embodied by early 1761, and significant military victories, the King and Newcastle were concerned for domestic security in expressing misgivings over the Belleisle expedition.[83] The number of effective militia troops in 1760 is difficult to state precisely but official estimates appear optimistic, ranging from 19,205 in January to 21,524 in August. Of 32,000 voted for militia service, half at most were ready for service by June.[84] As the militia did not receive bread from contractors, the cost of contracts was reduced, for this also meant a reduced number of wagons were necessary. Although sixty-four were provided in 1760 they were, unlike in 1759, discontinued during winter months despite the contractor's willingness to provide them.[85]

The reduced number of regular troops allied to a receding invasion threat encouraged economy. In 1761, Hume suggested that the bread contractor should be obliged to deliver bread without incurring the cost of a wagon contract. An extra allowance would be made in the price of bread. Wagons for carrying sick men to hospital could be hired for the necessary time before being discharged. Ligonier approved the proposal after Hume convincingly demonstrated considerable savings would be made.[86] With the exception of wagons, all other articles were provided under contract, although a separate bread contract was concluded.[87] Hume's proposals were implemented, with the contractor agreeing to supply settled and 'flying camps'.[88] The latter appears to have been camps that were regularly moved. In 1762 the contractor agreed to supply troops provided the distance was less than ten miles. If above ten miles the contractor was allowed payment for wagons. The Treasury resisted proposals that any wagon contract must be for six months certain.[89] Nevertheless, the Family Compact and the re-emergence of an invasion threat allied to concern over the estimated 26,000 French prisoners in England made it prudent to retain the option of procuring wagons.[90]

Other minor adjustments were made during the course of the war. The amount of hay contained in the forage ration was found insufficient in 1759, with the Commander-in-Chief given discretionary power to decide an appropriate amount. On Barrington's advice, the Treasury resisted making a permanent alteration for fear of the precedent.[91] Another change came in 1762 when loaves of 4½lb instead of 6lb were supplied.[92] By 1762, the nature of encampment supply had changed commensurate with military developments. No wagons were provided and the amount of bread supplied was reduced, but the volume of forage, wood and straw supplied was maintained at a reasonably high level. This partly emanated from supplying forage to Guards regiments at St Marylebone mobilized for encampment.[93]

Somewhat surprisingly, quality of provisions was seldom the subject of complaint. Although bread was the only food article provided under contract, sutlers and butchers were assigned booths or huts at the rear of camps. Quarter Masters and sergeants, or from 1748 commanding officers, examined the quality and prices of goods.[94] Sutlers were often criticized in the same terms as contractors, as purveyors of poor quality, expensive goods. In Shakespeare's *Henry V*, Pistol related:

> For I shall sutler be
> Unto the camp, and profits will accrue.[95]

Earlier regulations warned sutlers against providing 'naughty' or 'unsound or unsavory Victuals'.[96] It would be surprising if sutlers did not attempt to exploit the captive market of an encamped army. In 1756, sergeants and corporals were reminded they were not permitted to act as sutlers.[97] Sutlers were threatened with ejection from camp if found collaborating with troops bringing stolen wood into camp. After receiving reports that petty sutlers intercepted small traders destined for camps, and purchased products which they then sold to troops at high prices, the military authorities ordered that if found guilty of such practices, sutlers would be punished and plundered.[98] Unsurprisingly, the sale of alcohol proved problematic. Sutlers' huts were often a scene of rowdy and boisterous behaviour, particularly abroad. Richmond informed Newcastle of twenty sutlers' huts 'full of Soldiers & whores singing, roaring, and dancing'.[99] The military authorities struggled to contain drinking. Troops were forbidden to drink alcohol in their tents, and restrictions on selling alcohol, not permitted between 9 p.m. and Reveille, were a regular feature of Articles of War. Part of the duty of Rear Guard troops was to ensure there were no disorders in sutlers' booths.[100] Close contact with troops perhaps enforced greater accountability in supplying provisions at reasonable prices. Nevertheless, that sutlers would attempt to exploit their position to the utmost may explain an additional clause in the 1749 Articles of War against violence towards them.[101]

With troops receiving a 6lb loaf every four days, the weekly ration of 10½lbs compares well against the 8lbs consumed by the average London artisan.[102] Whilst a full stomach was a safeguard against mutiny, there was sickness and fever. This arose from poor organization rather than poor quality provisions, and was a familiar feature of encampments.[103] On encamping at Blandford, James Wolfe wrote optimistically of the 'good care taken of the men in the necessary articles of wood and straw, bread and meat, and the regiment will all be newly clothed very soon'.[104] There were hospitals nearby with a resident physician general and surgeon for inspection of troops. Nevertheless, after ten weeks the strain was beginning to tell. Wolfe complained that regiments with the longest marches remained the longest encamped, resulting in sickness arising from overexposure to cold weather.[105] Although Wolfe sought barrack accommodation, many of the worst cases of sickness were reported amongst those confined indoors for long periods. The Norfolk militia was reportedly 'all a dying of the bloody Flux'.[106] Another problem, present at Hilsea barracks, was the:

> Numbers of vagrant & dissolute Women lying in the Hedge Rows round the Barracks, by whom many of the Soldiers are distemper'd, become incapable of Duty, and several have died under Salivations.[107]

The main considerations in maintaining good health in or out of doors appear to have been the application of common sense in ensuring activity, and avoiding prostitutes, long confinement and exposure to extremities.[108] The consequence of insufficient organization can clearly be seen in the encampment near Cherbourg in 1758. The remains of upwards of 7,000 sheep and great numbers of cattle slaughtered since the arrival of British troops lay above ground, making the rear of the camp 'Noisome' in the heat.[109] No such complaints can be found relating to encampments in England.

How efficiently did contractors and government manage the wartime demands of encampments? Whilst the military authorities can be blamed for occasional inattention, the personnel administering camps, government officials and contractors alike, appear to have competently performed their tasks. The functions of contractors and commissaries were well-defined, there was a reasonable number of staff employed, and considerable initiative was displayed in surmounting problems. Throughout the war Hume played a pivotal role as the point of contact between contractors, War Office and Treasury. Regular consultation as to troop numbers, camp location, and organization occurred between the Commander-in-Chief, Hume, Barrington, and Quartermasters.[110] Hume communicated the details to contractors, and gave directions as to how contracts were to be performed.[111] Upon making contracts, the Treasury continued to request his assistance in assessing proposals.[112] In 1761, after five years' experience of encampments the Treasury continued to request his advice over payments to contractors.[113] In anticipating and resolving problems, Hume proved to be an excellent supervisor. A typical example concerned the supply of rye bread to German troops in 1756.[114] As winter approached, and with German troops remaining in England, Hume reminded the Treasury that the pending expiration of the contract meant further provision was necessary. The contractor continued supplying troops until their departure for Germany.[115] Simple initiative such as this counted for much and obviated many potential problems. The numerous factors that could affect the quality of provisions overseas were felt far less intensely within Britain. Shorter distances, more frequent deliveries, a shorter chain of supply with less intermediary staff, effectively enforced greater accountability. The blame for poor quality provisions could not so easily be laid elsewhere. Although problems could arise from storing a large amount of provisions, complaints concerning quality of provisions were rare within England.

The presence of German troops allowed contemporaries to comment on the superiority of English food, whilst hinting at the opportunism of contractors:

> We hear that strict Orders are given to see that the Bread furnished to the Men encamped at Chatham, be such as is fit for Englishmen.[116]

Such admonitions emanated from English distaste for rye bread. A foreign observer found that although rye was grown in England, wheat bread was always preferred. Rye bread was variously described as consumed by cattle, the poor, or those living in northern England.[117] Ligonier warned against supplying rye bread to British troops in Germany, believing that during Queen Anne's wars 'more men were lost by this kind of Bread than by the sword of the Enemy'.[118] This may have emanated from ergot poisoning to which rye flour is particularly susceptible.[119]

Concerns over type of provisions supplied were generally subordinate to concerns over quality. Allegations of poor quality forage in 1758 and 1759, perhaps motivated by jealousy, proved groundless.[120] Contractors themselves could be victims of unscrupulous practices. A House of Commons committee heard that purchasing forage was fraught with difficulty owing to the practices of salesmen and 'Hay Jockies'. The stable-keeper John Warrington claimed these men, purchasing hay in the country for the London market placed wet rubbish in the middle of trusses, which if not immediately discovered spoiled the hay by heating.[121] Contractors were also at the mercy of employees. In employing bakers in different counties, contractors utilized tradesmen rapidly displacing home-based domestic activity.[122] Yet specialization was not unproblematic. Bread adulteration was a serious problem in the mid-eighteenth century, for by these means bakers cut costs and increased profits. Nevertheless, unlike society at large, few problems appear to have arisen with bread supplied under contract.[123]

Fraud allegations were even rarer than that of poor quality provisions but in February 1760, the contractor John Willan and several officers were accused of colluding to inflate the number of forage rations issued in 1759. The case demonstrates that involvement in such practices was not confined to civilian officials or contractors, but could also encompass army officers and contractors' agents.[124] In 1756, the forage rations allowed for staff and regiments were established, alongside a warning that forage was allowed for effective horses only, and that government would not pay for excess rations. Monthly returns of regimental numbers and effective horses were to be sent to Hume who would report to Cumberland.[125] In 1759 these orders were reiterated, with weekly returns to be made to commanding officers at each camp.[126] A deputy commissary attended each camp as a 'check upon the Contractor, both as to the goodness of the Forrage, and the sufficiency of the Weight and measure'. His responsibilities did not include checking the number of forage rations drawn by officers against the number of effective horses, which was conducted 'upon honour'. If regiments received more forage, although within the regulation of eighty-two horses per regiment, they were to pay the contractor the difference. If drawing less, they could claim the shortfall or an allowance in lieu based on government allowance to the contractor of 10¼d. per ration.[127] Difficulties arose over application of the order. Barrington considered it applicable only to regiments who encamped late in summer or not at all but had kept their horses in readiness. He also pointed out that the order expressly forbade regiments from receiving more forage than for their effective horses, even if within the regulation. Nevertheless, many regiments had drawn excess forage or money.[128]

The affair emerged in a letter from the Duke of Richmond to Barrington.[129] Richmond's regiment had thirty-nine effective horses, and having received fewer rations that their entitlement, in conformity with Ligonier's order, applied for the remaining quantity. On approaching Willan's agents, Richmond was informed they would pay the regiment only 3s. for every seven rations, despite the contractor receiving 10¼d. per ration from government. A letter from one of the contractor's agents to the regimental paymaster suggested officers alter the return to 'any number they pleased'. Richmond refused, and informed the War Office. If enacted, this would have allowed the regiment and contractor to profit at the government's expense. The regiment would have received £238 instead of the alternative amounts proposed by contractor and government respectively: £93 or £187. The contractor would receive £236 instead of £93, and the cost to government would be £475 instead of £187. Many officers signed false returns but the subsequent inquiry mainly attributed the contractor with fraudulent intent.[130]

Even those responsible for implementing forage regulations were confused by their application, with the regimental agent John Calcraft informing Lord Tyrawley:

> I saw Mr Cox last Night, who tells me Lord Ligonier takes his forrage in kind and only for 40 Horses, which he has Effective; I ask'd what was the Use of the Regulation ... He Reply'd the Comr. In Chief & Secretary at War had differed so much in Opinion on this Subject that to avoid further altercation, He had come to this Resolution.[131]

The complex forage regulations and the complicity of officers played a large part in the decision not to prosecute. The Attorney General argued deductions from the contractor's account was sufficient punishment.[132] Willan repeatedly denied fraudulent intent, claiming he misunderstood the regulations.[133] By the time the case was considered many regiments were abroad thus allowing the authorities to act with greater leniency in reprimanding officers for acting 'inadvertently'.[134] It appears far from certain Willan was guilty of fraud, and more evidence exists against his agent and the officers.

A tightening up of contract regulations, including the insertion of a clause against any composition between officers and contractors was implemented.[135] All Colonels, even those uninvolved, were reminded of the need for accuracy in completing regimental returns, whilst professions of innocence were met by a War Office rejoinder that officers should know that signing a false return was a breach of duty.[136] The affair illustrates that the activities of agents and officers allied to contractors' accountability to government often meant contractors were unjustly blamed for the activities of subordinate officials. For extensive encampment contracts, minor peculation or occasional problems with quality might be expected. Yet the relative rarity of such problems is striking. Lack of discovery may partly account for this, but the available evidence makes it difficult to support the association of contractors with fraud, sharp practice, or purveyors of poor quality provisions.

The competent performance of encampment contracts partly emanated from the vibrancy and rising productivity of English agriculture. Harvest quality remained the barometer of the economy, with an estimated 51 per cent of the population of England and Wales engaged in agriculture in 1759.[137] The extent to which harvest quality influenced contract prices is very marked, with market price movements reflected in contract proposals. Competitive tendering meant potential contractors were aware of price movements even if the Treasury was not. Forage prices fluctuated considerably in the period 1756–62, peaking at 14d. per ration in 1758. Yet a succession of good harvests reduced and stabilized prices from 1759 until 1762, when scarcity caused by drought, again raised prices, although not to the extent of earlier in the war. Nevertheless, higher contract prices in 1762 appear justified. Straw and wood prices were subject to less fluctuation. Contract prices were reduced in 1760 and 1761 but remained stable in 1762, a pattern consistent with market prices.[138]

A similar pattern characterized bread prices. From a peak of 11d. per loaf in 1757, caused by dearth in 1756 and deficiency in 1757, prices gradually fell before rising slightly in 1762.[139] In the period 1759–61, the average price of a peck loaf (17lb 6oz) remained fairly stable at 20d, computing at 6.9d. per 6lb loaf. The reduction in contract price from 6d. to 5d. in 1760 therefore appears a good bargain for government, despite the doubtful accuracy of averages. In

1756, with the market price of bread at 8.2*d*. per 6lb loaf, Oswald contracted for bread at 75 per cent of market price.[140] In 1759, it was 86.9 per cent of cost price, but in 1760 and 1761, reduced to 72.5 per cent. The rising price of a peck loaf in 1762 to 23*d*. meant an average of 7.9*d*. per 6lb loaf, and with the contract made at 5½d per loaf this meant 69.6 per cent of cost price.[141] Through bulk purchase and local price variation, contractors probably paid less.[142] Weekly returns from the London Corn Exchange illustrate significant price fluctuation in 1759, with the price of 100 quarters of wheat falling from £1 10*s*. to £1 4*s*. between April–June.[143]

The years when a serious threat of invasion existed, 1756 and 1759, proved to be most expensive. In the latter years of the war, a declining invasion threat and a reduced number of encamped troops facilitated reductions. In these terms, annual renewal of contracts was sensible and well-tailored towards meeting variable economic and military conditions. Despite the successful performance of encampment contracts, the entire area of camp supply was reformed later in the century. The supplier of camp equipage, Trotter, established a contracting dynasty. From 1794 his son supplied practically all non-perishable military supplies. With the central base at his factory in Soho Square, the business comprised 109 depots in 1807. Trotter stored articles such as blankets and tents at the end of each conflict, and reissued them to the army when needed, thus undercutting regimental agents and contractors by peacetime purchasing. Yet with no definite agreement, and Trotter fixing his own prices and charging 10 per cent profit, objections were raised over the propriety of the provision, issue and custody of articles belonging to the same man. These objections were removed by returning to open contracting, and converting Trotter's business into the Store Keeper General's Department with custody of all military stores, except the Ordnance.[144]

The method of making contracts for bread, wagons and forage was also reformed. Significantly, reform did not encompass methods of advertising and tendering, but only localized contracts in order to cut costs. Whilst a Select Committee of 1797 implicitly accepted that competitive tendering reflected some concern for economy, the method of making a single contract was criticized on the basis of multiplication of employees.[145] The implementation of this reform earlier in the century may have reduced costs. It can also be surmised that, in presenting opportunities to men over a wider geographical area, wealth derived from encampment contracts would have been distributed more widely.[146] Making contracts on a district basis continued to inform domestic contracts into the nineteenth century.[147] In the mid-eighteenth century, there seems little reason to doubt provincial merchants and wholesalers were capable of supplying local camps. However, the proposals of provincial applicants, usually for selected items or selected camps, appear to indicate their incapacity to supply a wide range of camps. Such proposals indicate limited resources of capital and credit, with less capacity for extensive economic enterprise. Whilst employing a single contractor may have increased costs, the likely effectiveness of a system reliant on a large number of local suppliers is open to considerable doubt, and the success of the adopted method appears to vindicate the Treasury in awarding contracts to 'organizing middlemen'.

In the mid-eighteenth century the government managed encampment supply competently, but such efficiency was gained from the experience and extensive knowledge of a handful of men. Domestic mobilization on an unprecedented scale raised difficulties that were compounded by bad harvests. The ability to surmount difficulties demonstrates the organizational abilities of government and contractors. That men were consistently found who were capable of meeting extensive demands indicates that within the agricultural sector there existed resourceful men possessed of organizational, even entrepreneurial abilities. Alongside the establishment of an efficient administrative structure, the requisite infrastructure and personnel were established to ensure this was a successful area of military supply during the Seven Years' War. There clearly existed a number of men who concerned themselves in encampment supply, and whose related interests entitle them to be considered a community of contractors in this sector. In considering that foreign countries managed military supply cheaper and better than Britain, Jenkinson was not entirely correct in stating:

> That the sort of men who are fit to manage Concerns of this sort are more easy to be found in those countries than they are here; There are men who are bred up to this Business, As the Force of these Countries consists chiefly in Land Armies their attention is principally turned to this Object, They have Men for this purpose always ready, We are forced to find them when occasion calls for them.[148]

By 1756, on the basis of experience in recent conflict and related business expertise, Britain also possessed capable men.

[Table 5.2: Payment for Encampment Contracts, 1756–62]

Year	Contractor	Sums Received
1756	Richard Oswald	£81,807[149]
1757	Do.	£27,374[150]
1758	Do.	£12,574[151]
1759	John Willan	£50,817[152]
1760	Archibald Fraser	£18,675[153]
1761	John Boghurst & John Martyr	£11,092[154]
1762	Samuel Tewkesbury	£15,241[155]

[Table 5.3: Total Supplies to Encampments, 1756–62[156]]

	Bread	Wagons	Forage	Wood & Straw
1756	994,756	200	1,059,707	N/A
1757	343,396	100	N/A	89,837
1758	312,450	N/A	76,120	30,763
1759	215,167	84	310,536	55,394
1760	U	64	137,070	70,976
1761	U	N/A	201,868	44,781
1762	66,165	N/A	212,793	54,009 (wood)
				64,308 (straw)
Total	1,931,934	448	1,998,094	345,760 (wood)
				356,059 (straw)

Key:
Bread: 6lb loaves
Wagons: four horses and one driver per wagon; payment per day
Forage: complete rations (15lb hay, 8lb oats)
Wood: complete rations (105lb) & Straw (36lb) per man per week
N/A: Not supplied under contract
U: Supplied but account unavailable

[Table 5.4: Prices of Encampment Articles[157]]

	Bread	Wagons	Forage	Wood & Straw
1756	6¼d (wheat)	11s. 6d. per wagon	11d. per ration	N/A
	5½d (rye)			
1757	11d. per wheat loaf	8s.	N/A	2s. 2d.
1758	8d. do.	N/A	14d.	1s. 9d.
1759	6d. do.	10s.	10¼d	2s.
1760	5d. do.	9s. 6d.	10½d	1s. 11d.
1761	5d. do.	N/A	8¾d	1s. 6d.
1762	5½d do.	N/A	12d.	1s. 6d.

[Table 5.5: Volume of Encampment Articles, 1756–62 (lbs)]

	Bread	Hay	Oats	Wood	Straw
1756	5,968,536	15,895,605	8,477,656	N/A	N/A
1757	343,396	N/A	N/A	9,432,885	3,234,132
1758	1,874,700	1,141,800	608,960	3,230,115	1,107,468
1759	1,291,002	4,658,040	2,484,288	5,816,370	1,994,184
1760	U	2,056,050	1,096,560	7,452,480	2,555,136
1761	U	3,028,020	1,614,944	4,702,005	1,612,116
1762	396,990	3,191,895	1,702,344	5,670,945	2,315,088
Totals	11,591,604	29,971,410	15,984,752	36,304,800	12,818,124

Excluding bread provided in 1760 and 1761, for which accounts are missing.

[Table 5.6: Total Weight of Encampment Articles, 1756–62 (lbs)]

Bread	11,591,604
Hay	29,971,410
Oats	15,984,752
Wood	36,304,800
Straw	12,818,124
Total	106,670,690

6 A DOMESTIC CONTRACTOR: JOHN WILLAN

At the beginning of the Seven Years' War, Britain possessed few men with direct experience of supplying field armies, and men whose business experience made them particularly well-equipped to perform encampment contracts assumed these functions. The logistical and distributive difficulties inherent in this type of supply meant contracts in this sector were not merely underwriting operations where the credit facilities of contractors assumed prime importance. In supervising supply operations, a variety of skills were required relating to procurement and distribution, and encompassing managerial skills in negotiating with sub-contractors and employing agents and staff. The work of contractors in this sector indicates that in terms of the daily functioning of the fiscal military state, it was not only sophisticated financial operations that contributed towards military victories. For many contractors, business competence and ability outweighed political considerations of patronage and place. Neither this type of contract nor this type of contractor should be indiscriminately consigned to history as elements of 'Old Corruption', or more appositely, included within the description of the eighteenth century as an age of horseflesh and political jobbery.[1]

John Willan is a good example of this type of contractor, for despite an apparent lack of connections he was recognized as a highly capable man. An examination of his business life reveals something of a community of contractors centred on supplying horses and forage, whilst also indicating that fortunes could be made in this sector of contracting. Willan was a horse-dealer who performed an extensive contract supplying encampments in 1759. Reputedly worth £200,000 at his death in 1792, his wealth arose from related business interests of which the supply of horses to the army was a central component. Anecdotal evidence relates:

> Willan, the great horse contractor and occupier of the Bull and Mouth Inn, in the year 1745 was hostler at the Lion Inn at Barnet. The then Duke of Cumberland, when on his route to the north, happened to have a horse for his own riding brought to him to look at this inn; his Royal Highness had doubts of the horse's answering

his purpose, and with his usual good humour asked everybody's opinion – among others Jack's, and John immediately pronounced him unfit. He was then requested by his Royal Highness to assign his reasons, which John stated. Upon which John was asked whether he knew of a horse that he could recommend, and John replied in the affirmative, and went and fetched a horse into the inn-yard which upon trial gave the Duke much satisfaction. On the Duke's return from Scotland he found John in the same capacity, and commending his skill in horseflesh, asked him if he was disposed to take a contract for furnishing a few artillery horses. John bowed, and said he 'needed the one thing needful.' This want his Royal Highness supplied; and from this circumstance John, when he departed from this world, had accumulated 200,000*l*.[2]

The veracity of this account is questionable, particularly since it confuses John Willan (1711–92) with his eponymous nephew (1746–1822) of the Bull and Mouth Inn. The latter held mail coach contracts in the late eighteenth and early nineteenth century.[3] It was perhaps an understandable mistake, for both were successful in similar lines of business and both examples of how relatively modest men in agriculturally related sectors of the economy could benefit from government contracts.[4] For the Willan family such contracts facilitated upward social mobility. John Willan was clearly of the 'middling sort' interested in improvement and accumulation resulting from the application of capital and labour.[5] Essentially gentleman farmers in the eighteenth century, by the nineteenth century the Willan family had acquired the familiar middle-class trappings of university education, appointments as JPs, and professional careers.[6] Despite having no children, the elder John Willan was the central figure in this transformation.[7] It is difficult to say whether notable Willans from earlier centuries were directly related to John Willan's family, who hailed from Westmorland.[8] It seems clear that the family, as opposed to individuals, did not feature in any significant economic or political activity in earlier centuries. Much of Willan's activity as a contractor occurred in the largely unrecorded world of sub-contracting. The encampment contract of 1759 appears to be the only one where he was the named contractor but sufficient evidence has survived to indicate he was a major supplier of artillery horses.[9] This sub-contracting confirms obituary notices stating he was 'many years a contractor with government'.[10]

Willan held an extensive amount of land and was instrumental in the business success of his nephews, John and Thomas, who followed his example, blending agriculture and government contracts. Although Willan did not possess a diverse portfolio of economic interests, he skilfully adapted his expertise towards different uses. Such expertise was a valuable commodity in a pre-industrial society where agriculture was central to the military supply system. Willan was undoubtedly very wealthy. In his will he provided £3,000 in direct legacies, £4,300 in contingent legacies and approximately £1,700 in annuities.[11] He also possessed freehold and copyhold property in Essex, Warwickshire, Oxfordshire,

Middlesex, and the City of London. Respect for his character and integrity were not compromised by his wealth:

> His great prosperity through a very long life seemed to have been marked by the peculiar favour of heaven; the tongue of envy or malevolence never attempted to blacken a character guarded by a probity that feared not strictest scrutiny, and adorned by a general openness of heart and nobleness of conduct that would not have dishonoured the most exalted station.[12]

Such praise, testimony of the high esteem in which Willan was held by respectable county society, displays sentiments not normally associated with contractors. Willan appears to have been respected for traditional John Bull-type straightforwardness and honesty. A dispute over his will occasioned friends and acquaintances to comment on his character. Servants and friends spoke warmly of him, with the parish curate considering him a man of 'strong natural abilities'.[13] Towards the end of his life, after purchasing a small Essex estate in 1782 and retiring from business, Willan lived in the manner of a country gentleman.[14] This was appropriate, for his business success was based on a lengthy career in agriculturally related interests in and around London. This intermingling of rural and urban interests is characteristic of an age where no stark dichotomy existed between town and country. Wealth thus gained is a reminder of those twin poles of eighteenth-century wealth creation noted by Daniel Defoe and repeated by modern historians: military provisioning and the metropolitan economy.

The second son and fourth child of William Willan and Jane Thornborrow, John Willan was christened at Casterton, Westmorland on 9 February 1711.[15] He probably came south at an early age. Although his precise role during the 1745 Jacobite Rebellion is unclear, Willan appears to have been employed in some governmental capacity. During the Carlisle expedition, Cumberland's secret service accounts record payments made to a Willan for 'Messages' and a 'Journey made & gratification'.[16] A list of 'Riders' of Light Horse of the Westmoreland militia in 1745 includes a John Willan.[17] A recent writer considers it unlikely this was the same man who purchased land around London in the period 1746–77.[18] This is probably true but not certain. Most importantly, in accounting for Willan's prosperity, this brief account entirely omits Willan's government contracts.[19] In Willan's case, land was acquired for business purposes rather than prestige or status. A 1746 rate book describes him as 'John Willan of the White Horse in Holborn', and in possession of Barrow Hill Farm, consisting of sixty-four acres.[20] In 1751 he rented land on the undeveloped north side of Green Street on the Grosvenor Estate. The usage is clear, with most of the ground let to Willan 'a stable-keeper, who built stabling around a yard named North Row Mews'.[21] In 1752 the remaining ground was made over by Willan to Joseph Kell.[22] Willan lived in North Row until 1760, renting house and stables at annual rents of £30 and £32 respectively.[23] This property was in an area 'almost entirely taken up with stables and other appendages of buildings'.[24] In Willan's correspondence with the Treasury, Green Street was always the address given. Despite the close proximity of Willan's house and stables to the aristocratic political elite there is no evidence of favourable political connections, and Willan's friendship with Sir John Jervis, later Earl of St Vincent began much later.[25] By 1756 Willan had acquired farming land, stables, and a residence on the Grosvenor estate. He was clearly a successful businessman but he was not notably or ostentatiously wealthy.[26]

Willan's first recorded interest in contracting occurred in 1757 when he proposed to supply wood and straw for encampments in England:

> The Proposal of John Willan, Farmer and Dealer … He Engages to furnish every Tent of 5 Men to each Tent, with 3 Trusses of good dry wheat Straw each Truss to weigh 36lb. at their first coming in to Camp, and one Truss every week following to refresh their beds, as also 15lb. of good dry Wood, each day to Every Tent of 5 Men, at the Rate of 4 pence each Tent … a day.[27]

In correctly estimating rations and delivery times, the proposal suggests familiarity with encampment contracts, whilst Willan's self-description indicates varied business interests. The proposals varied, from the incumbent contractor Oswald proposing to supply all articles to all camps to others offering specific articles for specific camps. With his proposals considered 'the most reasonable and at the cheapest rates' Oswald obtained the contract.[28] Oswald offered wood and straw at 2s. 2d. per week for each tent of five men. Willan's proposal amounted to 2s. 4d. An estimate of costs over seven weeks indicated Willan's proposals would cost £3,704 8s. against Oswald's £3,439 16s.[29] The priorities of government in awarding the contract were cheapness and the ability to supply all articles to all camps. Willan could lay claim to neither.

Willan succeeded to the 1759 contract by submitting the lowest proposals for all articles to all camps. A month separated consideration of proposals, and originally Willan did not propose to supply wood and straw.[30] In March, the Treasury was informed contracts would be necessary, with advertisement following shortly afterwards.[31] Ligonier named eight locations where magazines were required, with 320,000 forage rations to be provided and maintained.[32] Willan was somewhat fortuitous in obtaining the contract. As the incumbent contractor Oswald was in Germany, he chose not to make proposals.[33] Of the six proposals made, two were solely concerned with the Isle of Wight, one with supplying wood and straw, and one proposed to serve camps on commission. Willan and John Warrington submitted the two comprehensive proposals, supplying all articles to all camps. It appears likely that an agreement existed between them that if either won the contract, the other would be involved.[34]

Augmentations, militia embodiment, and embarkations to Germany make it difficult to state with precision the exact number of encamped troops. The War Office estimated 26,953 troops in South Britain in May 1759, including 4,000 invalids guarding garrisons and 6,000 troops in London. Estimates of 18,000 troops appear approximately correct. There were also 6,280 militiamen on active service.[35] By early June, it was reported that all regular forces would be encamped as quickly as possible.[36] Seven camps and fourteen magazines were established at important strategic points throughout the southern counties. Camps were formed at Chatham, Dartford, Warley Common, Sandheath, Winchester, Bedhampton and South Sea Common, with magazines erected in close proximity.[37] Purchase and distribution across a wide geographic area required considerable planning and foresight, and prospective contractors would have seriously assessed their capability of fulfilling the contract before submitting proposals.[38]

With 215,167 loaves of bread, 55,394 rations of wood and straw, and 310,536 rations of hay and oats provided, the contract was extensive. In addition, sixty-four wagons were provided in the period 20 June–18 July 1759, with an additional twenty from 19 July–14 November 1759. The full complement of eighty-four wagons continued in service from 15 November 1759 until 6 June 1760. With four horses and a driver per wagon, 256 horses and sixty-four drivers were employed 20 June–18 July 1759. The additional wagons make a total of 336 horses and eighty-four drivers in the period July 1759–June 1760.[39] Awarding the contract, the Treasury directed:

> Let the Contract be made with Mr Willan as the lowest Bidder, if he can give sufficient Security for the whole sum. Mr Willan comes in, and proposes Mr Baldwin, and Mr Godfrey, or any other Security that might be liked better, and the Contract is to run for such Quantities, and in such places, and at such times, as Lord Ligonier shall think fit to direct.[40]

Baldwin appears to be William Baldwin, a partner of John Warrington in an artillery horse contract of 1755–7. Godfrey is almost certainly William Godfrey, the commissary for firing and straw in 1756–7.[41] Experience, trustworthiness and good judgment were excellent qualifications for such a role. Contract duration was unspecified, the only proviso being fourteen days' termination notice by either party. Reflecting the temporary expedient of establishing encampments to meet the invasion threat, the contract would be performed only as long as the government required it. The first camp was formed on 16 June, and Willan began supply from 20 June until the last camp dispersed on 19 November.[42] Widespread panic and the hasty preparation of preventative measures pervade contemporary documentation. John Calcraft reported the invasion scare throughout May and June but was sanguine 'as there are 24 Stout Ships ready for Sea I am very Easy – We are going to Encamp most of the Troops in

England'.⁴³ Establishing encampments, amidst extensive military mobilization, instilled confidence in Britain's ability to defeat any invasion attempt. Newcastle informed Hardwicke of Pitt's good temper, as the latter 'laughs at everything the French can do, though he thinks they will make an attempt'.⁴⁴

Alongside more overt military measures such as the erection of batteries on the south coast and further land purchase for fortifications at Chatham, Portsmouth and Plymouth, men such as Willan provided the organizational apparatus productive of such confidence.⁴⁵ Willan must have expended considerable sums in the initial weeks of the contract. In July 1759 he requested an advance of £12,000, claiming he had furnished £25,000 worth of provisions. The Treasury was fairly regular with payments, and despite issuing only £10,000 on this occasion, followed this with payments of £7,000 and £15,000 in October 1759 and March 1760.⁴⁶ The Treasury agreed to Willan's proposal that eighty-four wagons be kept in service at a reduced rate of 5s. per day each between 15 November 1759 and 1 April 1760.⁴⁷ At £21 a day this amounted to £2,940, but with wagons hired until 6 June, the total cost was £4,305 for 205 days. Wagons were retained in readiness 'in case the Service should have required it', before Edward Hawke's naval victories temporarily dispelled the invasion threat.⁴⁸ The re-emergence of the invasion threat induced caution, and wagons continued to be necessary after Willan's contract ended, with the new contractor supplying sixty-four from 10 June 1760.⁴⁹ Willan's presence at the Treasury on the day the 1760 contract was awarded suggests he hoped to submit proposals, but fraud allegations, although inconclusive, damaged his prospects, with the Treasury stating 'My Lords will not proceed with those Contractors even for Wagons and Horses'.⁵⁰ Responding to Willan's professions of innocence, the Treasury stated 'Mr. Willan will have an opportunity of being heard in his defence if the Attorney and Sollicitor General should think the Case demand a prosecution'.⁵¹ Although there was no prosecution, there was no renewal of the contract. Despite submitting proposals in 1762, Willan did not perform another encampment contract.⁵² Yet in supplying horses at the very time he was being censured, Willan was not proscribed in the way the Treasury intended. The application of 1762 indicates that Willan had found the earlier contract profitable.

[Table 6.1: Sums Received for 1759 Encampment Contract⁵³]

Date	Amount
10 July 1759	£10,000
29 October 1759	£7,000
12 March 1760	£15,000
14 January 1761	£8,862
11 February 1761	£9,954
Total	£50,816

[Table 6.2: Approximate Costs of 1759 Encampment Contract[54]]

Forage	£33,787
Bread (government part of payment)	£899
Wood and straw	£5,539
Bread wagons (to 14 January 1760)	£7,228
Do. (14 January–6 June 1760)	£3,003
Total	£50,456

Any prospect of loss appears to have been covered by Treasury payments, with the discrepancy in accounts between the sums Willan claimed and those he received explicable by the application of allowances and disallowances. Allowances were made for losses on 38,144 rations of unused hay and oats, amounting to approximately £1,650, and government paid the wages of labourers and agents employed at magazines, rental of buildings, and construction of ovens at Westerham and Dorking that were unused.[55] Total disallowances amounted to £1,266 including £45 deducted for bread that did not conform to the new regulation weight of 4½lb.[56] Money received from government added to disallowed sums amounted to upwards of £52,083. This was not the only money Willan received. The contract price for bread was 6d. a loaf, with troops paying 5d. and government 1d. Only government payments are recorded in official accounts. The remainder, £4,495 of a total of £5,394, was paid by stoppages from troops' pay. Contract payments thus amounted to £55,311. Profitability is difficult to assess. After poor harvests in 1756–7, successive fine harvests reduced the cost of agricultural produce, and Willan received less for forage, bread and wagons than Oswald received in 1756.[57] It appears likely that Willan owned the requisite wagons and horses as part of his equine business interests. Procuring forage was in all likelihood relatively easy. Willan's friendship with Godfrey, the former commissary, appears significant, for he was likely to possess knowledge pertaining to procurement of cheap and plentiful forage. He appears to be the man described as from Paddington, and possessing freehold and copyhold land in Middlesex and Essex, and may be the same man employed as a meal-weigher at London Corn Exchange.[58]

Willan's personal wealth appears to have been augmented by the contract. In 1760 he acquired a residence in Park Street, near his premises at North Row, where he remained until approximately 1773.[59] In 1761–2 he held £3,700 in 3 per cent Consols, probably representing part payment of the contract. Having received the stock in October 1761, he sold out by March 1762. This appears to indicate a lack of interest in stock-holding, but perhaps also a need for working capital.[60] Contract profits appear to have facilitated land purchase. In 1760, Willan acquired the lease on Marylebone Park, consisting of 282 acres at £152 per annum. In 1761, he was paying an additional rent of £60 for 'Mist's Farm'.[61] Willan perhaps needed to extend his landholding, for he was one of a number of contractors for artillery horses between 1760 and 1762. John Warrington was the named contractor, but the contract was performed by a group of London horse dealers. The contrast between contracts for horses and victualling contracts is striking. Whereas victualling contractors coordinated and organized supply rather than being the suppliers of the goods themselves, the pattern of supplying horses was entirely different.

Contracts for horses were made with substantial London dealers. For those outside the trade, extensive procurement could be problematic.[62] Such difficulties also illustrate why horse dealers became involved in encampments. Horses were seldom mentioned alongside encampment articles, for it was perhaps too obvious that they were required for wagons. With four horses per wagon, 1,792 horses were provided for encampments between 1756 and 1762.[63] Contractors supplying horses were familiar with camps, for horses were used both for Artillery Trains and for transporting ammunition and gunpowder.[64] Thus Warrington, a horse-dealer, is found submitting proposals for encampment contracts in 1758, 1759, 1761 and 1762.[65] Willan belonged to a distinct community of large London horse dealers. Partnerships amongst them were common and probably necessary to meet extensive demands. For example, the partnership of Warrington and Baldwin supplied artillery horses for the Field Train in England between 1755 and 1757. Initially supplying 130 horses, the number rose to 500 amidst a higher degree of military mobilization.[66] This contract was made without advertisement and only after an approach to two 'considerable Dealers in Horses' who refused to contract at 2s. 6d. per horse per day. The dealers are unnamed but such private approaches indicate that the method of making contracts for horses was not dissimilar from foreign victualling contracts. The leading men in the trade were well-known, thus obviating any need for advertisement. Ligonier, impressed with the horses' performance, considered them 'the Cheapest & I think a Good Bargain'.[67] Nevertheless, advertisement in 1757 resulted in a contract with George Grisewood for 406 horses at 1s. 9d. per horse per day, representing a weekly saving of over £90 on the previous contract.[68] Advertisement reduced the cost of horse contracts more widely during the Seven Years' War. In Germany, Oswald supplied horses at 36 per cent less than Warrington and Grisewood in July 1758, and a similar pattern occurred in Scotland.[69] Grisewood and Warrington supplied horses in Germany and for coastal expeditions to France as well as at home.[70] In 1760, contracts with Grisewood and Warrington for horses attending the Field Train and Battalion Guns in England appear to have run concurrently.[71] Both were terminated and superseded by a contract with Warrington for horses, conductors and drivers for the Artillery Train in England. The contract was performed from 14 June 1760 until 10 December 1762.[72] Horses were employed in moving entrenching tools, artillery guns, and ammunition.[73] Six men supplied horses for the contract, although Willan appears to have been working in partnership.

[Table 6.3: Division of Contract for Artillery Horses, 1760–27[74]]

William Hollamby	£5,196 (18.2%)
John Benson	£1,619 (5.7%)
George Grisewood	£1,619 (5.7%)
John Willan & co	£8,066 (28.3%)
Joseph Gibson	£2,083 (7.3%)
John Warrington	£9,942 (34.8%)
Total	£28,525

As the named contractor Warrington supplied the most horses, but the extensive nature of the contract illustrates he was not merely accommodating business associates. For example, in the period 14 June–3 October 1760 Willan provided 110 horses, thirty-four drivers, and one conductor of a total of 611 horses, 194 drivers, and four conductors. During the course of the contract, the number of horses supplied fluctuated between 561 and 611, the number of conductors between 156 and 194, with either two or four conductors employed. Whilst Willan and Warrington between them received just over 63.1 per cent of the proceeds, they were not necessarily the most considerable dealers. Several others were substantial businessmen. To complicate matters there were three men named George Grisewood. The horse contractor was the eponymous nephew of an inn-holder, of the White Swan, near Holborn Bridge, who was involved in horse racing.[75] The nephew died in 1761, and contract payments were made to his Executor.[76] Both uncle and nephew were long-established London innkeepers.[77] The third Grisewood, cousin of the nephew, described himself as a 'Sadler' at the Stirrup, Moorfields. He was also involved in horse breeding and in running thrice-weekly coaches to Bath.[78] Hollamby was an inn-holder in Crutched Friars.[79] Gibson also appears to have been an innkeeper, although it is difficult to differentiate his activities from that of William Gibson, the son of the famous surgeon-farrier.[80] William Gibson appears to have had connections with John Calcraft.[81]

The ability of these men to cooperate and coordinate supply was vital, for there was a great demand for horses throughout the war. In June 1756 'a great number of Light Horse were purchased for the service of Government for the newly raised troops'.[82] In September, the purchase of horses at Newbury Fair brought forth the comment 'There has not been so Great a Fair, for a Demand of horses, ever known in the Memory of Man, as this last was'.[83] Although the importance of horses to the pre-motorized economy has long been recognized, men skilled in horseflesh possessed scarcity value, and were equally important.[84] An advertisement of 1756 requested any 'Countrymen' formerly apprenticed to smiths and farriers to contact the Friendly Society of Master Farriers in London where they would be 'immediately employed'.[85] With an estimated eightfold increase in horses in the metropolis between 1752 and 1765, the need for such men becomes readily apparent.[86] With no government studs, even horses for officers and cavalry and dragoon regiments could only be procured on the open market.[87] Such extensive military demands tested the resources of London horse dealers, but by the mid-eighteenth century the trade was vibrant. Approximately 42 per cent of the 3,200 fairs in England and Wales included horses.[88] The emergence of the great London repositories was only the most obvious sign of this vibrancy.[89] In other respects, the expansion of the trade did not alter its earlier characteristics, notably the prevalence of partnerships and related business interests.[90]

In two and a half years Willan received upwards of £63,378 from encampment and horse contracts. This was 'grassroots' contracting, where skilled tradesmen from a social milieu very different from merchant contractors engaged in military supply. Knowledge in a specialized sector of the economy, not the Namierite route of patronage and influence, was fundamentally important in determining the profile of contracting personnel in this sector. Political influence was not entirely absent. The extensive nature of horse contracts proved attractive to men possessing predominantly mercantile interests, with the London merchant Nicholas Linwood soliciting contracts in Germany.[91] There was no barrier to such men possessing horse contracts, provided they possessed adequate connections in procurement. Linwood was connected with Fox and Calcraft, with the latter promoting his claims. Given Calcraft's connection with Gibson, he was probably concerned in procuring horses for Linwood.[92]

Despite a modicum of mercantile involvement, supplying horses remained mainly an area for specialist dealers. There was a great difference between the world to which Willan belonged and that of merchant contractors such as Dundas and Oswald. The latter two possessed a wide mercantile portfolio, where supplying horses was a stage in their careers rather than a reflection of occupational status. As they became wealthier their interest waned, although Oswald kept horses on his Ayrshire estate, and Dundas subscribed to the first *Racing Calendar*.[93] Keeping horses for estate management and leisure was not the same as gaining one's livelihood from horses. The latter was the province of men such as Willan and Warrington. Willan appears to have known his limitations and concentrated on the business at which he was most competent. He and others in this sector did not aspire to supplying troops abroad, or consider themselves as merchants.[94] Concentration on the domestic economy was the defining characteristic of their business activity. Willan's personal estate illustrates both his extensive wealth and the nature of his business activity. His possessions included furniture, plate, jewels, rings, watches, linen, china, and books. The source of his wealth was detailed in directions that his wife was to receive his:

> Coach Horses, my Saddle Horses, Cart Horses, Coach Chaise and other Carriages and the Flannels, Saddles, Bridles, Furniture, and other things belonging to and

appurtenant thereto together with the Live and dead stock, Farming Utensils and Implements of Husbandry.[95]

After his death, a protracted legal dispute emerged over the lease of the Brownswood Estate, Hornsey, between his eponymous nephew and William Willan, his great nephew.[96] The dispute concerned an agreement made days before his death between Willan and his nephew, by which the latter would receive a new twenty-one year lease for the farm at Hornsey and other farms at £565 per annum. In 1796 a surveyor valued the annual rental of the estate at £1,040, with fines to be paid out of the elder Willan's estate. In terms of acreage the agreement meant the renewal of a lease of 122 acres and an additional 311 acres.[97] William Willan objected that his great uncle was of unsound mind when making the agreement, and conflicting evidence existed as to his intentions. The case reveals the central role of the elder Willan in the business activities of the family. His eponymous nephew related how his uncle acquired the sub-lease of Brownswood estate in 1781 and occupied the 122 acres himself, in connection with a contract for artillery horses. At his retirement in 1784, Willan sold the lease, horses, and other stock to his nephews John and Thomas, and Bright Hemming.[98]

In 1788 the younger John Willan, lacking ready cash, suggested to his uncle that his uncle purchase the lease of another tenant, whilst the younger man became tenant of most of the leasehold property. The transaction was concluded, with the lease renewable every seven years upon payment of a £9,500 fine to St Paul's prebendary. The elder John Willan now held the leasehold of Brownswood manor and estate, comprising three farms, tavern, public buildings, garden, premises called Hornsey Wood house, and 540 acres. His nephew remained tenant of 122 acres at £210 a year rental. The elder John Willan indicated to his nephew the utility and convenience of the land for his business as coach master and innkeeper. In following his uncle to London, John Willan undoubtedly needed guidance and advice from an experienced businessman.[99] The activities of the elder Willan appear to have been important in the business activities of his nephews, and he appears to have introduced his nephews to prominent horse dealers. A witness to the marriage of Thomas Willan on 23 July 1778 was Thomas Fitzherbert MP, a prominent contractor during the American Revolution.[100] A connection between the elder Willan and Fitzherbert can be assumed from evidence relating to a contract held by Warrington for horses at Portsmouth fortifications. At his death in 1774, Fitzherbert, who held a contract for horses to the navy at Portsmouth, assumed the contract at the request of Warrington's widow.[101]

Evidence relating to a contract for artillery horses in 1782 offers a further indication of a connection between the Willan family and Fitzherbert. The latter relinquished the contract as a consequence of 1782 Contractors Bill. Fitzherbert related how, pending a new contract, those he engaged with for horses allowed them to be temporarily continued in use.[102] He was alluding to Willan and Hemming, as they supplied 391 horses between 10 and 16 October, before another partnership were awarded the contract.[103] Willan and Hemming had earlier submitted proposals for the contract.[104] When considerable savings were made under the new contract, Fitzherbert was criticized in Parliament. Offering a spirited defence, Fitzherbert alluded to the short time to procure nearly 1,700 horses, possible early discharge, and loss on sale of horses as factors indicating that 1s. 9d. per horse per day was not a high price.[105] However, with a new contract made for 1s. ¾d., it was bound to appear so. The new contractors proved unable to perform the contract, citing obstructions from 'Persons connected with Mr. Willan'. Hemming continued the contract until 28 October. It is unclear what was behind this sequence of events, but it appears likely the new contractors were relying on Willan and Hemming as sub-contractors.[106] There was clearly a close relationship between Hemming and the Willan family. Hemming was an Executor to the will of William Willan, a London innholder and nephew of the elder John Willan, and later performed an artillery horse contract in partnership with John and Thomas Willan.[107]

The main activity of the younger John Willan was running stage and mail coaches from the Bull and Mouth Inn to locations throughout Britain. He was one of the original mail coach contractors when the system was established in 1784.[108] The inn's colourful motif, represented on his coaches, provoked contemporary comment.[109] Willan had a long career as a mail coach contractor, and was active at the Bull and Mouth until his death in 1822.[110] At his death, he was described as an 'eminent coach master'.[111] These activities confirm the importance of the elder Willan in establishing the family in economic sectors relating to horses and transportation. The elder Willan's activity afforded him the opportunity to forge friendships with men in governmental and military capacities, most notably the Earl of St Vincent, an executor to the will, who gave a moving account of Willan's final illness.[112] The estate administrator, Cuthbert Fisher, was Deputy Treasurer of the Ordnance. He left the residue of his estate to Fitzherbert, further evidence of the network of friendships forged by employment in military supply.[113] Sir Ferdinando Poole was another friend, originally an Executor but removed in the final codicil.[114] An ancient Roman Catholic family related to the Pelhams, the Pooles were recipients of Pelhamite patronage.[115] Ferdinando was a Treasury Under-Clerk between 1756 and 1762, before obtaining a Chief Clerkship, which he held until 1782.[116] After Willan's death, he leased portions of his land, and appears to have been interested in breeding horses.[117] Although tempting to speculate on the political connections Willan may have had, it appears unlikely that the Pooles were influential. Ferdinando was in a minor position at the Treasury when Willan was awarded the 1759 contract, although an undated list detailing the responsibilities of Treasury clerks indicates that contracts were later added to his responsibility.[118] The Pooles were impoverished, with Newcastle providing for them as they were 'Starving, by the Loss of Their place in Minorca'.[119] With an estate of £800 per annum they were reliant on patronage.[120] This evidence depicts a family useful for electoral purposes in Sussex, but from the many favours bestowed upon them, unlikely to be in a position to command favours.

Despite the absence of a precise valuation, some indication of John Willan's wealth can be reconstructed from land sales and estate administration. In 1798–9, part of the freehold estates in Thundersley, Rayleigh and Billericay, all in Essex, were sold for £4,846. In January 1798, seventy-two acres in Thundersley and Rayleigh was conveyed to the Neave family for £31,000, and £55,600 received for six leases in Dean Street, London, from the Dean and Chapter of Westminster.[121] The sales proved inadequate to meet the payment of legacies and annuities directed in the will, with William Willan claiming he paid £8,300 of his own money to make these payments.[122] He requested the Trustees to convey and settle the freehold and manors vested in them, except How Hatch and Frieze Hill, Essex.[123] In June 1829 the final portion of land, How Hatch comprising 115 acres was sold for £10,024.[124] These land sales, relating to Essex and Middlesex alone, amount to £101,470. Only after thirty years generous dispersal of annuities and legacies was Willan's money eventually expended. Willan's career illustrates that domestic contracting could have a great impact on family wealth and status. Although John and Thomas Willan continued within related sectors, their children and grandchildren joined the ranks of the gentry, attending universities and establishing county residences.[125]

The main inheritor of John Willan's wealth, William Willan, does not appear to have been active in business. He attended Oxford, and his son kept two terms at Cambridge.[126] The last Willan who worked the land appears to have been Thomas, grandson of John Willan (1746–1822) who continued farming until his death in 1865.[127] With the death of the younger John Willan in 1822, the Bull and Mouth Inn and coaching house were briefly taken over by Thomas Willan, before being conveyed to the coaching magnate Chaplin.[128] With the development of Regent's Park, land previously used for meeting the supply of artillery horses was subject to urban development. The old landmarks of the Willan family's association with agriculture and coaching had disappeared by the second quarter of the nineteenth century. John Willan left his farms and lands on the Marylebone estate to his nephew Thomas Willan, who continued to occupy this land and a smaller estate at St John's Wood.[129] In 1789 he was tenant of 398 acres, and by 1804 remained in possession of approximately 300 acres, consisting entirely of dairy farms.[130] Thomas Willan maintained his family's military connections. In 1804, he sub-let part of St John's Wood estate to the Ordnance for the Battery Guns of the Royal Artillery Drivers at £150 per annum.[131] Barracks and stabling were built on the land. As the Treasury would not extend his lease, Thomas Willan moved from Marylebone to St John's Wood in 1812, temporarily displacing the Ordnance from rented premises, before relinquishing the farm and moving to West Twyford, Middlesex.[132]

No longer reliant on agriculturally-based pursuits the economic activities of the family reflected in microcosm the passing of an older agricultural England. Family members increasingly turned to the army, the professions, or gentlemanly leisure promoted by financially sound marriages, but the prosperity of the family owed much to the elder Willan. From humble beginnings, he used his knowledge and expertise to establish his nephews in business, whilst his wealth enabled the family to acquire the trappings of upper middle-class gentility. Social mobility may not have been possible for John Willan in his lifetime, but the generously wide dispersal of his wealth ensured the prosperity of the Willan family in the nineteenth century.

Contractors such as Willan did not harbour political ambitions, or seek social acclaim and approval. Little wonder such humility and modesty has led to neglect of their importance. The historical tendency to view contractors as rapacious mainly applied to those whose wealth and ambition propelled them into public life, where, viewed as vulgar parvenus, they represented the unacceptable face of 'new wealth'. Yet the largely hidden world of sub-contracting reveals many men of modest ambition who worked hard for their financial rewards. Contractors of this type can also be found in Scotland, where military supply presents a considerable contrast to England.

7 DOMESTIC SUPPLY AND CONTRACTING IN SCOTLAND, 1746-62

The divergent nature of military supply and composition of contracting personnel within Britain was nowhere better illustrated than in Scotland. Emanating from different rates of economic development and differences in the nature of the military presence throughout Britain, the unique military experience of Scotland justifies separate examination. Variability in terms of available mercantile expertise and agricultural resources produced variable supply methods. In England, a thriving mercantile community and a productive agricultural sector meant there was no shortage of potential contractors. In Scotland, mercantile organization, as opposed to Scottish merchants in London, was less developed and agriculture less productive.[1] Despite extensive road building, the Scottish communications network was notably poor, and in terms of supply infrastructure English merchants possessed considerable advantages over their Scottish counterparts.[2]

One area where Scottish contractors possessed an advantage was experience, obtained during periods of military activity in the years preceding 1756. An important procedural difference in making contracts partly emanated from the 1745 Jacobite Rebellion. The formal procedure which accompanied annual encampment contracts in England was not followed in Scotland. The position was somewhat analogous to that of foreign campaigns, with military commanders assuming greater involvement both in recommending contractors and in making contracts, although subject to Treasury approval. Distance and familiarity with the country made decentralization sensible, although logistical considerations were also important. In Scotland, the army was rarely concentrated in encampments. Diversity in military operations and mode of accommodation contributed towards localized supply methods, which in turn meant Scottish contractors. No English merchants appear to have considered applying for contracts in Scotland. It is difficult to see insufficient profitability as an explanation. Although troop numbers fluctuated in the post-Rebellion period, many more troops were resident in Scotland than most foreign garrisons. With far greater distances traversed in the performance of foreign victualling contracts, albeit by sea, distance is not a sufficient explanation. For London-based merchants, difficulties that appear to have prohibited English merchants from performing encampment contracts applied also to Scotland. These sectoral divisions were accompanied by distinctly national considerations. An important consideration for any potential contractor was how far contracts complemented other business interests. With widely dispersed and not easily accessible garrisons, Scotland was something of a backwater.[3] Logistical and distributive problems associated with troop dispersal, when contrasted with troop concentration in encampments and foreign garrisons appear to have been a factor in the absence, not only of English merchants but English men.

Political considerations accompanied supply difficulties in determining contracting personnel. Loyalty to the Hanoverian dynasty was fundamental, and it was demonstrably loyal Scots who supplied the army after 1746. Despite reservations over whether Scots could be trusted with military responsibilities, marked displays of loyalty effectively undermined such distrust.[4] Whilst many political and economic difficulties existed which were inapplicable in England, these should not be overemphasized. Contractors did not heroically manage supply in the face of a hostile population. During the Rebellion, military victories made the task easier, and in its aftermath Jacobitism rapidly and irreversibly declined.[5] Moreover, the relative quiescence of Scotland between 1756 and 1762 meant supply was conducted on a smaller scale than in England. Nevertheless, after the events of 1745/6, success in this sphere was a considerable achievement.

The absence of a centralized supply organization in Britain led to a high degree of decentralization in Scotland. During the 1715 Rebellion it was initially necessary to rely on the Scottish Whig establishment and aristocracy to raise the militia, and provide horses, arms, accoutrements and provisions.[6] The interaction of location and season compounded difficulties that affected the mobility and strategy of both armies.[7] Although winter campaigning introduced additional supply difficulties, procurement problems were a constantly recurring theme in Scottish military campaigns.[8] The skeletal military presence in Scotland in 1715 estimated at 1,788 troops, resulted from extensive reductions made in 1713.[9] However, after 1715 the number of resident troops remained reasonably impressive, in terms of the overall size of the British army. Jacobite scares and civil disorder led to extensive military deployment, whilst government measures aimed at pacification included the periodic reconstruction of a chain of Highland forts and barracks and extensive road-building.[10] In attempting to overcome the physical isolation of the Highlands such plans were well-conceived but badly executed.[11] Building was delayed and many garrisons neglected.[12] The existence of barracks led to the Barrack Master General, a commissioned officer appointed by the Ordnance Board, assuming particular importance in supply matters. The singular nature of the position is apparent upon comparison with England and

Ireland, where no corresponding position existed until 1792 and 1800 respectively.[13] The corollary of this divergence was that although billeting on private houses was legal, the existence of barracks made billeting less important and less politically contentious in Scotland.[14]

In Scotland, Deputy Barrack Masters and Storekeepers resided at barracks but the Barrack Master General possessed the proprietary right to supply provisions, fuel, and brewing and baking utensils.[15] Combining the duty of maintaining and supervising barracks the position encompassed military and mercantile responsibilities. As a public accountant, the Barrack Master managed the supply of garrisoned troops by making sub-contracts with merchants.[16] Beyond the position of Barrack Master there was no supply organization, and with less than 4,000 widely dispersed troops in 1745 little need for one.[17] The 1745 Rebellion transformed this situation, and illustrated the difficulties of supplying a large army quickly, at short notice, in winter, and in inhospitable country. As in 1715, the severity of the military situation necessitated a higher degree of state planning. The absence of a coordinating figure was an acute problem. Whereas Continental armies employed officials solely concerned with supply, the absence of corresponding officials in Britain meant military officers assumed some responsibility for supply matters. In the early stages of the Rebellion this was particularly apparent, with Sir John Cope responsible for the Highland army, and Joshua Guest, Barrack Master, responsible for the Lowlands.[18] Cumberland's later performance as a 'Providore' was praised, alongside complaints that he should not have to perform such tasks, although the disparate nature of military operations meant the continual involvement of officers when necessary.[19]

The key figure in the supply organization was the Commissary General of Provisions, Stores and Forage. The position was not a permanent one on the British establishment but periodically revived when necessary, most recently in 1742 for the Flanders army when Abraham Hume held the position. By 1745 Hume was employed as Commissary for the Exchange of Prisoners.[20] Appointed in lieu of his previous position, Hume was instructed to attend the commanding officer Henry Hawley and ensure contracts were fully complied with, particularly for forage which it was feared would be scarce.[21] Arriving in January 1746, Hume's immediate task was to obtain an accurate assessment of conditions, including available resources and provisions required. Resources could then be allocated according to time and place. A report on the condition of magazine provisions at Inverness, Stirling, Perth and Leith exemplified the variability in quantity and quality of conditions in Scotland generally.[22] These shortcomings bespoke a system lacking coordination where accurate information was sparse, leading to alternate overstocking and scarcity. Hume's appointment was immediately recognized as the first step in remedying an unsatisfactory state of affairs.[23]

In Scotland, the limitations of reliance on local procurement in inhospitable territory were cruelly exposed. A soldier present at Falkirk related 'he could get nothing but oatmeal and water for some days together and at other times such victuals as no Englishman could eat, except hunger drove him'.[24] Yet by late January 1746, with the army concentrated, the Rebels retreating and the requisite officials employed, supply became less problematic. The supply methods that emerged as most appropriate for the Hanoverian army comprised an admixture of traditional practices and the strategic use of sea power. In localities, forage was purchased from landowners and farmers at regulated county rates.[25] Local government officials procured shipping and provisions, whilst attempting to prevent the Rebels receiving supplies.[26] Amongst significant London suppliers were the Sephardic Jews Abraham and Jacob Franco, who shipped nearly 8,000 sacks of flour.[27] Voluntarist efforts from loyal associations supplied clothing, although clothing contracts remained necessary.[28] Whilst government was prepared to obtain supplies from a wide geographical area it remained important to procure as much as possible in Scotland. Having personally presented proposals in London to supply forage, Lawrence Dundas and his elder brother Thomas made a contract in January 1746 with Hawley for '1 million Rations of Forage or so much as is required'.[29] Magazines were to be established throughout Scotland, with the first at the strategically important points of Edinburgh and Leith. An indication of procurement problems was a clause stipulating oatstraw as an acceptable substitute should hay be unavailable. Nevertheless, the contract was not formally ratified. Hawley complained that having heard nothing since sending the contract to London he had empowered the contractors to act until the contract was formally concluded.[30] This appears to account for the curious status of Lawrence Dundas during the Rebellion. He is described as a commissary after 31 January, an appointment made retrospectively on 22 March by Cumberland's warrant.[31] Thomas Dundas, married to a daughter of the sixth Earl of Lauderdale, played a subordinate role as his younger brother's agent and correspondent.[32]

As commissary, Lawrence Dundas procured supplies from a variety of sources rather than contracting to supply a specific amount of specific articles for a fixed period. Dundas needed to identify sources of supply before organizing collection, delivery and distribution. To accomplish this, it was necessary to establish a working relationship with local officials whilst adopting a degree of improvisation. Forage magazines were located in churches at Falkirk and Stirling, whilst bread was delivered to the Town House at Stirling.[33] Establishing a forage magazine at Stirling, Dundas indicated to the bailie of Alloa that he required his cooperation in collecting all available local hay, for which Dundas issued receipts and paid the regulated county price.[34] The appointment of Dundas has been attributed to the influence of Colonel Masterton, Cumberland's Aide-de-Camp.[35] Yet Hume's recommendation of Dundas as a 'Person of

Substance capacity & integrity' appears to have been vital.[36] Despite difficulties of distance, terrain, scarcity, and local hostility, in his dotage Dundas happily recalled the experience, and 'talked a great deal of his adventures, as I may call them, with the Duke of Cumberland's army in 1745-6'.[37]

Dundas managed an extensive supply organization encompassing commissaries, sub-contractors, and agents. The Portuguese retained an involvement, with Jacob Gomez Serra acting as commissary for bread, and at least three others employed as assistants.[38] Commissaries and their agents operated across a wide area employing labourers, and renting magazines, horses and carriages, and were an essential component of a system heavily reliant on sub-contractors. Dundas assumed considerable responsibility in supply matters. At Perth an officer and twenty men of each regiment were instructed to cut wood under his instructions, whilst at Inverness he supervised foraging parties. Although his main activity consisted of procuring meal and forage, he also sold beef and delivered livestock.[39] Dundas also shipped coals coastwise, and imported hay from Holland.[40] Dundas clearly possessed an aptitude for business allied to indispensable local and European mercantile connections. Conscious of making himself popular, Dundas ingratiated himself with those possessing influence and authority, even arranging Edinburgh accommodation for the Earl of Albemarle, the commanding officer in Scotland.[41] Cumberland and Albemarle, neither renowned for partiality towards Scots, recommended his further employment.[42] With such recognition and support the Rebellion constituted the 'making' of Dundas, and marked the beginning of a spectacularly successful career, with a contracting and commissarial portfolio embracing England, Flanders and Germany.

Despite concerns over the rapidity and scale of military disengagement after Culloden, the rebuilding of forts, extension of Highland roads, and general policing activities ensured the army remained a significant presence. In late 1746, 13,000 troops remained.[43] Vigilance remained the basis of government policy but maintaining a large army conflicted with the need to reduce expenditure, and even Cumberland accepted that 18,990 troops in Britain represented more troops than any previous period of peace.[44] Although in 1747 it was planned that 12,056 troops should remain in Scotland, incomplete regiments and postwar reductions depleted numbers until by 1752 only 6,275 remained.[45]

[Table 7.1: Forces in Great Britain, 1742-8[46]]

Year	No. of men	Cost
1742	23,316	£623,555
1743	23,610	£647,862
1744	19,028	£561,794
1745	15,768	£499,936
1746	49,229	£1,298,100
1747	33,030	£856,066
1748	27,451	£760,061

Loyalty to the Hanoverian dynasty was vitally important in determining contracting personnel in the post-Rebellion period. During the Rebellion the chaotic situation precluded any scramble for places but afterwards government loyalists sought recompense. Individuals and local areas supplying the army but remaining unpaid and those who suffered from Jacobite impositions were foremost in seeking reimbursement.[47] Amongst governing circles, some sought to reward loyal men and the emphasis on loyalty occasioned disputes over the political management of Scotland.[48] At Ministerial level, Pelham faced accusations of tolerating the continued employment of Jacobites and acquiescence in the dismissal of loyal men. When the King raised the subject 'Mr. Pelham said, The Attack against Him, was, for being for the Constitution, against Military Power, or a Military Government'.[49] Whilst Scotland became the focus of aristocratic factionalism, Pelham was confident the result of the inquiry would undermine the designs of Cumberland's faction. Yet, it was increasingly clear that an important legacy of the Rebellion was a renewed emphasis on loyalty as an essential quality towards employment in Scotland.[50] Whilst it was acknowledged that some Jacobites were employed in governmental positions, in the potentially sensitive area of military supply, loyalty was particularly apparent.[51] Experience was no less important, for with barracks, forts and encampments all used to accommodate troops, the variegated and dispersed military presence demanded familiarity with topography, people and resources. The twin pillars of loyalty and experience are apparent in the careers of three men who dominated military supply in Scotland for a generation.

After the Rebellion Dundas, with Cumberland's approval, received a contract providing bread, wagons and forage for the Fort George encampment of 1747, and for troops quartered along the coast.[52] Despite wheat and oatmeal prices having fallen considerably, Dundas contracted at the same price as 1746.[53] This contract was perhaps the type of reward Albemarle intended.[54] Dundas agreed to purchase fifty wagons belonging to the Ordnance, covering and maintaining them at his own expense, and fitting them with horses. With Dundas paid for five months certain, he was given an immediate opportunity to recoup the purchase price. However, Dundas's failure to secure the post of Barrack Master General indicates there were limits to his advancement. With the elderly Guest willing to allow him to succeed to the position, Dundas only required Cumberland's approval.[55] For political reasons this consent was withheld.[56] Nevertheless, in 1748 Dundas travelled to Flanders as Deputy Commissary General at £3 per day, having the same year been appointed Commissary of Stores in Scotland at 10s per day. This position superceded his earlier position, and Dundas retained it until 1759.[57]

Dundas's activities in Scotland were marked by suspicion of inordinate gain from fraudulent practices, and although never conclusively proved, the allegations against him appear convincing. An ex-employee, to whom Dundas owed money, outlined numerous frauds, including issuing receipts for forage, coals and peat for amounts over the quantity delivered. On signing receipts the Quartermaster received a 'consideration'. Dundas was also accused of making a post-dated 'sham Contract' with one of his clerks. Although the informer could not estimate the extent of fraud he confidently cited twenty people capable of providing further information.[58] The specificity of the allegations was impressive, bolstered by widespread amazement at the rapidity with which Dundas made a fortune.[59] The disruption occasioned by military operations facilitated such practices, by providing justification for missing documentation.[60] That Dundas survived such allegations owed much to a good relationship with the military triumvirate of Cumberland, Albemarle and Bland. The latter supported Dundas's argument that the 'Urgency of the Service during the Heat of the Rebellion' allowed no time for formally issuing warrants or receipts, and that it was standard practice to issue money to Dundas on account.[61] On Dundas settling accounts with the informer, the latter was unwilling to appear before the Treasury, and Pelham allowed the affair to drop.[62] The difficulty of initiating proceedings five years after the event, the support Dundas received from officers, and perhaps an appreciation that the Rebellion occasioned many irregularities, may have influenced his decision.[63]

Whilst Dundas's activity in Scotland declined in the following years, the loyalty of two other men ensured their continued employment. In 1746 Dundas received considerable assistance from Robert Gardiner, the eldest son of a Linlithgow merchant.[64] Before the Rebellion, Gardiner was 'well established in business before the Court of Session' before being entrusted by the Lord Justice Clerk and Barrack Master 'with the Execution of several important Commissions'. Relinquishing business and devoting himself to the 'Publick Service' Gardiner, owing to his 'Assiduity and Success' was 'insulted and abused' by the Rebels when taken prisoner at Preston. Appointed a commissary before the battle of Falkirk, Gardiner claimed that on Dundas's appointment in January 1746 he was requested to act as his deputy as Dundas was unfamiliar with the business.[65] He continued to work for Dundas in the following years and appears to have conducted Dundas's business as Commissary of Stores.[66] Gardiner was involved in gathering intelligence and monitoring Rebel movements, and was particularly interested in capturing the Pretender, but his duties as a commissary proved to be of more long-term consequence.[67] At the end of 1745 Gardiner was employed to travel to Linlithgow, Falkirk and Stirling to assess forage availability. He also paid workmen constructing stables, hired baggage horses, and ensured provisions were available at Linlithgow and Borrowstoneness.[68] For the forced march of regiments from Linlithgow to Edinburgh, Gardiner hired 515 horses from the Linlithgow Volunteers, loyal troops for whom he acted as manager and representative.[69] Gardiner worked hard during the Rebellion. Following the army, he often stayed behind a day after their departure to settle outstanding forage and firing accounts.[70] He claimed that working eighteen-hour days left no time to report military movements, having earlier done so.[71]

When Dundas's office of Commissary General of Provisions was abolished in February 1748, Gardiner continued on the orders of commanding officers to act as Commissary and Paymaster. General Bland employed him to provide barrack provisions at the end of 1747. Bland described Gardiner as Dundas's 'Chief Clerk', and recommended his employment to the new Barrack Master as 'thoroughly skill'd in these Affairs' and 'an Able & an Honest man'.[72] This advice was heeded, for Gardiner was later described as his principal agent.[73] Bland reiterated Gardiner's 'great service to the Troops during the time of the late Rebellion' and considered that he rather than Dundas ensured efficient supply operations.[74] Gardiner did not however possess a commission and this proved to be an obstacle towards obtaining employment. To leave the option open to the new Barrack Master should he wish to undertake supply on the same terms Bland would not employ Gardiner for more than one year, thus indicating the inherent advantage of a position on the military establishment.[75] Gardiner however continued to supply troops, particularly when a larger military presence was required such as supplying oatmeal to troops building roads in 1750–1 and for encamped troops employed in building Fort George.[76]

In 1749, the cost of wagons and Gardiner's travelling expenses were questioned, and as he had sole privilege of supplying bread it was expected he should pay for transport.[77] With a view to economy the government proposed to construct a bakery, storehouse and ovens near Fort George. As this could not be accomplished in 1750 the previous supply method was continued, amidst admonitions over controlling expenditure.[78] Gardiner himself proposed constructing temporary 'sod Hutts', a suggestion supported by the Ordnance as cheaper, as Gardiner was less likely to be imposed on by local people.[79] Despite criticism over costs Gardiner was more often praised. Gardiner acted as a contractor at Fort William but on directions from commanding officers in other areas.[80] General Churchill supported Gardiner's application for renewal of the Fort William contract on the basis of previous competence.[81] In 1752 Gardiner began supplying isolated Highland detachments, and his willingness to conduct difficult supply operations made him popular.[82] Gardiner was involved in managing supply, a type of 'grass-roots' contracting similar to English encampment and horse contractors. Indeed, he unsuccessfully applied for the English encampment contract in 1759, and held an Ordnance contract for artillery horses between 1755 and 1759.[83] Successive military commanders found him reliable, capable and honest, and these qualities ensured his continual involvement in supplying troops.[84] Yet, as the career of the third figure in Scotland demonstrates, merit as a factor within the supply system must be offset against the influence of patronage.

Thomas Leslie MP, a younger brother of the tenth Earl of Rothes, used ministerial connections to obtain contracts and a position on the military establishment. Leslie came from a military family of Hanoverian loyalists. In 1715 the ninth Earl commanded cavalry volunteers at Sheriffmuir, and despite Jacobite attacks on the family seat in Fife, Defoe later noted its magnificence.[85] The tenth Earl, Leslie's brother, ended a distinguished military career as Commander-in-Chief in Ireland from 1758 until his death in 1767.[86] Leslie was a Captain in Murray's regiment in 1745, and was imprisoned at Prestonpans but rescued in January 1746. Recalled to London on account of his brother's health, he does not appear to have fought at Culloden.[87] As a younger son Leslie needed, and received, considerable aid from his father and brother. In 1722 he was unseated as MP on petition after his father, as Returning Officer, proclaimed him elected when he was clearly defeated. In 1742, Leslie was appointed an equerry to the Prince of Wales with an annual salary of £300.[88] In 1743 he was elected to Parliament, and in 1744 was appointed Aide-de-Camp to Sir Robert Rich's regiment.[89]

A 'patriot Whig' connected with the Marquis of Tweeddale and the anti-Argyll Squadrone, Leslie's loyalty to the Hanoverian dynasty and support for the Pelhams were never in doubt.[90] Leslie proved his anti-Jacobite credentials in civil and military terms, by presenting, as district MP, a 'loyal and dutiful address' from Dundee Magistrates and Town Council six weeks after the Jacobites left town.[91] Learning that the post of Barrack Master General was vacant, Leslie requested Newcastle's assistance:

> My Lord Rothes's attachment and his family's to your Grace's, makes me flatter my self with your assistance ... Mr. Dundas who was Commissary for provisions or forage in Scotland had made some proposals to General Guest but a Stop was put to it. I think my pretensions Are Much Better than any he can have, I am told that he is Applying for this Employment.[92]

Leslie obtained the £365 per annum position, and the lucrative nature of the position was enhanced by the likelihood that, acting on precedent, the holder would succeed to further contracts for bedding, barrack furniture, and provisions.[93] When the post was vacant, Dundas temporarily assumed the task, but sought to make it permanent.[94] Dundas was reportedly 'carrying on a project of being barrack master in another name and has employed a noble Lord for that purpose'.[95] After defeating a government candidate at the 1747 election, Dundas was subsequently unseated for bribery. His activities enraged Pelham and Argyll.[96] The latter requested Pelham to delay appointing a Barrack Master and settling Dundas's accounts. Pelham needed little encouragement, informing Argyll he would complain of Dundas's conduct to Cumberland.[97] Dundas's credit with Cumberland was insufficient to secure the position, and Leslie, whose loyalty was never in doubt and whose brother was a trusted subordinate officer to Cumberland was appointed.[98]

Unlike commissaries the post of Barrack Master was not deemed incompatible with the possession of contracts. Leslie's official position proved advantageous, for when Gardiner offered to supply barracks in 1752 difficulties arose from commitments made to Leslie 'that if he served well he should at the expiration of the present Contract, supply all the Barracks'. Although Cumberland was convinced of Gardiner's 'extraordinary merit', Leslie succeeded to further contracts.[99] Rival claims were disposed of. As Commissary of Stores, Dundas claimed a proprietary right as previous Barrack Masters had never supplied Fort William and Fort George, and there was nothing in Leslie's commission relating to provisions. Bland however assured Leslie he would succeed to everything his predecessor possessed.[100] An earlier informal agreement made with Gardiner to supply barracks was easily disposed of.[101] Governors and Lieutenant Governors were another group with a claim to supply barracks; particularly those not previously supplied by the Barrack Master. This claim was invalidated by prohibition of officers' involvement in supplying troops contained in the 1748 Articles of War, although examples of Lieutenant Governors providing fire and candle, a long-standing perquisite, persisted.[102]

Leslie initially furnished barracks at Fort Augustus, Bernera, Inversnaid, Braemar, Duart, and Corgarff Castles, with oatmeal, malt, liquor, firing, candles and other articles.[103] The sole right of supplying provisions was a privilege Leslie sought to maintain, accusing the Lieutenant-General of Fort Augustus of allowing interlopers to brew and sell ale within the fort. Leslie met counter-accusations that he failed to keep six months' provisions in store, by arguing that as provisions were shipped the short distance from Inverness via Loch Ness, it was unnecessary to provide the specified amount.[104] Despite Leslie's insouciance towards contract regulations he appears to have heeded the criticism, for his agent applied to have storehouses repaired in order that six months' provisions could be stored. Commanding officers were instructed to ensure the regulations were complied with.[105] With contracts due to expire in 1753 the Lords Justices directed Leslie to continue supplying barracks, including those previously supplied by Gardiner.[106] They also advised Leslie that in future he should submit proposals to commanding officers for any new Scottish garrisons.[107] In promoting Gardiner's claims, Bland received an extraordinary response from Fox conveying Cumberland's approval of Leslie:

> His Royal Highness returns me your Letter & his opinion in these words <u>Mr Lesslie has undoubted right to furnish all the barracks and Fort George tho' not finished yet</u>

certainly belongs to him. Be assur'd that this Decision comes not from either favour to Mr. Lesslie or Dislike to Mr. Gardner but Justice only.[108]

A recipient of Newcastle's 'Secret Service Money', Leslie's impecunious nature was placated by contracts. Indeed, Leslie often linked contract payments to enhancement of his electoral prospects.[109]

Although considered vulnerable to French invasion, the quiescence of Scotland between 1756 and 1762 led to a steady decline in the number of resident troops. As troops were transferred to active theatres of war, troop numbers fell from 7,008 in March 1756 to 5,417 in January 1760.[110] The Artillery Train sent to Scotland in 1755 was miniscule. Gardiner supplied twenty horses, with the entire cost for 1757 only £821, compared to £4,192 for horses and drivers attending sixteen battalions of foot in England between January–June 1757.[111] More widely, the contrast with England, and Scotland during the Rebellion, is striking. Dundas's accounts as commissary and contractor for 1745–7 amounted to £128,789. In the period 1747–67 payments to Gardiner and Leslie amounted to £34,231 and £41,614 respectively.[112]

Even for a small number of troops supply could be precarious. Famine was feared in 1757 when the mob obstructed the transportation of grain, and troops waiting to embark for Ireland were saved by the arrival of a ship at Port Patrick laden with oats.[113] The presence of 338 French prisoners in Scotland exacerbated the pressure on resources with only a limited number of safe areas capable of providing cantonments.[114] By 1759, the invasion threat was serious, exacerbated by anxiety over the estimated 1,000 French prisoners.[115] In May, earlier plans for cantonments were abandoned and anti-invasion preparations began, with troops ordered to carry camp equipment in case of encampment.[116] In June, regiments were ordered to provide themselves with bat and baggage horses for encampment, with troop disposition and warrants for horses following shortly afterwards.[117]

Camps were formed in July at Fort George and Musselburgh, and continued until October.[118] The locations were predicated on defending Edinburgh and the east coast against a 'Sudden Descent' from Dunkirk or Ostend.[119] Gardiner had regularly supplied troops encamped near Fort George, and appearing the natural choice to supply encampments, the commanding officer Lord George Beauclerk requested him to begin supply before contracts were officially made.[120] Although the Treasury approved Gardiner's appointment as commissary in July 1759, he chose, on the advice of Argyll and Barrington to become a contractor for the encampments. The conflict of interest meant he could not hold both positions.[121] His understanding that he would be appointed commissary once his contracts ended influenced his decision. A new commissary, George Munro, was temporarily appointed.[122] Gardiner came to regret this decision, for when the encampments ended, despite having no duties to perform Munro refused Gardiner's requests to resign in his favour.[123] This was particularly galling, as Gardiner had advised Munro to apply for the position. Gardiner attributed Munro's continued employment to the influence of the Treasury Secretary, James West.[124] Gardiner sought the position on the basis that he was effectively 'Acting Commissary' between February 1748 and December 1758. The Auditors and previous commanding officers were consulted relative to his status, and the former accepted Gardiner's claim that he performed commissarial functions without a commission.[125] Gardiner's activities were mostly in response to the orders of commanding officers with payment from annual Contingent Bills. Although paid for provisions issued, Gardiner did not receive a salary for himself or the clerk he employed.[126]

Gardiner had other grievances relating to the contract. Haste in organizing supply perhaps explains the delay in making advance payments. Gardiner argued that the absence of this payment, important in reducing the purchase price of provisions, would deleteriously affect profitability:

> Mr Gardiner the Contractor complains much of the want of the Impress applied for, to enable him to carry on the business, & says, he will be a considerable looser by both contracts.[127]

The contract terms reflected supply difficulties in Scotland.[128] Transport difficulties impacted on costs, with bread supplied north of the Tay costing 7½*d*. per loaf, 1*d*. more than south of the river.[129] Deliveries were made weekly. Eighteen wagons were contracted for Musselburgh only, with wagons removed from government stores at Fort William and Edinburgh Castle appearing to have been used at Fort George.[130] In an example of local variation, the forage ration consisted of 18lb hay, 8lb oats and 4lb straw, with peat or coals an acceptable alternative to wood.[131] The ration prices for wood and straw, 1*s*. 11*d*., and for wagon hire, 4*s* per day, were cheaper than in England. Gardiner provided 66,520 forage rations, 75,372 6lb loaves of bread (452,232lb), and 798 36lb trusses of straw (28,728lb) under contract. With three infantry regiments and an artillery detachment Musselburgh was larger, and received larger amounts, but the need to pay for sea carriage meant the proportionate cost of Fort George was higher.[132]

One week after the camps dispersed, intelligence was received of a French plan to invade Scotland.[133] Troops had been cantoned for easy assembly but the invasion threat effectively ended with the defeat of Thurot's squadron in February 1760.[134] Gardiner contributed further towards military operations by supplying wagon horses accompanying troops from Edinburgh to western Scotland.[135] With a long coastline and a shortage of troops, Scotland was vulnerable.

An unwelcome reminder of this came from Charles Townshend, who visited Scotland in 1759. Debating the Scotch militia bill:

> C: Townshend Spoke Violently for it, as having been a Witness last Summer to the unprepared State of the Country & that It was impossible To be against letting those defend Themselves when You could not Spare a Sufficient Force to protect Them.[136]

Fear of arming Jacobites played a part in defeating the bill, but Townshend raised other serious issues.[137] With reports circulating in London of disease and distress prevailing in Scottish encampments, Newcastle informed Hardwicke of Townshend's claim:

> That Hanover, America & c. were to be defended, & Scotland abandon'd & deserted, And That He had seen the Troops there, which had more, the Air of a Hospital, than of a Camp of Soldiers.[138]

The commanding officer denied this, although admitting small pox, fluxes and fevers, prevalent throughout the country, affected some troops. Officers defended the contractor by emphasizing the freshness of provisions.[139] Of three regiments encamped at Musselburgh composed of 2,640, thirty-one died and forty-one deserted.[140] These figures indicate particular cases of sickness rather than a general malaise. The camps were competently supplied, and the sickliness of troops exaggerated, at least partly for factional purposes. Important information was regularly conveyed to the contractor and a satisfactory delineation of functions achieved.[141] The invasion threat of 1759 was the high point of military activity in Scotland during the war. With little significant military activity afterwards, troops continued to be sent abroad.[142] The necessity of continuing Gardiner's contract for thirty-six horses and eighteen wagons was questioned.[143] Although admitting limited usage, the commanding officer argued that low cost made it prudent to maintain them, particularly as difficulties might arise from a necessity to acquire them suddenly. On this basis, the contract was continued until the end of 1762.[144]

During the war, Leslie continued to dominate garrison contracts. The garrisons in the Great Glen linking Inverness with Fort William represented the base of Hanoverian power in the Highlands.[145] Aside from Fort William the forts suffered badly during the Rebellion.[146] Post-Rebellion reconstruction included the new Fort George, the rebuilding of Fort Augustus, and conversion to barracks of two small castles at Corgarff and Braemar.[147] Work proceeded slowly, with insufficient storehouses and granaries in 1748, and Fort George uninhabitable until 1752.[148] Scottish garrisons were ill-prepared to accommodate a large army. Insufficient barrack capacity prompted the Ordnance to prepare Stirling Castle as a garrison for three companies in 1756.[149] The Artillery Company based at Perth suffered from a lack of barrack furniture including bedding, and sutlers' quarters at Edinburgh Castle were uninhabitable.[150] At the height of the war, Fort William was described as in a 'most ruinous state'.[151] Even the much-vaunted Fort George possessed barracks for only 1,600 men. Despite their proliferation, these defences were, by contemporary standards 'toy forts', although sufficiently large to impress local inhabitants.[152]

Cost was a great consideration in supplying garrisons. During the war, price movements in Scotland were similar to England, with high prices in 1757 followed by a progressive decline until prices began to rise in 1762.[153] In 1757, the War Office directed no new charge should be incurred except from absolute necessity.[154] The commanding officer in Scotland initiated the search for economies. Examining Leslie's accounts, he was struck by a clause in the contract stipulating when the price of oatmeal exceeded 8d. per peck, Leslie should notify the commanding officer in order to receive an additional allowance. He advocated a fixed sum in place of the annual surcharge, but no action was taken amidst the dearth of 1757.[155] As government possessed no control over the surcharge, the system did not encourage economy, and reform was clearly necessary. Although meal was cheap in 1759 the provision of six months' supply in store meant another surcharge would be levied. The surcharge cost the government £3,072 18s. over five years, including £1,110 in 1757 and £881 in 1758. The possible savings of a fixed charge were clearly demonstrated on the basis of previous years.[156] Leslie made counter-proposals, and both sets of proposals, together with Barrington's observations were presented at the Treasury.[157] A fixed sum was agreed on, and any higher price required the commanding officer's approval.[158] Leslie also agreed to supply utensils in return for an annual allowance, including a sum for damages. Considerable distance between Highland barracks and markets and towns meant there was little opportunity to hire utensils as in Lowland Scotland.[159] These arrangements occurred amidst a period of heightened military activity. A survey of June 1759 indicated divergent supply methods between Lowland and Highland forts. The former, comprising the castles of Edinburgh, Stirling, Dumbarton and Blackness held 1,075 troops. As troops in these areas purchased provisions daily, no magazines were established and no one was employed to supervise supply. No more than two days provisions were stored.[160] In contrast, Highland garrisons, accommodating 1,350 troops, always had six months' provisions in store. Leslie supplied oatmeal, firing, candles and ale under contract, whilst troops provided themselves with other food products including cheese, potatoes, butter, and meat.

Cost and availability underpinned this divergence in supply methods. Fear of enemy attack induced the anonymous author to recommend all articles for Highland garrisons should be supplied under contract, whilst small magazines should be established at Lowland garrisons, with troops receiving provisions at prices regulated by the commanding officer.[161] With Scotland threatened with invasion, an artillery train was dispatched to Fort George.[162] Ligonier informed the Treasury of the immediate necessity of providing provisions for 1,000 men for six months at Fort George, and Leslie was instructed to begin purchasing and storing provisions before presenting proposals. The Treasury used estimates prepared by Gardiner to reduce pork and meal prices.[163] Whilst the extensive amount of provisions proved superfluous, indicative of governmental overreaction, such a problem was less serious than dearth.[164]

It is unsurprising that in a small country those engaged in the same business were acquainted. In London, most Scots involved in contracting inhabited the same area, and only Gardiner did not have a London residence. Together, they comprised a distinctive sub-section of the Scottish mercantile community in London.[165] In the early 1750s Dundas, Robert Haldane and George Ross, the London agent of Gardiner and Leslie, were resident in Conduit Street, with Leslie resident in nearby Sackville Street.[166] Leslie and Gardiner appear to have been on cool although not hostile terms with Dundas. This probably emanated from Dundas's ambitious nature, and competition for the position of Barrack Master.[167] Leslie and Gardiner appear to have been on friendly terms. Alongside Ross, Leslie stood surety of £1,000 for Gardiner's contract for horses in 1755. Leslie also nominated Ross to stand surety for a bedding contract of 1760.[168] Ross appears to have been an important figure. Formerly clerk to Duncan Forbes, the Lord President of the Court of Session, he received Argyll's patronage after Forbes's death.[169] From 1754, Ross was London agent of the Convention of the Royal Burghs, a position he held for twenty-five years.[170] Possessing political, legal and military interests, Ross was well-connected. In 1746 he acted as solicitor for the Rebel Lords Balmerino, Kilmarnock and Lovat, but seven years later represented the Crown over Forfeited Estates.[171] Ross promoted the loyalty of the sons of Jacobite Rebels, and the sons of Lovat and Kilmarnock recovered family estates.[172] Forbes appointed Ross agent to the independent companies during the Rebellion, and in London Ross acted as a regimental agent. By 1763 he possessed eight agencies.[173] Acting as middleman between colonels and contractors, Ross managed the supply of camp necessaries and clothing for regiments under his care.[174] Rival agents viewed his ministerial connections with jealousy, Calcraft informing Loudoun 'Lord Bute has made Ld. George Sackville give Ross his Agency which is Politically as well as otherwise Unpleasant'.[175]

Ross also acted as an agent to Scottish contractors, transacting business on their behalf. He personally attended the Ordnance Board in 1755 and agreed terms on Gardiner's behalf whilst two clerks in his London office witnessed Leslie's barracks contract of 1759.[176] Ross was connected with Lawrence Dundas whilst the latter was in Germany, and served as a channel of financial and political intelligence.[177] Even General Bland, seeking payment for expenditure incurred in suppressing Highland lawlessness, requested Ross's assistance, as he 'could not think of a fitter Agent to Negotiate it at the Treasury'.[178] The nature of his business, the services he provided, and the connections he possessed, indicate Ross should be viewed as a 'Merchant-Attorney' alongside those employed by foreign contractors.

By 1762, the mid-century contractors in Scotland were approaching the end of their careers. Whilst Dundas was sufficiently wealthy after 1762 to retire from business, Gardiner received his final payments early in 1764.[179] Post-war demobilization affected Gardiner more than Leslie, for the temporary expediencies which characterized his involvement in supply no longer existed. There were limits to advancement by merit. In 1762, Beauclerk appointed Gardiner to supply Edinburgh Castle with coals and candle, with an estimated £400 annual profit.[180] When a new Lieutenant Governor was appointed, he requested supply on the basis of precedent.[181] Beauclerk denied partiality towards Gardiner, arguing the appointment was for the good of the service, as the previous Lieutenant Governor defrauded the men, and Gardiner's appointment meant there would be a check on prices. Nevertheless, proprietary right and custom prevailed, and Gardiner's appointment was revoked.[182]

Leslie's contracts, based on a permanent military presence, continued into the post-war period, although his loyalty to Newcastle did not survive the latter's fall from power.[183] He did not relinquish the post of Barrack Master until 1769, when he was succeeded by Dundas's friend James Masterton.[184] Leslie's career illustrates patronage was a factor in awarding contracts in post-Rebellion Scotland, but it was never all-encompassing. Distance from London and procurement and distribution difficulties narrowed the range of prospective contractors. The careers of Gardiner and Dundas illustrate the importance of recommendations from military commanders. Although the open competition of English encampment contracts was not applied in Scotland, merit, ability, and reliability were not completely precluded. In the immediate post-Rebellion period contracts do not appear to have been advertised in newspapers, but were awarded to those who had rendered loyal service. Gardiner was awarded an artillery horse contract 'in Consequence of a Letter from General Bland' in April 1755.[185] In this case, military recommendations worked against Dundas, who offered horses at the same price. This example of indirect influence in contract allocation, indirect as it only became operative with identical tenders, was at least partly based on Gardiner's proven reliability. There is evidence that competition reduced costs. In 1759 after advertisement in Scottish and English newspapers, the lowest bidder of seven proposals was accepted.[186] Awarding contracts as a reward for loyalty was not always the cheapest supply method. Nevertheless, proven reliability, satisfactory performance, and a sense of gratitude and obligation amongst military commanders and politicians towards those who served during the Rebellion perhaps had their place in post-Rebellion Scotland.

In recognizing greater opportunities existed outside Scotland, Dundas was the most successful. It was Dundas's German contracts that made him the 'Nabob of the North'. In post-Rebellion Scotland, Leslie and Gardiner divided most of the contracts. The contrast between them reflects in microcosm the profile of contractors in their entirety. Leslie, of an aristocratic family, accustomed to the rewards of patronage, and Gardiner, the modest merchant who established a reputation for reliability and trustworthiness. The longevity of this triumvirate is impressive, with Dundas and Gardiner active for seventeen years each, and Leslie for twenty-two. All were active against the Pretender, with only Dundas escaping the indignity of Jacobite imprisonment. Although difficult to attribute how much weight should be attached to the praise they received from military officers, it should not be ignored. In hostile conditions, the knowledge and connections of these men made them a valuable asset to Ministries unfamiliar with Scottish conditions, and they contributed towards facilitating government control of Scotland.[187]

If the gains from contracting in Scotland were limited, the career of Lawrence Dundas is sufficient indication that this was not so in more active theatres of war. No account of contracting can ignore issues of profitability, wealth, and social advancement. It was the social effects of large-scale contracting that disturbed many eighteenth-century observers, and such concerns have been revived by the recent interest amongst historians into the sources of wealth creation and social mobility in pre-industrial economies.

8 PROFIT AND WEALTH

> Examine a little this chain of causes. We have been twenty years engaged in the two most expensive wars that Europe ever saw. The whole burthen of this charge has lain upon the landed interest during the whole time. The men of estates have, generally speaking, neither served in the fleets nor armies, nor meddled in the public fonds, and management of the treasure. A new interest has been created out of their fortunes, and a sort of property, which was not known twenty years ago, is now encreased to be almost equal to the terra firma of our island.[1]

To eighteenth-century observers the relationship between possession of contracts, wealth creation and social mobility was a simple one, wherein a causal link was established between possession of contracts and the acquisition of riches and social status. It was widely believed that supplying the British army was more financially lucrative than military service. As early as 1726 Defoe pointed the contrast between Britain and Europe, with British contractors 'rais'd to immense estates' by wealth obtained from supplying the armed forces.[2] Defoe made these assumptions upon the basis of highly visible palatial mansions and broad acres of the very wealthiest contractors of the early eighteenth century. How representative these magnates were of contractors generally is highly questionable.[3] Nevertheless, these observations proved highly influential and adaptable in their application, with the mid-eighteenth century being characterized as a period when 'Fortunes were made and the greatness of families founded in army magazines and bread waggons'.[4] Such application might be more justifiable later in the century, purely on the basis of more extensive contracts. Yet the nature of contracting was also important. It is indicative of the restricted opportunities for extensive contracting earlier in the eighteenth century that Defoe named only financiers and clothing contractors. These were elite contractors, whose ability to operate on a sufficiently large scale ensured commensurately large rewards.[5] Yet, by the mid-eighteenth century the language used by Defoe was applied to what can be termed 'non-elite' contractors.

In the eighteenth century, contractors' wealth was a subject arousing much passion, although generating more heat than light. For Horace Walpole, the Seven Years' War was a crucial period when from 'inattention' and 'rapacity' there appeared 'those prodigious private fortunes which we have seen suddenly come forth'.[6] Despite the assertion that 'Government contracting was always a lucrative, if shady, way to make a great deal of money', few studies have attempted to explore the relationship between wealth and contracting.[7] Never entirely ignored, it has become something of an unspoken assumption requiring no systematic study. In terms of the claim that the sector of business activity was of greater consequence towards wealth creation than social background, religion or entrepreneurial effort, contracting appears a particularly apposite area for further examination.[8] Adopting this sectoral approach, it appears that contracting was undoubtedly profitable and could be an important component in the wealth of individuals. However, the impact of this wealth measured by the number of families whose fortunes were transformed by it was limited. Nevertheless, Namier's observation is particularly appropriate, for in citing 'magazines and bread waggons', he perhaps inadvertently drew attention to a sector of contracting where the impact of new wealth was strongly felt, and where in several cases it proved most enduring.[9]

There are three areas where methodological and evidential problems exist in establishing a causal link between possessing contracts and wealth accretion. The first concerns the financial status of men before they performed contracts. The second and third relate to the absence of reliable data concerning contract profitability and wealth valuation. As procedures for awarding contracts indicate, government actively sought men of wealth and credit. Moreover, by its very nature, that is, the dependence on a large army, contracting could never be a full time occupation or constitute a sole source of income. Difficulties disentangling contract profits from other business ventures are compounded by an absence of reliable data. Profits varied from contract to contract and little direct evidence such as contractors' account books has survived. Similarly, the absence of probate data prohibits analysis on this basis. Although offering some indication of relative wealth, wills reveal little of the sources of wealth or economic experience.[10] As a quantitative analysis of wealth-holding for 1809–39 illustrates such an approach presents formidable methodological problems. The discovery of ten contractors amongst 905 persons leaving upwards of £100,000 in this period has been accompanied by acknowledgement that this almost certainly underestimates the economic importance of contracting, in terms of providing employment, and in relation to the role of the state in engendering wealth.[11]

Such methodological problems have not proved insuperable. Studies of eighteenth-century wealth-holding suggest sectoral disparity, with fortunes arising from a variety of business operations. Nevertheless, most were made within the variegated complex of commercial and financial sectors of the City of London. Industrial and provincial fortunes were fewer and lower.[12] Within the context of metropolitan wealth, the bias towards London merchants possessing contracts appears to indicate it was a facet of the regional imbalance in the wealth structure of eighteenth-century Britain. A 'sectoral' approach into the relationship between contracting and wealth creation is therefore viable, and in examining a sector of economic activity and a clearly delineated group of men, possesses some value. In the absence of comprehensive statistical data, indirect evidence of wealth, such as land ownership and conspicuous consumption, when assessed alongside possession of contracts, can indicate the wealth-creating propensities of contracting. By assessing the longevity of the possession of contracts, it is possible to establish whether contracts were deemed particularly lucrative, for men would not continue performing contracts if they were unprofitable. Conversely, a reluctance to relinquish contracts can be viewed as indicative of significant profitability. Although incomplete, such evidence can provide more than an impressionistic account of contractors' wealth. It would be an impossible task to assess every contractor for the armed forces.[13] Whilst any sampling method cannot claim to be comprehensive, an analysis of mid-century contractors is sufficiently wide to provide evidence of the effect of contracting on the wealth of contractors and their families.[14]

It would be tempting to surmise that contracts played a pivotal role in 'rags to riches' stories. Such dramatic transformations of fortune were rare, although relatively modest, not impoverished, men acquired fortunes from contracting. An examination of social origins indicates that many contractors were rich or at least moderately wealthy before performing any contracts. Pre-existing wealth is most notable amongst remitters and foreign victuallers, with many descended from wealthy mercantile families. For example, the Fonnereau brothers were sons of a wealthy Hamburg merchant who purchased land and established a parliamentary interest in Suffolk. He left £165,000 to his nine children, including £60,000 to the two brothers.[15] Similarly, more than twenty years before performing remittances, John Gore was a Hamburg merchant and South Sea Company Director, whose extensive mercantile activities included purchasing sugar, wheat and indigo at Nantes for sale in Hamburg and Amsterdam. He also appears to have supplied tin, for in 1721 the Treasury owed him £22,793 for 760 tons lying at Hamburg. In 1720 his estate was valued at £38,936.[16] Similarly, John Bristow's grandfather made a fortune in the Virginia trade, whilst his father moved in financial and Court circles. Bristow's career saw him blend high finance with government contracts.[17] George Amyand, second son of a Huguenot refugee, received a mercantile apprenticeship before succeeding to a banking partnership.[18] Arnold Nesbitt also moved in this direction, whilst others such as the Colebrookes were born into banking families.[19] For many mid-century contractors, a notable shift in their axis of economic operations towards finance, indicative of business success and pre-existing family wealth, is readily apparent.[20]

Contractors whose interests remained predominantly mercantile were also notably wealthy. Amidst war with Spain, Nicholas Linwood petitioned government for a licence to ensure freedom from 'Molestation or Obstruction' from British ships, in seeking to export £180,000 worth of woollen goods and other manufactures to America via Cadiz.[21] In 1769 he was described as 'formerly a very considerable merchant in the city' who retired with an estimated fortune of £100,000.[22] His occasional associate Brice Fisher was a substantial cloth exporter to Portuguese merchants and the East India Company.[23] The export of cloth was extremely lucrative, particularly for the Blackwell Hall factors in London, 'the great mercantile capitalist agency' of the trade.[24] However, the cloth trade encompassed various gradations of wealth. Sir William Baker was the son of a successful London draper, whilst Samuel Touchet belonged to a family of prominent Manchester cotton merchants.[25] Two of the richest eighteenth-century contractors began in the cloth trade. Humble employment at his father's Edinburgh shop was a constant source of amusement for those wishing to debunk the genteel pretensions of Sir Lawrence Dundas.[26] Likewise, Sir Samuel Romilly recalled Sir Samuel Fludyer and his brother Thomas beginning their mercantile careers 'in very narrow circumstances, but by extraordinary industry, activity, enterprise, and good fortune they acquired inordinate wealth'. Although Fludyer's progress from 'rags to riches' was clearly exaggerated, he, for example, was educated at Westminster, the extent of his wealth, reputedly £900,000 at his death, indicates remarkable success.[27] Nevertheless, in terms of relatively humble origins and the extent of their wealth, Fludyer and Dundas are untypical of contractors generally.

The mercantile background of contractors supplying troops abroad, predominantly in banking and textiles, appears narrow. Several contractors were earlier described as wine merchants but this appears to have been a temporary or subsidiary sphere of activity.[28] Specialization in the wine trade tended to be a prelude to economic diversification.[29] Nevertheless, as an area where knowledge pertaining to foreign trading houses and correspondents could be acquired, it was an appropriate environment for potential contractors. Not all contractors came from a mercantile background. Peregrine Cust, a younger son of the Lincolnshire family received a vigorous mercantile apprenticeship before becoming a contractor. He made a virtue of a necessity in arguing that business activity was essential to maintaining a gentrified lifestyle.[30] Pre-existing wealth amongst remitters and foreign victuallers could also be facilitated by marriage. Thomas Walpole, a nephew of Sir Robert, married a daughter of the financier Sir Joshua Vanneck. Similarly, Joseph Mellish's marriage to his cousin, John Gore's daughter, was the defining moment of his business life, leading to a partnership with his father-in-law. The marriage in 1754 of Sir George Colebrooke to the heiress of an Antigua planter was another example of a judicious and financially lucrative match.[31]

An indication of the wealth these men possessed is apparent from government loan subscriptions. For the 1744 loan, Gore, Burrell and Bristow subscribed £390,000 between them. For these men, the award of contracts was dependent on the credit at their disposal, with wealth a prerequisite towards possessing contracts, not the reverse.[32] Similarly, for the 1757 loan of £3,000,000, Linwood and Nesbitt each subscribed £20,000, Touchet subscribed £25,000, and James Colebrooke £50,000.[33] Although Nesbitt and Colebrooke began a remittance contract in 1756, such sums were clearly not solely derived from contract profits. Colebrooke subscribed £20,000 to the 1742 loan, and was a major stockholder.[34] Linwood possessed no contracts until 1761 and Touchet's contracts did not begin until 1758.[35] Victualling contractors subscribed considerably lower sums than financiers did.[36] Despite clear City divisions between the rich mercantile and financial classes and lesser merchants, financial and victualling contractors both belonged to the former group, although the gradations of wealth are readily apparent.[37] Both groups contained Directors of Chartered Companies, with twenty of twenty-nine (68.9 per cent) contractors closely connected with City of London financial institutions and companies.[38] For the mercantile-financial elite, contracting may have contributed towards their wealth, but it appears unlikely it was the most important component. Contracts were not so much a means towards making a fortune as a means towards maintaining one. Nevertheless, as a component of mercantile portfolios, contracting should not be underestimated. The perception of maximum gain and minimum loss was the fundamental reason contracts were sought after. It was commercially attractive to supply a large number of men for a fixed duration, secured against competitors, and with payment guaranteed. The privilege of a captive market meant this was commercial enterprise with a higher degree of security than other mercantile ventures.[39]

Remittances were often cited as the most lucrative contracts. When Newcastle attempted to raise opposition to Bute, he was disappointed that Zachary Fonnereau felt insufficiently rewarded for political services:

> His Brother & He, had spent Thirty Thousand pounds in Elections; That He had got but little, from my Brother, & me, & That He must look out to His Interest. – I suppose His Price is, Some Valuable Remittances to Minorca & c. When a Man owns Himself, That He is bought, One has Nothing to say to Him.[40]

As the Pelhams partly created a situation where political loyalty was likely to accrue to the man at the head of the office awarding contracts rather than the man himself, this amounted to Newcastle being hoist by his own petard. That remittances were profitable can be surmised from the longevity of contractors during mid-century wars. In the period 1739–48, remittances of pay and subsidies were dominated by partnerships of Gore and Gulston, and Bristow and Burrell.[41] Gulston was later dropped, Burrell died in 1756, but Gore and Bristow continued into the later war.[42] There is no example of a remitter voluntarily relinquishing a contract. As the spectacular row over distribution of Gibraltar remittances demonstrates, competition for them could be intense.[43] Significantly, complaints over remittances concerned Ministers' unsuccessful attempts to promote equitable distribution, or the removal of remitters from contracts.[44] The removals of 1762 led Newcastle to draw parallels with the removal of Marlborough's allies during the 'rage of party' in 1710.[45] Newcastle also indicated the propriety and proprietary elements in employing contractors:

> The removing a Gentleman of Credit & Reputation, from a Contract, which He has had for ten Years; & had performed with great Care, Exactness & Fidelity, without the least Pretence of a Complaint, or any Cause assigned, is still a stronger Fact, than Turning any Man out of a Common Employment; Such a Contractor ought in Justice to be continued; & even to have the Preference of any Other, If The Terms of The Contract are to be alter'd, which does not appear to be the Case.[46]

The logical conclusion to draw from the dissatisfaction of contractors at being removed is that these contracts were financially lucrative.[47] In 1739, estimated annual profit on Gibraltar and Minorca remittances was £2,500.[48] Profits were dependent on the number of troops, and the rate and method by which the Treasury chose to contract. A large military presence was obviously most lucrative, as the larger the number of troops, the larger the profit by contract or commission.[49] The most salient point concerning remittances was their ease of performance. For those with financial interests and correspondents in relevant areas, remittances were easily accomplished and almost incidental to their business.[50]

Men lower in the social scale, lacking the privileges many financiers possessed, offer a better example of the potential for profit-making. Thomas Revell began his career as the navy's Agent Victualler at Port Mahon and Lisbon, before his appointment as a Victualling Board Commissioner at £500 per annum. He succeeded to the Gibraltar contract in 1734.[51] In 1739, the estimated annual profit from the contract was £1,500.[52] As Revell was paid £167,332 between 6 January 1735 and 13 July 1740, the profit computes at approximately 5 per cent, a sum receiving approximate confirmation from the proceeds of the first year of the contract, £29,091.[53] This estimate, published alongside Revell's name, aimed at displaying Walpole's method of purchasing support in the Commons. If anywhere near accurate, it is curious, for it neither indicates inordinate gain nor accounts for Revell's fortune. At his death in 1752, Revell was very wealthy, but this wealth probably owed more to his career in naval administration. Although the 1742 Place Act led to his resignation as a Victualling Commissioner in 1747, Revell continued the Gibraltar contract.[54] There is evidence that Revell's earlier activities provided a larger part of his fortune. At Port Mahon in 1720, Revell was agent to the captors of Spanish prizes, and seeking election to Parliament in 1734, he spectacularly treated the poor of Dover.[55] In 1738, he married a daughter of a younger brother of the first Duke of Bridgewater. He also purchased the 100-acre Fetcham Park estate, Surrey, with advowson, mansion, gardens and park. As early as 1732 he was an assistant with the Royal African Company.[56]

It was widely felt that Revell possessed a lucrative contract, for on his death, several applications were made to succeed him. The competition for Gibraltar contracts resembled a scramble for places, as well as indicating the difficulty for politicians in meeting obligations and expectations inherent in the patronage system.[57] Chauncy Townsend informed James West, 'Mony Support I allways declined – half Gibraltar was my object'.[58] Abraham Hume also applied, but found 'the present Undertakers had got so far the preference that unless he would lower the price two or three thousand pounds a Year, He could not succeed'. Hume considered this too hazardous, and his offer to lower the price by £500 was refused.[59] The suggestion of lowering the price by between £2,000 and £3,000 was probably made in the knowledge that Hume could not comply with it. His thinking it too hazardous suggests this may have been the approximate annual profit, or at least his perception of it.

It is difficult to state contract profitability with any confidence, for profits not only varied from contract to contract, but within each contract according to price variations and the difficulties, and hence cost, of performing specific contracts.[60] Attempts to use market prices are fraught with difficulty, for it is unlikely contractors paid these prices. There are occasions when contractors themselves estimated profitability, but these must be treated with caution, for it appears likely conservative estimates were submitted to avoid accusations of indecent profiteering. In 1745, Townsend assessed the profit on £2,281 worth of provisions at £320, approximately 14 per cent, whilst Woodford in 1760 estimated the annual profit on his contract as £387 of a total of £3,285, approximately 11.7 per cent. For the latter contract, Woodford demonstrated that a reduction of ¼d. per man per day would reduce the profit to £251 or 7.6 per cent.[61] Although a reasonable profit remained, the significant reduction demonstrated the effect of nominally marginal sums on costs and profitability. These estimates were based on rather small contracts.[62] Larger contracts, with greater economies of scale and proportionally lower administrative costs, would operate more in the contractors' favour.

The most convincing evidence as to contract profitability is the continuing mercantile interest in performing contracts. With few contractors willingly relinquishing contracts, there was no rapid 'turnover' of personnel, except for encampment contractors subject to annual competition.[63] Many contractors sought to extend their interest in contracts or introduce relatives into them.[64] A few, such as Anthony Bacon, Arnold Nesbitt, and John Willan possessed contracts during the Seven Years' War and the American Revolution.[65] Although somewhat remarkable, such longevity was only an extreme manifestation of a common phenomenon. There were few occasions when government could not find a contractor. This indicates a perception of profitability amongst applicants that may have been based on unrealistic expectations. Yet the many men possessing contracts over a long period positively indicates that experience demonstrated contracts were profitable ventures. There could however be disadvantages in possessing a contract. The fixed formula and set rates could act in a way to prevent excessive profiteering whilst simultaneously checking economy.[66] Rising prices could reduce or even eliminate profits, for whilst the Treasury was willing to raise wartime prices, they were reluctant to do so at other times, as this would interfere with the 'ordinary commercial speculation' of the contractor.[67] Many contractors claimed they lost money, and given the possibility of rising prices and lengthy delays in repayment, this may not be as fanciful as it first appears.[68] The varied extent and duration of contracts meant variable profitability. Yet although there was no certainty of profit, there were few occasions when losses were sustained over a long period or were anything other than temporary. The fear of temporary loss tempered by long-term gains is illustrated in a contractor's memorial:

> It may not perhaps be improper to observe that ye Proceeds of my Contract cannot reasonably be look'd on as extraordinary it being for all kinds of Risques exclusive of the Dangers of the Seas, Enemys & Pyrates, wch are provided for by ye contract such as ye Chance of the Market Price of Provisions Accidents, & other contingent Articles; the Trouble of corresponding, keeping ye Accounts & passing them thro' ye several Offices; & many Uncertaintys & difficultys attending this Business; All which being justly admitted of the Profits of this contract may be look'd on only as a proper Consideration for such a precarious Service.[69]

The risk and trouble were insufficiently powerful to induce the contractor to terminate the contract. He was in fact protesting against the termination notice served by the Treasury.[70] This type of complaint indicates the Treasury had achieved a correct balance between offering sufficient financial inducement for contractors, whilst ensuring government was not accountable for the entire attendant expenses of the contract.

For foreign victuallers and remitters, two features are particularly striking: most possessed a modicum of wealth before performing contracts, and contracting represented an additional source of income in a varied mercantile portfolio. A clear difference in origins and commercial activity is discernible for contractors supplying field armies or encampments. These men appear not to have possessed a significant amount of pre-existing wealth, and their economic activity was in most cases narrower and less concerned with finance than other contractors. Within a narrower business portfolio, contracting assumed greater importance to the economic activity of these men, and contributed towards their success, for in concentrating on their area of expertise, they built a reputation based on specialization. Although contracting was considered one of the quickest ways to make a fortune, for contractors in this sector, this process appears to have been much more incremental.[71] Three contractors in this sector became notably wealthy. Richard Oswald, Lawrence Dundas and John Willan were said to be worth £500,000, £900,000 and £200,000 respectively at their deaths.[72] Others made more modest gains. Samuel Tewkesbury held the 1762 encampment contract, and later supplied horses to the Ordnance, but he does not appear to have been notably wealthy.[73] Similarly, Gardiner and Leslie in Scotland, despite long careers, were not rich. As a younger son of an aristocratic family, Leslie possessed no estate.[74] Gardiner owned leasehold tenancies on tenements in Canongate, Edinburgh, but does not appear to have been notably wealthy.[75] The simple possession of contracts was not enough to guarantee a fortune. Operations on a suitably large scale, and over a long period, were necessary. Dundas, Oswald and Willan were all involved in contracting over a long period. Oswald's six years represent the shortest duration of this group, but the importance of contracting to his wealth has been clearly demonstrated.[76] Similarly, contracting was important to the wealth of John Willan.[77]

Abraham Hume is a rare example of a man predominantly concerned in mercantile activities who became involved in this sector. A contractor in 1742, he graduated to the position of Commissary General at £3 per day, or £1,095 per annum. Hume possessed a significant fortune prior to his involvement in military supply. He and his brother belonged to the 'flotsam of British Jacobitism cast upon the Flemish shores by the whig triumph of 1714'.[78] His involvement with the Ostend Company in the Brabant trade, and later with the East India Company, to whom he leased ships, indicates considerable mercantile experience and wealth.[79] As early as 1736 he was a Director of the Royal Exchange Assurance, and by 1740, the South Sea Company.[80] As his letters to Carteret with intelligence from the Swedish Court indicate, Hume also possessed political connections.[81] Although active in domestic supply, Hume's mercantile portfolio and pattern of wealth-holding is more typical of victuallers and remitters.

The most outstanding example of riches gained from contracting is Sir Lawrence Dundas, whose fortune provoked much contemporary comment. Dundas was the 'Nabob of the North', a term conveying the envy, jealousy, and hostility he effortlessly aroused.[82] Although much was made of the wealth Dundas obtained from contracts in Germany between 1759 and 1763, he had worked within the supply system since 1746, when similar accusations of inordinate gain were made.[83] His wealth was based on a long career, with the financial rewards apparent as early as 1749 when he purchased the lands and baronies of West Kerse, Stirlingshire.[84] Nevertheless, Dundas's accounts from German contracts between 1759 and 1763, amounting to upwards of £1,900,000, illustrate the astonishing sums involved in contracting on this scale.[85] Moreover, Dundas himself attributed his fortune to his contract for horses for the Hanoverian Artillery Train, despite the contract being 17.5 per cent cheaper than the contract with Oswald for the British Artillery.[86] Whilst any assessment of profitability is extremely difficult, it does appear that the scale of Dundas's contracts rather than huge profit margins account for his wealth.

In his post-contracting business life, Dundas invested in shipping, the East India Company, and government loans. Before 1760 he was not a loan subscriber, but in that year subscribed £20,000 and £50,000 in 1761 and 1762 respectively.[87] Between February and April 1763 Dundas possessed between £235,050 and £310,775 in the funds.[88] Despite subsequently sales, Dundas remained a major stockholder.[89] He particularly interested himself in East India stock, splitting it at the government's request. By February 1771 he held £82,500, whilst also expending large sums purchasing property and building a political interest.[90] When Fox removed Newcastle's friends from office, Newcastle cited Dundas's alignment with the Court as part of the electoral maneuvers of Fox and Bute, with the sarcastic comment that the selection of Dundas, who had 'got 300,000£ out of the Publick', was a 'Proof of the Sincerity of These Reformers of Publick Abuses, & Corruption'.[91] Dundas's wealth and ambition made him many enemies, nationally and in Scotland. The source of his wealth, and his social ambitions and pretensions were attacked, alongside his 'oligarchy' and neglect of local issues. How newly wealthy contractors should behave was commented on, with Dundas being unfavourably compared with Richard Oswald:

> You acquired a very princely fortune, to be sure, and you wished to be a great man on the merit of it. You took a very different line from your brother Commissary O—d, who chose to conceal the extent of his riches, and to play the patriot by improving his estate.[92]

Dundas was even ridiculed on the London stage in Samuel Foote's farce 'The Commissary'.[93] This was one of the ways in which contemporaries made the connection between wealth and contracting.[94] Although untypical of contractors generally, the wealth obtained by Dundas illustrated the gains that could be made.

The display of worldly success offer an insight into the wealth, or at least, conspicuous wealth, of contractors. Although a crude indicator, plate duties indicate sectoral divisions between contractors. Whereas elite contractors such as Colebrooke, Fisher and Bristow possessed 2,000–4,000oz, lesser contractors held substantially smaller amounts. Oswald increased his holding from 300 to 1,000oz in the period 1756–66, whilst owning 400oz in Scotland. Robert Gardiner owned 600oz in the same period. Warrington and Baldwin, horse contractors, owned 300 and 600oz respectively.[95] Others, such as Willan, Tewkesbury, Boghurst and Martyr possessed none at all. A similar pattern emerges relative to carriage duties. Elite contractors such as Fonnereau and Fludyer owned three four wheeled carriages, whilst men such as Baldwin, Willan and Oswald owned one.[96] Conspicuous wealth does not necessarily equate with total wealth. Men such as Willan could acquire a fortune unobtrusively, with less need for the ostentatious display accompanying activity in political and financial circles.

Although most contractors appear to have profited from contracts, this did not automatically translate into business fortunes. A significant minority ended their business lives poorer than when they began. John Bristow sustained estimated losses of £120,000 by the Lisbon earthquake of 1756 and the inability or unwillingness of the Portuguese Court to repay debts owed to him.[97] Chauncy Townsend expended his fortune in coal mining, whilst Sir George Colebrooke's attempt to corner the market in alum was a spectacular failure.[98] Temperament and the capacity for risk-taking were undoubtedly important. Greater risk was attached to the business transactions of elite contractors. Ambitious risk-taking entrepreneurs were likelier to experience extremes of riches and poverty, and fortunes were lost through indulgence in multifarious economic activity.[99] For most elite contractors, possessing contracts did not create their fortunes. Equally, financial ruin did not result from the loss of contracts. The wider economic activities of these men were more important in the extent of, and the use and misuse of wealth. The variability of contractors' wealth illustrates the importance of the economic volition of individuals. Prudence, frugality and extravagance impacted on the ability to make and maintain a fortune. The ability of several contractors in this area to use income from their contracts to invest carefully rather than attempting risky business ventures, illustrates temperamental, as well as sectoral, differences.

Although extensive purchase of country estates by merchants declined in the late seventeenth century, successful London merchants in the eighteenth century usually obtained a county residence, which remained for many a desirable, even necessary accoutrement to gentlemanly status and outward display of worldly success.[100] As most estates were purchased after contracts were held, the income from contracts appears to have contributed towards land purchase. Yet for most contractors, land purchase was complementary to business not a substitute for it.[101] Men whose environment and experience had been predominantly urban do not appear to have been temperamentally inclined to adopt a country lifestyle. Purchasing rural property was not for them a prelude to full acceptance of rural domesticity. Most divided their time between town and country, and the vast majority, even at an advanced age, remained active in business and retained a London residence.[102] Despite his purchase of Ayrshire estates, Richard Oswald, remained active in business in London.[103] Aged seventy-nine, Oswald was keen for market intelligence relating to the sale of an African island he previously owned.[104]

For many contractors, the enjoyment of country life and society represented a temporary escape from urban life. Merrick Burrell kept fallow deer at his 350-acre Sussex estate, and established a stud farm for hunting horses, whilst Brice Fisher enjoyed participation in rural social activities such as horse racing from his Berkshire estate.[105] The importance of proximity to London is apparent on analysis of contractors' landholding. Whether contractors purchased land for residence or investment, they displayed a preference for counties surrounding London. The landholdings of twenty-nine contractors in parliament in the mid-eighteenth century reveal that Surrey, Hertfordshire and Middlesex were the most popular counties, followed by Essex, Sussex and Kent.[106] Few contractors possessed property in more distant southern counties such as Wiltshire or Hampshire. Northern counties are poorly represented, although Dundas and Fisher possessed Yorkshire estates. Adam Drummond possessed English property, although his will does not specify the location.[107] Several contractors owned land in several counties but displayed a clear preference for southern counties. For example, Peregrine Cust owned property in Lancashire, but also Middlesex, Surrey, Sussex, Essex and Oxford Street/Piccadilly.[108]

Many properties were fully-fledged estates, such as Sir William Baker's 3,000 acres at Bayfordsbury or the 550 acres of Gatton Park, Surrey, purchased by Sir James Colebrooke in 1751.[109] Others such as John Gore purchased land in several counties, alongside an older family estate. The Gore family had been resident at the 300 acres estate of Tring Park since 1705.[110] For others such as Abraham Hume, possession of an estate was the result of sibling inheritance.[111] A few contractors, such as Dundas and Nesbitt owned land in Ireland, whilst mining operations account for land acquired by Townsend and Bacon in South Wales. Many contractors also possessed American land.[112] This even applied to the non-parliamentary contractor Richard Oswald, with 20,000 acres in Nova Scotia.[113] Although less likely to purchase an estate, non-parliamentary contractors were just as likely to purchase rural property. Oswald and John Trotter held large estates in Ayrshire and Surrey respectively, and Archibald Fraser succeeded to the restored estates forfeited from his father.[114]

In such a variegated business as the purchase of property, this portfolio is probably incomplete. Nevertheless, sufficient information exists to indicate that proximity to London was an important consideration for most contractors. Land purchase outside southern counties usually emanated from affinity with a particular location, provincial origins, or as part of a wider property portfolio. The dispersal of mercantile wealth and property, as opposed to primogeniture and strict settlement characteristic of the aristocracy, has been considered a notable feature of mercantile wealth-holding.[115] Although most estates passed to the eldest son or nearest relative, many were sold to meet legacies, annuities or debts. Most of Arnold Nesbitt's property, including 1,200 acres at Sussex, was sold to meet debts of over £120,000.[116] In the year of his death, Nicholas Linwood's wife sold his Hampshire estate. All Samuel Fludyer's property, except Downing Street, was sold.[117] Even Moor Park, the Hertfordshire estate advertised as one of the most desirable residences in the country, comprising 400 acres of freehold estate and 180 acres of freehold farmland was sold after Sir Lawrence Dundas's death for £13,000 less than he paid for it.[118] The extravagance of Joseph Gulston's son led to the loss of a fortune including Hertfordshire, Middlesex, and London property and an estimated £250,000 in the funds.[119] Many estates did not even survive the lifetime of the purchaser. Financial difficulties forced Sir George Colebrooke to sell Gatton Park and other Surrey properties in 1774, and Thomas Walpole to sell houses at Lincoln's Inn Fields and Carshalton.[120] John Bristow's bankruptcy led to the seizure of Norfolk and Middlesex estates to pay Crown debts.[121]

Land sales and the rapid dissolution of estates in some cases emanated from the dissipation of descendants, but often resulted from provisions made in wills. As most contractors outside Parliament held land for business purposes rather than for prestige or social status, much tended to be sold after their death. In the wills of Willan and John Warrington, directions were given that land should be sold to meet legacies and annuities. Warrington directed that his Southwark livery stables and Surrey freehold estate should be sold.[122] As much of this land was used for stabling and exercising horses, once the business necessity was relinquished, there was little reason to retain it. Conversely, Abraham Hume left £30,000 for purchasing land in England, and in the event of his son's death, land sales were prohibited until his grandson was twenty-one.[123] For most contractors, land represented comfort, a welcome retreat from urban life, and an investment, in making provision for their families after their death. There was no wholesale gentrification of contractors arising from the purchase of rural property. The wills of many contractors unambiguously displayed their mercantile and urban mentalité in benevolence towards urban commercial, religious and social institutions. Both Gore and Mellish left legacies to the Merchant Adventurers, religious foundations, and hospitals.[124] During their lifetime, many contractors were involved in urban charitable ventures. Fisher, Linwood and Baker were Governors of Christ's Hospital, with Gore Vice-President of London Infirmary.[125]

What was the legacy bequeathed by mid-eighteenth century contractors? As a sector contracting has been classified, alongside trade and finance, as a 'medium fast' avenue of upward social mobility between the sixteenth and mid-eighteenth century.[126] Immense wealth could, but did not always, lead to social mobility in the next generation. There are cases where wealth transmission was relatively straightforward. In the absence of a male heir, Thomas Revell's daughter inherited her father's fortune. She then married George Warren, 'The Great Mr. Warren of Cheshire who married Miss Revel; Has an immense Estate'. Their daughter and heir married Viscount Bulkeley in 1777.[127] The marriage of new wealth and aristocracy was far from novel, but the relationship between the most successful contractors and the aristocratic political elite is particularly notable. In his will Revell, with a combination of gratitude and deference, left 300 guineas to Henry Pelham, 100 guineas each to Lord Vere and the Earl of Scarborough, and twenty guineas to Sir Richard Lloyd 'if he pleases to accept of them'.[128]

The marriage of contractors' daughters to the nobility was not uncommon. It is not difficult to discover why. Prior to his daughter's marriage to Lord Carnarvon, John Major paid £21,000 of the noble family's debts. His daughter was notable 'for a sweet disposition and a fortune of £30,000'.[129] Two daughters of John Bristow married sons of the Earl of Buckinghamshire and Lord Lovat respectively.[130] Similarly, two daughters of Sir George Amyand married the Earls of Malmesbury and Minto.[131] Probably the most spectacular example was the marriage of the second Earl of Ashburnham to Elizabeth Crowley, daughter and co-heiress of John Crowley, London Alderman, and granddaughter of the great ironmaster Sir Ambrose Crowley. Her fortune was estimated at £200,000.[132] Abraham Hume's son had no male heir and the estates passed to the children of his daughter Sophia, wife of the second Baron Brownlow. His other daughter married Lord Farnborough in 1793.[133] Some contractors did not have to wait until their children made aristocratic marriages. By marrying Lady Katherine Paulet, second daughter of the Duke of Bolton, Adam Drummond married into the English aristocracy. His sister married the second Duke of Atholl.[134]

Despite such fraternization with the aristocracy, it seems clear that not all merchants wished to enter landed society.[135] Contractors aiming to enter landed society were in an ambiguous position. The wealth necessary for this transformation arose from mercantile activity that was both a vehicle and barrier towards it. Contractors possessed a means towards social advancement, but as Lord George Sackville informed Viscount Irwin there were limits to such advancement, and wealth alone was not enough:

> I am glad Sir Lawrence Dundas is known to Lord Chesterfield. Approbation from such men as his Lordship must be most acceptable, as it cannot be purchased even by his great fortune.[136]

Social acceptance could not be purchased. Even in terms of receiving honours, contractors were not particularly notable, for in this period, only nine, all MPs, were created baronets.[137] The status of baronet appears to be as far as contractors could go in their lifetime. There was no possibility of ennoblement.[138] This required the preservation of a fortune, discontinuation of trade, and continued political services. Above all, sufficient time had to elapse in order to remove the stain of trade. When all these conditions were met 'a coronet was within the reach of the children or grandchildren of the successful Government contractors'.[139] There are several examples of this process. John Henniker received an Irish peerage in 1800, and the grandson of Peter Burrell and son of Lawrence Dundas were created barons in 1794 and 1796.[140] Not until 1838 did Dundas's grandson obtain a peerage.[141] How far the wealth of contractors contributed towards the dual process of social mobility and gentrification of their heirs is perhaps more relevant.

By the nineteenth century, the social legacy bequeathed by mid-eighteenth century contractors was a general upward social mobility. Amidst the inevitable vicissitudes of families and with notable failures, this process did occur. Despite considerable and well-founded doubt as to the extent of upward social mobility and the openness of the landed classes to 'new wealth', it appears that contracting was an avenue towards entry into landed society. The pattern of maintaining a gentlemanly lifestyle whilst entering occupations coterminous with their new status in society clearly occurred. However, wealth thus gained was rarely self-sustaining. At best, it laid a foundation upon which later generations built.

The most obvious difference was education. Whilst only one mid-eighteenth century contractor attended Oxford or Cambridge, and one other Leyden, many of their children attended university.[142] Four wealthy financial contractors had elder brothers who attended university, perhaps indicating that it was their status as younger sons that determined their absence from university.[143] Yet for most mid-century contractors, university education was not a serious option. This may not have arisen from financial reasons, but simple inability to see the relevance of a university education towards a mercantile career. Significantly, the only contractor who attended university, Peregrine Cust, was a younger son, but of a gentry not a mercantile family.[144] A university education was a symbol of prosperity, and many sons of affluent contractors were free to pursue cultural, artistic, and political ambitions. A minority however continued in business, with a few following their fathers as contractors.[145] For the latter men, something of a shift towards financial concerns is apparent, with the sons of Henniker and Gulston, predominantly, although not exclusively, involved in remittances rather than supplying naval stores.[146] Ten contractors sent a total of fourteen of their children to university. Seven sent one son, two sent two, and one sent three.[147] In the nineteenth century the grandsons of Sir Samuel Fludyer and

John Major attended Oxford.[148] For contractors outside Parliament, few were wealthy enough to bestow a university education on their descendants, although John Willan is an exception.[149] Fourteen male descendants of twelve contractors, including one younger son and three nephews, became MPs, nine of whom had attended university. A wider sample would reveal more, for sons of men such as John Sargent and Joseph Curtis, predominantly naval contractors, also became MPs.[150] Sir William Curtis, between 1785 and 1796 successively Alderman, Sheriff and Lord Mayor of London, was the son of a Wapping biscuit baker. As with Dundas, this rapid mobility occasioned much ribaldry and mockery.[151] Those contractors who died possessed of little wealth had often made prior provision for their children. Colebrooke's sons secured positions as Judges in India, and one became the first great European Sanskrit scholar.[152] Similarly, Townsend was instrumental in the careers of his socially prominent sons, as an Alderman and Lord Mayor of London, and a 'popular preacher among the Calvinistic Methodists' respectively.[153]

Wealth accrued in one generation was rarely sufficient for the next. Although many merchants sought to provide comfort and wealth for their heirs this did not preclude the need of many to continue in business. Those such as Hume, Dundas and Baker were sufficiently wealthy to ensure their sons did not have to engage in any kind of productive industry. Baker's eldest son was 'bred up to be a country gentleman' although younger sons, in a mercantile imitation of aristocratic practice, continued in business.[154] Hume's son abandoned politics to concentrate on artistic pursuits, possessing a fine collection of minerals and precious stones.[155] His daughter married James Hare, the wit and politician, whose fortune was 'much augmented' by the marriage settlement, stipulated by Hume in his will to be £20,000.[156] At his death in 1781 Dundas owned land in England, Scotland, Ireland, and Dominica, as well as the Earldom of the Orkneys and the lordship of Zetland.[157] Acquisition of property was one sign of wealth and upward social mobility. Marriage was perhaps a more permanent sign. Dundas's son Thomas married Lady Charlotte Fitzwilliam, a niece of the Marquess of Rockingham, in April 1764. With Dundas providing a handsome £4,000 per annum marriage settlement, this marriage of 'new wealth' to aristocracy proved sufficiently notable to provoke contemporary comment, and the wealth obtained from contracts, somewhat exceptionally, proved to be enduring.[158]

It seems clear that the simple possession of contracts was insufficient to guarantee making a fortune. The most significant reasons for this were pre-existing wealth, variation in contract profitability, and wider mercantile portfolios. Competition for contracts and the longevity of those possessing them indicates more than a mere perception of profitability. Yet the idea that contracts made the fortunes of many contractors is misplaced. For this to happen, two conditions were necessary: long duration and high profitability, and neither could be guaranteed.

This is not to say that fortunes were not made from contracts. Both factors were present in the careers of Willan, Oswald and Dundas, all within the same sector of contracting. Wider mercantile portfolios tended to dilute the effect of profits from contracts. The most surprising aspect of mid-eighteenth century contracting is the relatively small number of men for whom the wealth obtained proved to be enduring. By 1833 the number of identifiable descendants of contractors amongst those possessing the highest rated homes in Britain is disappointingly small, with only three men clearly connected to mid-eighteenth century contractors: Trotter at the Soho Bazaar and Brice Pearce and William Mellish in Essex. All continued in some form the work of their antecedents.[159]

There were spectacular failures where the wealth of mid-eighteenth century contractors rapidly disappeared. The economic volition of individuals was always fundamentally important in the usage of wealth. One can conclude that although contract profitability was of short-term financial significance, the longer-term impact, in terms of the number of gentrified families, was negligible. There were simply too many factors surrounding the application and usage of money for a simple connection to be made between possessing even the most lucrative contracts and inter-generational upward mobility. Qualified acceptance, because of limited application, can therefore be given to the idea of an 'open elite' as a 'hoary old myth'. This was a difference of degree, not kind, and does not invalidate the process of upward social mobility.[160] It could and did happen.

CONCLUSION

By 1763, after upwards of twenty years of intermittent warfare, a coherent supply structure had emerged within which contractors played a pivotal role. A sustained period of warfare made supply organization a high priority, a tendency most apparent in the establishment of the Commissariat in Germany. Despite a higher degree of state organization, no permanent supply corps was established. In a sense, the opposite happened. Lacking the resources and personnel to establish a supply organization, government became increasingly reliant on contractors. The short term, urgent priorities of war only heightened a proliferation of contracts and delegation of responsibility to contractors received further encouragement, thus further delaying state organization. Clearly constituting an 'interest' group of some importance to the war-making capacity of the state, the employment of contractors illustrates that in terms of resources, the operation of the fiscal military state required men as well as money. With an extensive array of services provided and considerable variation in personnel, contract performance was always likely to be variable. It was a difficult task to supply large armies without later technological advances in machinery, transport, communications and refrigeration. The speed of delivery, quality of provisions, and overall administrative efficiency and supervision could all have been improved upon.[1] Yet based on available resources, the system was impressively efficient and one finds little mid-century criticism of the actual performance of contracts based on solid evidence of contractors' mismanagement or negligence. Criticism that emerged in the aftermath of the Seven Years' War was somewhat delayed and indirect.[2] The astonishing increase in the National Debt led to calls for a strict examination into wartime accounts, alongside the exclusion of contractors from the Commons. The underlying suspicion of rampant profiteering by contractors gathered force when a connection was made between levels of government expenditure and the fortunes made by a handful of prominent contractors.[3] This connection was perhaps an inevitable consequence of the obvious tension existing between performing contracts in the 'national' interest whilst making private profit, a tension most acute during wartime.[4] As wars occasioned a marked increase in the number of contracts, the work of contractors was inextricably linked to the martial fortunes of the British army. However, military success did not bring gratitude and goodwill towards those supplying the troops: quite the reverse. Victories were bought at a considerable price, and hostility emerged towards perceived beneficiaries of escalating military expenditure.[5]

Military victories may account for the relatively small volume of criticism aimed at contractors, for as a historian of contracting during the American Revolution has pointed out:

> Where demanded by circumstances, the same basic contracting methods had been followed in the Seven Years War, without attracting the same volume of criticism.[6]

Military defeat allied to crippling military expenditure focussed attention more quickly and directly on contractors. Ministers were attacked for incompetence, the making of improvident bargains, and of being motivated by political considerations in allocating contracts, with Lord North bearing the brunt of attacks for rum contracts made at the Treasury.[7] When North suggested there was no design in paying high rates, it indicated lack of vigilance assessing prices and carelessness in awarding contracts.[8]

Wealth, or more accurately money, was always a controversial aspect of contracting. In the eighteenth century, politicians and contractors alike shared the obloquy of the inflated cost of war. With modern concepts of public administrative theory and practice, Economical Reformers refurbished the ideological and practical agenda in reforming public administration. Yet despite a more explicit concern with economy and official probity during 1776–82, ideas of the public interest and accountability were consistently if unevenly maintained throughout the eighteenth century.[9] The rhetoric of the campaign to exclude contractors from the Commons has cast a long shadow over the reputation of contractors and contracting generally. The powerful critique of Edmund Burke and the Earl of Shelburne, incorporating constitutional purity and economic equity, pointed to contractors and government deriving mutual benefit from contracts made at the public expense. Facing a torrent of exquisite oratory, it was always going to be difficult for those seeking to defend contractors.

Yet there was a defence. Well-publicized abuses pertaining to individual cases on particular occasions cannot be taken as representative of an entire system. For the mid-eighteenth century such a view of contracting is not only inadequate, but also positively misleading. Clear instances of abuses, illustrating the fine line between legitimate influence and illegitimate pecuniary gain, contributed towards the notoriety of the system but were not typical of it. The controversy over the rise of contractors as an interest encompassed accusations of political influence, favouritism, excessive profiteering, varying degrees of sharp practice, and hints at outright corruption. Given the disparity between the level of economic organization required and the administrative apparatus possessed by government, a degree of defalcation and misappropriation of funds appears inevitable. This was probably less extensive than many believed. There appears to have been a higher incidence of fraud amongst minor officials, and long before Economical Reformers campaigned on such issues, government was issuing directives against collusion. Such practices were difficult to eradicate but later in the century the problem appears to have declined, although such generalizations are perhaps unwise given evidential problems. There is little evidence to suggest politicians received money from contractors, although absence of evidence should not be taken as evidence of absence. Closed procedures, patronage and the longevity of many contractors performing contracts raised suspicions of a mutually profitable pecuniary relationship. Yet it appears to have been the nature of the system more often than specific, proven examples that created the association in the public mind between contracting and corruption.

The Contractors Act of 1782 disqualified Members of Parliament from possessing or having an interest in a government contract.[10] Such a specific Act would have been unthinkable thirty years earlier. The torrent of criticism against contractors was not new, for the patriotic opposition had long argued contractors were little more than placemen. Nevertheless, earlier Place Bills had not excluded contractors.[11] The specificity of the Contractors Act indicates the rise to prominence of contractors as an interest within the state during the intervening period. It is symptomatic of the prevailing historical orthodoxy that the growth of contracting in the eighteenth century has been noted by reference to the number of contractors in the House of Commons.[12] This concentration on political issues has led to an overemphasis on connections and abuses, and more seriously, relative neglect both of contracting as an area of economic activity, and of sectors of contracting where contractors possessed few, if any, political connections.

It is perhaps more pertinent that the greater prominence of contractors in the mid-eighteenth century reflected the greater prevalence of military activity. If a period of warfare had existed earlier it appears likely more contracts would have been made and more contractors would have entered Parliament. In the period 1715–54, 24 of 198 (*c.* 12 per cent) merchant members of parliament and 25 of 43 (*c.* 58.1 per cent) 'principal industrialists' have been designated contractors. These figures are an underestimate. Lawrence Dundas is inexplicably absent, whilst the identification of contractors solely with trade and industry excludes military men such as Thomas Leslie. Others such as Arnold Nesbitt held contracts later in their career, whilst those such as William Beckford are not primarily known as contractors.[13]

The presence of contractors in Parliament was in general symptomatic of the unreformed political system.[14] However, their political influence was rather negligible, and undoubtedly subordinate to their business activities. Even wealthy remitters connected with great Chartered Companies were consulted for financial expertise rather than political weight or judgement.[15] Hardwicke emphasized these separate spheres, informing Newcastle of 'the little consequence of Mr. Burrell, other ... than as Subgovernor of ye So: Sea Company'.[16] The financial and mercantile expertise of many contractors was displayed in parliamentary speeches, pamphlet publications, and advice tendered to politicians on predominantly commercial matters.[17] Yet such activity was a handicap inasmuch as despite illustrating commendable expertise, it was a narrow expertise imbued with interest, and thus far removed from contemporary notions of the disinterested statesman. Whilst unrealistic to expect contractors to rise to the elevated heights of statesmanship, government office was a more attainable and realistic aspiration. Yet the few contractors who held office, mostly connected in some form with supply matters, is indicative of the negligible impact they made on governing circles.[18] Substantial merchant contractors held few positions, although governmental bodies possessing mercantile and commercial responsibilities included experienced merchant contractors.[19]

There were even limits to the advancement of contractors to positions of a business character, particularly if these involved the exercise of a degree of political authority.[20] This is not to dismiss contractors as mere lobby fodder.[21] Many clearly possessed forceful, articulate views, and contrary to the stereotype of contractors as warmongers, some opposed the expansive military operations in the latter years of the Seven Years' War.[22] Although most contractors failed to make any political impact, this may have emanated as much from lack of desire as it did from a design to exclude merchants from political office. As most contractors entered Parliament later in life, there was in any case, less opportunity for advancement.[23]

Viewed as the 'aristocracy of the bourgeoisie' by neo-Namierite historiography, elite merchants have, in social and political terms, been considered clients of the aristocracy. A necessary corrective to this view has been provided by Marxist historians who emphasis the reciprocal nature of the relationship, and the extent to which great landed proprietors were 'circumscribed by the imperatives of an ebullient capitalist economy'.[24] Although clientage undermined a middle-class challenge to aristocratic political authority in the eighteenth century, financial and mercantile activities were respected. By mid-century, contractors combining victualling and financial operations were referred to as 'Gentleman Contractors', and expertise and genteel respectability could overcome residual aristocratic prejudice against mercantile pursuits.[25] Even contractors outside Parliament, such as Richard Oswald, were accorded considerable respect from members of the landed interest.[26]

The social and economic importance of contractors was arguably much greater than their political role, although this can easily be obscured when the focus of attention is Parliament, division lists, and patronage. Whilst the Contractors Act marked a watershed in terms of contractors' political role, it also confirmed their economic value to the state. Despite the high-flown rhetoric characteristic of much of the debate, it was reform of the system, not its existence that was at issue. It was no part of the reformers' argument that politicians should cease awarding contracts, or that private contracting should be anything other than a central component of the supply system. A concern with economy and the exclusion of contractors from the Commons rather than termination of the contract system concerned reformers.[27] Administrative reform was necessary to insert a higher degree of supervision and accountability, but these measures implicitly recognized contractors as essential to the effective functioning of the armed forces.

The emergence of larger armies in the seventeenth century, particularly since the War of Spanish Succession, led states to turn towards contractors to meet heightened military demands. Such a policy orientation was rational and necessary. Militarily, it was necessary to insert some certainty into supply, for logistically it was increasingly untenable to rely on ad hoc supply methods. With larger armies necessitating more extensive supply operations than previous centuries, the employment of contractors was implicit recognition of the vibrancy of Britain's mercantile community. In this sense, logistical and economic factors were motivating factors on the demand side in employing contractors, but the supply side factor of mercantile expertise ensured that demands were met. In providing economic organization and infrastructure, contractors were important in enhancing military capability. With warfare testing the economic capacity and resources of states, financial solvency was always important, for credit-worthy merchants and financiers possessed the means for government to conduct military operations far in excess of what could be paid out of ordinary government revenue. The credit facilities of contractors were highly important to the British military effort, for war was increasingly financed by credit, and there were limits to the sums that could be raised from Parliament. One of the more important effects of the persistent 'Country' critique was that it induced something of an 'opposition mentality' in government.[28] Recognizing a limit to the amount of taxation that could be levied, and with military expenditure consistently outrunning sums voted in annual estimates, there was little alternative to deferring payment of necessary services. If government was in a sense forced into this position by parliamentary control of army finance, there was also an element of compulsion in supply methods. Two factors were important here: the increasing number and concentration or distribution of troops in the mid-eighteenth century. Extensive troop concentration strained the economic resources of surrounding areas. Equally, the distribution of the British army in relatively unproductive areas, or where local markets were relatively undeveloped, called for resources to be provided from a wider area, which in turn required extensive economic organization and supply infrastructure.

One of the more important reasons for contractors assuming an important role in supplying the British army was one of omission. The absence of an army supply corps meant no governmental organization, other than the navy's Victualling Office, was equipped to supply troops. With a cheese-paring Treasury, and widespread resistance to the establishment of military institutions, it was unlikely such an organization would be established. Intermittent demand and diversity in military operations meant contracts were a suitable, and perhaps more efficient supply method. A fully developed commissarial structure assuming procurement functions only emerged during sustained and extensive military activity in certain theatres of particular complexity. The European campaigns of the British army in both mid-century wars witnessed a higher degree of state organization, but in areas of continual military activity, such as Scotland and Gibraltar, there was continued reliance on contractors.

It is difficult to see an alternative to contractors in filling the lacunae in supply organization. It would have required the creation of a supply organization with qualified personnel and the establishment of a sophisticated and complex system of purchasing, delivery and distribution. The cost of such an organization may have been great and its efficiency doubtful. One of the advantages for government in making contracts was cost. As salaried officers procuring provisions, commissaries possessed little incentive to keep costs down. Conversely, the cost of articles supplied under contract was a key element in contracting, for this influenced award and renewal, and determined profitability. The danger was that contractors would attempt to cut costs by providing poor quality provisions, but such activity endangered renewal or continuation of the contract. Establishing a link between profitability and efficiency, government appealed simultaneously to the self-interest of contractors and the patriotic duty of efficiently supplying troops.

Cost was also important at the termination of contracts. Once the necessity for contracts passed, there was no large body of staff on half-pay after cessation of hostilities.[29] As the size of the British Army fluctuated considerably during the eighteenth century, this was perhaps sensible, but can be criticized as somewhat myopic. Despite appearing well-suited towards British military needs, this approach meant a great deal depended on the ability of merchants to supply the army at short notice. How far this compromised government is open to considerable doubt. Underpinning the system was an implicit assumption of reasonable profitability. It was unreasonable to expect contractors to advance capital, employ labour, organize supply, and assume the risk of losses merely to break even. The nature of the system demanded that profit accrue to contractors for the attendant labour and risk. Yet profits do not appear to have been excessive, although contract variability, and the ability of contractors to secure cheap supplies, could mean considerable profits.

The often-criticized cost of contracts may have been reduced with greater competition. Yet there was much resistance to, and suspicion of competitive tendering. The monopolist East India shipping interest was not alone in maintaining 'We know of no instance of a thoroughly good and efficient article furnished by competition or open contract'.[30] Applied to all contracts, competitive tendering could result in incapable men securing contracts they were unable to perform merely on the basis of submitting the lowest tender.[31] Such a view did not emanate solely from interested parties or defenders of those succeeding to contracts through closed procedures. The Ordnance Board noted:

> In some Cases Advertizing may prevent or break Combinations, in others it may form and strengthen them, By Advertizing you are tied down to admit the cheapest without regard to Credit or substance, but by the other method you treat with none but reputable and Substantial People, and it is apprehended that by advertizing a door would be open to more abuses, than by the other method mostly Practised by the Office.[32]

A combination of experience, ability and a creditable reputation were therefore required. Financial solvency alone was no proof of capability, although even Shelburne accepted this should be more important than the lowest bid in determining allocation of contracts.[33] Although sureties may have induced confidence that contracts would be competently performed, in terms of supply efficiency 'disappointment to the Service by an ignorant Contractor, may produce very bad consequences not to be ballanced with any forfeiture he might incurr'.[34]

Despite opposition to competitive tendering, it was the chosen method of allocating encampment contracts, and in assessing proposals, the Treasury possessed something of a safeguard in having the Commissary General examine their viability.[35] The Treasury struck a judicious balance between ensuring capable men were awarded contracts, whilst reserving the power to reduce prices. Treasury control of allocation and renewal meant contract performance counted for much. Moreover, even under 'closed' contracts, competition was rarely completely excluded. In the performance of contracts, equipped with an array of administrative safeguards, financial penalties, and numerous officials assessing contract terms and accounts, the Treasury attempted to enforce economy over a range of fronts. From 1763, governments sought to curb military expenditure. Towards the end of the war, Pitt asked 'Will a little saving in a Contract make any mighty difference in the National Expence?'[36] Whilst the war 'decisively shifted British governmental thinking in a more decidedly imperial direction', post-war governments answered in the affirmative.[37] Whilst noting the increase in peacetime military expenditure, one estimate offset this against savings made from the reduction of the domestic army, and the great diminution in contract prices.[38]

George Grenville's ministry claimed to have reduced the annual cost of Gibraltar remittances by £25,000, but the most notable reduction concerned the Gibraltar victualling contract.[39] Since 1715 the contractor was paid 3s. 1¼d. per man per week.[40] The new contract was made at 2s. 8d., a reduction of 14.1 per cent. The Treasury's termination of the contract in December 1762 was a device to reduce prices.[41] Further termination notices were issued in 1763 either because many places supplied in wartime were no longer so in peacetime or termination was used as a device to reduce prices.[42] Contracts for new territories were made at significantly lower rates, and an assertive note of stringent economy struck in the firm rejection of compensation claims for unfit provisions.[43] Another notable reform was the shift towards payment by commission at 2 per cent for remittances to foreign garrisons.[44] These reductions were presented in order to exemplify the financial probity and rectitude of a ministry conscious of the need for economy.[45] The willingness of contractors to accept reductions does not necessarily indicate exorbitant profiteering during hostilities. Contingent expenses such as insurance and freight were always higher in wartime, and a modicum of profit was an essential incentive. Perhaps significantly, given the emphasis placed by the Grenville administration on economy and reducing the cost of contracts, there was no wholesale removal of contractors. Continuity in contracting personnel perhaps indicates the value of mercantile activity, or at least a desire to avoid the disruption of changing contractors. Although Fox removed Newcastle loyalists, other contractors transferred political allegiance, and continued in their contracts or were awarded others.[46] For many contractors, as Newcastle discovered, political loyalty meant loyalty to the head of the Treasury.[47]

The impressive correlation between contractors' business interests and the contracts they performed indicate the Treasury's success in finding suitable men to perform contracts. The sectoral vibrancy and geographical diversity of the British mercantile community is readily apparent from the profile of contractors during mid-century wars. Patronage was only a dimension in awarding contracts. Despite being indiscriminately cited amongst the Court patronage of sinecures and places, for officials administering contracts, and for contractors performing them, it was clear that contracts were not sinecures.[48] Amidst legitimate fears arising from competitive tendering, methods of awarding contracts appear entirely appropriate in an age where recommendation and influence were important components of social and political relationships.[49] At every level of contracting, business experience and competence were important, and considerable emphasis was placed on the capability of contractors. In administrative terms the award of contracts in the eighteenth century does not correspond with modern notions of formalized competition based on merit. Yet the efficiency of the system is readily apparent from the negligible number of supply failures, a factor most striking when set alongside the number of contracts performed and difficulties in performing many of them. Alongside the Treasury's concern for economy, this evidence indicates that a simple equation between contracting and 'Old Corruption' is misleading and inaccurate.

That varying methods of awarding contracts could co-exist with simultaneous effectiveness is readily apparent from domestic military supply. In England and Scotland, the type of contractor and type of supply differed from that of foreign garrisons. In England, open competition for encampment contracts, including advertisement was adopted. Advertisement was necessary, for the most suitable men to perform these contracts were not primarily merchants, nor Members of Parliament. The Treasury's preference for a single contractor appears, on the basis of successful performance, to have been vindicated.

Despite examining encampment supply of 1756–62 as a precedent for the camps of 1778, the Treasury eventually chose to contract separately for encampment articles.[50] The ensuing difficulties illustrated the problems of reliance on local suppliers.[51] Employing multiple suppliers always increased the possibility of supply failures, and in dispersing profits, may have adversely affected contract performance. Such problems did not emerge between 1756 and 1762, when the most pressing problem concerned surpluses, emanating from an understandable overreaction and overestimation of requirements. Difficulties in assessing supply and demand were exacerbated by uncertain duration. Although invasion could only seriously be attempted in summer, mild weather and the strategic value to the French of tying down British troops by maintaining the threat made it difficult to plan dispersal with any precision.[52] Despite these complicating factors, there never appears to have been any risk of shortages. Despite food riots in the early years of the war, the relative quiescence of Britain was an obvious contribution towards efficient domestic supply.

In terms of procurement, delivery and distribution, encampment supply was clearly efficient, but was it cost-effective? It may have been cheaper to employ a contractor for every article, but this is not certain. Such a mode of proceeding may have encouraged combinations. Although supply was localized from the late eighteenth century onwards, even in 1856, with forty-six separate bread and forage contracts throughout Britain, the Director-General of the Commissariat warned against an excessive division of contracts, as smaller tradesmen would charge retail prices.[53] Extraneous strategic and economic factors, a receding invasion threat, and better harvests were important in lowering costs later in the war, and prices do not appear high. In terms of prices and regularity of deliveries, the system attained a high level of efficiency and accomplishment.

The success of encampment supply in the mid-eighteenth century demonstrated that problems of inexperience could be surmounted, although there were some experienced men. Dundas, Hume, Godfrey and Gardiner were involved in this sector between 1739 and 1748. This experience proved invaluable during the Seven Years' War, in allowing them to apply their knowledge in different capacities, as contractors and commissaries, in the various locations of Scotland, England, Flanders and Germany. The ability of these men has often been overlooked. Whilst Prince Ferdinand's threat to hang Dundas for late deliveries under contract and his vast accretion of wealth were much commented on, Dundas's execution of contracts on cheaper terms than others and the praise he received are often overlooked.[54] Direct experience was supplemented by skills based in related sectors, where expertise could be either sectoral or geographical, or both. The number of contractors for horses who also supplied encampments indicates a sector where the skills of men engaged in transport and agriculture converged with the needs of government. Men such as John Willan, whose skills encompassed expertise with horses and transport, allied to considerable organizational ability, were well-suited towards supplying encampments.

The profile of contracting personnel in this sector indicates success based on longevity, application to business and hard work. Encampment contractors appear to have been more closely concerned in daily management than foreign garrison contractors. Whilst a recent historian has considered contractors as not forming a distinct subset of London merchants, such a view is applicable to the wider mercantile portfolios of financial and victualling contractors.[55] For encampment contracts, a 'contracting community' of organizing middlemen within the domestic economy, encompassing horse dealers, large farmers, and a number of Scottish merchants, does appear to have existed. Such variety indicates the vibrancy and complexity of domestic economic activity. Over a considerable period, this group of men devoted considerable time and resources to this sector. The extent of their activities is somewhat submerged, owing to the extensive nature of sub-contracting, but glimpses of it are apparent from examination of encampment and horse contracts. The convergence in personnel for both types of contract indicates the considerable expertise at the service of government, whilst offering an illuminating insight into grass roots contracting. Although contracts in this sector were made for basic necessities, it was a particularly specialized form of supply. Many operations were functionally similar to garrison supply, but distribution was more complex. Moreover, the articles supplied under contract, encompassing food and transport, required extensive knowledge of a number of areas. The importance of contractors in this sector, and their value to the state, is readily apparent. That these men formed the nucleus of an unofficial supply corps is reinforced both by the longevity of men such as Willan, Dundas and Oswald, and by the activities of descendants of Willan, Gardiner and Trotter in the same sector. The general competence of encampment supply was buttressed by a small but significant number of experienced military officers. A number of military and governmental personnel drew upon the experience of previous wars to ensure a degree of continuity in methods and planning. Whilst the employment of contractors obviated greater governmental involvement, it was a collaborative effort between contractors and governmental and military personnel that ensured successful encampment administration.

Similar accomplishment is apparent in Scotland, where the events of 1745–6 proved crucial to the evolution of the supply structure and composition of contracting personnel. During the Rebellion, the combination of shipment of supplies and an admixture of local requisitioning and sub-contracting from a wide geographical area was curiously reminiscent of earlier Scottish campaigns. Although bearing no trace of modernity, it proved highly effective. In the following years, although supply methods and the use of contractors were regularized, no attempt was made to replicate English procedures in awarding contracts. In planning supply, considerable authority was delegated to military commanders, with such delegation curiously similar to methods applicable to foreign campaigns.

The importance of contractors to the British military supply system was fundamentally a consequence of the British aversion to a large standing army and proliferation of military institutions. Whilst this led to an informal, temporary supply system, solid economic and financial reasons also existed for the extensive employment of contractors in the mid-eighteenth century. One could perhaps say exactly the same about the early eighteenth century, yet mid-century contractors were arguably more important. With a period of peace between 1713 and 1739 there was little continuity in personnel from earlier wars, and the demands made of contractors were both geographically wider and more extensive.

A new generation of contractors emerged in the mid-eighteenth century, with many continuing into the American and French Revolutionary wars. It almost appears as if an unofficial supply corps of contractors and commissaries emerged, one based on experience of previous wars. The importance of mid-century contractors, encompassing different areas at different times in different conflicts, was not therefore constrained by time, distance, or geographical considerations. In a sense, it was the strength and weakness of the system that it encouraged men in different areas of business and governmental capacities to participate in it. With no established supply organization, various forms of sectoral knowledge and experience were required and effectively utilized.

In contrast to the significance of mid-century contracting in supply terms, the impact of contracting upon contractors' wealth is more ambiguous. There are cases where contract profits appear to have been of great importance in the wealth of individuals. This is most apparent in those performing contracts over a long period and with a narrow portfolio of business interests. A notable feature in the relationship between wealth creation and contracting is the success of many contractors involved in domestic supply. This owed something to humble origins in accentuating their gains, but also emanated from longevity, experience and expertise.

Despite the emphasis in historical works given to the political role of contractors, the importance of contractors to the state did not emanate from their political position. Even contractors' wealth, an even older preoccupation, appears unremarkable. The importance of contractors to the state appears, in fact, to reside in their primary function, of supplying the army. For different reasons, this has been somewhat obscured by political and military historians. The remarkable feature of contracting in eighteenth-century Britain was its efficiency. The few failures that occurred only serve to illustrate that most contracts were competently performed. Contract performance was dependent on a number of factors, many beyond contractors' control. Bad weather, enemy seizure, and employee peculation were amongst the more obvious. Together these factors constituted a formidable array of variables obstructing efficient performance. Accounts that solely blame contractors for supply failures are therefore simplistic and inadequate. Whilst one historian has suggested that, through naval expansion, long-term credit, and improvements in governmental and colonial administration Britain possessed 'an efficient means for mobilizing her resources', army contractors often provided supply infrastructure and used their own resources.[56]

The more extensive use of contractors neither amounted to a revolution in economic organization or a revolution in government. This may account for the lack of consideration given to the economic activities of contractors and the overemphasis on patronage. Yet an examination of lesser-documented areas of contracting and contractors reveals their economic and military value to the state. A modern estimate assessed supply of bread, forage, and fuel as constituting over 90 per cent of an eighteenth-century army's supply requirements.[57] Together with transport, these articles comprised the basic operational equipment of the military forces. In organizing supply in this sector, contractors effectively organized a privatized mercantile military machine, playing a vital role in the modus operandi of the eighteenth-century British army. Whilst patronage and jobbery clearly existed, they do not, and did not, imply inefficiency and incapacity. One can see a glaring double-standard in historical studies relating to contractors. Most historians would reject the view that the achievements of William Pitt are fatally undermined by the method of his election to Parliament. Why then assess contractors on the basis of how contracts were awarded or who their political friends were? If one assesses contractors on the basis of their performance of contracts, it seems clear they deserve to be viewed in more generous and accurate terms than as rapacious beneficiaries of a corruptsupply system.[58]

APPENDIX A: SAMPLE OF ARMY CONTRACTORS IN PARLIAMENT

[Table A.1: Age at First Contract and on Entering Parliament[1]]

Contractor	Dates	First contract	Entered Parliament
George Amyand	1720–66	36 (1756)	34 (1754)
Anthony Bacon	c. 1718–86	40 (1758)	46 (1764)
William Baker	1705–70	41 (1746)	42 (1747)
John Bristow	1701–68	38 (1739)	33 (1734)
Merrick Burrell	1699–1787	53 (1752)	48 (1747)
Peter Burrell	1692–1756	47 (1739)	30 (1722)
G. Colebrooke	1729–1809	30 (1759)	25 (1754)
J. Colebrooke	1722–61	36 (1758)	29 (1751)
Peregrine Cust	1723–85	39 (1762)	38 (1761)
A. Drummond	1713–86	51 (1764)	48 (1761)
L. Dundas	1710–81	36 (1746)	37 (1747)
Brice Fisher	d. 1767	Unknown (1744)	Unknown (1754)
Samuel Fludyer	1704–68	60 (1764)	50 (1754)
T. Fonnereau	1699–1779	53 (1752)	42 (1741)
ZP Fonnereau	1706–1778	46 (1752)	41 (1747)
John Gore	1689–1763	53 (1742)	58 (1747)
Joseph Gulston	c. 1694–1766	c. 48 (1742)	c. 43 (1737)
John Henniker	1724–1803	39 (1764)	37 (1761)
Abraham Hume	1703–72	39 (1742)	44 (1747)
Robert Jones	d. 1774	Unknown (1762)	Unknown (1754)
Thomas Leslie	1701–72	47 (1748)	33 (1734)
N. Linwood	1709–73	54 (1763)	52 (1761)
John Major	1698–1781	66 (1764)	63 (1761)
Joseph Mellish	1717–90	42 (1759)	44 (1761)
Arnold Nesbitt	1721–79	37 (1756)	32 (1753)
Thomas Revell	d. 1752	Unknown (1733)	Unknown (1734)
Samuel Touchet	1705–73	53 (1758)	56 (1761)
C. Townsend	1708–70	36 (1744)	40 (1748)
Thomas Walpole	1727–1803	25 (1752)	27 (1754)

[Table A.2: Age Groups at First Contract and on Entering Parliament]

Age groups	Performed first contract	Entered Parliament	Combined totals
20–29	1 (3.8%)	3 (11.5%)	4 (15.3%)
30–39	8 (30.8%)	8 (30.8%)	16 (61.6%)
40–49	9 (34.6%)	10 (38.5%)	19 (73.1%)
50–59	6 (23.1%)	4 (15.4%)	10 (38.5%)
60 +	2 (7.7%)	1 (3.8%)	3 (11.5%)

The sample consists of twenty-nine men who held army contracts from the Treasury and who sat in Parliament during the three middle decades of the eighteenth-century. Nineteen (65.5 per cent) were MPs before possessing contracts, a clear illustration of contracts as a reward for political loyalty. Ten (34.5 per cent) held contracts before entering Parliament. Most of the latter were active in mercantile rather than financial circles, and came from a more modest, though not impoverished background. Hume, Dundas, Fisher and Bacon in particular fit this category. Gore and Walpole, predominantly financiers, were exceptions. Active merchants such as Touchet, Townsend, and Baker are also in this group, although it did not take them long to enter Parliament.

The figures suggest that those voting for Administration were shown favour but perhaps more importantly, that contracts were awarded to experienced and wealthy businessmen. The date of birth of three contractors in the sample (Fisher, Jones, and Revell) is unknown but for the remaining twenty-six men, the average age of entering Parliament computes at just over forty-one (41.4). Average age of possession of first contract, with aforementioned omissions, is forty-four. Twenty-one (80.8 per cent) held their first contract between the ages of thirty-six and fifty-three. The oldest was John Major at sixty-six, although he previously performed navy contracts. The youngest was Thomas Walpole at twenty-five, precocity explicable by his 'political' family.

Unsurprisingly, the date when contractors held their first contract was heavily influenced by whether the nation was at war. Eighteen (approximately 62 per cent) held their first contract during wartime. A small but significant number (four) performed their first contract after 1762, as a direct result of ministerial changes and political partisanship. In addition, two others began contracts towards the end of the war. Those succeeding to peacetime contracts concerned Gibraltar and Scotland, both places accustomed to a permanent military presence. The safest inference to draw from the data is that the first priority of government was to ensure active men of business were selected to perform contracts. The operation of political influence was variable and dependent on the type of contract. The mere existence of non-parliamentary contractors should induce a degree of caution as to a simple equation between votes in Commons lobbies and contract allocation.

These figures corroborate Namier's view that 'merchants' entered parliament relatively late in life.[2] This certainly applies to merchants from relatively modest backgrounds. Wealthier merchants could, by a combination of wealth and connections, enter Parliament at a relatively young age. Thus, Thomas Walpole entered Parliament aged twenty-seven and the Colebrooke brothers at twenty-five and twenty-nine. Equally, a younger son of an aristocratic family, such as Leslie, was likely to enter Parliament early. These qualifications aside, the idea that merchants entered Parliament later in life is confirmed.

Appendix A: Sample of Army Contractors in Parliament

[Table A.3: Duration of Parliamentary Career]

	Age	Duration (years)
Amyand	34	12
Bacon	46	20
Baker	42	21
Bristow	33	34
M. Burrell	48	31
P. Burrell	30	33
G. Colebrooke	25	20
J. Colebrooke	29	10
Cust	38	23
Drummond	48	24
Dundas	37	11
Fisher	Unknown	14
Fludyer	50	14
T. Fonnereau	42	33
ZP Fonnereau	41	27
Gore	58	14
Gulston	43	28
Henniker	37	17
Hume	44	14
Jones	Unknown	20
Leslie	33	25
Linwood	52	12
Major	63	7
Mellish	44	19
Nesbitt	32	22
Revell	Unknown	18
Touchet	56	7
Townsend	40	22
Walpole	27	30

Twenty-nine contractors served a total of 582 years in parliament, an average of just over twenty years. The Septennial Act, support for government, and the ability of many to pay their electoral expenses rather than relying on government patronage accounts for such longevity. Only two contractors sat for less than ten years. Even for those entering Parliament later in life, long careers were possible, as the careers of the Fonnereau brothers and Merrick Burrell demonstrate.

Constituencies

The analysis is based on English constituencies. A few contractors (Drummond, Dundas, Leslie, and Townsend) sat for Scottish constituencies, and there are similarities with English constituencies inasmuch as they all sat for burghs with very small electorates. The omission of Scottish constituencies, being few, is not fatal to the analysis. No contractors sat for Welsh constituencies. Thirty-eight English constituencies, all boroughs, albeit with various franchises, were represented by contractors. No contractor sat for a constituency with what could be considered a large electorate. The Cinque Port of Dover was the largest with 1,000 voters.

[Table A.4: Location of Seats by County]

Wiltshire	5
Devon	4
Cornwall	4
Sussex	4
Yorkshire	3
Buckinghamshire	2
Surrey	2
Lincolnshire	2
Dorset	2
Hampshire	2
Suffolk	2
Huntingdonshire	1
Kent	1
Norfolk	1
Shropshire	1
Somerset	1
Staffordshire	1

Predictably, there is an imbalance in representation towards constituencies in southern England. Some indication of the type of seat held by contractors can be obtained by examining the results of the 1832 Reform Act. Two constituencies, New Shoreham (1771) and Grampound (1824) were disfranchised before 1832. Of the remaining thirty-six, fifteen were retained as two member constituencies, seven reduced to one-member, and fourteen abolished.[3]

[Table A.5: Constituencies of Contractors]

	Constituency	1832 status
Amyand	Barnstaple	Ret. (Retained as two-member constituency)
Bacon	Aylesbury	Ret.
Baker	Plympton Erle	A (Abolished)
Bristow	Bere Alston	A
	St Ives	Red. (Reduced from two to one member constituency)
	Arundel	Red.
M. Burrell	Great Marlow	Ret.
	Grampound	D (Disfranchised pre-1832)
	Haslemere	A
	Great Bedwyn	A
P. Burrell	Haslemere	A
	Dover	Ret.
G. Colebrooke	Arundel	Red.
J. Colebrooke	Gatton	A
Cust	Bishop's Castle	A
	New Shoreham	D
	Ilchester	A
	Grantham	Ret.
Drummond	St Ives	Red.
	Lymington	Ret.
Dundas	Newcastle-u-Lyme	Ret.
	Richmond	Ret.
Fisher	Malmesbury	Red.
	Boroughbridge	A
Fludyer	Chippenham	Ret.
T. Fonnereau	Aldeburgh	A
ZP Fonnereau	Aldeburgh	A

Appendix A: Sample of Army Contractors in Parliament

	Constituency	1832 status
Gore	Great Grimsby	Red.
Gulston	Tregony	A
	Poole	Ret.
Henniker	Sudbury	Ret.
	Dover	Ret.
Hume	Steyning	A
	Tregony	A
Jones	Huntingdon	Ret.
Linwood	Stockbridge	A
	Aldeburgh	A
Major	Scarborough	Ret.
Mellish	Great Grimsby	Red.
Nesbitt	Mitchell	A
	Winchilsea	A
	Cricklade	Ret.
Revell	Dover	Ret.
Townsend	Westbury	Red.
Touchet	Shaftesbury	Red.
Walpole	Sudbury	Ret.
	Ashburton	Red.
	King's Lynn	Ret.

APPENDIX B: THE LEGACY

Baronets[1]

James Colebrooke: 12 October 1759
Samuel Fludyer: 14 November 1759
William Baker: 3 November 1760
George Colebrooke: 10 May 1761
Lawrence Dundas: 20 October 1762
George Amyand: 9 August 1764
John Major: 8 July 1765
Merrick Burrell: 15 July 1766
Abraham Hume: 20 March 1769

Male Descendants of Contractors who Became MPs[2]

John Amyand (1751–80)
Sir William Baker (1743–1824)
Sir Peter Burrell (1754–1820)
William Burrell (1732–96)
Sir George Cornewall (c.1749–1819)
Sir Thomas Dundas (1741–1820)
George Fludyer (1761–1837)
Martyn Fonnereau (1741–1817)
Phillip Fonnereau (1739–97)
John Henniker (1752–1821)
Abraham Hume (1749–1838)
William Mellish (nephew) (c.1764–1838)
John Nesbitt (nephew) (c.1745–1817)
James Townsend (1737–87)

Sons of Contractors Attending University[3]

William Baker (Camb.)
Jacob Baker (Camb.)
John Baker (Camb.)
Peter Burrell (Camb.)
William Burrell (Camb.)
Sir George Cornewall (Oxon)
Sir Thomas Dundas (St Andrews)
Phillip Fonnereau (Camb.)
Joseph Gulston (Oxon)
John Henniker (Camb.)
Abraham Hume (Camb.)
James Townsend (Oxon)
Joseph Townsend (Camb.)
Thomas Walpole (Camb.)

APPENDIX C: THE BUSINESS LIFE OF CONTRACTORS

[Table C.1: Contractors and Chartered Companies[1]]

Key: BE: Bank of England; EI: East India Company; RAC: Royal African Company; REA: Royal Exchange Assurance; RC: Russia Company; SSC: South Sea Company; SFO: Sun Fire Office

Amyand	i. RC Assistant 1756.
	ii. EI Dir. 1760–3, 1764
Baker	i. EI Dir. 1741–5, 1746–50, 1751–3
	Deputy Ch. 1749, 1751–2; Ch. 1749–50, 1752–3
	ii. Hudson's Bay Co. Deputy Gov. 1750–60; Gov. 1760–70
Bristow	SSC Dir. 1730–3, Deputy Gov. 1733–56; Sub-Gov. 1756–62
M. Burrell	BE Dir. 1742–56; Deputy Gov. 1756–8; Gov. 1758–60; Dir. 1760–4
P. Burrell	i. SSC Dir. 1724–33, 1756.
	ii. REA Dir.
G. Colebrooke	EI Dir. 1767–71, 1772–3; Deputy Ch. 1768–9
	Ch. 1769–71, 1772–3
Cust	i. RAC Delegate (Bristol) 1755–65.
	ii. EI Dir. 1767–9; Deputy Ch. 1769–70
Fisher	i. SSC Dir. 1753–5.
	ii. SFO Dir. 1734–67
Fludyer	BE Dir. 1753–5, 1756–8, 1759–62, 1763–6
	Deputy Gov. 1763–8
ZP Fonnereau	EI Dir. 1753, 1754
Gore	SSC Dir. 1711–12, 1715–21
Gulston	SSC Dir.
Henniker	London Assurance Dir.
Hume	i. SSC Dir. 1738–45.
	ii. REA Dir. 1736–45
Jones	EI Dir. 1754–8, 1765–9
Linwood	i. EI Dir. 1749–51, 1752–4
	ii. SSC Dir. 1758–64
	iii. SFO Dir. 1760–73
	iv. REA Dir. 1749
Major	i. SSC Dir.
	ii. RC Deputy Governor 1752
Revell	RAC Assistant 1731–2
Touchet	i. SFO Dir. 1756–64
	ii. RAC Commissioner (Liverpool)
Walpole	EI Director 1753–4

Government Employment

Abraham Hume[2]
Commissary General of Stores, Provisions and Forage (Austrian Netherlands), December 1742–25 December 1745.
Do. HM Forces home and abroad, 25 December 1745–8?
Do. 1 February 1756–70?

Lawrence Dundas[3]
Commissary for forage (Scotland), 1746–7.
Commissary for stores and provisions (Flanders), 1747–8.
Commissary for stores (Scotland), 1748–59.
Superintendent of forage magazines (England), 1757–8.
Commissary of bread for foreign troops (Germany), 1759.

Thomas Leslie[4]
Barrack Master General (Scotland), 1748–69.

Nicholas Linwood[5]
Commissioner for sale of French prizes, August 1756–March 1761.

Adam Drummond[6]
Inspector General of forfeited estates, 1780.

Thomas Revell[7]
Victualling Commissioner, 9 May 1728–23 June 1747.

Samuel Touchet[8]
Commissioner for sale of French prizes, August 1756.

APPENDIX D: PROPERTY-HOLDING

London residence, either a dwelling house or office, is assumed. Where London property-holding was particularly notable it has been included, although not counted within the analysis, which concentrates on counties.

Amyand: Surrey[1]
Bacon: Essex, Merthyr Tydfil, and Virginia[2]
Baker: Hertfordshire, and North America[3]
Bristow: Norfolk, and Middlesex[4]
M. Burrell: Sussex[5]
P. Burrell: Kent, and Sussex[6]
G. Colebrooke: Surrey, Middlesex, Hertfordshire, and North America[7]
J. Colebrooke: Surrey, Middlesex, and Hertfordshire[8]
Cust: Lancashire, Middlesex, Surrey, Sussex, Essex, and Oxford Street/Piccadilly[9]
Drummond: Perthshire[10]
Dundas: Hertfordshire, Yorkshire, London, Scotland, Ireland, and West Indies[11]
Fisher: Berkshire, Yorkshire, and North America[12]
Fludyer: Kent, Middlesex, and Downing Street[13]
T. Fonnereau: Suffolk[14]
ZP Fonnereau: Surrey[15]
Gore: Hertfordshire, Middlesex, and Berkshire[16]
Gulston: Middlesex, and Hertfordshire[17]
Henniker: Essex, Suffolk, Kent, Ireland, and North America[18]
Hume: Berwickshire, Hertfordshire, Essex, and Lincolnshire[19]
Jones: Cambridgeshire[20]
Leslie: Scotland[21]
Linwood: Hampshire, and North America[22]
Major: Suffolk, Essex, Sussex, Grosvenor Estate, Yorkshire, and North America[23]
Mellish: Middlesex[24]

Nesbitt: Kent, Sussex, Huntingdonshire, Ireland, West Indies, and North America[25]
Revell: Surrey[26]
Touchet: Essex, and East Florida[27]
Townsend: Wiltshire[28]
Walpole: Surrey[29]

NOTES

Introduction

1. J. Brewer, *The Sinews of Power: War, Money and the English State 1688–1783* (London: Unwin Hyman, 1989); P. K. O'Brien and P. A. Hunt, 'The Rise of a Fiscal State in England, 1485–1815', *Historical Research*, 66:160 (1993), pp. 129–76.
2. L. Stone (ed.), *An Imperial State at War: Britain from 1689–1815* (London: Routledge, 1993), p. 6; cf. 'Military history is more than the account of the accountants', J. Black, *Britain as a Military Power 1688–1815* (London: University College London Press, 1999), p. 293.
3. N. Baker, 'Changing Attitudes towards Government in Eighteenth-Century Britain', in A. Whiteman, J. S. Bromley and P. G. M. Dickson (eds), *Statesmen, Scholars and Merchants: Essays in Eighteenth-Century History Presented to Dame Lucy Sutherland* (Oxford: Clarendon Press, 1973), pp. 203–19; p. 203.
4. Recognition of the vital partnership between the state and private interests underpins the important work of Stephen Conway: see *War, State and Society in Mid-Eighteenth-Century Britain and Ireland* (Oxford: Oxford University Press, 2006).
5. For naval contracting, see B. Pool, *Navy Board Contracts 1660–1832: Contract Administration under the Navy Board* (London: Longmans, 1966); D. Crewe, *Yellow Jack and the Worm: British Naval Administration in the West Indies 1739–1748* (Liverpool: Liverpool University Press, 1993).
6. L. B. Namier, *The Structure of Politics at the Accession of George III*, 2nd edn (London: Macmillan & Co., 1957), pp. 45–58; P. G. M. Dickson, *The Financial Revolution in England: A Study in the Development of Public Credit 1688–1756* (London: Macmillan, 1967), pp. 393–8; for acknowledgement that contracts covered 'a vast range of services', see J. Childs, *The British Army of William III, 1689–1702* (Manchester: Manchester University Press, 1987), p. 175.
7. J. Norris, *Shelburne and Reform* (London: Macmillan & Co., 1963), pp. 65, 127, 158–9; I. R. Christie, *The End of North's Ministry 1780–1782* (London: Macmillan & Co., 1958), pp. 182–4.
8. Namier, *Structure of Politics*, p. 51.
9. D. Chandler, *The Art of Warfare in the Age of Marlborough* (London: Batsford, 1976); R. E. Scouller, *The Armies of Queen Anne* (Oxford: Clarendon Press, 1966); Martin van Creveld, *Supplying War: Logistics from Wallenstein to Patton* (Cambridge: Cambridge University Press, 1977); A. Corvisier, *Armies and Societies in Europe, 1494–1789* (Bloomington and London: Indiana University Press, 1979).
10. Childs, *Army of William III*, p. 247.
11. Namier warned against overstressing the relationship (*Structure of Politics*, p. 47).
12. N. Baker, *Government and Contractors: The British Treasury and War Supplies, 1775–1782* (London: Athlone Press, 1971); N. Baker, 'The Treasury and Open Contracting, 1778–1782', *Historical Journal*, 15:3 (1972), pp. 433–54; H. Little, 'The Treasury, the Commissariat, and the Supply of the Combined Army in Germany during the Seven

Years War (1756–1763)', (Phd dissertation, University of London, 1981); D. Hancock, *Citizens of the World: London Merchants and the Integration of the British Atlantic Community 1735–1785* (Cambridge: Cambridge University Press, 1995), pp. 221–39.
13. Baker, 'Changing Attitudes', p. 205; J. Hoppit, *Risk and Failure in English Business 1700–1800* (Cambridge: Cambridge University Press, 1987), p. 95.
14. Brewer, *Sinews of Power*, p. xvii.
15. For military material, see J. West, *Gunpowder, Government and War in the Mid-Eighteenth Century* (London: Royal Historical Society, 1991).
16. For 'industrialists' as contractors, R. Sedgwick, *The House of Commons 1715–1754*, 2 vols (London: HMSO, 1970), vol. 1, p. 151; for those interested in both areas, see below, pp. 50 and 131.

1 The Supply System of the British Army from the Seventeenth Century

1. Ireland possessed a separate military establishment. 'Britain' and 'British' refers to the British military establishment. A. J. Guy, 'The Irish Military Establishment, 1660–1776' in T. Bartlett and K. Jeffrey (eds), *A Military History of Ireland* (Cambridge: Cambridge University Press, 1996), pp. 211–30.
2. Brewer terms the period 1688–1783 the 'second Hundred Years War' (*Sinews of Power*, p. 41); see also B. Lenman, *Britain's Colonial Wars, 1688–1783* (Harlow: Longman, 2001).
3. Public Income and Expenditure 1688–1801, *Parliamentary Papers* [hereafter *PP*], (1868–9), xxxv [366–I], pp. 99–149.
4. Between 1713 and 1763, the number of troops voted in Britain rose from 15,851 to 111,553 (1 June 1713, *House of Commons Journals* [hereafter *HCJ*], 17, p. 383; A. J. Guy, *Oeconomy and Discipline: Officership and Administration in the British Army 1714–1763* (Manchester: Manchester University Press, 1985), p. 9).
5. C. H. Masse, *Predecessors of the Royal Army Service Corps* (Aldershot: Gale and Polden Ltd., 1948), p. xv.
6. G. Perjes, 'Army Provisioning, Logistics and Strategy in the Second Half of the 17th Century', *Acta Historica Academiae Scientiarum Hungaricae*, 16 (1970), pp. 1–52; pp. 49–51.
7. F. Redlich, *The German Military Enterpriser and his Work Force: A Study in European Economic and Social History*, 2 vols (Wiesbaden: Franz Steiner Verlag, 1965), vol. 2, pp. 21–2; for Prussian field bakeries administered by military officers, see Little, 'Commissariat', p. 10; for the wider contrast between Britain and Prussia, see J. Childs, 'The Army and the State in Britain and Germany during the Eighteenth Century', in J. Brewer and E. Hellmuth (eds), *Rethinking Leviathan: The Eighteenth-Century State in Britain and Germany* (Oxford: Oxford University Press, 1999), pp. 53–70.
8. C. S. L. Davies, 'Provisions for armies, 1509–1550; a Study in the Effectiveness of Early Tudor Government', *Economic History Review*, 17:2 (1964–5), pp. 234–48; p. 239.
9. C. H. Firth, *Cromwell's Army: A History of the English soldier during the Civil Wars, the Commonwealth and the Protectorate*, 2nd edn (London: Methuen, 1912), appendix L: 'Articles of War' (1643), p. 420; *London Gazette* [hereafter *LG*], 12–16 August 1718; the 1748 Articles of War prohibited Governors and officers from selling provisions at

Notes to pages 8–9

garrisons, Section 8, Article 4, Public Record Office, London, War Office papers [hereafter PRO, WO] PRO, WO 72/2.

10. C. Duffy, *The Army of Maria Theresa: The Armed Forces of Imperial Austria, 1740–1780* (Vancouver and London: David and Charles, 1977); in France, a state corporation provided forage but 'munitionnaries' supplied bread to the entire army (L. Kennett, *The French Armies in the Seven Years War, A Study in Military Organization and Administration* (Durham, NC: Duke University Press, 1967), pp. 99–112.
11. For the supply system as 'informal, irregular and inefficient', Hancock, *Citizens of the World*, p. 224.
12. For a nuanced approach to the early modern state, see M. Braddick, 'The Early Modern English State and the Question of Differentiation, from 1550 to 1700', *Comparative Studies in Society and History*, 38:1 (1996), pp. 92–111.
13. Childs, *Army of William III*, pp. 252–3; D. W. Jones, *War and Economy in the Age of William III and Marlborough* (Oxford: Basil Blackwell, 1988), p. 9.
14. For the Seven Years' War as 'The First World War', see W. Churchill, *A History of the English Speaking Peoples*, 4 vols (London: Cassell & Co., 1956–8), vol. 3, p. 123; P. Kennedy, *The Rise and Fall of British Naval Mastery*, 3rd edn (London: Fontana, 1991), p. 115.
15. Viscount Barrington to W. Pitt, 21 January 1761, Chatham papers, PRO 30/8/18, f. 209.
16. G. Parker, *The Military Revolution: Military Innovation and the Rise of the West, 1500–1800* (Cambridge: Cambridge University Press, 1988), p. 16; J. H. Stocqueler, *The Military Encyclopaedia; a Technical, Biographical and Historical Dictionary, Referring Exclusively to the Military Sciences, the Memoirs of Distinguished Soldiers, and the Narratives of Remarkable Battles* (London: William H. Allen, 1853), pp. 253–6. Battles were scarce during the Nine Years' War (1688–97) (Childs, *Army of William III*, p. 240).
17. J. Black, 'A Military Revolution? A 1660–1792 perspective', in C. J. Rogers (ed.), *The Military Revolution Debate: Readings on the Military Transformation of Early Modern Europe* (Boulder, CO: Westview Press, 1995), pp. 95–114; M. J. Braddick, 'An English Military Revolution?', *Historical Journal*, 36:4 (1993), pp. 965–75.
18. Cited in Parker, *Military Revolution*, p. 16.
19. Ibid., p. 16.
20. F. Tallett, *War and Society in Early Modern Europe, 1495–1715* (London: Routledge, 1992), p. 62; Corvisier, *Armies and Societies*, p. 113.
21. Davies, 'Provisions for Armies', pp. 235–6.
22. For seventeenth-century *Kontributions* and *Brandschatzung*, see F. Redlich, 'Contributions in the Thirty Years War', *Economic History Review*, 12:2 (1959–60), pp. 247–54; *Brandschatting* was burning of towns and villages slow in paying contributions (Childs, *Army of William III*, p. 242).
23. Sir J. Fortescue, *The Royal Army Service Corps: A History of Transport and Supply in the British army*, 2 vols (Cambridge: Cambridge University Press, 1930–1), vol. 1, p. 6; Childs, *Army of William III*, p. 248; for regulations for sutlers serving the British army, see Articles of War (1718–49), PRO, WO 72/2; for regulations of States General, see *Daily Courant*, 8 April 1706.
24. Sir J. Fortescue, *A History of the British Army*, 13 vols (London: Macmillan & Co., 1899–1930), vol. 2, p. 606; C. G. Cruikshank, *Elizabeth's Army* (Oxford: Oxford University Press, 1946), p. 37; for earlier problems, see J. Gillingham, *The Wars of the Roses: Peace and Conflict in Fifteenth-Century England* (London: Weidenfeld and Nicolson, 1981), pp. 44–7.

25. G. R. Elton (ed.), *The Tudor Constitution: Documents and Commentary*, 2nd edn (Cambridge: Cambridge University Press, 1982), p. 41.
26. Sir W. Beveridge, *Prices and Wages in England from the Twelfth to the Nineteenth Century*, vol. 1 [no further volumes published] (London: Longman's and Co., 1939), p. 319.
27. The Restoration effectively established an English standing army under the guise of the King's 'Guards and Garrisons' (Braddick, 'English Military Revolution?', p. 965); for England's reliance on the navy and militia before 1660, see *Craftsman*, 6 January 1733.
28. J. S. Nusbacher, 'Civil Supply in the Civil War: The Supply of Victuals to the New Model Army on the Naseby Campaign, 1–14 June 1645', *English Historical Review*, 115:460 (2000), pp. 145–60.
29. Articles of War (1718–49), PRO, WO 72/2; Stocqueler, *Military Encyclopaedia*, pp. 274, 306. Clausewitz noted four different methods of subsistence; three involved some form of local procurement (C. von Clausewitz, *On War* (1832), tr. J. J. Graham, rev. F. N. Maude (Ware, Hertfordshire: Wordsworth, 1997), pp. 267–72).
30. Childs, *Army of William III*, p. 248.
31. Gentles, *The New Model Army in England, Ireland and Scotland, 1645–1653* (Oxford: Blackwell Publishing, 1991), p. 41 ff.; Fortescue, *Royal Army Service Corps*, vol. 1, p. 9.
32. Parker, *Military Revolution*, p. 76; F. D. Dow, *Cromwellian Scotland, 1651–1660* (Edinburgh: John Donald, 1979), p. 124; Gentles, *New Model Army*, p. 388.
33. Dow, *Cromwellian Scotland*, p. 124; cf. similar method for troops attacking French coastal towns, *The Journal of Corporal William Todd, 1745–1762*, ed. A. Cormack and A. Jones (Stroud: Army Records Society, 2001), p. 32 (entry for 26 September 1757).
34. van Creveld, *Supplying War*, p. 33.
35. Ibid. pp. 19–21; Tallett, *War and Society*, pp. 63–5.
36. Cited in Parker, *Military Revolution*, p. 67; Clausewitz dated magazine development from the final quarter of the seventeenth-century (*On War*, pp. 270–1).
37. Childs, *Army of William III*, pp. 243–4. Possessing territory was important in peace bargaining. Witness Pitt's determination to hold African territory previously held by the French, 'Memos for the King', 31 July 1759, BL, Add. MS 32893, f. 391; Duke of Newcastle to Andrew Stone, 1 August 1759, ibid., ff. 403–12.
38. Col. M. Hazenkampf, 'The Supply of an Army in Time of War', *Journal of the United Services Institution*, 21 (1877), pp. 1017–50; pp. 1028–9.
39. Supply failures emanated from wider governmental and military disorganization: J. Childs, 'The Williamite War, 1689–1691', in Bartlett and Jeffrey, *Military History of Ireland*, pp. 188–210; J. Childs, *The Army, James II, and the Glorious Revolution* (Manchester: Manchester University Press, 1980), p. 98; Childs, *Army of William III*, p. 249; S. B. Baxter, *William III* (London: Longmans, 1966), pp. 284–5.
40. Jones, *War and Economy*, pp. 34–7; Childs, *Army of William III*, pp. 230, 249–50; Scouller, *Queen Anne*, pp. 27, 225; for victualling and cavalry horse contracts made with 'the Jew Opponheimer', see *Post-Boy*, 14–16 March 1706.
41. C. Dalton, *George the First's Army 1714–1727*, 2 vols (London: Eyre and Spottiswoode, 1910–12), vol. 1, pp. 230, 244 n. 10; see below, pp. 105–6; R. Browning, 'The Duke of Newcastle and the Financial Management of the Seven Years War in Germany', *Journal of the Society for Army Historical Research* [hereafter *JSAHR*], 39 (1971), pp. 20–45; p. 29.
42. Commissaries of Stores resident at Gibraltar, Minorca and Annapolis Royal from 1715, Dalton, *George the First's Army*, vol. 1, pp. 238, 240–1.
43. Commissioners of Public Accounts, Seventh Report, 19 June 1782, *HCJ*, 38, p. 1071.

44. Warrants, 11 June 1761, Public Record Office, London, Treasury papers [hereafter PRO, T] PRO, T 52/52, pp. 324–5; Little, 'Commissariat', pp. 87–8.
45. 'Instructions to Pierson', 9 May 1760, BL, Add. MS 32905, f. 358; for Treasury rejection of a commissary's claim that his commission entitled him to the bread contract, Charles Jenkinson to William Courtenay, 9 November 1764, Liverpool papers, BL, Add. MS 38304, ff. 83–4; see below, p. 113.
46. Jones, *War and Economy*, p. 32.
47. Conversely, 'some of the problems of the Crimean War arose from the fact that William III had used Machado and Periera rather than setting up a supply system of his own' (Baxter, *William III*, p. 285).
48. Instructions to Deputy Lieutenants, 29 September 1715, Hume of Marchmont papers, National Archives of Scotland [hereafter NAS], GD158/403; Duke of Argyll's instructions, 2 October 1715, *Flying Post*, 15–18 October 1715; Argyll to Lord Polwarth, 16 November 1715, Historical Manuscripts Commission, [hereafter HMC] *Manuscripts of Lord Polwarth*, 5 vols (London: HMSO, 1911–61), vol. 1, p. 27; Robert Pringle (War Office) to Treasury, 17 June 1718, *Calendar of Treasury Papers* [hereafter *CTP*], *1714–19*, ed. J. Redington (London: Longmans and Co., 1883), pp. 384–5.
49. J. Baynes, *The Jacobite Rising of 1715* (London: Cassell, 1970), p. 172.
50. Scouller, *Queen Anne*, p. 25.
51. 28 May 1712, *HCJ*, 17, p. 245.
52. 18 May 1715, *HCJ*, 18, p. 124; *Calendar of Treasury Books* [hereafter *CTB*], (1714–15), pp. 85, 264, 274, 277; Report on army debts, 14 January 1715, Liverpool papers, BL, Add. MS 38330, f. 8; Dickson, *Financial Revolution*, pp. 396–7; Scouller, *Queen Anne*, pp. 222–5.
53. J. Swift, *The Conduct of the Allies, and of the Late Ministry, in Beginning and Carrying on the Present War*, 4th edn (London: John Morphew, 1711), p. 54; cf. 'war is become rather an expense of money than men, and success attends those than can most and longest spend money', Lord Haversham, 6 November 1707, W. Cobbett, *Cobbett's Parliamentary History of England: From the Norman Conquest, in 1066, to the year 1803* [hereafter *PHE*], 12 vols (1806–12), vol. 6, c. 598.
54. Swift, *Conduct of the Allies*, pp. 47–52.
55. For financial pressures across Europe, see Perjes, 'Army Provisioning', p. 50.
56. William Blathwayt to Lowndes, 15 July 1697, *CTP* (1697–1702), p. 73; see also Memorial of Valemon de Medina, 24 July 1694, stating contractors could not continue unless £24,000 arrears were paid, *CTP* (1556/7–1696), p. 381.
57. Dickson, *Financial Revolution*, pp. 400–2; interest on victualling bills was reduced from 5 to 4 per cent in 1749, Treasury to Navy & Victualling Commissioners, 16 March 1749, PRO, T 27/26, p. 408; an Act of 1763 allowed contractors to exchange debts for a 4 per cent annuity charged on the Sinking Fund, 7 February 1763, *HCJ*, 29, p. 437.
58. 19 January 1747, PRO, WO 46/7.
59. Dickson, *Financial Revolution*, pp. 379, 402; D. Hancock, '"Domestic Bubbling": Eighteenth-Century London Merchants and Individual Investment in the funds', *Economic History Review*, 47:4 (1994), pp. 679–702; p. 696; the danger was that merchants selling bills at discount would reduce the price of long term stocks and thus threaten loan subscriptions (R. Middleton, *The Bells of Victory: The Pitt-Newcastle Ministry and the Conduct of the Seven Years' War, 1757–1762* (Cambridge: Cambridge University Press, 1985), p. 89).

60. 'Memorial relating to Navy Bills & c.', n.d., unsigned, BL, Add. MS 33047, ff. 381–2; Sir J. Barnard, 'Some Maxims Relating to the Funds', in M. Postlethwayt, *Universal Dictionary of Trade and Commerce*, 3rd edn, 2 vols (London: H. Woodfall, A. Millar, J. and R. Tonson et al, 1766), vol. 2 [unpaginated], Entry for 'money'.
61. See Thomas Leslie to Newcastle, 11 June 1760, BL, Add. MS 32907, f. 155; n.d., received 22 June 1760, ibid., f. 343; 23 January 1760, PRO, T 29/33, p. 273; 12 February 1760, ibid., p. 285; 3 July 1760, ibid, p. 339.
62. Perjes, 'Army Provisioning', p. 50.
63. J. Childs, *Armies and Warfare in Europe 1648–1789* (Manchester: Manchester University Press, 1982), p. 176.
64. H. Roseveare, *The Treasury: The Evolution of a British Institution* (London: Allen Lane, 1969), p. 89; Sedgwick, *Commons*, vol. 1, p. 4.
65. 9 April 1717, Cobbett, *PHE*, vol. 7, c. 440.
66. Roseveare, *Treasury*, p. 93.
67. Sir E. Knatchbull, *The Parliamentary Diary of Sir Edward Knatchbull (1722–1730)*, ed. A. N. Newman, *Camden Society*, 3rd series, 94 (London: Royal Historical Society, 1963), p. 81 (entry for 27 January 1729).
68. In 1713, Robert Harley advised the Secretary at War to present extraordinary expenditure in a 'favourable manner', 2 May 1713, *Calendar of Treasury Books and Papers* [hereafter *CTBP*], (1713), p. 199.
69. Francis papers, BL, Add. MS 40759, f. 222.
70. n.d., [*c.* 1760], BL, Add. MS 33039, f. 422.
71. Hansard, *The Parliamentary Debates*, [hereafter *PD*], vols 13–36 (1812–20), vol. 15, cc. 1213–16.
72. 'Account of Extraordinary Expenditure of the Army provided during the last peace' (1754), PRO, T 1/357, f. 389; accounts: 1748–54, *HCJ*, 25, pp. 779–81, 957; *HCJ*, 26, pp. 72–3, 349, 529, 930; *HCJ*, 27, pp. 86–7.
73. See below, p. 18.
74. Typically £20,000: 23 November 1749, *HCJ*, 26, p. 898; Yonge informed Stair any contingent charges exceeding £10,000 must be justified by precedent or absolute necessity to be included within extraordinary expenditure, 13 August 1742, PRO, WO 4/37, pp. 358–9.
75. Francis papers, BL, Add. MS 40759, ff. 251–2; Guy, *Oeconomy and Discipline*, p. 70.
76. 'A Million has been usually granted during this War by a Vote of Credit, to supply unexpected demands, for Services unforeseen, and for which no provision was made by Estimate.' Lord Barrington's paper on supplies and expenses, 31 March 1762, BL, Add. MS 33040, f. 317.
77. R. Browning, 'The Duke of Newcastle and the Financing of the Seven Years' War', *Journal of Economic History*, 31:2 (1971), pp. 344–77; pp. 371–2.
78. 19 May 1757, *HCJ*, 27, p. 901; 16 March 1758, *HCJ*, 28, pp. 154–5; 23 May 1759, Hansard, *PD*, vol. 15, cc. 938–40; 5 December 1759, *HCJ*, 28, p. 675; 5 December 1760, *HCJ*, 28, p. 966.
79. 2 October 1757, BL, Add. MS 32874, f. 409.
80. Barrington to Newcastle, 27 March 1762, BL, Add. MS 32936, f. 162.
81. Dyson to Barrington, 31 March 1762, ibid., f. 233.
82. Little, 'Commissariat', p. 20; Commons debate, 20 May 1782, *Gentleman's Magazine* [hereafter *GM*], 52 (1782), p. 467.
83. Roseveare, *Treasury*, p. 128.

84. 47,776 troops were in British pay on 18 April 1713; by 20 November 1718 only 17,866 were voted on the estimates; *HCJ*, 17, p. 296; *HCJ*, 19, p. 17.
85. Brewer, *Sinews of Power*, p. 32.
86. One writer argued military needs were 'openly and deliberately neglected' between 1713 and 1739 (H. Gordon, *The War Office* (London: Putnam, 1935), p. 33).
87. Judged correctly so by a wide body of opinion from Bolingbroke to Blackstone (Kennedy, *British Naval Mastery*, p. 4); cf. Whig commitment to land forces in Europe (L. B. Namier, *England in the Age of the American Revolution* (London: Macmillan, 1930), p. 354).
88. L. G. Schwoerer, *"No Standing Armies!": The Anti-Army Ideology in Seventeenth-Century England* (Baltimore, MD: John Hopkins University Press, 1974), pp. 192–4; G. Quilley, '"All Ocean is her Own": The Image of the Sea and the Identity of the Maritime Nation in Eighteenth-Century British Art' in G. Cubitt (ed.), *Imagining Nations* (Manchester: Manchester University Press, 1998), pp. 132–52.
89. C. Barnett, *Britain and her Army, 1509–1970* (London: Allen Lane, 1970), p. 166; Schwoerer, *'No Standing Armies!'*, pp. 189–92.
90. J. Childs, *The Army of Charles II* (London: Routledge and Kegan Paul, 1976), p. 232.
91. *Parliamentary Diary of Sir Edward Knatchbull* (entry for 28 January 1730).
92. The larger peacetime army led an anonymous pamphleteer to claim many 'educated in Revolution-Principles' had 'long feared the approach of a MILITARY GOVERNMENT' ([Anon.], *Seasonable and Affecting Observations on the Mutiny-Bill, Articles of War, and Use and Abuse of a Standing Army: in a Letter from a Member of Parliament* (London: W. Owen, 1750), p. 12); for fear of a Cumberland-Fox 'Military Administration', see Namier, *American Revolution*, p. 49 n. 3.
93. Barrington considered Britain too frugal in peacetime, whilst Egmont considered extensive peacetime mobilization an attempt to introduce military government. Debate on a plan for speedily manning the navy, 14 April 1749, Hansard, *PD*, vol. 14, cc. 538–42.
94. Guy, *Oeconomy and Discipline*, p. 10.
95. Charles Yorke to Newcastle, 27 December 1762, BL, Add. MS 32945, ff. 390–2.
96. S. B. Baxter, *The Development of the Treasury 1660–1702* (London: Longmans, Green and Co., 1957), p. 59; 6 February 1734, *The History and Proceedings of the House of Commons from the Restoration to the Present Time*, 14 vols (London: Chandler, 1741–4), vol. 3, pp. 69–88; 6 December 1742, HMC, *Diary of the Earl of Egmont*, 3 vols (London: HMSO, 1920–3), vol. 3, p. 268; debate on land forces, 28 November 1751, Hansard, *PD*, vol. 14, cc. 1086–127; for opposition in the Irish House of Commons to raising regiments, see Rigby to Newcastle, 20 January 1760, BL, Add. MS 32901, f. 379.
97. Viscount W. Barrington, *An Eighteenth-Century Secretary at War: The Papers of William, Viscount Barrington*, ed. T. Hayter (London: Bodley Head for Army Records Society, 1988), p. 26.
98. Baxter, *Development of Treasury*, pp. 73–4; D. A. Baugh, *Naval Administration in the Age of Walpole* (Princeton, NJ: Princeton University Press, 1965), pp. 469–70.
99. For an example of the Admiralty being warned off giving directions over contract allocation, see Baugh, *Naval Administration in the Age of Walpole*, pp. 88–9.
100. Browning, 'Newcastle and Financial Management', p. 21; Little, 'Commissariat', pp. 15–16.
101. When troop augmentations necessitated increasing supplies, the War Office issued the requisite instructions. Barrington to Mr. Bowerbanks, 17 March 1756, PRO, WO 4/51, p. 284; 29 November 1757, PRO, WO 4/55, p. 93; coal for Gibraltar: Yonge to Revell,

17 September 1741, PRO, WO 4/37, p. 30; Barrington to John Calcraft, 14 June 1757, PRO, WO 4/54, p. 127.

102. Scouller, *Queen Anne*, pp. 36–7; G. W. Morgan, 'The Impact of War on the Administration of the Army, Navy and Ordnance in Britain, 1739–1754' (Phd dissertation, University of Leicester, 1977), p. 71.

103. Morgan, 'Impact of War', p. 360.

104. The Paymaster General and Treasury received copies before presentation of estimates to Parliament, Fox to James West, 17 September 1754, PRO, WO 4/50, p. 39; Barrington to Treasury, 14 November 1758, PRO, WO 4/57, pp. 31–2.

105. Corvisier, *Armies and Societies*, p. 76; on governmental conduct of the war, see Middleton, *Bells of Victory*, p. 212.

106. Pitt, as Secretary of State, asked Barrington what orders should be given to execute troop movement from Scotland to Ireland. For Barrington's reply, see 16 March 1757, Chatham papers, PRO 30/8/18, ff. 172–5.

107. West to Barrington, 27 February 1756, PRO, T 27/27, p. 198; see below, p. 62.

108. Barrington, *Eighteenth-Century Secretary at War*, pp. 26–8; Ordnance protest at War Office order to supply bedding for Chatham hospital, 5 June 1760, PRO, WO 47/55, p. 107.

109. Encampment contracts inexplicably omitted in Roseveare, *Treasury*, pp. 92–3.

110. Browning, 'Newcastle and Financial Management', p. 21.

111. Treasury minutes, 18 November 1714 and 31 July 1759, relating to orders for the more regularly keeping of papers and dispatch of business at the Treasury [Copy], Minto papers, National Library of Scotland [hereafter NLS], MS 11040, ff. 29–32. Contracts only specifically mentioned at latter date.

112. Guy, *Oeconomy and Discipline*, pp. 26–8; although even Cumberland exercised limited authority over the army in Ireland (Middleton, *Bells of Victory*, p. 46).

113. Fortescue, *Royal Army Service Corps*, vol. 1, p. 12; regiments were numbered from 1751 but years afterwards were still known by the names of their proprietary colonels (J. A. Houlding, *Fit for Service: The Training of the British Army 1715–1795* (Oxford: Clarendon Press, 1981), p. xx).

114. 1 July 1856, Report from the Select Committee on Contracts for Public Departments, *PP*, 1856, vii.117 [362], pp. 138–9; off reckonings were abolished in 1854.

115. Calcraft to Amherst, 9 June 1759, PRO, WO 34/99, f. 28; Calcraft to Loudoun, 7 January 1757, Calcraft papers, BL, Add. MS 17493, f. 27; A. J. Guy, 'Regimental Agency in the British Standing Army, 1715–1763: A Study of Georgian Military Administration', *Bulletin of the John Rylands University Library of Manchester*, 62:2 (1980), pp. 423–53; D. J. Smith, 'Army Clothing Contractors and the Textile Industries in the 18th Century', *Textile History*, 14:2 (1983), pp. 153–64; p. 156.

116. Warrants: 22 April 1757, PRO, T 52/48, p. 220, 18 April 1761, PRO, T 52/52, pp. 196–7; Fox to Agents, 17 April 1755, PRO, WO 4/50, p. 245; Barrington to Calcraft, 17 August 1756, PRO, WO 4/52, p. 175; Barrington to George Ross, 16 August 1757, PRO, WO 4/54, p. 306.

117. R. C. Jarvis, 'Army Transport and the English Constitution: With Special Reference to the Jacobite Risings', *Journal of Transport History*, 2:2 (1955–6), pp. 101–20.

118. Ibid., pp. 111–12.

119. Marlborough is credited with introducing contracts instead of 'sporadic hiring and impressment' (Scouller, *Queen Anne*, p. 203); Morgan, 'Impact of War', p. 37; Little, 'Commissariat', p. 19; Articles of War (1718–49), PRO, WO 72/2; Scouller, *Queen*

Anne, p. 206. The 1756 Mutiny Act did not permit billets in public houses for foreign troops. This required an Act of Parliament (30 Geo. II c.2) (C. M. Clode, *The Military Forces of the Crown: Their Administration and Government*, 2 vols (London: John Murray, 1869), vol. 1, p. 238; W. Y. Baldry, 'Notes on the Early History of Billeting', *JSAHR*, 13:50 (1934), pp. 71–3; p. 73.
120. C. Winslow, 'Sussex Smugglers' in D. Hay, P. Linebaugh, J. G. Rule, E. P. Thompson, and C. Winslow (eds), *Albion's Fatal Tree: Crime and Society in Eighteenth-Century England* (New York: Pantheon, 1975), pp. 119–66.
121. Impressment warrants: 26 July 1759, PRO, WO 26/24, f. 25; 1 February 1760, PRO, WO 26/24, f. 110; 16 October 1760, PRO, WO 26/24, f. 259; a transport corps was not established until 1784 (Jarvis, 'Army Transport', p. 101).
122. H. G. de Watteville, *The British Soldier* (London: J. M. Dent & Sons, 1954), p. 57.
123. 'This is intended to increase the number of lodging-houses for the soldiery, who are now more numerous than ever in England', 30 April 1757, *GM*, 27 (1757), p. 187. Freemen of the Vintners Company admitted before 1757 were exempt (Francis Grose, *Military Antiquities Respecting a History of the English Army, from the Conquest to the Present Time*, 2 vols (London: S. Hooper, 1786–8), vol. 2, p. 175).
124. 10 February 1757, *HCJ*, 27, p. 75; Barrington to Mayor of Southampton, 22 June 1756, PRO, WO 4/52, p. 73; Memorial of Mayor of Winchester, 24 July 1759, Public Record Office, London, State papers [hereafter PRO, SP] PRO, SP 41/23, f. 118; Peter Burrell to Barrington, 23 July 1759, PRO, WO 4/58, p. 289. Pitt threatened publicans with revocation of licences if they closed their public houses (Pitt to Mayor of Winchester, 25 July 1759, PRO, SP 41/23, f. 180).
125. J. R. Western, *The English Militia in the Eighteenth Century: The Story of a Political Issue, 1660–1802* (London: Routledge & Kegan Paul, 1965), pp. 381–2.
126. Jarvis, 'Army Transport', p. 102.
127. 'War was the motor behind the rapid growth of public spending during the long eighteenth century' (P. Harling and P. Mandler, 'From "Fiscal-Military" State to Laissez-Faire State, 1760–1850', *Journal of British Studies*, 32:1 (1993), pp. 44–70; p. 49).
128. Childs, *Armies and Warfare*, p. 175.
129. N. A. Brisco, *The Economic Policy of Robert Walpole* (New York: Columbia University Press, 1907), pp. 78–9, 84–5. During the Seven Years' War the land tax was 4*s*. in the pound (W. R. Ward, *The English Land Tax in the Eighteenth Century* (London: Oxford University Press, 1953), pp. 75–6).
130. Percentages calculated from B. R. Mitchell, *British Historical Statistics* (Cambridge: Cambridge University Press, 1988), pp. 575–7.
131. Brewer, *Sinews of Power*, p. 119.
132. E. Hughes, *Studies in Administration and Finance 1558–1825: With Special Reference to the History of Salt Taxation in England* (Manchester: Manchester University Press, 1934), pp. 154–5; Brewer, *Sinews of Power*, p. 126.
133. Calculated from 'History of the Early Years of the Funded Debt from 1694–1786', *PP* (1898), lii.269 [Cm. 9010], pp. 24–8; cf. £51,500,000 for loans 1756–63, see Baker, *Government and Contractors*, pp. 225–7.
134. Browning, 'Financing Seven Years War', p. 348; Harling and Mandler, 'From "Fiscal-Military" State', pp. 47–8.
135. H. Walpole, *The Yale Edition of Horace Walpole's Correspondence*, ed. H. Lewis, 34 vols (New Haven, CT: Yale University Press, 1937–83), vol. 21, p. 549 (entry for 16 November 1761).

136. Anon to [Robert Harley?], 10 March 1701/2, HMC, *Portland MSS., V: Harley Papers*, III (London: HMSO, 1899), vol. 8 (1907), p. 96; cf. 'fattened ... on the blood of the nation', T. Smollett, *The Expedition of Humphry Clinker* (1771), ed. L. M. Knapp, rev. P. Gabriel-Boucé (Oxford: Oxford University Press, 1984) p. 36; S. Conway, *The War of American Independence 1775–1783* (London: Edward Arnold, 1995), pp. 195–6.

137. Despite accepting the 'money-mongers must be kept a little in temper', Legge suggested to Newcastle the exclusion of the 'Gallo-Batavian', financier Joshua Van Neck, as he cared nothing for the country except its money (15 July 1758, BL, Add. MS 32881, ff. 327–8). Newcastle replied 'I neither love the Man, nor His Practices; but We must consider our Situation. We shall want immense sums of Money, next Year; We may even be put to difficulties as to the taxes to raise them upon' (15 July 1758, ibid., ff. 321–2).

138. Brewer, *Sinews of Power*, p. 143; for persistent opponents, see J. Hoppit, 'Attitudes to Credit in Britain, 1680–1790', *Historical Journal*, 33:2 (1990), pp. 305–222; p. 320.

139. P. O'Brien, 'The Political Economy of British Taxation, 1660–1815', *Economic History Review*, 41:1 (1998), pp. 1–32.

140. D. A. Baugh, 'Maritime Strength and Atlantic Commerce: The Uses of a "Grand Marine Empire"', in Stone (ed.), *Imperial State*, pp. 185–223; p. 190.

141. Guy, *Oeconomy and Discipline*, pp. 39–42; in 1815, thirteen offices were concerned with some aspect of military administration; six remained in 1854 (Gordon, *War Office*, pp. 32–3).

142. Little, 'Commissariat', p. 28.

143. Parker, *Military Revolution*, p. 147; Corvisier, *Armies and Societies*, pp. 74–5.

144. Fortescue, *Royal Army Service Corps*, vol. 1, pp. 20–1.

145. J. Hoppit's review of Brewer pointed to this analytical shift, *Historical Journal*, 33:1 (1990), pp. 248–50.

146. Newcastle to Hardwicke, 15 December 1759: 'The very Principles of Government, and Liberty, are changed These last Three Years. All parts of this Kingdom are, or seem To be, for a Military Standing Force; When, formerly, That was The Point The most dreaded' (BL, Add. MS 32900, ff. 88–9); J. Douglas, *A Letter Addressed to Two Great Men, on the Prospect of Peace; And on the Terms Necessary to be Insisted upon in the Negociation*, 2nd edn (London: A. Millar, 1760), pp. 45–6.

2 The Growth of Army Contracting

1. Childs, *Army of William III*, p. 230; Scouller, *Queen Anne*, pp. 25–7, 222–5.

2. G. Granville to Lord High Treasurer, 15 November 1711, *CTP* (1708–14), p. 330; Admiralty to Earl of Dartmouth, 13 December 1711, PRO, T 1/140, f. 112.

3. Treasury to Victualling Commissioners, 25 April 1712, PRO, T 27/20, p. 177; 30 April 1712, ibid, p. 180; Victualling Commissioners to Taylour, 3 May 1712, *CTP* (1708–14), p. 385.

4. 4 and 7 October 1712, *CTP* (1708–14), p. 430; Treasury to Commissioners for Inspecting the Affairs of War in Spain and Portugal, 24 April 1713, PRO, T 27/20, p. 408; 30 March 1714, PRO, T 29/20, p. 193.

5. Victualling Board to Lord High Treasurer, 2 December 1713, PRO, Adm. 110/6, p. 237; 19 January 1715, PRO, Adm. 110/7, pp. 11–12.

6. Victualling Office [hereafter VO] to Treasury, 18 January 1715, PRO, Adm. 110/7, p. 9; 9 February 1715, *CTB* (1714–15), p. 251; 11 February 1715, ibid., pp. 18–20; 9 January 1716, ibid., p. 412; cf. 5 March 1741, PRO, T 29/28, pp. 296–7.

7. 'Observations on the Importance of Gibraltar and Minorca; written in the Year 1748', *GM*, 27 (1757), pp. 105–9; 'Abstract of the 10th Article of Peace between Britain & Spain in which cession of Gibraltar formally made', *GM*, 18 (1748), p. 379; for Spanish refusal to sell fresh provisions, *London Evening Post*, 11–13 May 1758.
8. 4 October 1712, *CTP* (1708–14), p. 430; 5 February 1713, ibid, p. 463; 12 December 1712, Portland Loan, BL, Add. MS 70171, ff. 44–135; proposals for Gibraltar and Minorca, 3 October 1713: 'The forces in both these Places being at this time in very great straits for Provisions', ibid., ff. 44–161.
9. Henry Neale to Lord High Treasurer, 15 July 1714, *CTP* (1708–14), pp. 607–8.
10. 'State of the several subsisting contracts' (1764), Liverpool papers, BL, Add. MS 38338, ff. 109–11.
11. 13 April 1713, PRO, T 29/20, p. 72; Victualling Board to Treasury, 6 May 1713, PRO, Adm. 110/6, p. 104; 14 May 1713, ibid., p. 144; VO to Treasury and Secretary at War, 18 March 1715, PRO, Adm. 110/7, pp. 74–5.
12. VO to Admiralty, 20 August 1715, PRO, Adm. 110/7, pp. 157–8; VO to Treasury, 21 December 1715, ibid, pp. 209–10; VO to Navy Treasurer, 13 December 1716, ibid., p. 348; Comptrollers to Treasury, 21 June 1718, PRO, Adm. 110/8, pp. 76–7.
13. 10 May 1715, *Journals of the Commissioners for Trade and Plantations* [hereafter *JCTP*], (1714/15–1718), pp. 5–6; 12 May 1715, ibid., p. 26; 22 February 1716, ibid., p. 115.
14. VO to Stanhope, 30 July 1718, PRO, Adm. 110/8, pp. 77–9; VO to Admiralty, 31 July 1718, ibid, pp. 79–80; VO to Comptrollers, 13 April 1720, ibid, p. 283.
15. VO to Treasury, 7 September 1719, PRO, Adm. 110/8, p. 220; September 1737, AO 1/187, f. 575.
16. Newcastle to Blakeney, 5 April 1740, PRO, SP 41/12; Newcastle to Spotiswood, 5 April 1740, BL, Add. MS 32693, ff. 134–9; Newcastle to Vernon, 18 April 1740, ibid., ff. 217–22; Vernon to Sir Charles Wager, 26–31 May 1740, B. McL. Ranft, *The Vernon Papers* (London: Navy Records Society, 1958), p. 101.
17. Georgia and Rattan: Treasury to Victualling Board, 19 May 1742, PRO, T27/26, p. 43; 26 April 1744, ibid., p. 132; Treasury to Secretary at War, 8 February 1744, ibid., p. 122; the Victualling Office was directed to send provisions to Jersey in case of siege, Treasury to Huske, 19 July 1756, PRO, T 27/27, p. 216; Belleisle: Treasury to Victualling Commissioners, 26 January 1762, PRO, T 27/28, p. 45; 16 February 1762, ibid., p. 252; 10 June 1762, ibid., pp. 295–6.
18. Articles of Agreement, 22 September 1737, BL, Add. MS 33028, ff. 350–2; exemption warrants, 4 December 1740, *CTBP* (1739–41), p. 285; 17 December 1740, ibid., p. 357.
19. Report from the Committee appointed to consider The State of His Majesty's Land Forces and Marines, 6 June 1746, *House of Commons Committee Reports 1715–1803* (16 vols, 1803-6), vol. 2, pp. 73–112; p. 99.
20. 15 January 1746, *HCJ*, 25, p. 29; 'Expense of the Army 1760', BL, Add. MS 33047, ff. 375–7.
21. Comptrollers Reports on Victualling lists, April 1734–March 1735: 12 August 1734, PRO, AO 17/35, pp. 33–4; 10 September 1734, ibid., pp. 43–4; 28 October 1734, ibid., pp. 45–7; 18 December 1734, ibid., pp. 48–50; 20 February 1735, ibid., p. 52; 15 April 1735, ibid., p. 57; 3 May 1735, ibid., p. 59; 19 May 1735, ibid., p. 66; 9 July 1735, ibid., p. 70; Calculated from warrants, *CTBP* (1735–8), pp. 104, 110–12, 125, 127, 134, 139.
22. 24 January 1732, *HCJ*, 21, p. 777; 3 February 1741, *HCJ*, 23, p. 627.

23. During 1739–48, the largest number of troops in the 'Plantations, Minorca & Gibraltar' was 15,027 between 1746–8, BL, Add. MS 33047, f. 137.
24. 11 February 1746, PRO, T 54/34, pp. 368–72; Treasury to Baker, 18 April 1746, T 27/26, p. 221; Memorial, 18 September 1746, PRO, T 1/321, f. 76.
25. 9 October 1733, PRO, T 29/27, p. 220; 5 February 1734, PRO, AO 17/35, p. 533; 12, 22 and 30 March 1743, *CTBP* (1742–5), pp. 248, 253, 258; 12 July 1748, PRO, AO 1/189, f. 585; Rattan: 17 April 1744, PRO, T 29/30, p. 10; Treasury to Townsend, 25 March 1746, PRO, T 27/26, p. 216; Nova Scotia: 23 October 1744, PRO, T 54/34, pp. 272–4.
26. Order of Council, 2 February 1744, PRO, T 1/313, ff. 13–16; Articles of Agreement, 17 April 1744, PRO, T 54/34, pp. 227–8; the colony failed, and was returned to Spain in 1748 (R. Pares, *War and Trade in the West Indies 1739–1763* (Oxford: Clarendon Press, 1936), p. 104).
27. Treasury to Secretary at War, 18 December 1747, PRO, T 27/26, p. 326.
28. 11 August 1747, PRO, T 29/31, p. 47.
29. Morgan, 'Impact of War', p. 356.
30. 1 July 1764, Liverpool papers, BL, Add. MS 38304, f. 31.
31. The Low Countries incorporated seven provinces of the Dutch Republic, various districts of the Austrian Netherlands and parts of northern France (M. S. Anderson, *The War of the Austrian Succession* (London: Longmans, 1995), p. 14).
32. Jones, *War and Economy*, pp. 28–43.
33. Ibid., pp. 36, 191; 31 January 1712, PRO, AO 17/1, p. 77; 31 July 1742, PRO, T 54/34, pp. 79–83; 19 January 1748, PRO, T 54/35, pp. 1–6; Treasury to Wade, 16 February 1743, PRO, T 27/26, p. 123.
34. 1 July 1741, PRO, T 29/28, pp. 342–6; contracts: 31 January 1743, PRO, T 54/34, pp. 206–7; 6 March 1743, ibid., pp. 208–14; 19 February 1745, PRO, T 29/30, p. 124; 3 June 1746, ibid., p. 288; Lord Carteret reminded Stair of this: 8 April 1743, PRO, SP 87/12, ff. 8–10; 9 January 1711, PRO, T 29/18, pp. 124–5; Memorial of Honywood, n.d., minuted 3 June 1741, PRO, T 1/305, f. 114; 28 July 1742, *CTBP* (1742–5), p. 60.
35. Revision of 'Ammunition' bread contract, *CTBP* (1742–5), pp. 44, 61–2, 68–9, 89, 262, 519; forage contract in Ligonier to Chesterfield, 25 November 1746, PRO, SP 87/21, ff. 200–1; Carpentier's contract in Ligonier to Treasury, 12 February 1745, PRO, T 1/316, f. 14; 'Memorandums for Lord Rothes', n.d., [*c.* April 1746], PRO, SP 87/20, ff. 141–2.
36. West to Boyd, 11 March 1758, PRO, T 1/384, f. 38; West to Hatton, 20 September 1758, PRO, T 1/385, f. 100; Treasury instructions [extract] in Hunter to Oswald, 14 February 1759, PRO, T 1/397, f. 173.
37. Hatton to Samuel Martin, 21 August 1758, PRO, T 1/384, f. 51; Marlborough to Newcastle, 29 August 1758, BL, Add. MS 32883, f. 154; Newcastle to Boyd, 27 October 1758, PRO, T 1/385, f. 111; Hume to Treasury, 23 October 1758, PRO, T 1/384, f. 63; Treasury to Marlborough, 26 October 1758, PRO, T 1/385, f. 108.
38. Governors and commanding officers abroad were instructed that any bills drawn on the Treasury or Paymaster must specify usage and necessity for the sum drawn, Hardinge to Tyrawley, 7 June 1756, PRO, T 27/27, p. 217; Treasury to Governors, 15 April 1761, PRO, T 27/28, p. 152.
39. Articles of Agreement, 31 July 1742, PRO, T 54/34, pp. 79–83; 6 March 1743, ibid., pp. 208–14; 5 February 1745, PRO, T 29/30, p. 118; 19 February 1745, ibid., p. 124; 13 May 1746, ibid, p. 282; 3 June 1746, ibid, p. 288; cf. contract with Francis Lopes Suasso on behalf of Abraham Prado, 19 January 1748, PRO, T 54/35, pp. 1–6; at Carpentier's

death, the respective Attorneys negotiated transfer of the contract, Treasury to Paymaster, 16 February 1748, PRO, T 27/26, p. 337.
40. 7 June 1746, PRO, SP 87/20, ff. 149–51.
41. Rothes to Harrington, 17 June 1746, ibid., f. 167.
42. Stair to Carteret, 12 April 1743, PRO, SP 87/12, ff. 11–16.
43. 21 August 1742, West papers (Treasury), BL, Add. MS 34736, ff. 23–6; 31 July 1742, PRO, T 54/37, p. 79; 19 August 1742, ibid, p. 87.
44. J. G. Parker, 'The Directors of the East India Company 1754–1790' (Phd dissertation, University of Edinburgh, 1977), pp. 73, 408; in lodgings 1738–49: *Intelligencer, or Merchant's Assistant*, 3 (1738), p. 113; *Compleat Guide*, 7 (1744), p.121; *Compleat Guide*, 9 (1749), p. 159.
45. Ligonier to 'My Lord', 23 December 1746, PRO, SP 87/21, ff. 216–17; I. Pauchard to Fawkener, 10 February 1747, Duke of Cumberland papers, Royal Archive, Windsor, Box 20, f. 208 [hereafter RA Cumberland].
46. Barrington papers, BL, Add. MS 73654, f. 6.
47. 27–29 July 1742, *CTBP* (1742–5), pp. 59–61; 30 July 1742, ibid, p. 62.
48. Yonge to Stair, 13 August 1742, PRO, WO 4/37, pp. 358–9.
49. Black, *Military Power*, p. 62.
50. 'List of General Officers & their First Commission', 6 December 1742, *HCJ*, 24, pp. 352–3.
51. Bland to Carteret, 27 April 1742, PRO, SP 87/8, ff. 82–3; Carteret to Stair, 4 May 1742, ibid., ff. 106–10; Bland to Carteret, 5 May 1742, ibid., ff. 120–1; Bland to Stair, 13 May 1742, ibid., ff. 184–5; *Ipswich Journal*, 15 May 1742.
52. The contractor at Ghent wished to terminate his contract. Stair to Carteret, 14 November 1742, PRO, SP 87/10, ff. 173–5; 20 December 1742, Carteret papers, BL, Add. MS 22537, ff. 105–8.
53. Carteret to Stair, 11 Mar. 1743, Carteret papers, BL, Add. MS 22537, ff. 174–80; Ligonier to Carteret, 3 September 1744, Carteret papers, BL, Add. MS 22358, f. 279; Harcourt to Newcastle, 30 June 1743, BL, Add. MS 32700, ff. 225–6; J. M. Graham, *Annals and Correspondence of the Viscount and the First and Second Earls of Stair*, 2 vols (Edinburgh and London: Blackwood, 1875), vol. 2, pp. 290–1.
54. 11 June 1743, PRO, SP 41/14; Carteret to Newcastle, 23 June 1743, BL, Add. MS 32700, ff. 201–3; W. Coxe, *Memoirs of the Administration of the Right Honourable Henry Pelham*, 2 vols (London: Longman, Rees, Orme, Brown and Green, 1829), vol. 1, p. 66.
55. Loudoun to Newcastle, 11 July 1743, BL, Add. MS 32700, ff. 268–70; Newcastle to Walpole, 22 July 1743, ibid., ff. 314–18.
56. Robert Hay Drummond to Newcastle, 20 August 1743, BL, Add. MS 32701, f. 3.
57. Drummond to Andrew Stone, 22 August 1743, ibid., f. 9.
58. Honywood to Carteret, 1 April 1742, PRO, SP 87/8, f. 26.
59. Alexander Hume to Carteret, 9 August 1742, Carteret papers, BL, Add. MS 22542, f. 218; Coxe, *Pelham*, vol. 1, p. 62.
60. Newcastle to Hardwicke, 24 October 1743, BL, Add. MS 32701, ff. 202–17; J. B. Owen, *The Rise of the Pelhams* (London: Methuen & Co., 1958), p. 137.
61. Hardwicke to Joseph Yorke, 10 October 1742, 'we understand very well *sacks to forage corn in* to be a kind of thieving utensil legitimated by the practice of war' (*The Life and Correspondence of Philip Yorke, Earl of Hardwicke, Lord High Chancellor of Great Britain*, ed. P. C. Yorke, 3 vols (Cambridge: Cambridge University Press, 1913), vol. 1, p. 308).

62. 2 May 1745, *CTBP* (1742–5), p. 687; 5 February 1745, PRO, T 29/30, pp. 118–26; 6 March 1743, PRO, T 54/34, pp. 208–14.
63. 13 March 1744, *HCJ*, 24, p. 614; MS Yorke Journal, 19 March and 10 April 1744, Hansard, *PD*, vol. 13, cc. 675–83, 698–702; Bath to Newcastle, 4 October 1742, doubted Parliament would accept the expenditure incurred, BL, Add. MS 32699, ff. 432–3.
64. Carteret to Wade, 26 June 1744, Carteret papers, BL, Add. MS 22538, ff. 171–3, Arch Dutchess Governess to George II, 15 July 1744, ibid., ff. 211–13; Joseph Yorke to Hardwicke, 14 July 1744, Hardwicke papers, BL, Add. MS 35354, ff. 60–2; 25 July 1744, ibid., ff. 64–5; 'Orders in relation to the whole Army's foraging', (1747), RA Cumberland, Box 20, f. 14; Cumberland to Chesterfield, 30 May 1747, PRO, SP 87/21, ff. 280–2.
65. 'Minutes relating to Magazines', 25 January 1744, Carteret papers, BL, Add. MS 22538, ff. 9–10.
66. Carteret to Honywood, 31 January 1744, ibid., f. 21.
67. Pelham considered 1,300,000 rations sufficient for British and Hanoverian troops, but was refuted by Ligonier and Hawley who considered this sufficient for only one fixed magazine. Pelham's enclosure in Harrington to Cumberland, 19 April 1745, RA Cumberland, Box 2, f. 105; Hawley & Ligonier to Cumberland, n.d., received 23 April 1745, RA Cumberland, Box 2, f. 155.
68. Ligonier to 'My Lord', 13 August 1746, PRO, SP 87/21, ff. 1–2.
69. 19 August 1742, PRO, T 54/34, pp. 79–83; Stair to Carteret, 20 December 1742, Carteret papers, BL, Add. MS 22537, ff. 109–10.
70. Dunmore to Harrington, 3 January 1746, PRO, SP 87/20, ff. 1–2; Rothes to Harrington, 7 June 1746, ibid., ff. 149–51; 1 July 1746, ibid., ff. 193–4; 3 June 1746, PRO, T 29/30, p. 288.
71. 'Observations', August 1742, Carteret papers, BL, Add. MS 22537, f. 12; cf. 210 loaves per wagon, *Journal of Corporal William Todd*, p. 310 n. 178 (entry for 2 November 1761).
72. Fortescue, *History*, vol. 2, pp. 92, 156–7; Cumberland to Chesterfield, 28 April 1747, PRO, SP 87/22; 5 May 1747, RA Cumberland, Box 21, f. 375; Hume to Fawkener, 8 May 1747, RA Cumberland, Box 21, f. 418.
73. 15 December 1747, PRO, T 29/31, p. 71; 482 wagons were provided in 1747, 12 September 1747, RA Cumberland, Box 27, f. 41.
74. Hume to Fawkener, 9 November 1747, RA Cumberland, Box 29, f. 183; protesting against the war's expense, the *Craftsman* noted the cost of wagons (6 and 13 August 1748, *GM*, 18 (1748), p. 369).
75. 'The Remembrancer', 22 July 1749, *GM*, 19 (1749), p. 322.
76. Hume to Fawkener, 29 August 1747, RA Cumberland, Box 26, f. 376; Dundas to Fawkener, 6 August 1748, ibid. Box 38, f. 15.
77. 8 November 1747, RA Cumberland, Box 29, f. 165; towards the end of the war Cumberland relied on Hume and Huske to assess proposals, Fawkener to Huske and Hume, 17 November 1747, ibid. Box 30, f. 22; Huske and Hume to Fawkener, 3 November 1747, ibid. Box 29, f. 259; 28 November 1747, ibid. Box 30, f. 10.
78. Lawrence Dundas to Fawkener, 4 February 1749, RA Cumberland, Box 43, f. 86.
79. Colonel Madan to Fawkener, 19 October 1745, RA Cumberland, Box 6, f. 79; Quarter Master's Accounts, 24 June 1747, ibid. Box 23, f. 483; A. N. Campbell-Maclachlan, *William Augustus Duke of Cumberland* (London: Henry S. King, 1876), pp. 67–9, 75–6.

80. Carteret to Stair, 11 May 1742, PRO, SP 87/8, ff. 136–7; Appointments: 20 August 1743, PRO, SP 41/14; 20 September 1743, *CTBP* (1742–5), p. 421; Yonge to Carteret, 8 March 1744, PRO, SP 41/15, f. 107; 13 March 1744, *HCJ*, 24, p. 614.
81. Dundas to Fawkener, 21 January 1749, RA Cumberland, Box 43, f. 39; Auditor's Report, 11 January 1758, PRO, T 1/383, f. 8; Hume to Barrington [Copy], 17 January 1759, PRO, T 1/451, ff. 198–200.
82. Hume to Fawkener, 25 March 1748, RA Cumberland, Box 33, f. 72; Fawkener to Dundas, 21 April 1748, ibid., f. 380; Dundas to Fawkener, 17 May 1748, RA Cumberland, Box 35, f. 81.
83. 'A Scheme for the more readily knowing the State of the Magasins of Forrage', 12 January 1747, RA Cumberland, Box 20, f. 89.
84. Staff 1740 and 1749 (1749), Chatham papers, PRO 30/8/75, ff. 131, 135.
85. Stair to Carteret, 1 September 1742, PRO, SP 87/10, f. 17; Dunmore to Harrington, 10 February 1746, PRO, SP 87/20, ff. 85–6; Hume to Fawkener, 12 March 1746, RA Cumberland, Box 12, f. 79; Anderson, *Austrian Succession*, p. 44.
86. Pelham to Newcastle, 29 July 1748, BL, Add. MS 32715, f. 478.
87. Treasury to Baker and Townsend, 12 December 1748, PRO, T 27/26, p. 388; Treasury to Lords of Trade, 12 December 1750, ibid., f. 480; 31 January 1750/1, ibid., f. 483; 13 January 1752, *HCJ*, 26, p. 347.
88. 19 November 1751, PRO, T 1/345, ff. 26–7.
89. Vernon to Victualling Board, 4 October 1740, Ranft (ed.), *Vernon Papers*, p. 361.
90. Fox to Albemarle, 17 February 1747, PRO, WO 4/43, p. 115.
91. Lord George Beauclerk to Barrington, 7 July 1759, PRO, WO 1/614, f. 141.
92. Little, 'Commissariat', p. 103.
93. 'Superintendent of Forage', supervising forage contracts, noted as entirely new in the British army, Martin to Hatton, 29 April 1760, BL, Add. MS 32905, ff. 157–8.
94. 26 March 1756, PRO, WO 34/69, f. 86; Kilby to Captain Christie, 3 September 1758, ibid., ff. 81–2.
95. West to Baker, 27 December 1758, PRO, T 27/27, p. 412; 'Memos for the King', 14 January 1760, BL, Add. MS 32901, ff. 226–7; Amherst to Kilby, 24 March 1760, PRO, WO 34/69, f. 127.
96. 20 December 1759, PRO, T 54/37, pp. 123–8; 27 February 1760, ibid., ff. 379–81.
97. 'Charge of the War 1755–1761', BL, Add. MS 33048, f. 174.
98. Warrant, 22 February 1757: PRO, T 1/375, f. 23; Articles of Agreement, 27 April 1757, ibid., f. 32; 3 February 1758, PRO, T 1/386, f. 3; Council meeting, 8 September 1757, BL, Add. MS 32874, f. 42.
99. Hatton to Newcastle, 9 September 1758, PRO, T 1/384, f. 55; Hume was the obvious candidate, but pleading a leg injury refused to go, West to Newcastle, 20 October 1758, BL, Add. MS 32884, f. 455; he was requested to offer advice on supply methods and prices, West to Hume, 23 October 1758, PRO, T1/386, f. 72; Newcastle to Hardwicke, 1 May 1760, BL, Add. MS 32905, f. 197.
100. 28 June 1758, BL, Add. MS 33047, f. 164; *LG*, 11–15 July 1758.
101. Details of sub-contracting for horse and wagon accoutrements in letters to Abraham Prado, Letter Book of David Mendes de Costa, 1757–9: 30 August 1758, BL Egerton MS 2227, f. 71; 11 September 1758, ibid., ff. 73–4.
102. Dundas to Archibald Fraser, 14 June 1759, Sir Lawrence Dundas papers, Zetland Archive, North Yorkshire County Record Office [hereafter ZA], ZNK X1/1/159, f. 86; 'Mr. Commissary Faber has ordered the add[itiona]l Field Ovens; Mr Dundas is build-

ing the 33 Waggons which they require to transport them', Hatton to Martin, 9 April 1760, PRO, T 64/96, p. 326.
103. 'Account of British Forces 1742–1748', BL, Add. MS 33047, f. 137; Hunter to Treasury, 25 March 1759, PRO, T 64/96, pp. 77–80; Hunter to Martin, 29 April 1759, ibid, pp. 100–2; Newcastle to Granby, 12 May 1760, HMC, *Rutland*, 3 vols (London: HMSO, 1888–94), vol. 2, p. 211.
104. Barrington papers, BL, Add. MS 73654, ff. 2–9; the 1761 total (£5,784,807) was even higher, 'Charge of the War in Germany' (1764), BL, Add. MS 33048, f. 331;'A Million is a Trifle now', Newcastle to Mansfield, 22 August 1761, BL, Add. MS 32927, ff. 173–4.
105. West to Newcastle, 12 May 1762, citing Pitt: 'It was the nature of the war [that] has caused the Expence', BL, Add. MS 32938, ff. 185–8; Granby's argument, 11 February 1763, on Sir John Philips's motion for a Committee of Public Accounts into Treasury supervision of wartime expenditure, Barrington to Newcastle, 7 February 1763, BL, Add. MS 32946, f. 351, Barrington to Philips, 9 February 1763, ibid., f. 365, West's report, 11 February 1763, ibid., ff. 381–4.
106. Little, 'Commissariat', pp. 144–5, 220.
107. 13 May 1762, Hansard, *PD*, vol. 15, c. 1222; cf. Hardwicke to Newcastle, 26 January 1761, considered Granby 'ignorant of every thing relating to Contracts, Oeconomy, & Accounts', BL, Add. MS 32918, ff. 70–1.
108. Newcastle to Yorke, 29 May 1760, BL, Add. MS 32906, f. 353; Newcastle to Barrington, 27 December 1761, BL, Add. MS 32932, f. 377.
109. 'Expense of the War in Germany', PRO, T 1/425, f. 89.
110. 'Memos for the King', 15 August 1760, BL, Add. MS 32910, f. 46.
111. 9 September 1760, BL, Add. MS 32911, ff. 263–4; 'Memos for the King', 8 October 1760, BL, Add. MS 32912, f. 458.
112. Nine remittance contractors subscribed £1.2 million of the £1.8 million loan of 1744 (*GM*, 14 (1744), p. 225); of twenty-two subscribers to the £8 million loan of 1759, £3 million was supplied by seven remittance contractors (Brewer, *Sinews of Power*, p. 208).
113. George Amyand's list amounted to £924,000, January 1760, BL, Add. MS 32900, ff. 242–3; Namier, *Structure of Politics*, p. 54 n. 3.
114. Lawrence Dundas was on Sir George Colebrooke's list, Dundas to Mr Lesingham, 31 October 1761, Letter Book of Lawrence Dundas, NLS, Acc. 8425, f. 89; Dundas to Colebrooke, 12 November 1760, ZA, ZNK X1/1/160, ff. 206–7; Dundas to Sir James Colebrooke, 5 December 1760, ibid, f. 219; Bank books 1759–64, ZA, ZNK X1/12/1.
115. Calculated from 1757 Loan: PRO, E 401/2598; 1760: BL, Add. MS 32901, f. 238; Namier, *Structure of Politics*, p. 55; 1761: BL, Add. MS 33040, f. 79; 1762: BL, Add. MS 32931, ff. 383–4.
116. 'The State of Great Britain at the end of 1762', BL, Add. MS 33040, ff. 399–400; cf. 'Funded Debt' *PP* (1898), lii [Cm. 9010], pp. 27–9.
117. Newcastle to MG Yorke, 7 December 1759, BL, Add. MS 32899, f. 355.
118. Newcastle to Mansfield, 22 August 1759, BL, Add. MS 32894, ff. 366–71; 'Memos for the King', 4 September 1759, BL, Add. MS 32895, f. 155.
119. Newcastle to Hardwicke, 18 October 1760, BL, Add. MS 32913, f. 187; the 'open' loan of 1757 failed, Sedgwick, *Commons*, vol. 1, p. 437.
120. West to Newcastle, 11 May 1760, BL, Add. MS 32906, ff. 10–11.
121. 'State of Payments', n.d., [*c*. 1760], BL, Add. MS 33039, ff. 382–5.
122. 26 November 1759, ibid., f. 297; 29 January 1760, ibid., f. 360.

123. 'State of Charge on Supplies', 17 April 1762, BL, Add. MS 33040, f. 322; Newcastle to Barrington, 5 August 1762, BL, Add. MS 32941, ff. 160–1.
124. As the Treasury owed him £130,000, Dundas informed Arnold Nesbitt that he could not assist with remittances, 8 July 1762, Dundas Letter Book, NLS, Acc. 8425, f. 180.
125. As the Trade and Plantations Commissioners did not have a map of Nova Scotia, the King's Brewer at Portsmouth was requested to lend them his, 4 June 1719, *JCTP* (1718–22), p. 72.
126. Thomas Missing to Treasury, 3 October 1715, *CTB* (1714–19), pp. 144–5.
127. R. B. Westerfield, *Middlemen in English Business* (New Haven, CT: Yale University Press, 1915), p. 202.
128. The Victualling Office supplied Gibraltar between March–June 1715, 17 February 1715, PRO, Adm. 110/7, p. 21.
129. VO to Treasury, 15 June 1715, with enclosure detailing commissary's mismanagement, PRO, Adm. 110/7, pp. 123–4; 30 August 1715, excusing late delivery by contrary winds, as the Victualling Office ship was similarly delayed, ibid, pp. 163–4; James Craggs junior to Treasury, 30 August 1717, *CTB* (1714–19), p. 318; Missing to Treasury, 4 October 1717, ibid, p. 322.
130. Treasury proposal for reducing advance payments, [misdated 20 December 1725: after 1727], *CTP* (1720–8), p. 372.
131. Two provisions ships were lost in 1720, 26 October 1721, *HCJ*, 29, p. 656.
132. Martin to Governor of Louisbourg, 19 October 1758, PRO, T 27/27, p. 390; Martin to Governor Whitmore (Quebec), 15 April 1761, PRO, T 27/28, p. 151.
133. Governor Lawrence to Treasury, 20 April 1759, PRO, T 1/396, f. 163.
134. Auditors Report, 4 February 1742, PRO, T 54/34, pp. 109–10.
135. Missing to Scrope, 15 May 1717, *CTB* (1714–19), p. 295; September 1735, PRO, AO 1/183, f. 558.
136. 29 June 1731, PRO, T 29/27, p. 40; 4 January 1732, ibid, p. 179; 13 March 1734, ibid, p. 308; 8 July 1735, ibid, p. 338; 1 April 1733, *CTBP* (1731–4), p. 373; 2 January 1734, ibid., p. 527; work commenced five years after initial complaints, 21 September 1736, PRO, T 29/27, p. 406.
137. Revell to Yonge, 24 April 1741, PRO, T 1/305, f. 89; Treasury to Governor, 4 June 1741, PRO, T 27/26, p. 3; affidavit, 23 April 1747, PRO, AO 17/38, p. 134; Engineers Report, 26 July 1744, ibid., p. 144; Comptrollers Report, 15 July 1747, ibid., pp. 158–9.
138. Compensation for damage by inadequate storage, 29 May 1754, PRO, T 29/32, p. 201.
139. 7 May 1747, PRO, T 29/31, p. 10; 6 August 1747, ibid., p. 37; Treasury to Ordnance, 7 August 1747, PRO, T 27/26, p. 298.
140. 9 April 1747, PRO, T 29/31, p. 1; Treasury to Baker, 9 April 1747, PRO, T 27/26, p. 283; Treasury to Corbet, 8 May 1747, ibid., p. 289.
141. Treasury to Townsend, 14 July 1748, PRO, T 27/26, p. 363; Treasury to Ordnance, 18 October 1748, ibid, pp. 375–6; the Mediterranean Fleet supplied Minorca with beef when the contractor failed to deliver, Treasury to Burchett (Adm.), 11 April 1740, PRO, T 27/25, p. 533.
142. 24 November 1741, PRO, T 29/28, p. 385.
143. H. W. Richmond, *The Navy in the War of 1739–1748*, 3 vols (Cambridge: Cambridge University Press, 1920), vol. 1, pp. 83–90.
144. Treasury to Comptrollers, 8 March 1747, PRO, AO 17/38, p. 309; Master's Affidavit, 23 January 1747, ibid., p. 310; 12 July 1748, PRO, AO 1/189, f. 585.

145. In 1745, the young John Calcraft was employed as Deputy Paymaster collecting revenue from northern counties of England and distributing pay to Cumberland's army, PRO, T 52/45, p. 42; Calcraft to Henry Fox, 16 December 1745, Holland House papers, BL, Add. MS 51398, f. 5; Chatham papers, PRO 30/8/75, f. 69; Guy, *Oeconomy and Discipline*, p. 58.
146. 29 January 1741, PRO, T 29/28, p. 289; Burrell and Bristow to Treasury, 10 February 1741, PRO, T 1/305, f. 37; 5 June 1741, PRO, T 29/28, p. 326.
147. Cope to Pelham, 17 August 1745, Newcastle papers, (Clumber), [hereafter NeC], MS Department, Nottingham University Library, NeC 1634/2; Captain Thorne to Churchill, 22 August 1749, Blaikie papers [hereafter Blaikie], NLS, MS 307, ff. 236–7; Fox to Pitt, 22 August 1749, Chatham papers, PRO 30/8/77, f. 79; Royal Bank of Scotland Memorial, n.d., ibid., f. 51; Treasury to Paymaster General, 10 May 1750, PRO, T 27/26, p. 454.
148. Treasury to Townsend, 14 August 1753, PRO, T 27/27, p. 94; 23 April 1755, ibid, p. 158.
149. 5 May 1752, PRO, T29/32, p. 38; 11 October 1752, ibid, p. 71.
150. Memorial, n.d., [*c.* 1757], PRO, AO 17/42, p. 26; Warrant: 17 February 1757, ibid, p. 27; Treasury minute, 10 May 1757, ibid, p. 82.
151. 6 February 1752, PRO, T 29/32, p. 13; Treasury to Paymaster, 7 February 1752, PRO, T 27/27, pp. 38–9.
152. Pitt to Treasury, 12 February 1752, PRO, T 27/27, pp. 41–2; Treasury to Pitt, 26 February 1752, ibid, p. 42.
153. Treasury to Paymaster, 10 July 1755, PRO, T 27/27, p. 171.
154. Thomlinson and Hanbury to Treasury, 31 December 1757, PRO, T 1/379, f. 85.
155. Treasury to Secretary at War, 25 September 1755, PRO, T 27/27, p. 176; Treasury to Paymaster, 16 October 1755, ibid, pp. 179–80.
156. Treasury to Secretary at War, 5 March 1756, PRO, T 27/27, p. 199; West to Amyand, 5 March 1756, PRO, SP 36/133; Treasury to Loudoun, 9 December 1756, PRO, T 27/27, p. 251.
157. Thomas Sherwin to LG Onslow, 20 June 1755, PRO, WO 4/50, p. 333; Barrington to Onslow, 31 March 1756, PRO, WO 4/51, p. 336.
158. Calcraft to Townshend, 3 September 1761, PRO, WO 4/65, p. 418; West to Webb, 25 September 1761, PRO, T 27/28, p. 211; Martin to Webb, 20 October 1761, ibid, p. 221; Bristow to Newcastle, 28 August 1761, PRO, T 1/412, f. 44; Bristow's assets, 31 August 1761, BL, Add. MS 33055, f. 334; West to Paymaster, 1 January 1762, PRO, T 27/28, p. 239.
159. Failure of a financial house and legal opinion on contractors' liability, 24 March 1766, PRO, T 1/455, ff. 51–4; an Act of 1701 (12 & 13 Wm. III c.3) limited parliamentary privilege of MPs for Crown debts, Hughes, *Studies in Administration*, p. 192 n. 816.
160. Memorial of Fonnereau et al, 4 July 1757, PRO, T 1/372, f. 78; surveys: 31 January and 26 May 1757, ibid., ff. 79–80; 4 August 1757, PRO, T 29/32, pp. 479–80.
161. Tyrawley to Barrington, 25 July 1756, BL, Add. MS 32866, ff. 270–1; 2 October 1754, PRO, T 29/32, p. 236.
162. Treasury to Governor of Louisbourg, 7 November 1758, PRO, T 27/27, pp. 401–2.
163. West to Newcastle, 5 September 1760, BL, Add. MS 32911, f. 76; Memorial of Colebrooke, Nesbitt & Franks, 6 November 1761, PRO, SP 37/1, f. 232; Martin to Wood, 24 December 1761, ibid., f. 255.
164. Memorial of Colebrooke et al, 24 September 1761, PRO, T 1/408, f. 365.

165. West to Pitt, 16 October 1760, Chatham papers, PRO 30/8/66, ff. 228–9.
166. P. Bellivier to Colebrooke, [Copy], 9 June 1760, ibid., ff. 230–1; Memorial of Moses Franks, 30 August 1760, ibid., ff. 232–3.
167. Yonge to Revell, 6 May 1742, PRO, WO 4/37, p. 275.
168. Barrington to Calcraft, 17 June 1756, PRO, WO 4/52, p. 63; West to Barrington, 8 & 15 October 1756, PRO, T 27/27, pp. 239–40; Tyrawley to Barrington, 2 January 1757, PRO, WO 1/286, f. 55.
169. 29 April 1752, PRO, T 29/32, p. 34; Victualling lists, 27 September–19 December 1756, PRO, AO 17/42, p. 30; estimates: 27 November 1755, *HCJ*, 27, p. 317; 15 December 1756, ibid, p. 634.
170. Victualling lists: PRO, AO 17/43, p. 214; 'Memos for the King', 14/15 June 1759, BL, Add. MS 32892, f. 54; information of troop augmentations conveyed to contractor: Martin to Wood, 1 February 1759, PRO, T 27/27, pp. 423–4; Barrington to Holmes, 14 August 1759, PRO, WO 1/319, ff. 1–2; Treasury to Bacon, 16 October 1760, PRO, T 27/28, p. 102.
171. 'An Account of Ships that have Arrived at Senegal and Goree, under convoy 10 December 1758–31 July 1760.' Three ships delivered provisions before Bacon was directed to procede without convoy, PRO, AO 17/43, pp. 340–1.
172. 15 March 1759, PRO, T 29/33, pp. 155–7; L. B. Namier, 'Anthony Bacon, M.P., an Eighteenth-Century Merchant', *Journal of Economic and Business History*, 2:1 (1929), pp. 20–70; pp. 25–31.
173. Treasury to Bacon, 14 March 1760, PRO, T 27/28, p. 43; 11 August 1761, ibid., f. 203; 10 March 1762, PRO, T 1/415, f. 153; Townshend to Worge, 14 August 1761, PRO, WO 4/65, pp. 296–7.
174. Barrington to Martin, 12 June 1760, PRO, T 1/404, f. 71; Hospital Board Report, 8 June 1760, ibid., f. 74.
175. Namier, 'Anthony Bacon', p. 30; cf. North America: 'The army is undone and ruined by the constant use of salt meat and rum', Wolfe to Sackville, 24 May 1758, J. Wolfe, *The Life and Letters of James Wolfe*, ed. B. Willson (London: William Heinemann, 1909), pp. 367–8.
176. Barrington to Pitt, 2 June 1762, PRO, SP 41/24; Lieutenant Cary to Townshend, 8 June 1762, PRO, WO 1/319, f. 117.
177. For similar allegations, alongside blemished hogs and barrels of rice full of maggots, *GM*, 27 (1757), pp. 114–17.
178. Internal transports in North America were an exception if storage conditions were proved unsuitable, 31 July 1759, PRO, T 29/33, pp. 216–17; compensation, 19 January 1759, *HCJ*, 28, p. 361; 4 December 1759, ibid, p. 666.
179. For a controversy featuring these competing claims in which 1,953 barrels of flour were condemned, destroyed by weevils and worms, and 858 barrels through hot packing or age, see certificate of condemned provisions, 14 May 1762, PRO, T 1/415, f. 184; Comptrollers to Treasury, 7 July 1762, ibid., f. 182; Comptrollers Report, 13 December 1762, ibid., ff. 190–1; Colebrooke to Martin, 16 December 1762, ibid., f. 192.
180. Samples were taken before shipment in the aforementioned case. Affidavit, 13 December 1762, PRO, T 1/415, ff. 196–7; for Victualling Office procedures, *GM*, 6 (1736), p. 230; 21 July 1742, PRO, Adm. 111/28.
181. Regular inspections had been made since the beginning of the war. Robert Leake to Martin, 30 December 1759, PRO, T 1/391, ff. 3–4; D. J. Beattie, 'The Adaptation of the British Army to Wilderness Warfare, 1755–1763', in M. Ultee (ed.), *Adapting to Condi-*

tions: War and Society in the Eighteenth Century (Tuscaloosa: University of Alabama Press, 1986), pp. 56–83; pp. 61–5.
182. Treasury to Baker, 23 March 1748, PRO, T 27/26, p. 342; 22 March 1748, PRO, T 29/31, p. 100.
183. Stone (ed.), *Imperial State*, p. 9.
184. The rarity of supply failure is indicated in complaints over quality of provisions and non-performance of a bedding contract for troops embarking for Gibraltar, under the auspices of the Navy Board and Victualling Office. Fox had to inform Bland, who was by no means ignorant of military administration, of the procedure for punitive measures against contractors. 5 June 1749, PRO, WO 4/46, p. 230; 8 July 1749, ibid, p. 262.

3 Procedures and Patronage

1. 'Even for minor contracts, political recommendations were required' (Namier, *Structure of Politics*, p. 48 n. 3).
2. H. Perkin, *The Origins of Modern English Society 1780–1880* (London: Routledge & Kegan Paul, 1969), pp. 17, 48–9.
3. Ibid., pp. 17, 44–8; W. E. Minchison, 'The Merchants in England in the Eighteenth Century' in H. G. J. Aitken (ed.), *Explorations in Enterprise* (Cambridge, Mass: Harvard University Press, 1965), pp. 278–95; p. 278.
4. This tripartite division is apparent from Treasury sources, consistent with the practice of the Seven Years' War, and corresponds with a document in the Chatham papers: 'There are three Species of Contracts at present existing' (PRO 30/8/231, ff. 12–15, n.d. [*c.* 1782]); J. E. D. Binney, *British Public Finance 1774–1792* (Oxford: Clarendon Press, 1958), pp. 176–9.
5. Requesting the Russian subsidy for his son, Horace Walpole informed Newcastle 'the connections of our house with Baron Wolff the Consul at St Petersburg would enable us to Manage that afair so as not to affect the Exchange in the Least' (2 December 1755, BL, Add. MS 32861, f. 177); cf. John Gore to Newcastle, 30 November 1755, ibid., f. 157.
6. 'Remittance', Postlethwayt, *Universal Dictionary*, vol. 2 [unpaginated]; Office of Accounts Report, 18 June 1782, Seventh Report of the Commissioners of Public Accounts, *HCJ*, 38, pp. 1066–73.
7. 14 February 1749, PRO, T 29/31, p. 258; 22 November 1754, PRO, T 29/32, p. 253; 27 July 1758, PRO, T 1/387, f. 33; 15 May 1759, PRO, T 54/37, pp. 169–71.
8. For an example of the latter, see 12 May 1756, PRO, T 1/365, f. 51.
9. Charges of 20 per cent, see Memorial of Thomlinson and Hanbury, 5 November 1745, PRO, AO 17/37, p. 109.
10. C. Wilson, *Anglo-Dutch Commerce and Finance in the Eighteenth Century* (Cambridge: Cambridge University Press, 1941), p. 94; L. B. Namier, 'Brice Fisher MP: A Mid-Eighteenth Century Merchant and his Connexions', *English Historical Review*, 42:168 (1927), pp. 514–32; p. 528; for Namier they were 'Whigs *de par le roi*, Treasury Whigs' (*American Revolution*, p. 209).
11. 10 September 1761, BL, Add. MS 32928, f. 76; 16 April 1756, BL, Add. MS 32864, ff. 298–9; Newcastle to Burrell, 17 April 1756, ibid., ff. 318–19.
12. See below, appendices 1a & 3a, pp. 151 and 159.
13. 22 August 1758, BL, Add. MS 32883, f. 32.

14. Treasury to Gore, 6 April 1742, PRO, T 27/26, p. 43; Treasury to Thomlinson and Hanbury, 18 October 1745, ibid, p. 188.
15. Wilson, *Anglo-Dutch Commerce*, pp. 69, 75–6.
16. Jones, *War and Economy*, pp. 67, 84; Dickson, *Financial Revolution*, pp. 370–3.
17. 15 July 1697, *CTP* (1697–1702), p. 73; 10/11 June 1701, ibid., p. 497; n.d., *CTP* (1702–7), pp. 401, 482; 1 March 1711, PRO, T 29/19, p. 142; 17 June 1713, PRO, T 29/20, p. 97; 11 August 1713, ibid, p. 112; Furnese to Lord High Treasurer, 5 July 1711, Portland Loan, BL, Add. MS 70171, f. 44–228.
18. Baxter, *Development of Treasury*, pp. 49–50; H. Horwitz, *Parliament, Policy and Politics in the Reign of William III* (Manchester: Manchester University Press, 1977), p. 93.
19. Treasury direction for advertisement in the Gazette, at Royal Exchange and the Treasury, 18 December 1702, PRO, T 29/13, p. 296; *LG*, 17–21 December 1702.
20. 15 July 1730, *CTBP* (1729–30), p. 409.
21. Inquiry into the Conduct of the Earl of Orford, 30 June 1742, *HCJ*, 24, pp. 289–308; Further Report from the Secret Committee, BL, Add. MS 33032, ff. 210–24.
22. 9 July 1740, PRO, T 29/28, p. 234.
23. Evidence of James Knight, 30 June 1742, *HCJ*, 24, p. 308.
24. Charles Monson, MP, Deputy Paymaster, and related to the Pelhams, was a 'silent partner' holding one quarter of the contract according to profit and loss, with another official possessing a like amount (30 June 1742, *HCJ*, 24, p. 306); Namier, *American Revolution*, p. 23 n. 1.
25. 9 July 1740, PRO, T 29/28, p. 233.
26. The rate was raised on 5 June 1741 (ibid, p. 326).
27. 30 June 1742, *HCJ*, 24, p. 289; Pares, *War and Trade*, p. 40.
28. Treasury to Comptrollers, 22 January 1740, PRO, T 27/25, pp. 563–4; 15 April 1740, PRO, T 29/28, pp. 207–8.
29. City petition in William Maitland, *A History and Survey of London*, 2 vols (London: T. Osborne, J. Shipton and J. Hodges, 1756–7), vol. 1, pp. 593–5; *GM*, 9 (1739), pp. 304–10; Maitland calculated 234 of 262 MPs voting for the Convention were placemen, the annual value of whose employments was £212,956 (Maitland, *London*, vol. 1, p. 599).
30. See Earl of Wilmington to Pulteney, 28 June 1742, BL, Add. MS 32699, f. 303.
31. Debate on Remittance of Public Money, 10 March 1743, Cobbett, *PHE*, vol. 13, cc. 1–44; John Bance: 'Whether to call these remitting contracts a designed fraud, or only a piece of mismanagement, I am really at a loss to determine', ibid., c. 32.
32. 12 February 1746, HMC, *Egmont Diary*, vol. 3, p. 315.
33. For Newcastle's refusal to yield to City financiers, see Namier, 'Brice Fisher', pp. 524–7. Bristow 'after much grief, hesitation & concern' accepted Newcastle's remittance arrangements (West to Newcastle, 24 July 1756, BL, Add. MS 32866, ff. 268–9).
34. As a Jew, Samson Gideon's religion 'debarred him from rendering the political services that received their reward in profitable government contracts' (L. S. Sutherland, 'Samson Gideon and the Reduction of Interest', *Economic History Review*, 16:1 (1946), pp. 15–29; p. 21).
35. See below, p. 151 (Appendix A); L. B. Namier and J. Brooke, *The House of Commons 1754–1790*, 3 vols (London: HMSO, 1964), vol. 1, p. 135.
36. 'Reminiscences', Fox papers, BL, Add. MS 47589, f. 21; Fox may have planned their removal in any case. He wrote 'Sir Samuel Fludyer has my promise, & Mr. [Stephenson?]

has hopes, of some share in Contracts or Remittances that remain in Peace' ('List of Removals', n.d. [*c.* 1762], Francis papers, BL, Add. MS 40758, f. 278).
37. Sutherland, 'Samson Gideon', pp. 18–19; sensitivity, tempered by pragmatism, in Legge to Newcastle: 'I have always held that the Government might & ought to be masters of the market of money & not particular monied men Masters of the Government, but this too will in a great measure depend upon the Quantity demanded' (3 October 1759, BL, Add. MS 32896, ff. 237–42).
38. Newcastle to Earl of Bath, 12 December 1759, BL, Add. MS 32900, f. 16.
39. Joseph Gulston to Newcastle, 21 April 1758, PRO, T 1/388, f. 75.
40. For Winnington's reasons for making contracts at a fixed rate before troops embarked, see 10 March 1743, Hansard, *PD*, vol. 13, cc. 11–14.
41. For the refusal to share the Russian subsidy, see John Thornton to Newcastle, 6 December 1755, BL, Add. MS 32861, f. 208.
42. The Treasury requested John Gore's proposals for remitting subsidies (13 August 1740, PRO, T 29/28, p. 238; 6 April 1742, PRO, T 27/26, p. 37).
43. Legge to Newcastle, 9 July 1758, BL, Add. MS 32881, ff. 215–16.
44. Touchet to West, 29 July 1758, PRO, T 1/384, ff. 47–8; Walpole, Touchet and Mellish, 2 August 1758, ibid., f. 50; West to Newcastle, 29 July 1758, PRO, T1/385, f. 75.
45. Sir John Barnard criticized the 'undertakers' entrenched position and lucrative monopoly of government finance (Dickson, *Financial Revolution*, p. 290).
46. N.d., *c.* 19 September 1712, *CTB* (1708–14), p. 426; the Tangier contract had been advertised (*LG*, 1–4 October 1677).
47. 10 November 1714, *CTB* (1714–15), p. 25; *LG*, 27–30 September 1712, 9–13, 13–16, 16–19 November 1714; VO to Treasury, 18 January 1715, PRO, Adm. 110/7, pp. 9–10; 11 February 1715, ibid, pp. 18–20; 17 February 1715, ibid, p. 21; 26 February 1715, ibid, p. 55; 7 March 1715, ibid, p. 66.
48. *LG*, 23–27 September 1712; North American contract prices (1759), PRO, T 1/396, f. 25.
49. Beveridge incorrectly claimed they did not advertise during wartime for fear of raising prices (*Prices and Wages*, vol. 1, p. 515); cf. *LG*, 12–16 October 1756, 22–26 February 1757.
50. *Whitehall Evening Post*, 14–17 April 1759, 1–3 January 1761.
51. The one exception appears to be African garrison contracts (*LG*, 27 June–1 July 1758; 20 July 1758, PRO, T 29/33, pp. 73–5; 27 July 1758, ibid, p. 78); Jersey and Guernsey can be included if classified as 'overseas' (*LG*, 1–5 June 1756).
52. 9 May 1750, PRO, T 29/31, p. 282; 4 December 1750, ibid, p. 327; 11 December 1750, ibid, pp. 330–1; 29 January 1751, ibid, p. 341; West to Lords of Trade, 12 December 1750, PRO, T 27/26, p. 480.
53. Memorial of John Mason and John Simpson, 24 July 1733, PRO, T 29/27, p. 103; naval contractors in the West Indies, 3 September 1740, PRO, SP 42/33, f. 323; Crewe, *Yellow Jack*, p. 139.
54. For an example, in preparing an establishment for Rattan, Treasury to Secretary at War, 8 February 1743, PRO, T 27/26, p. 122.
55. 9 November 1759, PRO, T 29/33, pp. 239–40.
56. 2 April 1760, ibid, p. 310; cf. political influence discernible in Townsend's thanks to Newcastle for securing him a share of this contract, 8 May 1760, BL, Add. MS 32905, f. 347.
57. 22 April 1752, PRO, T 29/32, p. 32; 29 April 1752, ibid, p. 34.

58. Newcastle's rejection of Samuel Touchet's victualling proposals, Memorial, 21 June 1758, PRO, T 1/380, f. 32; Newcastle House meeting, 16 June 1758, ibid., ff. 33–4; Namier, 'Anthony Bacon', p. 26.
59. H. Walpole, *Horace Walpole's Memoirs of King George II*, ed. J. Brooke, 3 vols (New Haven, CT and London: Yale University Press, 1985), vol. 2, p. 209; Sir Roger Newdigate described the inquiry as a means to cover a 'scandalous bargain' (Namier and Brooke, *Commons*, vol. 3, p. 197); the controversy concerned high prices paid by Baker in purchasing provisions in England but, 'as Contractors will certainly Buy where the Commodity is the Cheapest ... America was not to be relyed on,' (West to Newcastle, 26 February 1757, BL, Add. MS 32870, ff. 222–8).
60. 14 & 22 February, 7, 9, 10 & 14 March 1757, *HCJ*, 27, pp. 706, 724–5, 754–5, 760–1, 768, 778.
61. Verified by Treasury minutes, 11 March 1756, PRO, T 29/32, pp. 376–7.
62. West to Newcastle, 26 February 1757, BL, Add. MS 32870, ff. 222–9; 14 March 1757, ibid., ff. 275–6; L. B. Namier and J. Brooke, *Charles Townshend* (London: Macmillan & Co., 1964), pp. 48–9.
63. Sedgwick, *Commons*, vol. 2, p. 260; 4 September 1733, PRO, T 29/27, p. 211; 9 October 1733, ibid, p. 220.
64. Woodford to Newcastle, 5 September 1757, BL, Add. MS 32873, ff. 496–7; Stanley to Newcastle, 6 January 1760, BL, Add. MS 32901, f. 105.
65. VO to Navy Commissioners, 3 September 1717, PRO, Adm. 110/7, p. 457; D. A. Baugh, *Naval Administration 1715–1750* (London: Navy Records Society, 1977), pp. 405 n. 1, 420–1, 498; J. B. Jones, *Annals of Dover* (Dover: Express Works, 1916), p. 389; Sedgwick, *Commons*, vol. 2, p. 381.
66. Although the Treasury insisted payment for the Georgia victualling contract must not exceed 2*d.* per man per day, 4 July 1738, *CTBP* (1735–8), p. 489; 28 August 1738, ibid., p. 503.
67. 14 August 1733, *CTBP* (1731–4), p. 396.
68. Revell obtained the Georgia contract largely because the regiment embarked from Gibraltar (Treasury to Revell, 6 April 1738, PRO, T 27/25, p. 468; Treasury to Comptrollers, 5 October 1738, ibid, p. 483; 12 July 1748, PRO, AO 1/189, f. 585).
69. With no contractor employed, shortages were feared, see Robert Gardner to Treasury, *CTB* (1714–19), pp. 473–4; Treasury minute, n.d. [both after 25 August 1719], ibid, p. 474.
70. Typically, Treasury to Thomlinson and Hanbury, 18 October 1745, PRO, T27/26, p. 188.
71. For competitive tendering reducing prices, see 26 October 1759, PRO, Adm. 111/49.
72. Hancock, *Citizens of the World*, pp. 13, 85–8; C. H. Wrigley, 'A Simple Model of London's Importance in Changing English Society and Economy, 1650–1750', *Past & Present*, 37 (1967), pp. 44–70.
73. For example, C. de Saussine, *A Foreign View of England in the Reigns of George I and George II: The Letters of Monsieur Cesar De Saussine*, trans. and ed. Madame Van Muyden (London: John Murray, 1902), pp. 216–17.
74. Applications for Ordnance and Victualling Office contracts could be submitted in locations where the contract was to be performed, and in London. Victualling Office contracts for Hull, Leith, Oporto, Vigo and Corunna, *LG*, 12–16 October 1756, 28 December 1756–1 January 1757; Ordnance contract in Scotland, ibid. 2–6 January 1759.

75. On 30 June 1742, the Secret Committee heard that merchants did not expect formal public notice, but that this information should be communicated to them – in London (*HCJ*, 24, p. 290).
76. Namier, 'Brice Fisher', pp. 514–15; Namier, 'Anthony Bacon', pp. 20–1; A. P. Wadsworth and J. de Lacy Mann, *The Cotton Trade and Industrial Lancashire 1600–1870* (Manchester: Manchester University Press, 1931), p. 244; C. Wilson, *England's Apprenticeship 1603–1763*, 2nd edn (London: Longman, 1984), p. 298.
77. Namier and Brooke, *Commons*, vol. 2, pp. 21, 41–2; *The Directory* (1736), p. 20.
78. *The Directory* (1736), p. 34; Namier and Brooke, *Commons*, vol. 3, pp. 194–5.
79. See below, p. 151 (Appendix A).
80. *North Briton*, 42 (19 March 1763), p. 141; 'The Battle of Cornhill', a satire featuring 'McGreedy, Van Scrip, and Isaac Loan', *Town and Country Magazine*, (March 1769), pp. 137–8; for controversy over the number of Scots in the army, see *GM*, 17 (1747), pp. 59–60; *St James's Chronicle*, 23–26 June 1764.
81. 11 September 1733, *CTB* (1731–4), p. 402; 9 October 1733, ibid, p. 408; 5 February 1734, ibid, p. 533.
82. 13 January 1741, *CTBP* (1739–41), p. 437; 5 March 1741, ibid, p. 449.
83. Memorials, 22 April 1752, (Fonnereau), PRO, T 1/348, f. 5; (Walpole), PRO, T 1/350, f. 35; North America, see below, pp. 49–50.
84. For the extensive river traffic in provisions, see [P. Kalm], *Kalm's Account of his Visit to England on his Way to America in 1748*, tr. J. Lucas (London: Macmillan & Co., 1892), p. 416.
85. Victualling Office advertisements for Warwickshire, Cheshire, or Gloucester cheese, *LG*, 8–11 August 1752.
86. Jenkinson to William Courtenay, 9 November 1764, Liverpool papers, BL, Add. MS 38304, ff. 83–4.
87. Treasury to Baker, Kilby and Baker, 3 March 1756, PRO, T 27/27, p. 201; Treasury to Paymaster General, 3 April 1745, PRO, T 27/26, p. 169; 3 June 1752, PRO, T 1/350, f. 78; Namier, *Structure of Politics*, p. 52.
88. Namier and Brooke, *Commons*, vol. 2, pp. 40–1, 358–61; vol. 3, pp. 536–7; Sedgwick, *Commons*, vol. 2, pp. 70–1; Dickson, *Financial Revolution*, p. 174 n. 10. All seven Members of 1742 who performed contracts were connected with Pelham, ('List of MPs and connections/patrons', in Fox to Newcastle, 16 October 1742, BL, Add. MS 32699, ff. 467–8; 'List of the Parliament 1747', BL, Add. MS 33002, ff. 440–6; Owen, *Pelhams*, p. 53 n. 1).
89. Treasury to Thomlinson and Hanbury, 18 October 1745, PRO, T 27/26, p. 188; 29 November 1754, Chatham papers, PRO 30/8/75, ff. 167–70; 17 May 1764, PRO, T 29/35, p. 394.
90. Nesbitt to Newcastle, 30 March 1756, BL, Add. MS 32864, f. 93; Calcraft to Loudoun, 12 February 1757, Calcraft papers, BL, Add. MS 17493, ff. 39–40; D. M. Clark, 'The Office of Secretary to the Treasury in the Eighteenth Century', *American Historical Review*, 42:1 (1936–7), p. 35.
91. The Colebrooke family's banking connections date from at least 1721 (F. G. H. Price, *A Handbook of London Bankers* (London: Guildford, 1876), pp. 40–1; Colebrooke, Rooke, and Hervey, 'Behind the Royal Exchange', *The Directory* 1736), p. 13; Namier and Brooke, *Commons*, vol. 3, pp. 194–5).
92. Namier, 'Brice Fisher', p. 517.

93. Gibraltar: 29 April 1752, PRO, T 54/35, pp. 339–45; Louisbourg and Guadeloupe: 30 October 1758, PRO, T54/37, pp. 123–8; 27 February 1760, ibid, pp. 379–81.
94. Admiralty to Newcastle, 22 September 1740, PRO, SP 42/23, f. 323; 10 December 1742, PRO, Adm. 106/2557; 17 December 1747, PRO, T 29/31, p. 72.
95. R. G. Albion, *Forests and Sea Power: The Timber Problem of the Royal Navy* (Cambridge, MA: Harvard University Press, 1926), pp. 56, 235; 17 May 1764, PRO, T 29/35, p. 394; 20 June 1764, ibid, p. 451.
96. Namier, 'Brice Fisher', p. 524.
97. L. Sutherland, *A London Merchant 1695–1774* (London: Oxford University Press, 1933), pp. 136–40.
98. 'Principal Merchants of the British Factory at Lisbon' petition, 7 February 1752, BL, Add. MS 32883, ff. 242–3; Jamaican remittance, 1740–2, Chatham papers, PRO 30/8/78, ff. 219–20; Memorial of M. Burrell, n.d., read 23 February 1744, PRO, T 1/313, ff. 52–3.
99. Treasury to Gore et al, 8 March 1756, PRO, T 1/367, f. 16; Gore and Bristow to Treasury, 14 April 1756, ibid., f. 25.
100. 28 March 1740, BL, Add. MS 32693, f. 121; Bacon mentioned that he had lived in America (9 November 1759, PRO, T 29/33, p. 240).
101. 11 February 1746, PRO, T 54/34, pp. 368–72; Treasury to Baker, 18 April 1746, PRO, T 27/26, p. 221; 1 October 1750–25 December 1760, PRO, T 1/401, f. 178; 26 March 1756, PRO, AO 1/191, f. 598.
102. 1 February 1743, BL, Add. MS 32700, ff. 19–21.
103. 26 March 1756, PRO, AO 17/41, pp. 202–7; Memorial, 28 October 1757, PRO, AO 17/42, pp. 173–4.
104. Memorial of Kilby, Barnard, and Parker, 17 October 1758, PRO, WO 1/975, f. 519; Baker to Newcastle, 21 September 1759, PRO, WO 34/69, f. 157; Amherst to Kilby, 6 May 1761, ibid., f. 159; Namier, *American Revolution*, p. 280; F. Anderson, *Crucible of War: The Seven Years' War and the Fate of the Empire in British North America, 1754–1766* (London: Faber, 2000), p. 131.
105. New England merchants memorial, *GM*, 19 (1749), p. 116; West to Kilby, 21 March 1749, PRO, T27/26, p. 409; West to Governor Cornwallis, 7 May 1750, ibid, pp. 453–4.
106. J. M. Price, 'What did Merchants Do? Reflections on British Overseas Trade, 1660–1790', *Journal of Economic History*, 49:2 (1989), pp. 278–9; Baker, *Government and Contractors*, p. 64.
107. Accounts of Peter Taylor, 1759–70, Bunbury papers, East Suffolk Record Office, E 18/853/18; merchants trading to or interested in 'His Majesty's Sugar Colonies', 1 April 1751, *HCJ*, 26, p. 160; his residence was used for distributing the Pondicherry prize (*LG*, 17–20 March 1759).
108. Declared accounts: 2 July 1771, PRO, AO 1/192, f. 602; 19 March 1790, PRO, AO 1/176, f. 519; Namier, 'Anthony Bacon', pp. 20–70.
109. R. Davis, *The Rise of the English Shipping Industry in the Seventeenth and Eighteenth Centuries* (London: Macmillan & Co., 1962), pp. 82–3, 100; Hancock, *Citizens of the World*, pp. 106–7.
110. Sutherland, *London Merchant*, pp. 136–40.
111. Contracts of Royal Hospital Chelsea, 1718–38, PRO, WO 247/1; C. G. T. Dean, *The Royal Hospital Chelsea* (London: Hutchinson & Co, 1950), pp. 193, 204; Sedgwick, *Commons*, vol. 2, p. 326.

112. The appointment occasioned a fascinating dispute between Newcastle and Fox in which 'spheres of influence' in awarding contracts was at issue: West to Newcastle, 10 October 1759, BL, Add. MS 32896, f. 424, Newcastle to Fox, 11 October 1759, BL, Add. MS 32897, ff. 18–19, Fox to Newcastle, 12 October 1759, ibid., f. 37, West to Newcastle, 13 October 1759, ibid., f. 63, Newcastle to Hardwicke, 15 October 1759, ibid., ff. 92–3, 'Answers to the Queries sent by R.H. Henry Fox', ibid., f. 103, Fox to West, 15 October 1759, ibid., f. 102.
113. Barrington to Calcraft, 17 June 1756, PRO, WO 4/52, p. 63.
114. Pay Office Ledger 1763, Bunbury papers, E 18/853/5; Calcraft to Earl of Home, 6 March 1759, Calcraft papers, BL, Add. MS 17494, ff. 73–4; 'The Right Hon. Lord Holland's Account with John Calcraft Esq.', 19 November 1763, Holland House papers, BL, Add. MS 51398, f. 125.
115. Calcraft to Tyrawley, 17 December 1763, Calcraft papers, BL, Add. MS 17496, f. 27v.
116. 26 April 1763, Holland House papers, BL, Add. MS 51398, f. 51.
117. Namier, *American Revolution*, p. 224.
118. For guilt by 'the extent to which the acts were kept secret by the power-holders themselves', see H. A. Brasz, 'The Sociology of Corruption' in A. J. Heidenheimer (ed.), *Political Corruption: Readings in Comparative Analysis* (New York and London: Holt, Rinehart, and Winston, 1970), p. 44.
119. 'An Ass Loaded with Trifles and Preferments' (1758) portrays Calcraft laden with scrolls inscribed with profitable positions he held as regimental agent and contractor including 'Coals for Gibraltar' (Anon., *A Political and Satyrical History of the Years 1756, 1757, 1758 and 1759*, 3rd edn (London: E. Morris, 1760), p. 68).
120. 30 June 1742, *HCJ*, 24, p. 308.
121. Sedgwick, *Commons*, vol. 2, pp. 513–14; 17 January 1712, *HCJ*, 17, p. 29.
122. 8 December 1711, HCJ, 17, p. 18.
123. 5 December 1711, PRO, T 27/20, p. 60; 18 February 1712, *HCJ*, 17, pp. 96–7; 16 April 1713, Cobbett, *PHE*, vol. 6, cc. 1198–1200, 1207.
124. 7 May 1713, *HCJ*, 17, p. 317.
125. W. Bromley to Earl of Oxford, 21 January 1712, HMC, *Portland* (London: HMSO, 1899), vol. 5, p. 139.
126. The Navy's customary usage also impinged upon army contracts, with Captains of men of war levying charges for carrying remittances (30 June 1742, *HCJ*, 24, p. 305, Treasury to Admiralty, 12 June 1759, T 29/33, p. 190); the Treasury decided public money should be shipped free (Treasury to Amherst, 26 January 1762, PRO, T 27/28, p. 246; N. A. M. Rodger, *The Wooden World: An Anatomy of the Georgian Navy* (London: Collins, 1986), pp. 318–19).
127. There were no Whig members of the Commissions of Public Accounts, 1702–14 (G. Holmes, *British Politics in the Age of Anne* (New York: St Martin's Press, 1967), pp. 137–8); cf. Whig conflict over transport costs of Dutch troops in Scotland (4 June 1717, Cobbett, *PHE*, vol. 7, cc. 466–8; Sedgwick, *Commons*, vol. 1, pp. 26–7).
128. See Treasury to Comptrollers, 22 January 1740, PRO, T 27/25, p. 563.
129. John Dick (Comptrollers Office), 'History of the Office', 20 November 1782, Chatham papers, PRO 30/8/231, ff. 130–4; Original Instructions, Comptrollers to Lord High Treasurer, 26 October 1705, PRO, AO 17/28, pp. 1–6. The 1746 Select Committee into the State of the Army noted the Comptrollers dealt mainly with victualling contracts (Morgan, 'Impact of War', p. 126).

130. The Comptrollers were appointed to the Committee examining Army Debts, 23 August and 19 October 1714, *CTB* (1714–15), p. 502.
131. Little, 'Commissariat', pp. 75–6; see below, p. 54.
132. Hughes, *Studies in Administration*, pp. 206–7.
133. J. Eatwell (ed.), *The New Palgrave: A Dictionary of Economics*, 4 vols (London: Macmillan, 1987), vol. 2, pp. 744–8.
134. 4 September 1733, PRO, T 29/27, p. 211; 29 April 1752, PRO, T 54/35, pp. 339–45.
135. 10 July 1758, PRO, T 29/33, p. 64; on this linkage, see Hoppit, 'Attitudes to Credit', p. 319.
136. Thirty-two provisions ships reached Gibraltar between 27 August 1757–27 August 1758, PRO, T 1/384, f. 147.
137. 23 February 1732, PRO, AO 1/183, f. 557; 28 July 1742, PRO, AO 1/184, f. 560; cf. £36,000 for North American contract for 12,000 men, 7 May 1756, PRO, AO 17/41, pp. 202–7.
138. 11 February 1745, PRO, T 54/34, pp. 368–72.
139. 17 April 1744, ibid, pp. 227–8.
140. 4 September 1733, *CTBP* (1731–4), p. 400.
141. Comptrollers Report, 3 March 1763, PRO, AO 17/45, p. 309; Reports, 12 May 1757, PRO, T 29/32, p. 462; 13 July 1757, ibid, p. 472.
142. Articles of Agreement, 22 September 1737, BL, Add. MS 33028, ff. 350–2.
143. In the period 1734–48, Government always owed Revell upwards of £9,000. Having received £10,000 advance, this was how the system was intended to operate. 28 July 1742, July 1748 and 16 June 1749, PRO, AO 1/184, ff. 560–2.
144. Memorial, 4 October 1737, PRO, T 29/28, p. 54; Treasury to Comptrollers, 4 October 1737, PRO, T 27/25, p. 452; Treasury to John Hampden, 14 May 1740, ibid, p. 538.
145. These perceptions permeate Woodford to West, 28 January 1760, PRO, T 1/393, f. 181; Woodford to Hans Stanley, 3 January 1760, BL, Add. MS 32901, f. 107.
146. Treasury to Revell, 10 June 1742, PRO, T 29/29, p. 60; Treasury to Burrell and Bristow, 1 December 1742, PRO, T 27/26, p. 73.
147. Comptrollers Report, 28 November 1748, PRO, AO 17/39, pp. 90–1; Revell received an extra allowance backdated to 5 October 1740 (13 January 1741, PRO, T 29/28, p. 283).
148. Revell successfully argued the wartime allowance should continue until provisions were consumed (5 October 1748, PRO, T 29/31, p. 55).
149. 21 and 28 September 1748, ibid, pp. 151–2; Treasury to Revell, Burrell & Bristow, 22 September 1748, PRO, T 27/26, p. 372; Treasury to Burrell and Bristow, 12 December 1748, PRO, ibid, p. 389; 30 May 1749, PRO, T 29/31, p. 205.
150. The explosion of a magazine at Goree in October 1762 was such an accident, with 32,480lb of beef and 5,350 gallons of brandy and rum destroyed (2 July 1771, PRO, AO 1/192, f. 602).
151. For rejection of claims submitted without documentation, see 5 March 1734, PRO, T 1/285, f. 27; 3 March 1763, PRO, AO 17/45, p. 308.
152. Captain's oath, 30 September 1746, PRO, AO 17/37, p. 295; Townsend's oath, 18 October 1746, ibid, p. 296.
153. Treasury to Comptrollers, 10 July 1745, PRO, T 27/26, p. 178; Comptrollers to Treasury, 26 August 1745, PRO, AO 17/37, pp. 60–1.

154. The contractor for Louisbourg claimed 18 per cent insurance from London and Ireland in 1746 (Memorial and schedule of ships, 10 February 1747, PRO, AO 17/38, pp. 88–91).
155. Comptrollers Report, 28 January 1741, PRO, T 29/29, pp. 190–1; 14 June 1744, PRO, T 29/30, p. 44.
156. William Baker to Treasury, 12 August 1746, PRO, T 1/321, f. 73.
157. Treasury to Admiralty, 7 January 1741, PRO, T 27/25, p. 558; the Auditors noted no insurance clause in Woodford's contract (26 March 1746, PRO, T 54/34, pp. 391–3).
158. Sutherland, *London Merchant*, p. 53; Burrell and Bristow to Treasury, 10 February 1741, PRO, T 1/305, f. 37; Treasury to Admiralty, 7 January 1741, PRO, T 27/25, p. 558; 23 January 1742, PRO, T 27/26, p. 26; 8 November 1745, ibid, p. 192; 20 July 1758, PRO, T 29/33, p. 75.
159. Treasury to Paymaster and Secretary at War, 31 December 1745, PRO, T 27/26, p. 199; Treasury to Townsend, 25 March 1746, ibid, p. 216.
160. Treasury to Revell, Burrell and Bristow, 22 September 1748, ibid, p. 372.
161. Memorial of Fonnereau et al, n.d., PRO, T 1/321, f. 95.
162. 29 April 1752, PRO, T 54/35, pp. 339–45.
163. Comptrollers Report, 25 January 1757, PRO, AO 17/42, p. 15.
164. Treasury minute, 10 February 1757, ibid, p. 205.
165. 27 September 1758, PRO, T 29/33, p. 89; Comptrollers Report, 26 July 1762, PRO, T 1/415, f. 188.
166. [R.] P. Crowhurst, *The Defence of British Trade 1689–1815* (Folkestone: Dawson, 1977), pp. 43–80; R. P. Crowhurst, 'The Admiralty and the Convoy System in the Seven Years War', *Mariner's Mirror*, 57 (1971), pp. 163–73; Fonnereau et al to Treasury, 14 February 1757, PRO, T 1/379, f. 18. Woodford usually sailed from Southampton to Placentia via Cork where he purchased provisions (PRO, T 54/34, pp. 391–3); contractors purchased dry provisions in and around London, and meat in Ireland (West to Clevland, 12 March 1756, PRO, T 27/27, p. 201; Fonnereau et al to Treasury, 26 April 1758, PRO, T 29/33, pp. 42–3).
167. Auditors Report, October 1744, PRO, T 54/35, pp. 411–14; Fonnereau to Treasury, 26 April 1758, PRO, T 29/33, pp. 42–3; Crowhurst, *British Trade*, p. 130; on Bills of Lading and Charter Parties, see 'Bill of Lading', Postelthwayt, *Universal Dictionary*, vol. 1, [unpaginated]; George Colebrooke to Martin, 3 February 1762, PRO, T 1/416, f. 170.
168. Corbett to Treasury, 8 August 1746, PRO, T 1/321, f. 72; for an almost identical letter sixteen years later, see John Clevland to Martin, 22 January 1762, PRO, T 1/416, f. 216.
169. Comptrollers Report, 20 March 1758, PRO, T 1/382, f. 53.
170. Martin to Clevland, 8 February 1759, PRO, T 27/27, p. 427; Treasury to North American contractors, 12 February 1759, ibid, p. 428; Colebrooke and Nesbitt to Treasury, 7 July 1762, PRO, T 1/415, f. 186; for continuing problems, 15 March 1759, PRO, T 29/33, p. 157; Treasury to Clerk of Council, 20 March 1759, PRO, T 27/27, p. 439.
171. Treasury to Colebrooke and Nesbitt, 27 April 1759, ibid, p. 445; 25 April 1759, PRO, T 29/33, p. 173.
172. *Read's Weekly Journal*, 8 February 1752; *LG*, 14–17 March 1752.
173. George Colebrooke to Treasury, 21 April 1761, PRO, T 1/412, ff. 57–8.
174. For mercantile complaints and 1742 Commons debate, see Crowhurst, *British Trade*, pp. 59–60; C. E. Fayle, 'Economic Pressure in the War of 1739–1748', *Journal of the Royal United Services Institution*, 68 (1923), pp. 434–46.

Notes to pages 55–9

175. 16 May 1761, BL, Add. MS 32923, ff. 123–5, cited Middleton, *Bells of Victory*, p. 182 n. 77.
176. 'That the public is a sufferer in almost every contract which regards the public service, may be suspected, without any breach of charity, when we reflect on the perfidies of that sort, which have been so often proved and so rarely punished' ('The Remembrancer', *GM*, 18 (1748), p. 72); cf. Brooke (ed.), *Memoirs of George II*, vol. 3, p. 52.
177. Articles of Agreement, 5 January 1761, PRO, T 54/38, pp. 28–32.
178. Comptrollers Report, 3 March 1763, PRO AO 17/45, p. 308.
179. Browning, 'Newcastle and Financial Management', pp. 23–7.
180. M. Peters, *Pitt and Popularity: The Patriot Minister and London Opinion during the Seven Years War* (Oxford: Clarendon Press, 1980), pp. 187–8; 11 July 1757, W. Pitt, *Correspondence of William Pitt, Earl of Chatham*, ed. W. S. Taylor and J. H. Pringle, 4 vols (London: John Murray, 1838–40), vol. 1, p. 237.
181. 'Reminiscences', 1729–1809, Fox papers, BL, Add. MS 47589, f. 6; cf. Horace Walpole: 'Newcastle revelled in a boundless power of appointing agents, commissaries, victuallers, and the whole train of leeches …' (*Memoirs of George II*, vol. 3, p. 52).
182. Bute to Newcastle, 24 April 1761, BL, Add. MS 32922, f. 171; [J. Douglas], *Seasonable Hints from an Honest Man on the Present Important Crisis of a New Reign, and a New Parliament* (London: A. Millar, 1761), p. 29; Newcastle to Barrington, 31 March 1765, BL, Add. MS 32966, f. 133, Onslow to Newcastle, 1 April 1765, ibid., f. 136, Barrington to Newcastle, 1 April 1765, ibid., f. 138; *North Briton*, 25 (20 November 1762), p. 78.
183. Newcastle to General Yorke, 19 February 1762, BL, Add. MS 32934, f. 437.
184. 23 December 1762, PRO, T 29/35, pp. 22–3.
185. Cf. 1776–82, Baker, *Government and Contractors*, pp. 250–1.
186. A typically blunt Anson advised Newcastle over appointing a new Victualling Commissioner, 'this gives me an opportunity of observing to your Grace that instead of adding to the useless people that are already in that office (if we should have a War with France) more people of business must be brought into it' (15 February 1755, BL, Add. MS 32852, f. 485); Middleton, *Bells of Victory*, pp. 33, 110–11.
187. Baugh, *Naval Administration in the Age of Walpole*, pp. 418–19; J. O'Donovan, *The Economic History of Livestock in Ireland* (Dublin and Cork: Cork University Press, 1940), p. 107; criticism during 1756–62 concerned the damage to Ireland's export trade (ibid, pp. 111–12).

4 Administration of Encampment Contracts in England, 1740–62

1. Notable exceptions include S. Conway, 'Britain and the Impact of the American War, 1775–1783', *War in History*, 2:2 (1995), pp. 127–50; Houlding, *Fit for Service*, pp. 322–46; Western, *English Militia*, pp. 372–403.
2. *Annual Register 1762* (1766), p. 93; cf. reviews by the King and Generals at Colchester, *Ipswich Journal*, 5 September and 24 October 1741; for military spectacle as 'positive enactments of national power', see K. Wilson, *The Sense of the People: Politics, Culture and Imperialism in England, 1715–1785* (Cambridge: Cambridge University Press, 1995), p. 198.
3. *LG*, 10–14 May 1757, 11–15 July 1758, 3–7 April 1759, 6–10 May 1760, 26–30 May 1761, 1–5 June 1762.

4. Late proposals were usually disregarded (23 May 1760, PRO, T 29/33, pp. 325–6; 11 June 1762, PRO, T 29/34, pp. 302–3); an exception was made for the 1742 Flanders contract (22 May 1742, *CTBP* (1742–5), p. 41).
5. For the procedure, 1756–62, see 1 April 1756, PRO, T 29/32, p. 382; 19 May 1757, ibid, pp. 464–5; 26 April 1758, PRO, T 29/33, pp. 41–2; 25 April 1759, ibid, pp. 171–2; 23 May 1760, ibid, pp. 325–7; 9 June 1761, PRO, T 29/34, pp. 95–7; 11 June 1762, ibid, pp. 302–3.
6. 'Sundry Articles necessary to be provided previous to the encampment of troops', n.d. [c. April 1757], PRO, T 1/375, f. 137; Little, 'Commissariat', p. 13.
7. H. Bland, *A Treatise of Military Discipline*, rev. W. Faucitt, 9th edn (London: R. Baldwin, 1762), pp. 287–8; 'Extracts of Cumberland's Orders during the late campaign and to be looked upon as Standing Orders', May 1755, Yester papers [hereafter Yester], NLS, MS 14512, f. 28; *Journal of Corporal William Todd*, pp. 40, 238 n. 201, 311 (entry for 23–24 May 1758 (South Sea Common); entry for 27 November 1761 (Germany)).
8. 'Ammunition' was used in a collective sense to signify articles issued from public stores, e.g. ammunition bread, ammunition boots (Stocqueler, *Military Encyclopaedia*, p. 11); it also appears to have meant bread made of one-third wheat and two-thirds rye flour, particularly prevalent in Europe (*Journal of Corporal William Todd*, p. 132 (entry for 5 May 1761)).
9. 'Extract of Orders given at Shroton Camp', 21 August 1756, Yester, NLS, MS 14513, f. 11v.
10. Bland, *Treatise*, pp. 295–6.
11. 29 June 1759, PRO, T 54/37, pp. 222–7.
12. 'Regulation of Wood and Straw', 23 July 1760, in Abraham Hume to Loudoun, 31 August 1762, Loudoun papers, BL, Add. MS 44072, f. 13.
13. In Germany, Marlborough was criticized for conceding a power the Commander-in-Chief always possessed, to employ wagons at his discretion, Hume to Treasury, 23 October 1758, PRO, T 1/384, f. 63.
14. Memorandum, 26 February 1756, RA Cumberland, Box 46, f. 169; Articles of Agreement, 15 April 1756, PRO, AO 17/41, pp. 243–52, 29 June 1759, PRO, T 54/37, pp. 222–7; cf. contract, 27 March 1710, for Low Countries with additional clause against selling horses to the enemy, PRO, T 64/132.
15. Barrington to Treasury, 2 April 1756, PRO, T 1/371, f. 33.
16. Allowed once, at Dover in 1759, Townshend to Colonel Napier, 24 November 1761, PRO, WO 4/66, p. 347.
17. 'Account and Regulation of Forage for General and Staff Officers', 9 July 1756, PRO, T 52/47, pp. 628–9; account for camp near Blandford, 9 March 1757, PRO, T 52/48, p. 165; 'Extract of Orders', 1 August 1756, Yester, NLS, MS 14513, f. 5; 2*d.* in the £ was deducted from forage money at home for agency (Guy, *Oeconomy and Discipline*, p. 102).
18. Bland to Beauclerk, 5 July 1755, Blaikie, NLS, MS 305, ff. 109–10; Beauclerk to Barrington, 19 May 1760, PRO, WO 1/614, f. 433; Martin to Barrington, 9 October 1760, PRO, WO 1/678, f. 403; Barrington to Beauclerk, 23 October 1760, PRO, WO 4/62, p. 322.
19. 'Estimates of the Amount of different proposals for supplying several Camps for seven weeks' (1757), PRO, T 1/375, f. 138.
20. Eighth Report of Commissioners appointed to inquire into fees in public offices, 17 April 1788, *PP*, 1806, vii [c.309], pp. 569–70; J. Ehrman, *The Navy in the War of Wil-*

liam III: Its State and Direction, 1689–1697 (Cambridge: Cambridge University Press, 1953), pp. 149–51.

21. 'Sundry Articles', n.d. [*c.* April 1757], PRO, T 1/375, f. 137; read 19 April 1757, PRO, T 29/32, p. 457.
22. 23 May 1760, PRO, T 29/33, pp. 325–7.
23. 23 May 1760, ibid, p. 326.
24. A fee of £24 10*s* was charged for every Treasury contract. Second Report of Commissioners appointed to inquire into fees in public offices, *PP*, 1806, vii [c.309], p. 84; Oswald paid over £101 in fees for his 1758 contract, 29 January 1813, PRO, AO 1/174, f. 511.
25. 19 May 1757, PRO, T 29/32, p. 464; cf. Oswald was given preference of renewal of bread and wagons contracts in Germany 'if he will do the service upon as reasonable terms as anyone else', Hunter to Treasury, 11 March 1759, PRO, T 64/96, p. 64.
26. Sackville to Bute, 10 September 1758, Bute correspondence, BL, Add. MS 36796, f. 63; cf. Oswald's partner John Mill's thanks to James Oswald for employing his interest at the service of friends, 27 December 1759, [No author], *Memorials of the Public Life of the Right Hon. James Oswald of Dunnikier* (Edinburgh: A. Constable, 1825), pp. 301–2; Hancock, *Citizens of the World*, p. 228.
27. 26 April 1758, PRO, T 29/32, pp. 41–3; 3 May 1758, ibid, pp. 44–5.
28. Based on a document in the Zetland archive by Lawrence Dundas, Oswald's partner in the contracts of 1756–7, 29 May 1756, ZA, ZNK X1/1/138.
29. 1 April 1756, PRO, T29/32, p. 382; the contract was not advertised.
30. Barrington to Treasury, 2 April 1756, PRO, T 1/371, f. 33; West to Barrington, 9 April 1756, querying wagon prices, PRO, T 27/27, p. 208. Forage for wagon horses was a factor in assessing contract prices in Germany (Hunter to Treasury, 20 January 1759, PRO, T 64/96, pp. 2–3).
31. 19 May 1757, PRO, T 29/32, p. 464; 26 April 1758, PRO, T 29/33, pp. 41, 44–5; 25 April 1759, ibid, pp. 171–2; 23 May 1760, ibid, pp. 325–6; 9 June 1761, PRO, T 29/34, pp. 95–7; 11 June 1762, ibid, p. 302.
32. Archibald Fraser was asked his profession and abode (23 May 1760, PRO, T 29/33, pp. 326–7).
33. Stair recommended a contract to Carteret, 'providing that those Jews could produce the Securitys they offered' (5 March 1743, Carteret papers, BL, Add. MS 22537, f. 172) it was; rejected 'on account of the insufficiency of himself and his securities' (18 March 1743, *CTBP* (1742–5), p. 250).
34. That is, 'the quantum of such advance is settled according to the nature and extent of the service' (Nineteenth Report from the Select Committee on Finance, 19 July 1797, *House of Commons Committee Reports*, xxii, p. 372).
35. A sum of £1 per man cited in Chatham papers, n.d., PRO 30/8/231, ff. 12–15; cf. £3 later reduced to £1 (Baker, *Government and Contractors*, pp. 39–40).
36. Barrington to Treasury, 2 April 1756, PRO, T 1/371, f. 33; Bonds, 15 April 1756, PRO, T 1/368, f. 35; Warrant, 20 May 1756, PRO, T 52/48, p. 104; cf. estimate for 22,680 troops for seven weeks encampment (1757), T 1/375, f. 138; 8 April 1756, PRO, T 29/32, pp. 382–3.
37. Articles of Agreement, 15 April 1756, PRO, AO 17/41, pp. 243–52; Memorial, 25 November 1756, PRO, AO 17/42, p. 2; approximately ninety days advance for wagon hire was normal (Hunter to Treasury, 11 March 1759, PRO, T 64/96, pp. 63–4).

38. Warrant, 20 May 1756, PRO, T 52/48, p. 105; Bonds, 29 April 1756, PRO, T 1/371, f. 41; earlier example of sureties double the advance, 19 April 1743, *CTBP* (1742–5), p. 263.
39. 21 July 1760, PRO, T 52/51, p. 94; 23 November 1762, *HCJ*, 24, p. 481.
40. In 1762 the contractor requested £6,000 but the Treasury, acting on the Commissary General's advice, issued £5,000. Hume to Treasury, 6 July 1762, PRO, T 1/416, ff. 160-2.
41. Baker, 'Open Contracting', p. 435.
42. 17 November 1757, PRO, AO 17/42, p. 183; 27 February 1758, ibid, p. 204.
43. Oswald Memorial, 30 May 1758, recounting losses sustained as the Treasury owed him over £10,000 from 1757, PRO, T 1/367, f. 84.
44. Oswald's accounts for 1756 and 1757 were settled by September 1757 (PRO, T 52/48, p. 376, and August 1758, PRO, T 52/49, pp. 159–60); Fraser's for 1760 by December 1761 (PRO, T 52/53, pp. 131–2).
45. 29 January 1813, PRO, AO 1/174, f. 511; his German accounts were not settled until after his death (Report of Commissioners of Public Accounts, 20 February 1795, *HCJ*, 50, pp. 249–55).
46. Anthony Bacon, a Manxman, was an exception, but it was his local knowledge and connections that facilitated his performance of a bread and forage contract on the island (Bacon to Charles Lowndes, 14 August 1765, PRO, T 1/439, ff. 145–6; 19 March 1790, PRO AO 1/176, f. 579).
47. Proposal of Abraham Cortissos, 25 September 1740, PRO, SP 41/19; Paper of W. Yonge, 14 August 1740, PRO, SP 41/12; 3 February 1741, *HCJ*, 23, p. 627; 15 March 1742, *HCJ*, 24, p. 126.
48. Treasury to Honywood and Ligonier, 27 July 1742, PRO, T27/26, p. 54; *LG*, 18–22, 25–29 May 1742, 24–28 January, 28–31 January, 31 January–4 February 1744; 3 June 1742, *CTBP* (1742–5), p. 44; 27 July 1742, ibid., p. 59; 30 July 1742, PRO, T 29/29, p. 92.
49. Honywood to Carteret, 1 April 1742, PRO, SP 87/8, f. 24; Stair to Carteret, 15 May 1742, ibid., ff. 118–19; 24 May 1744, *CTBP* (1742–5), p. 482.
50. Apparent from names and addresses of sureties, 10 March 1743, *CTBP* (1742–5), pp. 247–8; 18 March 1743, ibid, p. 250; 14 and 19 April 1743, ibid, pp. 262–3; ten de Costas, two Suassos and four Pereiras listed as merchants in directories of the 1730s and 1740s (*The Directory*, 2, pp. 11, 14, 36); in 1729 a foreign visitor noted the City synagogue of Sephardic Jews (Sausine, *Foreign View of England*, p. 329).
51. Maitland, *London*, vol. 1, pp. 634–5.
52. 'Proposals of Mr. Camber & c for furnishing in ye Camp at Hounslow Heath with bread' [misdated 30 December 1755; c. June 1740, see below, n. 54], PRO, SP 41/21.
53. Westerfield, *Middlemen*, pp. 150, 167, 171, 175.
54. Camber to Edward Loyd, 12 June 1740, BL, Add. MS 32693, ff. 375–6.
55. Obituary notice of Mr. Barker of Stradleigh, Berkshire, 'the greatest mealman and malster in England' worth £40,000, *GM*, 18 (1748), p. 236.
56. 19 December 1757–30 June 1763, PRO, AO 1/185, f. 565; between September 1755 and 29 August 1756, they received £31,860 (Comptrollers Report, 25 January 1757, PRO, AO 17/42, p. 15).
57. 20 December 1759, PRO, AO 1/174, f. 512; 'I am a whig and of a whig family Ready to serve your Grace and therefore ought to be taken care off' [sic] (Thomas Leslie to Newcastle, 14 October 1747, BL, Add. MS 32713, f. 265).

Notes to pages 64–6 195

58. The family association with the Isle of Wight was long-standing (Memorial of Thomas Holmes stating it was always the Lieutenant Colonel's duty to provide wood and straw for Isle of Wight camps, n.d. [*c.* 1714–15], *CTP* (1714–1719), p. 63); Holmes managed boroughs for Newcastle (23 May 1756, BL, Add. MS 32865, f. 100).
59. Memorial, 12 April 1744, BL, Add. MS 33052, ff. 278–94; first London directory entry in 1749 (*Compleat Guide*, 9, p. 148); Hancock, *Citizens of the World*, pp. 221–39.
60. 'Richard Oswald', *Notes and Queries*, 8:214 (1853), p. 549; cf. Mary Oswald to Oswald, 4 February 1761, 'I always Looked upon Goverment [*sic*] Service as a Sort of Slavery & now I know it by experience' (Oswald papers, NAS, GD213/52, f. 42).
61. Haldane, 'who stands in the place of Mr. Oswald in the management of the Forage Contract of last year', 27 December 1756, PRO, T 29/32, p. 427; Dundas to Andrew Mitchell, 7 July 1746, regarding a prospective loan to Haldane, Sir Andrew Mitchell papers, NAS (West Register House), Miscellaneous Letters RH4/70 (Reel 1: Bundle 53); Gen. Sir J. A. L. Haldane, *The Haldanes of Gleneagles* (Edinburgh and London: W. Blackwood & Sons, 1929), pp. 294–5.
62. See below, pp. 106–9 and 111–12; 'Sir Lawrence Dundas', *ODNB*, vol. 17, pp. 267–9.
63. 23 May 1760, PRO, T 29/33, pp. 326–7; Dundas to Ross, 3 June 1759, ZA, ZNK X1/1/159, ff. 66–7; 8 June 1759, ZA, ZNK X1/1/159, f. 86; 16 June 1759, ZA, ZNK X1/1/159, f. 91; 5 July 1759, ZA, ZNK X1/1/159, ff. 126–7; Dundas to Fraser, 14 June 1759, ZA, ZNK X1/1/159, f. 86; 25 June 1759, ZA, ZNK X1/1/159, ff. 103–5.
64. Listed in mercantile partnership in *Complete Guide*, 15 (1758), p. 126; [Kent], *Kent's Directory*, 16 (1759), p. 44.
65. A. H. Millar (ed.), *A Selection of Scottish Forfeited Estates Papers 1715* (Edinburgh: Scottish Records Society, 1909), p. 34; 'Archibald Campbell Fraser', *ODNB*, vol. 20, p. 824; MP for Inverness-shire, 1782–4 (Namier and Brooke, *Commons*, vol. 2, p. 469).
66. G. J. Bryant, 'Scots in India in the Eighteenth Century', *Scottish Historical Review*, 64:177 (1998), pp. 22–41.
67. Legal opinion, 29 May 1756, ZA, ZNK X1/1/138; Dundas informed George Ross of his determination 'never to have Partners' (26 April 1759, ZA, ZNK X1/1/48); see Dundas's disparaging comments to George Colebrooke on Oswald's performance of German contracts, 22 October 1760, ZA, ZNK X1/1/160, f. 179.
68. Oswald for British, Dundas for foreign troops: Hunter to Treasury, 11 March 1759, PRO, T 64/96, pp. 63–4; Hunter to Oswald, 19 March 1759, PRO, T 1/396, f. 51.
69. See above, p. 50.
70. Including 117 acres near Winchester for Hessian encampment; payments for damages: 10 May 1757, PRO, T 29/32, p. 462; 18 May 1757, PRO, T 52/48, pp. 203–4; 21 May 1761, PRO, T 52/52, p. 268; 3 February 1762, PRO, T 52/53, p. 206.
71. Probate registers, 28 February 1782, Public Record Office, London [hereafter PRO, PROB] PRO, PROB 11/1087, f. 92; Baker, 'Open Contracting', p. 444.
72. Houlding, *Fit for Service*, pp. 324–5.
73. Articles of Agreement, 15 April 1756, PRO, AO 17/41, pp. 243–52, 1 June 1757, PRO, AO 17/42, pp. 99–103.
74. Martin to Hume, 9 June 1761, PRO, T 27/28, p. 171.
75. 28 April 1756, PRO, T 29/32, p. 385.
76. For a dispute over buildings, see petition of John Sone, 1 January 1760, PRO, WO 4/59, p. 480; Colonel Robinson to Barrington, 7 January 1760, ibid, p. 503.
77. 15 April 1756, PRO, AO 17/41, pp. 243–52; 1 June 1757, PRO, AO 17/42, pp. 99–103.

78. Confirmation of muster, 21 July 1756, PRO, AO 17/41, pp. 255–6; for the 'frightfully large' wagons in England, see [Kalm], *Kalm's Visit to England*, pp. 11–12.
79. Articles of Agreement: 29 June 1759, PRO, T 54/37, pp. 222–7; 6 June 1761, AO 1/175, f. 515; 18 June 1762, PRO, T 54/38, pp. 448–53.
80. Hume to Treasury, 25 September 1756, PRO, T 1/369, f. 45; accounts, 2 February 1761, PRO, T 54/37, pp. 43–9; Articles of Agreement, 17 June 1760, ibid, pp. 418–21.
81. Proposals about Magazines of Forage, Flour, Wagons, Hospitals & c., 26 February 1756, RA Cumberland, Box 46, f. 169.
82. Abraham Hume to Barrington, 19 March 1756, PRO, T 1/367, f. 21; Reports of Messrs. Dundas and Haldane, 20 March 1756, RA Cumberland, Box 46, f. 199; 25 March 1756, ibid., f. 206; contractors' agents were reported as buying 170 quarters of wheat at London Corn Exchange in 1757. Guildhall Library, London: Bakers Company, Weekly Wheat Returns, 14 February 1757, MS 5183, f. 1.
83. Dundas to Barrington, 14 March 1756, PRO, T 1/367, f. 19.
84. Guy, *Oeconomy and Discipline*, p. 26; Morgan, 'Impact of War', p. 365.
85. 15 February 1757, PRO, T 29/32, p. 440; Warrant, 13 March 1756, PRO, T 1/368, f. 22.
86. 12 April 1756, PRO, T 1/370, f. 17.
87. Four men of each foot regiment were assigned to assist at magazines in making up forage rations, 'Extract of Orders' 29 July 1756, Yester, NLS, MS 14513, f. 3v.
88. Hume to Treasury, 7 April 1756, PRO, T 1/370, f. 19.
89. Barrington to Treasury, 12 April 1756, PRO, ibid., f. 18; Sherwin to Hume, 17 April 1756, PRO, WO 4/51, p. 387.
90. Memorial of Hume, 5 January 1757, PRO, T 1/374, f. 7.
91. 'List of persons employed in Services relating to the intended Encampment', 6 July 1756, PRO, T 1/367, f. 38.
92. 10 May 1757, PRO, T 29/32, p. 462.
93. Encampment papers, n.d. [*c.* 1757], PRO, T 1/375, f. 141; 10 May 1757, PRO, T 29/32, p. 462; 3 May 1758, PRO, T 29/33, p. 44; West to Hume, 4 May 1758, PRO, T 27/27, p. 332; Warrants: 8 March 1760, PRO, T 52/50, pp. 394–5; 29 Jan. 1761, PRO, T 52/51, p. 389; 18 February 1762, PRO, T 52/53, p. 233; 11 June 1762, PRO, T 29/33, pp. 302–3; Memorial, 17 January 1763, PRO, T 1/425, f. 208.
94. Hume to Barrington, 29 April 1756, PRO, T 1/370, f. 30.
95. 5 May 1756, PRO, T 29/32, p. 386; a corporal and six men from each infantry regiment were ordered to attend magazines, presumably collecting rations, 'Extract of Orders', 31 July 1756, Yester, NLS, MS 14513, f. 4v.
96. 21 July 1756, PRO, T 29/32, p. 398; described as a commissary in 'Account of the Application or Disposition of the £2000 paid to the Earl of Stair', 21 September 1745, PRO, T 1/319, f. 43.
97. 'List of Commissaries of Firing and Straw', n.d. [*c.* 6 July 1756], PRO, T 1/367, f. 39.
98. Namier, *Structure of Politics*, p. 17.
99. Undated, unsigned letter to Treasury [Barrington's handwriting], PRO, T 1/367, f. 40; 5 May 1756, PRO, T 29/32, p. 386; 21 July 1756, ibid, p. 398; Gomez Serra received the same salary during the Rebellion, Account Book, PRO, T 1/322, f. 29.
100. Godfrey to Hume, 29 April 1756, PRO, WO 4/51, pp. 414–15.
101. T. Hayter, *The Army and the Crowd in Mid-Georgian England* (London: Macmillan, 1978), pp. 57–8; Hume responded to post-war Treasury questioning over staffing lev-

Notes to pages 69–71 197

els by relating that Godfrey was frequently blamed for being under-staffed (14 January 1765, PRO, T 1/441, f. 32).

102. On 1 July 1756, Barrington informed Newcastle he viewed escalating expenditure with 'infinite concern', despite believing only expenses 'incident to Armies' were allowed (BL, Add. MS 32866, ff. 1–2).
103. Additions to staff account (1757), PRO, T 1/374, f. 85.
104. Later reissued: Barrington to Cathcart, 8 June 1757, PRO, WO 4/54, p. 119.
105. *Compleat Guide*, 10 (1752), p. 181; *Kent's Directory*, 12 (1754), p. 101; V. Orchard, *Tattersall's: Two Hundred Years of Sporting History* (London: Hutchinson, 1953), p. 84.
106. For Trotter as an 'Eminent & reputable Upholsterer', see 'Explanations upon Mr. Jenkinson's Queries upon the Extraordinaries' (1779) (Liverpool papers, BL, Add. MS 38343, ff. 303–4); cf. 29 June 1756, PRO, WO 47/47, pp. 695–6; Baker, *Government and Contractors*, p. 188.
107. Memorials: 25 July 1759, PRO, WO 1/980, f. 183; July 1759, PRO, T 1/396, f. 233; Payments: 4 December 1759, *HCJ*, 28, p. 671; 12 August 1762, PRO, WO 47/60, p. 118.
108. Wood and straw was sold in 1757 but Ligonier cautioned against selling wheat (7 December 1757, PRO, T 29/33, p. 2).
109. The position was held by Lawrence Dundas (1757–8) and James Pigott (1760–1), 23 May 1757, PRO, T 52/48, p. 215; 10 June 1760, PRO, T 29/33, p. 332; Accounts, 25 June 1760, PRO, T 54/37, pp. 425–7; 9 July 1765, PRO, AO 1/485, f. 53.
110. 11 May 1758, PRO, AO 1/174, f. 509.
111. 'Forage necessary for the Encampment of Troops', n.d. [*c.* February 1758], PRO, T 1/375, f. 141; 'An Account of where the camps are proposed to be', PRO, ibid., f. 140, n.d. [*c.* February 1757]; eighteen magazines listed in declared account, 7 June 1766, PRO, AO 1/485, f. 51.
112. Treasury to Hume, 15 July 1758, PRO, T 27/27, p. 358; 20 July 1758, PRO, T 29/33, p. 72; Treasury to Hume and Dundas, 21 July 1758, PRO, T 27/27, p. 363; Treasury to Excise Commissioners, 21 July 1758, PRO, ibid, p. 368; Treasury to Paymaster, 26 Sept. 1758, ibid, p. 383; 7 June 1766, PRO, AO 1/485, f. 51.
113. Accounts: 2 February 1761, PRO, T 54/38, pp. 43–9; 9 July 1765, PRO, AO 1/485, f. 53.
114. Treasury to Excise Commissioners and Commissioners of Taxes, 24 June 1756, PRO, T 27/27, p. 219.
115. Dupplin (Pay Office) to Newcastle, 15 June 1756, BL, Add. MS 32865, ff. 308–9.
116. Hume to Barrington, 31 January 1758, PRO, T 1/382, f. 43.
117. 'Qualities of a Commissary General', n.d. [*c.* February 1758], PRO, T 1/375, f. 44; read 15 February 1758, PRO, T 29/33, p. 15; cf. 'Duty of a Comptrolling Commissary', 24 June 1761, Minto papers, NLS, MS 11039, ff. 23–4.
118. 13 March 1756, PRO, T 1/368, f. 22; 18 January 1757, PRO, T 29/32, p. 432; 'Proposals for abating the expence of Preserving Magazines of Hay & Oats which have been provided for the use of HM Forces', 18 January 1757, PRO, T 1/375, f. 20.
119. Barrington informed the Treasury that Cumberland sanctioned £3 per day (15 February 1757, PRO, T29/32, p. 440; 19 May 1757, ibid, p. 464; 1 December 1757, ibid, p. 493).
120. 8 February 1758, PRO, T29/33, p. 14; 26 April 1758, ibid, p. 40.
121. In the Preface to his 1727 military textbook, Bland stated that personal knowledge of many military practices was dying out ('Humphrey Bland', *ODNB*, vol. 6, pp. 158–60);

sixty years later, Grose acknowledged his section on encampment organization owed much to Bland (Grose, *Military Antiquities*, vol. 2, pp. 204–45).

5 Performance of Encampment Contracts

1. 'The enemy threaten us with invasion from all ports, it is certain they are building and fitting numbers of large boats at a great expence all along the coast, but what can they do with them unsupported by a fleet?' (Holdernesse to Sackville, 5 June 1759, HMC, *Stopford-Sackville*, 2 vols (London: HMSO, 1904–10), vol. 1, p. 56).
2. Intelligence was received of simultaneous invasion of Scotland, Ireland and England in 1756 and 1759 (6 February 1756 (received 25 February), BL, Add. MS 32862, ff. 383–91, 13 February 1756, ibid., f. 476; 'Memos to the King', 19 November 1759, BL, Add. MS 32898, f. 362); for Ireland, see Guy, 'Irish Military Establishment', p. 225; Lord John Russell, *Correspondence of John, Fourth Duke of Bedford with an Introduction*, 3 vols (London: Longman, 1842–6), vol. 2, pp. 373–82, 391–3.
3. F. Wilkinson, *The Castles of England* (London: G. Philip, 1973), pp. 94, 131–3, 161, 163, 176; Sissinghurst Castle, Kent, was regularly used for French prisoners, *Whitehall Evening Post*, 5–7 June 1759; *Lloyd's Evening Post and British Chronicle*, 3–5 June 1761; 'A Freeholder' suggested troops occupy castles to relieve local burdens, *GM*, 27 (1757), pp. 150–1.
4. In 1741, regiments awaiting transports for Flanders were ordered to encamp at Lexden (25 June 1741, PRO, SP 45/3; *Ipswich Journal*, 20 June 1741).
5. Houlding, *Fit for Service*, pp. 322–3.
6. Public enthusiasm towards encampments: *Read's Weekly Journal*, 14 August 1756; 7 July 1757, *Journal of Corporal William Todd*, p. 18 (entry for 7 July 1757).
7. Col. C. Walton, *History of the British Standing Army 1660–1700* (London: Harrison & Sons, 1894), pp. 526–7, 697; W. C. Cunnington, *The Military Encampments of James II on Hounslow Heath* (Hounslow: Hounslow and District History Society, 1964), pp. 2–4; Masse, *Royal Army Service Corps*, p. xiv.
8. Chandler, *Art of Warfare*, pp. 107–8.
9. Clode, *Military Forces*, vol. 1, p. 222; Seventh Report from the Committee on Public Expenditure, 20 June 1810, *PP* (1810), ii. [370], p. 168.
10. Clode, *Military Forces*, vol. 1, p. 223; 'A standing army is therefore not only become a necessary evil, but it is also absolutely requisite for the ease of particulars and safety of the whole, that they should be lodged in barracks' (C.Dalrymple, *A Military Essay, Containing Reflections on the Raising, Arming, Cloathing, and Discipline of the British Infantry and Cavalry: With Proposals for the Improvement of the Same* (London: D. Wilson, 1761), p. 154).
11. Clode, *Military Forces*, vol. 1, p. 234; cf. Pulteney, 24 February 1741, Cobbett, *PHE*, vol. 11, c. 1443.
12. Six separate barracks listed near Portsmouth: Barrington to Fox, 17 August 1756, PRO, WO 4/52, p. 168; Barrington to Bowerbank (Barrack Master), 1 June 1756, ibid, p. 11; Sherwin to Bowerbank, 7 June 1756, ibid, p. 38; Portsmouth and Guernsey barrack furniture, 26 April and 3 July 1756, PRO, SP 41/22; barracks were built at Somerset House and 'the Old Playhouse' near Lincoln's Inn Fields (*London Evening Post*, 22–25 May 1756).
13. 'Providus' asked 'would not the Remedy be much worse than the Disease?' (*London Evening Post*, 12–15 January 1760).

14. 'Guards and Garrisons from 1714', Chatham papers, PRO 30/8/75, f. 137; C. T. Atkinson, 'The Army under the Early Hanoverians', *JSAHR*, 21 (1942), pp. 138–47.
15. P. S. Fritz, *The English Ministers and Jacobitism between the Rebellions of 1715 and 1745* (Toronto, ON: University of Toronto, 1975), pp. 83–4; B. Lenman, *The Jacobite Risings in Britain 1689–1746* (London: Eyre Methuen, 1980), p. 201.
16. Capt. Walter Molesworth to Hon. John Molesworth, 11 August 1722, HMC, *Various Collections*, vol. 8 (London: HMSO, 1913), p. 345.
17. Houlding, *Fit for Service*, p. 324 n. 3; Pares, *War and Trade*, pp. 158–60.
18. Fortescue, *Royal Army Service Corps*, vol. 1, pp. 20–1.
19. 24 June 1740, *CTB* (1739–1741), p. 277; 28 October 1740, ibid, p. 388; 5 February 1741, ibid, p. 408; 31 December 1741, ibid, pp. 566, 615; Yonge, the Secretary at War, recommended the commissary to Newcastle, 23 May 1740, PRO, SP 41/12; on Yonge's influence in appointments, Morgan, 'Impact of War', p. 361.
20. *LG*, 14–17 June 1740; Col. Leighton, 'Computation of the Expense to the Publick for Furnishing Bread to the Three Camps', enclosed in Wade to [Newcastle?], 25 September 1740, PRO, SP 41/12; Lords Justices minutes, 28 May 1741, PRO, SP 45/3.
21. 'An Account of the Several Camps 1740/41', Chatham papers, PRO 30/8/75, f. 5; the camps were approximately equal in size, Morgan, 'Impact of War', pp. 283–4; cf. 17,000 troops at Coxheath in 1778, Conway, *American Independence*, pp. 192, 201.
22. 3 February 1741, *HCJ*, 23, p. 627; 15 March 1742, *HCJ*, 24, p. 126.
23. 'The Champion' in *Ipswich Journal*, 17 April 1742; 'Number of Troops Sent Abroad', BL, Add. MS 33038, f. 234.
24. In 1744, Stair studied possible invasion sites, and 6,000 Dutch troops were brought over between February and June (Morgan, 'Impact of War', pp. 306–7; *General Evening Post (London)*, 22–24 March 1744; Newcastle to Cumberland, 21 May 1745, BL Add. MS 32704, f. 297; Black, *Military Power*, p. 68).
25. Newcastle to Lonsdale, 5 September 1745, calculated less than 6,000 troops in England (C. T. Atkinson, 'Some Letters about the 'Forty Five', *JSAHR*, 37 (1959), p. 114)
26. 'Proposed disposition of Forces around London', c. 24 October 1745, RA Cumberland, Box 6, f. 150; 'General St. Clair's report on Finchley Common for a Camp', n.d., c. 6 December 1745, responding to King's order for camp between Highgate and Whetstone, RA Cumberland, Box 7, f. 235; 'Disposition of the Forces near London', December 1745, ibid., f. 236; Lords Justices minutes, 6 December 1745, PRO, SP 45/5, ff. 143–4.
27. Richmond to Newcastle, 5 December 1745, BL, Add. MS 32705, f. 409; Stocqueler considered encampments consistent with Roman military practice, the object being 'every battalion or squadron may be enabled to form with ease and expedition at any given moment' (*Military Encyclopaedia*, p. 48).
28. For consideration of these fears, see Pelham to Horace Walpole, 12 June 1746, Hansard, *PD*, vol. 13, c. 1415; Richmond to Newcastle, 4 June 1746, BL, Add. MS 32707, f. 280.
29. Sir Benjamin Keene to Henry Fox [Extract], 13 February 1756, and Hague 'Advices', 10 February 1756, PRO, WO 30/54, ff. 145–6 (No. 52); R. Whitworth, *Field Marshal Lord Ligonier: A Story of the British Army 1702–1770* (Oxford: Clarendon Press, 1958), p. 207; two Irish camps were formed in 1755, *GM*, 25 (1755), p. 235; Walpole, *Memoirs of George II*, vol. 2, pp. 47–8.
30. *HCJ*, 27, pp. 539–40.
31. Newcastle recorded 15,406 additional troops in 1755 ('Several Augmentations of the Army', BL, Add. MS 33046, f. 360).

32. 'State of the Troops in Great Britain', March 1756, Hardwicke papers, BL, Add MS 35389, ff. 190–1; cf. slightly higher figures in BL, Add. MS 33047, f. 37, n.d.; Barrington to Clevland, 2 March 1757, PRO, WO 4/53, p. 296; the latter states 7,090 officers and men returning, 223 fewer than arrived, thus assuming a total of 7,313. The disparity appears to arise from some accounts omitting officers ('Number of Hessian troops in each county', (1756), PRO, T 1/375, f. 98; *Read's Weekly Journal*, 29 May and 19 June 1756).
33. 38,000 Hanoverians and 18,992 Hessians amongst 109,535 troops voted in British pay for 1759 (BL, Add. MS 32891, f. 71; 23 May 1759, Hansard, *PD*, vol. 15, c. 936); cf. 57,762 German troops were voted for 1760 (19 November 1759, *HCJ*, 28, p. 639.
34. Barrington to Amherst, 27 April 1756, PRO, WO 4/51, p. 402; Sherwin to Captains at Canterbury and Maidstone, 6 May 1756, ibid, p. 448; at Canterbury, barns, stables, and outhouses were prepared for Hessians, *Read's Weekly Journal*, 10 April 1756; London preparations included tents in St James's Park, and barns at Paddington and Southwark for horses and wagons, *London Evening Post*, 29 April–1 May 1756.
35. Barrington to Excise Commissioners, 10 May 1756, PRO, WO 4/51, p. 454.
36. Barrington to Clevland, 12 June 1756, PRO, WO 4/52, p. 42; Barrington to Captain Collingwood, 12 June 1756, ibid, p. 44; 'Memos for the King', 16 August 1756, BL, Add. MS 32866, f. 468.
37. Barrington to Cornet Abercrombie, 21 May 1756, PRO, WO 4/51/ p. 511; Barrington to Corporation and Inn Keepers of Southampton, and Recorder of Chichester, 22 June 1756, PRO, WO 4/52, p. 73; 29 June 1756, ibid, p. 85; refusals to quarter them and deny them 'small beer', Barrington to J. Cook, 10 August 1756, ibid, p. 155; Barrington to William Swanton, 24 August 1756, ibid, p. 179; *London Evening Post*, 23–26 October 1756.
38. Barrington to General Somerfield, 29 October 1756, PRO, WO 4/52, p. 355; Barrington to West & West to Barrington, 9 November 1756, ibid, p. 376; Godfrey to Barrington, n.d., enclosing tradesman's bills, PRO, WO 1/972, f. 83; M.G. Napier to Oswald, 9 November 1756, RA Cumberland, Box 48, f. 181; 11 May 1758, PRO, AO 1/174, f. 509; *GM*, 26 (1756), pp. 544, 592.
39. At Yarmouth, with 'disputes running high' a 'sharp action' occurred, wherein troops 'decided it with sword in hand' (*GM*, 29 (1759), p. 192).
40. Almost half of the £2,500 was allocated to Hampshire where the largest contingent of German troops were located (6 July 1758, PRO, T 52/49, pp. 109–10).
41. Houlding, *Fit for Service*, pp. 324, 329–31.
42. With little water, officers represented Blackheath as inappropriate (*Ipswich Journal*, 3 May 1740).
43. Thomas Tyrwhitt to Samuel Tewkesbury, 23 April 1761, PRO, WO 4/64, p. 204.
44. *Read's Weekly Journal*, 19 June 1756; 'David Watson', *ODNB*, vol. 57, pp. 606–8; he accompanied Ligonier surveying Sussex and Kent coasts, Thomas Pelham to Newcastle, 17 September 1759, BL, Add. MS 32895, f. 441, Ligonier to Newcastle, 19 September 1759, ibid., f. 493; Tyrwhitt to Holmes, 15 September 1759, requesting appointment of a person to find suitable ground and negotiate terms, PRO, WO 4/59, p. 57.
45. 4 April 1757, PRO, T 52/48, pp. 203–4; 12 May 1757, PRO, T 29/32, p. 462.
46. Watson to Barrington, 14 February 1758, PRO, WO 1/975, f. 75.
47. 'Extract of Orders', 26 July and 4 September 1756, Yester, NLS, MS 14513, ff. 1–2, 15v.
48. Bland, *Treatise*, pp. 285–97; 'Lieutenant Watson's Report on the most Convenient Ground for Encampments betwixt Dorchester and Petersfield', 8 June 1756, PRO, WO

30/54, ff. 117–18; 'Brackesh' water at South Sea Common, *Journal of Corporal William Todd*, p. 40 (entry for May 1758).
49. *Journal of Corporal William Todd*, pp. 14–15 (entry for 27 April 1756).
50. Houlding, *Fit for Service*, pp. 329–31.
51. Calculated from 'State of the Troops in Great Britain', March 1756, Hardwicke papers, BL, Add. MS 35389, ff. 190–1; Winter cantonment, ibid., f. 195; *Journal of Corporal William Todd*, pp. 14–15; cf. 34,547 in 'Disposition of the Troops in South Britain', 23 May 1756, Saltoun papers [hereafter Saltoun], NLS, MS 17505, f. 58a.
52. The Hessians departed 'to the great joy of the Innkeepers and Publicans in general' (*London Evening Post*, 26–28 April 1757).
53. Calculated from Declared Account, 11 May 1758, PRO, AO 1/174, f. 509; Articles of Agreement, 15 April 1756, PRO, AO 17/41, pp. 243–52.
54. Papers on iron ovens in Germany, n.d., PRO, WO 30/54, ff. 131–3 (No. 47).
55. David Mendes de Costa to Abraham Prado, 8 September 1758, on discovering the manufacturer of iron ovens 'on the Prussian model', Letter Book, BL, Egerton MS 2227, f. 73, 11 September 1758, ibid., ff. 73–4; described as 'a New Article of Expence Attending the Nature of the War in this Country', Hunter to Martin, 11 March 1759, BL, Add. MS 32889, ff. 1–5.
56. J. Stevenson, *Popular Disturbances in England 1700–1850* (London: Longman, 1979), p. 106; cf. medieval statutes prohibiting markets in neighbouring counties, in order that the army would be adequately provided with victuals (Grose, *Military Antiquities*, vol. 2, p. 166 n. C).
57. Barrington to Robert Haldane, 2 September 1756, PRO, WO 4/52, p. 199; 6 September 1756, ibid, p. 210.
58. Wilson, *England's Apprenticeship*, p. 370.
59. Cumberland insisted on rye bread for Hessians, Hume to Barrington, 19 March 1756, PRO, T 1/367, f. 21; Cumberland to Oswald, May 1756, RA Cumberland, Box 47, f. 37; Treasury to Oswald, 17 March 1757, PRO, T 27/27, p. 279.
60. Cumberland to Oswald, May 1756, RA Cumberland, Box 47, f. 36; Hume to Barrington, 25 September 1756, PRO, T 1/369, f. 45; Treasury to Oswald, 6 January 1757, PRO, T 27/27, p. 256.
61. Newcastle estimated £200,000 necessary for encampments, 'Estimates of supposed Services for 1756', n.d., BL, Add. MS 33038, f. 501.
62. *London Evening Post*, 18–20 January 1757; 11 May 1758, PRO, AO 1/174, f. 509.
63. E. P. Thompson, 'The Crime of Anonymity', in Hay, Linebaugh et al (eds), *Albion's Fatal Tree*, pp. 255–344; p. 280.
64. 30 Geo II c.1, 31 Geo II, c.1, 32 Geo II, c.2; W. G. Hoskins, 'Harvest Fluctuations and English Economic History, 1620–1759', *Agricultural History Review*, 16 (1968), pp. 15–31; p. 21; 'An Act to Permit the Importation of Salted Beef Pork & Butter from Ireland' (31 Geo. II, c.28), O'Donovan, *Economic History*, p. 110.
65. See below, p. 79.
66. James Wolfe to Lord Holdernesse, 27 October 1756, Leeds papers, BL, Egerton MS 3432, f. 9; *Journal of Corporal William Todd* (8 March 1757 and 25–30 April 1758), pp. 18, 39.
67. Barrington to Pitt, 1 July 1758, Chatham papers, PRO 30/8/18, ff. 188–9; Sir George Oxenden to Fox, 24 April 1757, Earl of Ilchester (ed.), *Letters to Henry Fox, Lord Holland* (London: Roxburghe Club, 1915), p. 106.
68. Treasury to Godfrey, 10 June 1757, PRO, T 27/27, p. 290.

69. With 400,000 rations of hay and 200,000 of oats remaining in magazines, Dundas advised against a forage contract, Dundas to West, 19 April 1758, PRO, T 1/383, f. 38.
70. Ligonier to Treasury, 15 April 1758, PRO, T 1/385, f. 115.
71. 11 November 1758, PRO, AO 1/174, f. 510.
72. *London Evening Post*, 19–21, 23–26 July 1757.
73. Hume to Treasury, 22 July 1757, PRO, T 1/379, f. 51; Treasury to Dundas, 2 August 1757, PRO, T 27/27, p. 297.
74. *London Evening Post*, 18–20 April 1758; 29 January 1813, PRO, AO 1/174, f. 511; Houlding, *Fit for Service*, pp. 329–31.
75. *London Evening Post*, 11–13 May 1758; troops ordered to Germany, 10 July 1758, PRO, T 29/33, pp. 62–3.
76. Treasury to Holmes, 19 May 1759, PRO, T 27/27, p. 454; 20 December 1759, PRO, AO 1/174, f. 512; in 1758, wood and straw contract prices at the Isle of Wight were identical to mainland camps (Auditors Report, 8 June 1759, PRO, T 54/37, pp. 202–4).
77. Colonel Parslow to Barrington, 28 June 1760, PRO, WO 4/61, p. 345.
78. 27 July 1757, BL, Add. MS 33047, f. 99; 9 January 1760, BL, Add. MS 33048, f. 7; 12 February 1760, ibid., f. 9; 20 April 1760, ibid., ff. 31–3.
79. Newcastle cited 120,000 land forces in England and Ireland, 'Memorandums for the King', 6 July 1759, BL, Add. MS 32892, f. 444; Newcastle to Granby, 23 November 1759, BL, Add. MS 32899, ff. 55–7.
80. Robert Napier to [Barrington?], 25 July 1759, PRO, WO 1/978, f. 459; John Cathcart to Barrington, 31 July 1759, ibid., f. 225; *Whitehall Evening Post*, 2–5 June 1759; Houlding, *Fit for Service*, p. 325; *St James's Chronicle*, 10–12 June 1762.
81. 'Memos for the King', 17 June 1759, BL, Add. MS 32892, f. 120; *Whitehall Evening Post*, 3–5 April, 5–7 June 1759; Western, *English Militia*, pp. 154–61.
82. Newcastle to Hardwicke, 1 May 1760, BL, Add. MS 32905, ff. 196–7; 2 May 1760, 'Memos for the King', ibid., f. 242.
83. Barrington to Newcastle, 3 January 1761, BL, Add. MS 32917, f. 75; Newcastle to Devonshire, 20 May 1761, BL, Add. MS 32923, ff. 200–2.
84. 'State of Troops', 9 January 1760, BL, Add. MS 33048, f. 7; Barrington's paper, 25 August 1760, BL, Add. MS 32910, ff. 274–5; Western, *English Militia*, p. 154.
85. Hume was directed to consult Ligonier, 3 November 1760, PRO, T 29/33, p. 371; Treasury to Hume, 8 October 1760, PRO, T 27/28, p. 98; 6 November 1760, ibid, p. 114; 21 November 1760, ibid, p. 119.
86. Hume to Treasury, 26 May 1761, PRO, T 1/408, f. 386; read 27 May 1761, ibid., f. 388.
87. Treasury to Paymaster, 9 June 1761, PRO, T 27/28, p. 171; accounts: 8 July 1761, PRO, T 54/37, pp. 478–81; 9 July 1762, PRO, T 1/412, f. 26.
88. 9 June 1761, PRO, T 29/34, pp. 95–7; cantonment of forces around London, 10 July 1761, PRO, SP 22/28, f. 41.
89. 11 June 1762, PRO, T 29/34, pp. 302–3.
90. Egremont to Ligonier, 27 May 1762, PRO, SP 44/192, f. 284; *St James's Chronicle*, 13–15 April, 29 April–1 May, 8–11 May, 11–13 May 1762; *Lloyd's Evening Post*, 7–10 May 1762; Newcastle to Clevland, 29 June 1762, BL, Add. MS 32940, f. 135; Hardwicke to Newcastle, 30 June 1762, ibid., f. 164.
91. 30 May 1759, PRO, T 29/33, pp. 187–8.
92. 23 December 1763, PRO, AO 1/175, f. 518; a similar order was issued in 1759, 8 January 1761, PRO, T 29/34, p. 12.

93. 11 June 1762, PRO, T 29/34, pp. 302–3; 23 December 1763, PRO, AO 1/175, f. 518; it was not usual for contractors to supply Guards regiments, as the latter rarely left London, Houlding, *Fit for Service*, p. 408 n. 1.
94. Bland, *Treatise*, pp. 287–8, 294–5; Section 8, Article 1, 1748 Articles of War, PRO, WO 72/2.
95. Cited in Davies, 'Provisions for Armies', p. 241. Sutlers were not always men; for a 'sutleress', see Fortescue, *History*, vol. 1, p. 574.
96. Firth, *Cromwell's Army*, p. 420; Article 41, Articles of War (1743), PRO, WO 72/2.
97. 'Extract of Orders', 26 July 1756, Yester, NLS, MS 14513, ff. 1–2.
98. 2 August and 1 October 1756, ibid., ff. 5v–6, 29.
99. 27 July 1743, BL, Add. MS 32700, f. 335.
100. Firth, *Cromwell's Army*, p. 421; Article 27, 1718 Articles of War, PRO, WO 72/2; 'Extract of Orders', 26 July 1756, Yester, NLS, MS 14513, f. 1.
101. Morgan, 'Impact of War', p. 349; included in 1743 Articles for the army abroad, Article 25, PRO, WO 72/2.
102. Stevenson, *Popular Disturbances*, p. 93.
103. *Ipswich Journal*, 19 September 1741; when encampments began in Germany in 1743 there were 300 men in hospital; by the end there were 740, Robert Hay Drummond to Newcastle, 3 February 1743, BL, Add. MS 32701, ff. 125–6.
104. Wolfe to father, 4 August 1756, *Life and Letters of James Wolfe*, p. 301.
105. 19 October 1756, ibid, pp. 303–4; for insufficient hospital capacity at the beginning of encampments, Report of Robert Adair, 12 July 1756, PRO, WO 1/974, f. 65; Cathcart to Sherwin, 23 July 1756, PRO, WO 1/972, f. 233.
106. Lady Townshend to Lady Ferrers, 2 October 1759, HMC, *Townshend and Dartmouth*, 3 vols (London: HMSO, 1887–96) vol. 1, p. 315; cf. 'Epistle of a Soldier in Hilsea Barracks', *GM*, 31 (1761), p. 135.
107. C. Hay to Barrington, 12 February 1759, PRO, WO 1/979.
108. Western, *English Militia*, pp. 393–7.
109. *Journal of Corporal William Todd*, p. 82 (entry for 15 August 1758).
110. 19 April 1757, PRO, T 29/32, p. 457; War Office Memorandum about Rochefort Expedition, n.d. [c. 1757], 'Mr. Commissary Hume to be consulted about bread and forage for the troops encamped or on the march', cited in Barrington, *Eighteenth-Century Secretary at War*, p. 73.
111. 9 June 1761, PRO, T 27/28, p. 171.
112. Hume to Treasury, 26 May 1761, PRO, T 1/408, f. 386; 9 June 1761, PRO, T29/34, pp. 95–7; 11 June 1762, ibid, pp. 302–3.
113. Treasury to Hume, 30 June 1761, PRO, T27/28, p. 190; 9 October 1761, ibid, p. 216.
114. For the arrival of sixteen Hanoverian bakers at Chatham, see *London Evening Post*, 20–22 May 1756.
115. Hume to Barrington, 10 December 1756, PRO, T 1/370, f. 88; 11 May 1758, PRO, AO 1/174, f. 509.
116. *London Evening Post*, 4–7 September 1756.
117. [Kalm], *Kalm's Visit to England*, pp. 55–6, 88, 360; on the continuing importance of rye, see W. Ashley, 'The Place of Rye in the History of English Food', *Economic Journal*, 31:123 (1921), pp. 285–308.
118. 20 July 1758, PRO, T 29/33, p. 71; cf. Marlborough to Treasury, 12 July 1758, PRO, T 1/384, f. 43; Treasury advertisement for rye bread and bread made of two-thirds wheat

and one-third rye flour, *LG*, 11–15 July 1758; mixing flour to make bread was common outside of the military (Ashley, 'Place of Rye', pp. 293–4).

119. M. K. Matossian, *Poisons of the past: molds, epidemics, and history* (New Haven, CT, and London: Yale University Press, 1989).
120. Martin to Newcastle, 20 July 1758, BL, Add. MS 32881, f. 426; 17 July 1759, PRO, T 29/33, p. 210.
121. 6 March 1758, *HCJ*, 28, pp. 118–19; Prompting 'An Act to Ascertain Weights of Trusses of Straw & c.' (31 Geo. II. c.40), 29 September 1758, *The Statutes at Large, from Magna Charta to 1869*, ed. O. Ruffhead, rev. C. Runnington, 43 vols (London: 1786–1849), vol. 7, pp. 244–9; this abuse remained prevalent in the nineteenth century, see Hay Contracts: Correspondence and Reports, *PP*, 1854, xli. [260] p. 76.
122. Kalm found English women did not bake at home as there was a baker in every parish (*Kalm's Visit to England*, p. 327).
123. S. and B. Webb, 'The Assize of Bread', *Economic Journal*, 14:54 (1904), pp. 205–6; alum was used to whiten bread (*London Evening Post*, 10–12 February 1758).
124. Barrington to Martin, 22 February 1760, PRO, WO 4/60, p. 168; some documentation relating to the case is printed in Barrington, *Eighteenth-Century Secretary at War*, pp. 164–76.
125. 'Extract of Orders', 9 September 1756, Yester, NLS, MS 14513, f. 17v.
126. Ligonier's order [Copy], 7 November 1759, PRO, WO 71/10, pp. 35–6.
127. War Office Report in Barrington to Martin, 23 April 1760, PRO, WO 4/60, pp. 586–94.
128. Officers in Scotland also drew excess rations, and were directed to reimburse the contractor: Barrington to Beauclerk, 6 November 1759, PRO, WO 4/59, p. 226; 21 November 1759, ibid, p. 303; Beauclerk to Barrington, 13 November 1759, PRO, WO 1/978, ff. 67–8; 27 November 1759, PRO, WO 1/689, f. 429; Barrington to Beauclerk, 6 December 1759, PRO, WO 4/59, p. 367; 8 January 1760, ibid, p. 491; Beauclerk to Barrington, 15 January 1760, PRO, WO 1/614, f. 235; 10 July 1760, ibid., f. 499.
129. 2 February 1760, PRO, WO 4/61, pp. 172–3.
130. War Office to Treasury, 23 April 1760, PRO, WO 4/60, pp. 586–94; Board of General Officers meeting, 20 June 1760, PRO, WO 71/10, pp. 41–5.
131. 2 July 1760, Calcraft papers, BL, Add. MS 17495, f. 92.
132. Barrington to Judge Advocate General, 29 May 1760, PRO, WO 4/61, pp. 166–7; 27 June 1760, PRO, WO 71/10, p. 46; Barrington to Martin, 27 June 1760, PRO, WO 4/61, pp. 338–9; 15 December 1760, PRO, T 29/34, p. 9.
133. Memorials: 23 May 1760, PRO, T 1/403, ff. 89–90; 3 June 1760, PRO, T 1/400, f. 239; 23 May 1760, PRO, T 29/33, p. 326.
134. Barrington to Whitman & Colonel La Fausielle, 27 June 1760, PRO, WO 4/61, pp. 340–1.
135. 21 May 1760, PRO, T 29/33, pp. 324–5; Treasury to Attorney General, 24 May 1760, PRO, T 27/28, p. 66; Articles of Agreement, 17 June 1760, PRO, T 54/37, pp. 418–21, 18 June 1762, PRO, T 54/38, p. 452.
136. War Office to Commanding Officers and Commander-in-Chief, 12 July 1760, PRO, WO 4/61, pp. 393–6; Barrington to LC Scott, 27 August 1760, ibid, p. 667.
137. P. O'Brien, 'Agriculture and the Home Market for English Industry', *English Historical Review*, 100:397 (1985), pp. 779, 784–5; itinerant harvest workers were exempt from recruitment between mid-May and mid-October in 'An Act for the Speedy and Effectual

Recruiting of H.M's Land Forces and Marines' (29 Geo. II.c.4), March 1756 (*Journal of Corporal William Todd*, p. 280 n. 111).
138. E. L. Jones, *Seasons and Prices, the Role of the Weather in English Agricultural History* (London: George Allen & Unwin, 1964), p. 142; hay and straw prices per load at London markets (*St James's Chronicle*, 13–15 April, 29 April–1 May, 3–5, 17–19 June, 13–15 July, 5–7 August 1762).
139. An estimate by the Victualling Commissioners indicated wheat prices of 1757 were almost double the average between 1752–6 (n.d., PRO, AO 17/42, p. 125).
140. Hancock, *Citizens of the World*, p. 236.
141. Average prices for peck loaves from *GM*, 30 (1760), pp. 48, 104, 156, 204, 252, 300, 347, 396, 444, 492, 544, 596; 31 (1761), pp. 48, 96, 144, 192, 240, 288, 336, 384, 432, 480, 540, 638; 32 (1762), pp. 48, 96, 148, 196, 244, 296, 344, 392, 450, 506, 524, 634; Beveridge, *Prices and wages*, pp. 199–200. See below (Table 5.4), p. 88.
142. Cf. 4.7*d*. for 4lb, or 7.05*d*. for 6lb (Mitchell, *Historical Statistics*, p. 770).
143. Bakers Company: weekly wheat returns on London Corn Exchange, 1756–1824, vol. 1, 1756–60, Guildhall Library, London; 2 & 30 April, 4 June 1759, MS 5183, f. 1.
144. Maj. Gen. A. Forbes, *A History of the Army Ordnance Services*, 3 vols (1929), vol. 1, pp. 177–80; George Harrison (Treasury) to Secretary at War, 15 June 1808 and Comptrollers Report, 13 June 1808: unnumbered papers, PRO, WO 40/29 Bundle 1808b; Report into the Civil Administration of the Army, 13 December 1833, *PP* (1837), xxxiv. [78], p. 135.
145. 19 July 1797, Appendix to Nineteenth Report from the Select Committee on Finance: Expenditure of Public Revenue, *House of Commons Committee Reports 1715–1803*, xii, p. 372.
146. Provincial merchants, millers, corn factors, and bakers were involved in encampment supply, 1778–82 (Baker, 'Open Contracting', p. 444).
147. Advertisements for tenders included established features, sealed proposals, bonds, no proposals received after deadlines, alongside innovations such as printed forms for tenders, and the stipulation that prices must be expressed in words, *The Times*, 12 December 1815; Director-General of Commissariat, 10 July 1856, Select Committee on Contracts, *PP* (1856), vii. [362], pp. 209–11.
148. Speeches of the First Earl 1778–82, n.d., Liverpool papers, BL, Add. MS 38383, f. 21.
149. 11 May 1758, PRO, AO 1/174, f. 509.
150. 11 November 1758, PRO, AO 1/174, f. 510; Oswald to Treasury, 30 May 1758, PRO, T 1/367, f. 84.
151. 29 January 1813, PRO, AO 1/174, f. 511.
152. 6 June 1761, PRO, AO 1/175, f. 515; 29 June 1759, PRO, T 54/37, pp. 222–7; 10 July 1759, PRO, T 29/33, p. 209; 29 October 1759, ibid, p. 237; 12 March 1760, ibid, p. 301.
153. 22 May 1762, PRO, AO 1/175, f. 516; 21 July 1760, PRO, T 52/51, p. 94; 20 December 1760, ibid, pp. 298–9; 16 January 1761, ibid, pp. 364–5; 17 December 1761, PRO, T 52/53, pp. 131–2.
154. 23 December 1762, PRO, AO 1/175, f. 517; 9 July 1762, PRO, T 1/412, f. 26.
155. 23 December 1763, PRO, AO 1/175, f. 518; including ground rent for 1761 encampments, 3 February 1762, PRO, T 52/53, p. 206.
156. Calculated from Declared Accounts, PRO, AO 1/174, ff. 509–11; PRO, AO 1/175, ff. 515–18.

157. 15 April 1756, PRO, AO 17/41, pp. 243–52; Hume to Treasury, 25 September 1756, PRO, T 1/369, f. 45; 1 June 1757, PRO, AO 17/42, pp. 99–103; 26 April 1758, PRO, T 29/33, p. 41; 29 January 1813, PRO, AO 1/174, f. 511; 29 June 1759, PRO, T 54/37, pp. 222–7; 17 June 1760, ibid, pp. 418–21; 8 July 1761, ibid, pp. 478–81; 9 June 1761, PRO, T 29/34, pp. 95–7; 18 June 1762, PRO T 54/38, pp. 448–53.

6 A Domestic Contractor: John Willan

1. Dickson, *Financial Revolution*, p. 23.
2. *The Times*, 9 May 1836.
3. An error repeated in B. Austen, *British Mail Coach Services 1784–1850* (New York: Garlands, 1986), p. 269.
4. The elder John Willan appears never to have been proprietor of the Bull and Mouth Inn. A John Willan, probably the nephew, is listed in *Kent's Directory*, 45 (1768), as a 'Factor' in Bull and Mouth Street. It has been claimed that John Willan Jr's association with the Bull and Mouth Inn dates from 1785 when he leased the inn and adjoining property for forty-one years (B. Lillywhite, *London Coffee Houses* (London: George Allen & Unwin, 1963), p. 141), but he was sworn into the Innholders Company on 1 July 1777 (Innholders Company Freedom Admissions, 1673–1820, Guildhall Library, London, MS 6651/1, f. 139).
5. P. Earle, *The Making of the English Middle Class: Business, Society and Family Life in London, 1660–1730* (London: Methuen, 1989), p. 5.
6. The Willan family archive details this shift from active farming to gentrification.
7. No children but possibly married three times, although identification is inconclusive. At his death his wife was Elizabeth Bradshaw, but a John Willan was married on 25 September 1762 to Elizabeth Stanley, and described as a widower. J. H. Chapman (ed.), *The Register Book of Marriages Belonging to the Parish of St George's Hanover Square, Vol. 1, 1725–1787* (London: Harleian Society, 1886), p. 114.
8. Leonard Willan, Mayor of Kingston-upon-Hull (1585–6), Merchant Adventurer; James Willan of Kingston-upon-Hull confirmed the family Grant of Arms in 1617; *Genealogical Quarterly*, 15:2 (1948), p. 61; Willan family archive: private collection [hereafter WFA], WFA 2/3/1 (Box 14); the name is recorded in Westmoreland in 1545 (J. Nicolson and R. Burn, *The History and Antiquities of the Counties of Westmoreland and Cumberland*, 2 vols (London: W. Strachan and T. Cadell, 1777), vol. 1, p. 474).
9. Account book of John Warrington, PRO, C 103/32.
10. *The Times*, 14 August 1792; *GM*, 62:2 (1792), p. 774.
11. 21 August 1792, W.F.1/1 (Box 1); PRO, PROB 10, f. 3217.
12. *Cheltenham Chronicle*, 17 August 1792.
13. Evidence of James Smith, House of Lords, 16 February 1805, WFA 1/3/3/27 (Box 1).
14. 'How Hatch estate papers', Indentures, 3–4 May 1782, 31 July 1783, Tower Family Archive, Essex County Record Office, [hereafter ERO], D/DTw/T43.
15. Willan Family Tree prepared by Peter J. Willan from family papers and notes by his father James H. G. Willan in Willan family archive; Kirkby Lonsdale Parish Register, Cumbria County Record Office, Kendal, WPR 19/2.
16. 12 January 1746, RA Cumberland, Box 9, f. 72; 23 January 1746, ibid., f. 140.
17. R. C. Jarvis, *The Jacobite Risings of 1715 and 1745* (Carlisle: Cumberland County Council, 1954), p. 263.

18. M. Brown, '"The Fields of Cows by Willan's farm": Thomas Willan of Marylebone (1755–1828)', *Westminster History Review*, 4 (2001), pp. 1–5; p. 1; A. Saunders, *Regent's Park: A Study of the Development of the Area from 1086 to the Present Day* (Newton Abbot: David and Charles, 1969), p. 57.
19. Brown identifies Willan as 'senior partner in a firm of mercers located from 1765 at 8 Chandos Street, Covent Garden', 'Willan's Farm', p. 1; PRO, PROB 11/1231 (1793) indicates this was a different man.
20. Parish of St Marylebone rate-books, Poor rate 1746, MF Reel 4, Westminster City Archives [hereafter WCA].
21. Middlesex Deeds Register, (Robert Andrews and John Willan), WCA, 1751/1/10; F. H. W. Sheppard, *The Survey of London, Vol. 40: The Grosvenor Estate in Mayfair, Part 2: The Buildings* (London: Athlone Press, 1980), p. 186.
22. Articles for building, 1 November 1752, Grosvenor Estate papers, WCA, Box 11/13/ f. 1094/3.
23. St George's Hanover Square rate-books (1752–73), WCA, C290–319.
24. Sheppard, *Survey of London, Vol. 40*, p. 195.
25. Jervis was a neighbour in the South Weald, Essex. There is no evidence they were acquainted before 1784 when Jervis moved to Essex, WFA 1/1 (Box 1); Alfred Hills, 'Lord St. Vincent at Rochetts', *Essex Review*, 44 (1935), pp. 8–15.
26. Not listed in those paying plate duties, 1756–62, PRO, T 47/5; 1762–4, PRO, T 47/4; between 1758–61 he owned a curricle; in 1761 a post-chaise, Carriage duty register, PRO, T 47/3, p. 72.
27. 19 May 1757, PRO, T 1/375, f. 108.
28. 19 May 1757, PRO, T 29/32, p. 464.
29. N.d. [*c.* May 1757], PRO, T 1/375, f. 138.
30. 'Proposals for Furnishing the Camps with Forage', 25 April 1759, PRO, T29/33, pp. 171–2; 30 May 1759, ibid, pp. 187–8.
31. Ligonier to Newcastle, 13 March 1759, PRO, T 1/389, ff. 99–100; *LG*, 3–7 April 1759.
32. Memorandum from Lord Viscount Ligonier, n.d. [*c.* May 1759], Chatham papers, PRO 30/8/76, ff. 64–5; 30 May 1759, PRO, T 29/33, pp. 187–8.
33. John Mill to Treasury, 24 April 1759, PRO, T 1/393, ff. 32–3.
34. With the Isle of Wight treated separately, competition was effectively reduced to four proposals, 25 April 1759, PRO, T 29/33, pp. 171–2; Willan's contract specifically excluded the Isle of Wight, PRO, T 54/37, pp. 222–7.
35. 'Disposition of the Army', *Scots Magazine*, 21 (1759), p. 385; 12 February 1760, BL, Add. MS 33048, f. 9.
36. *Whitehall Evening Post*, 2–5 June 1759.
37. 'The Present Camps', 13 July 1759, PRO, WO 1/869, f. 297; 6 June 1761, PRO, AO 1/175, f. 515; Houlding, *Fit for Service*, pp. 329–31; Whitworth, *Ligonier*, p. 283.
38. Yet Lord Royston informed Hardwicke that forage was scarce, 8 June 1759, BL, Add. MS 35352, f. 70.
39. 6 June 1761, PRO, AO 1/175, f. 515.
40. 30 May 1759, PRO, T 29/33, p. 188; the security provided is unstated.
41. 5 May 1756, PRO, T 29/32, p. 386; Baldwin unsuccessfully applied for an encampment contract, 26 April 1758, PRO, T 29/33, p. 41; on Godfrey, see above, pp. 68–9.
42. Ligonier's orders for winter quarters, 7 November 1759, PRO, WO 71/10, pp. 35–6.

43. Calcraft to Colonel Burton, n.d. [*c.* 22 May 1759], Calcraft papers, BL, Add. MS 17494, ff. 178–9; for 'unspeakable confusion' caused by false reports of a French landing, 7 July 1759, *GM*, 29 (1759), p. 343.
44. 12 June 1759, BL, Add. MS 32892, f. 27.
45. Warrants, 17 October 1759, PRO, SP 44/191, ff. 301–2; West, *Gunpowder*, p. 53.
46. 3 July 1759, PRO, T 29/33, p. 203; 29 October 1759, ibid, p. 237; 12 March 1760, ibid, p. 301.
47. 9 November 1759, PRO, T 29/33, p. 240.
48. 6 June 1761, PRO, AO 1/175, f. 515.
49. For the persistence of the invasion threat, Hardwicke to Newcastle, 4 October 1759, BL, Add. MS 32896, f. 266; cf. Intelligence (Paris), October 1759, ibid., ff. 330–3; 22 May 1762, PRO, AO 1/175, f. 516.
50. 21 May 1760, PRO, T 29/33, pp. 324–5; on fraud allegations, see above, pp. 83–5.
51. 23 May 1760, PRO, T 29/33, p. 326.
52. 11 June 1762, PRO, T 29/34, p. 302.
53. Paymaster General's papers, 1756–61, PRO, PMG 60/1; 11 December 1760, *HCJ*, 28, p. 974; 14 January 1761, ibid, p. 1020; 11 February 1761, *HCJ*, 29, p. 70.
54. Willan requested £15,000, citing costs to 14 January at £47,453 (Memorial, 14 January 1760, PRO, T 1/400, ff. 161–3).
55. Calculated total and details from PRO, AO 1/175, f. 515.
56. Hume to Treasury, 5 January 1761, PRO, T 1/407, ff. 151–2; 8 January 1761, PRO, T29/34, p. 12.
57. Jones, *Seasons and Prices*, pp. 141–2; 15 April 1756, PRO, AO 17/41, pp. 243–52; 29 June 1759, PRO, T 54/37, pp. 222–7.
58. St Paul's Cathedral Register of Prebendal Leases 1721–96, Guildhall Library, London, vol. 1: MS 25745, ff. 133–40; Probate, 7 April 1766, PRO, PROB 11/917, f. 137; Bakers Company (miscellaneous), Guildhall Library, Wheat prices at Corn Exchange, 13 & 20 November, 11 December 1758, MS 7801/1, ff. 30–2.
59. St George's Hanover Square rate-books 1759–61, WCA, C334–6; house and stables, North Row, 1753–73, C322–49, MF 485–9; C319, MF 2104.
60. Bank of England Archive, 3% Consols ledger (1761–4), AC 27/1422, f. 9469; A similar pattern discernible in the stockholding of John Warrington, Willan's erstwhile partner, 3% Consols ledger (1757), AC 27/1390, f. 4871; (1765), AC 27/1442, f. 10622.
61. St Marylebone rate-books (1760–1), WCA, MF 9; (1760 and 1761), MF 43; Howard De Walden (Portland) papers: Rentals 1779 lists Willan under 'Old Rents', paying £190, p.a., WCA, Acc. 449/3, f. 39.
62. Dundas to Barrington, 14 March 1756, PRO, T 1/367, f. 19.
63. See above (Table 5.3), p. 88.
64. Deliveries to Maidstone, Canterbury and Chatham, 2 June 1757, PRO, WO 47/47, pp. 603–4; 3 June 1757, ibid, p. 608; 20 June 1757, ibid, p. 662; Staff appointments to Artillery Train (Chatham), 21 June 1758, PRO, WO 46/8; West, *Gunpowder*, p. 85.
65. 26 April 1758, PRO, T 29/33, p. 41; 25 April 1759, ibid, pp. 171–2; 9 June 1761, PRO, T29/34, pp. 95–7; 11 June 1762, ibid, pp. 302–3.
66. 30 October 1755, PRO, WO 47/46, pp. 374–5; Charles Frederick to Ordnance Officers, 4 November 1755, PRO, WO 55/2, f. 25; 23 March 1756, PRO, WO 47/47, pp. 310–11; 12 December 1757, *HCJ*, 28, pp. 19–20.
67. Ligonier to Frederick, 27 October 1755, Ligonier papers, BL, Add. MS 57318, f. 45; 4 November 1755, ibid., f. 46.

68. *LG*, 31 May–4 June 1757; Expenditure of Public Money (Ordnance), 18 April 1763, *HCJ*, 29, p. 637.
69. *LG*, 11–15 July 1758; cf. contract for 1,000 horses for British artillery in Germany, 11 January 1760, PRO, WO 47/55, pp. 50–1; 11 January 1760, ibid, pp. 39–40; 18 April 1763, *HCJ*, 29, p. 637; for Scotland, see below, p. 118.
70. Ligonier to Frederick, 30 July 1757, Ligonier papers, BL, Add. MS 57318, f. 106; Frederick to Ordnance officers, 31 January 1758, PRO, WO 55/2, f. 120; West, *Gunpowder*, p. 115.
71. 1 April 1760, PRO, WO 47/55, p. 282; 2 May 1760, ibid, p. 358.
72. 30 May 1760, ibid, p. 454; 1 June 1760, ibid, p. 493; 13 June 1760, ibid, p. 498; 26 November 1762, PRO, WO 47/60, pp. 374–5.
73. 25 June 1760, PRO, WO 47/55, p. 536; 29 August 1760, PRO, WO 47/56, p. 158; 4 October 1760, ibid, p. 253; 10 October 1760, ibid, p. 270.
74. Calculated from Account book, PRO, C 103/202; after £1,724 deducted for 'expenses attending the contract', including fees, stationary, coach hire, expenses attending the Tower on business and Warrington's 'time for 2½ years attendance on Partnership account.'
75. *London Evening Post*, 3–5 April 1746, 12–14 October 1756; Probate, 11 May 1759, PRO, PROB 11/846, f. 168.
76. Account book, PRO, C 103/202; Probate, 17 February 1761, PRO, PROB 11/863, f. 55.
77. Guildhall Library: Innholders Company Court livery and members lists 1706–76, MS 6656/2; Innholders Company Freedom Admissions 1673–1820, MS 6656/1, ff. 55, 83.
78. *London Evening Post*, 25–27 May 1756, 17–19 August 1756, 12–14 February 1757.
79. Guildhall Library, Innholders Company Freedom Admissions, 1673–1820, MS 6651/1, f. 85; Probate, 21 August 1769, PRO, PROB 11/950, f. 283.
80. It appears likely Joseph Gibson was resident at the New Hercules Inn, Westminster Bridge (*London Evening Post*, 19–22, 24–26 March 1757); William Gibson bred horses at Brands, near Kilburn (*London Evening Post*, 26–28 February 1756); on his father, author of the 'Farriers New Guide', see *London Evening Post*, 6–9 October 1750, *Public Advertiser*, 11 March 1756.
81. Calcraft to Granby, 20 November 1758, Calcraft papers, BL, Add. MS 14794, f. 50.
82. *Read's Weekly Journal*, 5 June 1756.
83. *London Evening Post*, 4–7 September 1756.
84. K. Chivers, 'The Supply of Horses in Great Britain in the Nineteenth Century', in F. M. L. Thompson (ed.), *Horses in European Economic History: A Preliminary Canter* (Reading: British Agricultural History Society, 1983), pp. 31–49; F. M. L. Thompson, 'Nineteenth-century Horse Sense', *Economic History Review*, 29:1 (1976), pp. 60–81.
85. *London Evening Post*, 29–31 July 1756.
86. C. Smith, *Three Tracts on the Corn-Trade and Corn-Laws*, 2nd edn (London: J. Brotherton, 1766), p. 208; an estimated 6,000 quarters of oats were consumed weekly by an estimated 32,000 horses in London in 1764, *St James's Chronicle*, 29–31 March 1764.
87. Maj. G. Tylden, *Horses and Saddlery* (London: J. A. Allen & Co., 1965), p. 3; Guy, *Oeconomy and Discipline*, p. 125.
88. J. Thirsk, 'The Marketing of Agricultural Produce', in J. Thirsk (ed.), *The Agrarian History of England and Wales*, 6 vols (Cambridge, 1981–4), vol. 5:2, p. 437; based on W. Owen,

An Authentic Account Published by the King's Authority, of All the Fairs in England and Wales (London: W. Owen, 1756).
89. Chivers, 'Supply of Horses', p. 38; for examples of repositories, see *London Evening Post*, 29 April–1 May 1756, 24–26 February and 2–5 April 1757.
90. P. Edwards, *The Horse Trade of Tudor and Stuart England* (Cambridge: Cambridge University Press, 1988), pp. 81, 89.
91. Calcraft to Peter Taylor, 3 October 1760, Calcraft papers, BL, Add. MS 17495, f. 156.
92. Calcraft to Tyrawley, 2 July 1760, ibid., f. 57; Namier and Brooke, *Commons*, vol. 3, pp. 44–5.
93. Robert Doak to Oswald, 12 April 1766, Edinburgh University Library, Special Collections, Letters to Richard Oswald, Dk 1.30, f. 54; W. Page (ed.), *The Victoria History of the County of York*, 3 vols (Oxford: Oxford University Press, 1907–13), vol. 2, p. 513.
94. 'Merchant' indicated 'a function rather than an occupation', essentially involvement in foreign trade and finance, Minchison, 'Merchants in England', p. 279.
95. 21 August 1792, WFA 1/1 (Box 1).
96. Documents detailing estate and family history before the House of Lords, WFA 1/1 (Box 1); briefer account in *House of Lords Journals*, 47 (1809–10), pp. 270, 275, 323–4; 49 (1813–14), pp. 760, 804, 806, 868.
97. Plans and Alterations of Hornsey Wood House (1796), Willan v. Willan, PRO, C 171/48.
98. A stable keeper with stables in Curzon Street and leaseholds in Curzon Street and Clarges Street, his sister Isabel married James Willan, a younger brother of the elder John Willan. Thomas and John Willan, both Executors, are described in his will as nephews (Probate, 22 August 1800, PRO, PROB 11/1346, f. 602; *Public Advertiser*, 14 and 15 February 1770).
99. The younger John Willan was born in Westmoreland ('Case of the Respondents', January 1812, WFA 1/3/4 (Box 1)).
100. W. B. Bannerman and Capt. R. R. B. Bannerman, *The Registers of Marriages of St. Marylebone, Middlesex, 1775–1783, Vol. 51* (London: Harleian Society, 1921), p. 43; Namier and Brooke, *Commons*, vol. 2, p. 135.
101. Ordnance papers, BL, Add. MS 33116, f. 153; 8 and 9 August 1775, PRO, WO 47/86, p. 93.
102. Debate on Duke of Richmond's Report for the Ordnance Estimates, 10 March 1783, Hansard, *PD*, vol. 23, c. 635.
103. 16 October 1782, PRO, WO 47/100, p. 463.
104. 2 October 1782, ibid, p. 387.
105. 10 March 1783, Hansard, *PD*, vol. 23, cc. 615–40.
106. 4 December 1782, PRO, WO 47/100, p. 632, 6 January 1783, PRO, WO 47/101, p. 39.
107. Probate, 11 October 1780, PRO, PROB 11/1070, f. 498; PRO, PROB 10, f. 2820; 16 June 1795, PRO, WO 47/2559, pp. 674–5; 19 July 1797, Twenty-First Report of the Select Committee on Finance, Expenditure of the Public Revenue, *House of Commons Committee Reports 1715–1803*, xii, p. 434.
108. Report from the Select Committee on Mail Coach Exemption, *PP* (1810–11), iii. [212], p. 707; Austen, *Mail Coach Services*, p. 260; one of the 'most celebrated and widely used' inns for mail coaches (C. F. D. Marshall, *The British Post Office from its Beginnings to the End of 1925* (Oxford: Oxford University Press, 1926), p. 200); it is unclear whether the

Willan family had any connection with the Bull and Mouth livery stables, Hart Street, Bloomsbury (*Universal Register*, 7 January 1785).
109. Described as 'a man's head horribly opened, and over it a black bull', *Universal Register*, 11 January 1785.
110. British Postal Museum and Archives, London, Mileage Warrants (1789), POST 96/21, f. 29; (1792), POST 10, f. 245; Oil Account, 30 June 1796, POST 10, f. 27; petition of London mail coach contractors, 22 January 1817, Liverpool papers, BL, Add. MS 38379, ff. 221–5; in June 1822 he purchased horses from Dixon, proprietor of a Barbican repository (16 August 1822, Account Book of Bull & Mouth, WFA 2/2 (Box 1)).
111. *GM*, 92 (1822), p. 189; *The Times*, 29 July 1822.
112. Evidence to the Lords, 13 March 1805, WFA 1/1; 24 April 1805, WFA 1/3 (Box 1).
113. Probate, 27 September 1798, PRO, PROB 11/1312, f. 596; *GM*, 68 (1798), p. 817; previously 'Extraordinary Clerk' to the Ordnance Treasurer (*Court and City Kalendar* (1763), p. 178).
114. Sixth codicil, 6 August 1792, WFA 1/1 (Box 1).
115. Sedgwick, *Commons*, vol. 2, pp. 360–1; Namier, *American Revolution*, pp. 473–4, 476.
116. J. C. Sainty, *Office-Holders in Modern Britain: Treasury officials 1660–1870* (London: Athlone Press, 1972), pp. 6, 34, 76, 332, 516–17; West papers (Treasury), BL, Add. MS 34736, f. 121; Martin to Newcastle, 19 February 1762, BL, Add. MS 32934, f. 453; Probate, 23 June 1804, PRO, PROB 8/197.
117. Freehold estates at Warwick, Oxford, and Worcester held in exchange for £1,000 annual rental to Elizabeth Willan, 30 June 1795, ERO, D/DTw/T43; Arthur Young told how the manager of the East India Company stud at Barking bought a horse from Poole (*General View of the Agriculture of the County of Essex*, 2 vols (London: B. McMillan, 1807), vol. 2, p. 355).
118. Note Book 'Business at the Treasury', BL, Add. MS 30219, f. 25; 'Distribution of the Treasury Business to the Chief Clerks', n.d., Minto papers, NLS, MS 11040, ff. 33–4; 28 April 1778, T 29/47, pp. 93–4.
119. Newcastle to Rockingham, 23 August 1757, BL, Add. MS 32873, f. 244.
120. Sedgwick, *Commons*, vol. 2, pp. 360–1; Henry Poole to Newcastle, 14 January 1758, BL Add. MS 32877, f. 128; 3 May 1759, BL, Add. MS 32890, f. 460; Henry Poole to Jenkinson, Liverpool papers, 30 March 1765, BL, Add. MS 38204, f. 174.
121. 'Abstract of Willan Family Settlement', 3 June 1826, ERO, D/DTw/T43/33.
122. 'Willan Family Settlement', ERO, D/DTw/T43/36.
123. For a brief description of How Hatch and landscape garden with a 'fine avenue of elms', see G. A. Ward, *A History of South Weald and Brentwood* (Waddon: Spenser Press 1961), p. 24; W. Page et al (eds), *The Victoria History of the County of Essex*, 10 vols (Oxford: Oxford University Press, 1903–2001), vol. 8, p. 78; Young, *General View*, vol. 1, p. 34.
124. 'Particulars of a Valuable Freehold and Copyhold Estate of How Hatch, South Weald, Essex', 2 June 1829, ERO, D/DTw/E10; Statement on sale, King's Bench, 15 November 1828, ERO, D/DTw/T43.
125. The younger John Willan left £60,000, 5 October 1822; WFA 2/1 (Box 1); assessed under £70,000 when re-sworn, 27 October 1829, PRO, IR 26/936, ff. 829–31; Thomas Willan left £23,780, 16 April 1828, PRO, IR 26/1881, f. 37.
126. William Willan matriculated at Christ Church, 26 January 1790, J. Foster (ed.), *Alumni Oxonienses 1715–1886*, 4 vols (Oxford and London: Parker and Co., 1888), vol. 4, p. 1557.
127. Notice of sale by auction, 14 December 1865, WFA, EMW 3/6 (Box 14).

128. Account Book of Bull & Mouth, 18 July 1822–1 March 1824, WFA 2/2 (Box 1); H. W. Hart, 'Sherman and the Bull and Mouth', *Journal of Transport History*, 5:1 (1961), pp. 12–21; pp. 12–14; Lillywhite, *London Coffee Houses*, p. 141; W. J. Gordon, *The Horse World of London* (London: Leisure Hour Library, 1893), pp. 109–10.
129. 21 August 1792, WFA 1/1 (Box 1).
130. Marylebone Park, Manor of Marylebone papers, 1730–1805, Draft report, n.d. [*c.* January 1803], PRO, CRES 2/736; 'Mr. Potter's Sketch of Survey of Marylebone Park Estate', n.d., White papers, WCA, D/Wh/ f. 62; 'Quantities taken from the particulars of sale', ibid., f. 64.
131. 'Extract from Minutes', 9 July 1806, PRO, WO 44/299; J. Wanklyn (ed.), *Guns at the Wood: A Record of St. John's Wood Barracks* (Privately published, 1972), p. 10.
132. Thomas Willan to Colonel Neville, 5 June 1810; Treasury to R. H. Crew, 28 March 1812, Barrack Office to Crew, 2 April 1812, Thomas Willan to Crew, 12 April 1812, William Tull to Ordnance, 24 June 1812, PRO, WO 44/299; Wanklyn (ed.), *Guns at the Wood*, p. 13.

7 Domestic Supply and Contracting in Scotland, 1746–62

1. Discussing Scots in England, *Old England* asked, 'Is there a merchant among them?' (27 December 1746, *GM*, 16 (1746), pp. 633–4); in Scotland, a merchant is a retail shopkeeper (M. Robinson (ed.), *The Concise Scots Dictionary* (Aberdeen: Aberdeen University Press, 1987), p. 410.
2. Pack horses and panniers remained common at mid-century (H. Hamilton, *The Industrial Revolution in Scotland* (Oxford: Clarendon Press, 1932), pp. 226–7).
3. [E. Burt], *Letters from a gentleman in the North of Scotland to his friend in London*, 2 vols (London: S. Birt, 1754), vol. 1, pp. 310–11.
4. Cumberland argued even loyal Scots should not hold responsible *military* positions (Fox to Newcastle, 5 August 1748, PRO, SP 41/19).
5. On the dissolution of the Jacobite threat, see Fox to General Churchill, 31 May 1749, PRO, WO 4/46, pp. 213–14.
6. See above, p. 12.
7. 'The season of the year is bad: but that's bad for the enemy too' (Earl of Mar to Chevalier St George, 9 December 1715, HMC, *Mar and Kellie* (London: HMSO, 1904), p. 516); A. and H. Tayler, *1715: The Story of the Rising* (London: T. Nelson & Sons, 1936), p. 66; lack of provisions prevented pursuit of the rebels into the Highlands (*Daily Courant*, 25 January 1716).
8. Mar to Chevalier, 24 November 1715, HMC, *Mar and Kellie*, p. 514; *Flying Post*, 11–13 October 1715, *LG*, 8–12 November 1715; Baynes, *Jacobite Rising*, p. 172.
9. In July 1715, there were only 197 troops in four permanent Scottish garrisons (*HCJ*, 18, p. 407); independent companies were disbanded and offices abolished ('Anonymous Letter on Scottish Affairs in the Parliament', n.d. [*c.* 1713], HMC, *Laing*, 2 vols (London: HMSO, 1914–25), vol. 2, pp. 167–71; George Baillie to Earl of Marchmont, 26 May 1713, HMC, *Polwarth*, vol. 1, p. 13).
10. K. C. Corsar, 'The Garrison of Scotland, 1719', *JSAHR*, 22:85 (1943), p. 18.
11. 'Barracks & Forts Built, no Troops put in, and of little use, till the Communication was made', Bill for renewing the Highland bill 1725, BL, Add. MS 33049, f. 270; J. B. Salmond, *Wade in Scotland* (Edinburgh: Moray Press, 1934), pp. 41–51; Corsar, 'Garrison of Scotland', pp. 15–19.

12. Wade to Lord Townshend, 10 April 1727, HMC, *Townshend*, vol. 1, pp. 197–8; Tweeddale to Cope, 13 March 1744, PRO, SP 55/13, f. 98.
13. Clode, *Military Forces*, vol. 1, pp. 227, 240.
14. C. Tabraham and D. Grove, *Fortress Scotland and the Jacobites* (1995), p. 24; 'Memorial relating to Quartering of Forces in Scotland before the Union', January 1760, Saltoun, NLS, MS 17506, ff. 4–5; James Stewart (Aide-de-camp) to Quartermasters, 28 September 1751, Blaikie, NLS, MS 308, f. 19.
15. Treasury to Comptrollers, 3 October 1746, PRO, AO 17/38, pp. 9–10; Comptrollers Report, 11 February 1747, p. 24; cf. Bland to Thomas Leslie, 18 August 1748, Blaikie, NLS, MS 304, f. 95.
16. Innes to Ludovick Grant, 24 December 1746, Seafield Muniments, NAS, GD248/48/4, f. 81; Fort William was an exception. By custom, the Governor managed garrison supply, Bland to Leslie, 8 March 1748, Blaikie, NLS, MS 304, f. 44.
17. Lenman, *Jacobite Risings*, p. 249; R. C. Jarvis, 'Cope's March North, 1745', in R. C. Jarvis, *Collected Papers on the Jacobite Risings*, 2 vols (Manchester: Manchester University Press, 1971), vol. 1, p. 7.
18. Cope to Pelham, 27 August 1745, NeC 1631; Adam Bachop to Guest, 27 August 1745, PRO, SP 54/25, f. 101c.
19. Bland to [Pelham?] 9 June 1746, NeC 1725; Sir J. Fergusson, *Argyll in the Forty-Five* (London: Faber and Faber, 1951), pp. 74, 88; Brigadier-General Fleming to Newcastle, 27 March 1746, PRO, SP 36/82, ff. 91–2.
20. Dunmore to Fawkener, 27 December 1745, RA Cumberland, Box 8, f. 48; Alexander Hume to Fawkener, 21 December 1745, ibid., f. 86.
21. 25 December 1745, PRO, T 52/43, p. 449; *Scots Magazine*, 8 (January 1746), p. 50; Newcastle to Hawley, 4 January 1746, PRO, SP 54/27, p. 4.
22. Jacob Gomez Serra's Account of the State of the Magazines in Scotland, 6 January 1746, RA Cumberland, Box 9, ff. 36–7.
23. Wentworth to Newcastle, 9 January 1746, PRO, SP 36/80, f. 213; Yonge to Wentworth, 4 January 1746, PRO, WO 4/41, p. 190; John Huske to [Pelham?], 9 January 1746, NeC 1716, f. 1.
24. Lady Elizabeth Hastings [recounting letter she received] to Lord Hastings, 10 February 1746, HMC, *Hastings*, 3 vols (London: HMSO, 1928–34), vol. 3, p. 54.
25. Alexander Hamilton to Charles Mackie, 28 December 1745, HMC, *Laing*, vol. 2, p. 350.
26. W. B. Blaikie (ed.), *Origins of the 'Forty Five and Other Papers Relating to that Rising* (Edinburgh: Scottish History Society, 1916), pp. 335–69; Auditors Report, 6 February 1749, PRO, T 27/26, pp. 452–4.
27. Account Book of Jacob Gomez Serra, PRO, T 1/322, f. 56; Mayor of Newcastle to 'My Lord', 29 March 1746, PRO, SP 36/82, ff. 104–5; Edward Lloyd to Messrs. Franco, 4 March 1746, PRO, SP 54/29, f. 106.
28. Blaikie (ed.), *Origins*, pp. 429, 431–4; for transports in the Thames loaded with corn, shoes, stockings and waistcoats, see *London Evening Post*, 2–4 January 1746; Galfridius Mann to Edward Lloyd, 18 February 1745, PRO, SP 41/17, f. 45; L. Colley, *Britons: Forging the Nation 1707–1837* (New Haven, CT: Yale University Press, 1992), pp. 80–5, 376–7.
29. Fawkener to Hawley, 14 January 1746, RA Cumberland, Box 9, f. 78; 24 January 1746, PRO, SP 54/37, f. 41.

30. From January they delivered forage and coals, Hawley to Ligonier, 16 February 1746, PRO, SP 54/28, ff. 94–5; Hume considered a contract necessary for accounting purposes. Hume to Fawkener, 9 March 1746, RA Cumberland, Box 12, f. 18.
31. Account of provisions from Linlithgow, 31 January 1746, RA Cumberland, Box 10, f. 32; 19 June 1754, PRO, AO 1/485, f. 50; accounts: 14 March 1753, PRO, T 1/354, f. 1; January 1746–February 1747, ZA, ZNK X1/1/3.
32. Sir J. B. Paul (ed.), *The Scots Peerage*, 9 vols (Edinburgh: David Douglas, 1904–14), vol. 5, p. 317; M. I. Dundas, *Dundas of Fingask* (Edinburgh: D. Douglas, 1891), pp. 57–8.
33. Orderly Book of Lt. Col. Joseph Yorke 1746: Falkirk, 1 February, Stirling, 2 February, Hardwicke papers, BL, Add. MS 36257, ff. 5, 6v.
34. Dundas to John Erskine, 4 February 1746, Mar and Kellie papers, NAS, GD124/15, f. 1562.
35. Namier and Brooke, *Commons*, vol. 3, pp. 118–19; 14 December 1745 and 27 January 1746, Orderly-book of Cumberland's army, 23 October 1745–14 August 1746, Blaikie, NLS, MS 303, ff. 55 and 92.
36. Fawkener to Hawley, 14 January 1746, RA Cumberland, Box 9, f. 78.
37. 28 September 1780, J. W. Reed and F. A. Pottle (eds), *Boswell, Laird of Auchinleck 1778–1782* (New York and London: McGraw-Hill, 1977), p. 254.
38. See account book, PRO, T 1/322, f. 56.
39. Perth and Inverness, 12, 16 & 20 February, 17, 19, 20 & 24 April 1746, Hardwicke papers, BL, Add. MS 36257, ff. 12, 18–19, 20, 60, 64, 66, 72; Campbell-Maclachlan, *Cumberland*, p. 283.
40. Dundas informed the Montrose Customs Collector that Cumberland ordered army provisions to be shipped duty-free, but as the law was fixed by Act of Parliament, the Customs Commissioners demanded payment (Montrose Port Records, Dundee City Archives [hereafter DCA], Collector to Board, 27 February and 15 March 1746, Letter Book, DCA, CE 53/1/4; Board to Collector, 3 March 1746, Letter Book, DCA, CE 53/2/5; correspondence regarding 'large quantities of coals and hay' at Inverness, Customs Commissioners (North Britain) to Treasury, 19 September 1751, PRO, T 1/346, f. 37; Petition of Dundas, n.d., after July 1746, PRO, T 1/322, f. 29).
41. Dundas to Albemarle, 11 August 1746, W. A. Keppel, *The Albemarle Papers: Being the Correspondence of William Anne, Second Earl of Albemarle Commander-in-Chief in Scotland 1746–1747*, ed. C. S. Terry, 2 vols (Aberdeen: New Spalding Club, 1902), vol. 1, pp. 95–6.
42. Albemarle to Fawkener, 16 November 1746, RA Cumberland, Box 19, f. 40; Mordaunt to Albemarle, 4 August 1746, Keppel, *Albemarle*, vol. 1, p. 43; Albemarle to Newcastle, 5 March 1746, BL, Add. MS 32706, f. 257.
43. Houlding, *Fit for Service*, p. 34 n. 61; by 1767 there were over 1,000 miles of military roads. I. MacIvor, *Fort George* (Edinburgh: HMSO, 1970), p. 13.
44. Newcastle to Cumberland, 12 September 1747, BL, Add. MS 32713, f. 54; cf. Fox to Bland, 'every Saving (consistent with the good of the Service) to the Publick, is now necessary', 6 December 1748, PRO, WO 4/45, p. 292; Pelham to Newcastle, 9/20 September 1748, Coxe, *Pelham*, vol. 2, p. 31.
45. Approximately 8,811 troops fought at Culloden, *Scots Magazine*, 8, (1746), p. 216; 'Forces to remain in North Britain 1747', RA Cumberland, Box 20, f. 5; 'List of Quarters of HM Forces', indicates 10,767 troops in England, 5 May 1752, PRO, SP 41/20.
46. 'Account of British Forces', BL, Add. MS 33047, f. 137.

47. Petition of James Paterson, 4 September 1746, PRO, T 1/321, f. 74; Auditors Report, 22 February 1749, PRO, T 27/26, pp. 452–4; petition of George Ross, agent for Inverness inhabitants, n.d., PRO, T 1/321, f. 95; refused on the basis most claimants were Jacobite sympathizers, Report of Henry Fox, 26 May 1753, PRO, T 1/354, f. 18; Glasgow received £10,000 for Rebel impositions: Magistrates and Town Council Petition, 12 April 1749, *HCJ*, 25, pp. 826–7; 21 April 1749, Hansard, *PD*, vol. 14, cc. 497–538.
48. Newcastle to Andrew Fletcher, 8 October 1747 recommending 'Protection and Encouragement', PRO, SP 54/37, f. 12.
49. Newcastle to Hardwicke, 21 March 1751, BL, Add. MS 32726, ff. 314–15.
50. Andrew Stone to Newcastle, 8 May 1752, BL, Add. MS 32727, ff. 121–4; Walpole, *Memoirs of George II*, vol. 1, p. 186.
51. Jacobites employed: 'some there are and some there ever were', Pelham to Newcastle, 3 July 1752, BL, Add. MS 32728, f. 188; Newcastle to Hardwicke, 1 February 1753, BL, Add. MS 32731, ff. 131–2; for a detailed account, n.d., late 1752, BL, Add. MS 33050, ff. 130–93.
52. Fox to Albemarle, 17 February 1747, PRO, WO 4/43, p. 115; 3 March 1747, ibid, p. 138; accounts, 1 September 1746–23 September 1747, ZA, ZNK X1/1/1; 5 February 1748, Blaikie, NLS MS 306, ff. 4v–5.
53. 17 February 1747, PRO, T 29/30, p. 371; 26 February and 3 March 1747, ibid, p. 380; based on County Fiars averages of wheat and oatmeal prices, A. J. S. Gibson and T. C. Smout, *Prices, Food and Wages in Scotland 1550–1870* (Cambridge: Cambridge University Press, 1995), pp. 105, 148–9, 156–7.
54. 17 March 1747, PRO, T 54/37, pp. 437–9; £7,170 for bread and wagons, 19 June 1754, PRO, AO 1/485, f. 50.
55. Dundas to Fawkener, 28 April 1747, RA Cumberland, Box 21, f. 440.
56. See below, pp. 111–12.
57. Fawkener informed Dundas that Cumberland considered the Flanders appointment a trial of his ability (21 April 1748, RA Cumberland, Box 33, f. 380); Dundas was employed until 21 February 1749 (6 January 1750, PRO, T 52/45, p. 43); Scottish appointment (20 February 1748, ibid, p. 7).
58. David Doig to 'My Lord' in Drummond to Pelham, 19 July 1751, NeC 1976, ff. 1–2.
59. Drummond to Pelham, 25 June 1751, NeC 1975.
60. Upwards of £946 in Gomez Serra's accounts were unvouched for, PRO, T 1/322, f. 29.
61. Dundas to Treasury, 11 July 1751, PRO, T 27/27, p. 17; 'Mr. Harding's Observations on the Auditors State & Report of the Account of Lawrence Dundas', n.d. [*c*. 1753], T 1/321, f. 114; 20 June 1753, PRO, T 29/32, pp. 136–7.
62. Drummond to Pelham, 3 September 1751, NeC 1977.
63. 10 July 1751, PRO, T 29/31, p. 379; 16 May 1753, PRO, T 29/32, p. 127, 30 May 1753, ibid, p. 129; 20 & 27 June 1753, ibid, pp. 136–8, 8 November 1753, ibid, p. 162.
64. Probably the two 'Robert Gardeners' in C. B. B. Watson (ed.), *Roll of Edinburgh Burgesses and Guild-Brethren, 1701–1760* (Edinburgh: Scottish Records Society, 1930), p. 76.
65. Gardiner to Treasury, n.d. [*c*. June 1759], PRO, T 1/407, f. 101; Dundas's accounts state Gardiner acted as commissary between 16 December 1745 and 2 December 1746 at Guest's request, 19 June 1754, PRO, AO 1/184, f. 50; the will of Gardiner's father describes his eldest son as 'a writer in Edinburgh', February 1739/40, Edinburgh Commissary Court, NAS, CC8/8/102, ff. 619–20.

66. Gardiner to Robert Grant, 7 May 1747, Grant family papers, BL, Add. MS 25409, f. 224; Gardiner settled Dundas's accounts in 1749 and 1751, PRO, AO 1/485, f. 50; Fox to Bland, 1 July 1755, PRO, WO 4/50, p. 344.
67. Earl of Zetland MS, HMC, *First Report* (London: HMSO, 1870), p. 44; Gardiner to Andrew Fletcher, 18 December 1745, Saltoun, NLS, MS 16608, f. 3; 28 February 1746, Saltoun, NLS, MS 16622, ff. 232–3.
68. Accounts, 16 December 1745–3 January 1746, Saltoun, NLS, MS 17529, f. 30.
69. 23 December 1745, ibid., f. 49; Linlithgow Volunteers to Gardiner, 9 December 1745, Saltoun, NLS, MS 16608, f. 2.
70. Gardiner to Andrew Fletcher, 26 February 1746, Saltoun, NLS, MS 16622, ff. 229–30; Gardiner to Robert Brisbane, 16 April 1746, ibid., f. 236.
71. Gardiner to Andrew Fletcher, 24 March 1746, Saltoun, NLS, MS 16622, ff. 234–5; letters from Linlithgow, Edinburgh, Falkirk, Crieff, 7 & 27–28 January & 1, 3 & 5 February 1746, ibid., ff. 220–1, 221–3, 225–6, 227–8.
72. Bland to Leslie, 8 March 1748, Blaikie, NLS, MS 304, f. 44, Bland to Edward Lloyd, 31 May 1748, ibid., f. 77.
73. James Stewart to Captain Kempe, 11 April 1754, ibid., f. 150; Beauclerk to Charles Townshend, 8 March 1762, PRO, WO 1/615, f. 281.
74. Bland to Treasury, 30 October 1756, PRO, T 1/407, f. 103; Bland recommended Gardiner's employment, 10 August 1756, ibid., f. 102; Gardiner had a high regard for Bland, naming his son after him, NAS, Seisins Registers, Edinburgh 1781–1801, No. 350.
75. Bland to Leslie, 1 March 1748, Blaikie, NLS, MS 304, ff. 40–1.
76. 16 March 1750, PRO, T 52/45, p. 300; Certificates of R. Napier and Henry Fox, 28 and 29 June 1754, PRO, T 1/358, f. 362; Fox requested from General Churchill a copy of the contract 'if there is one' or 'acquaint me on what foot he is employed?' For an example of decentralization in making contracts in Scotland, see 15 August 1749, PRO, WO 4/46, p. 322; MacIvor, *Fort George*, p. 14.
77. Fox to Churchill, 26 September 1749, PRO, WO 4/46, pp. 344–6; Caulfield to Churchill, 14 September 1749, Blaikie, NLS, MS 307, ff. 249–50; Fox to Churchill, 30 January 1750, PRO, WO 4/47, pp. 74–5.
78. Fox to Ordnance Board, 13 March 1750, PRO, WO 4/47, p. 118; Fox to Churchill, 12 April 1750, ibid, p. 173.
79. Ordnance Board to William Skinner, 16 March 1750, Skinner papers, BL, Add. MS 17500, ff. 17–18.
80. Gardiner to James Stewart, 17 October 1749, Blaikie, NLS, MS 307, ff. 274–5; Bland to Gardiner, 23 July 1755, Blaikie, NLS, MS 306, f. 15v.
81. Churchill to Fox, 21 December 1751, Blaikie, NLS, MS 308, ff. 100–1.
82. See Leslie's complaints about supplying detachments, Churchill to Leslie, 28 December 1751, ibid., f. 107; James Stewart informed Gardiner that Colonel Howard 'Spoke very Handsomely' of him (24 October 1752, Blaikie, NLS, MS 309, f. 4).
83. 25 April 1759, PRO, T 29/33, pp. 171–2; see below, p. 117, for Ordnance contract.
84. Bland to Holdernesse, 17 April 1755, PRO, SP 36/130, ff. 60–1; Commissary for Stores, Fort William, 21 and 30 November 1752, Register of Deeds (July-December 1752), NAS, RD2/172, ff. 355 and 408; 13 January 1752, 17 January 1753, 28 January 1754, *HCJ*, 26, pp. 349, 529, 930; 19 January 1756, *HCJ*, 27, p. 385.
85. Col. J. Allardyce (ed.), *Historical Papers Relating to the Jacobite Period, 1699–1750*, 2 vols (Aberdeen: New Spalding Club, 1895–6), vol. 1, pp. xxxiv, 129–30; *LG*, 22–25 October

1715; *Flying Post*, 25–27 October 1715; D. Defoe, *A Tour thro' the Whole Island of Great Britain*, 3rd edn, 4 vols (London: J. Osborn, S. Birt et al, 1742), vol. 4, p. 153.

86. V. Gibbs (ed.), *The Complete Peerage by G. E. C.*, 14 vols (London: St Catherine Press, 1910–59), vol. 11, pp. 203–4; J. C. Sainty, *A List of Representative Peers for Scotland, 1707 to 1963, and for Ireland, 1800 to 1961* (London: House of Lords record office, 1968), p. 20.

87. 'Quarters of Officers taken Prisoner by Jacobites at Prestonpans', 21 September 1745, RA Cumberland, Box 5, f. 291; Yonge to Leslie, 1 March 1746, PRO, WO 4/41, p. 258.

88. 20 October 1722, *HCJ*, 20, pp. 32–3; 27 October 1722, ibid, pp. 48–9; Establishment of Prince of Wales, Michaelmas 1742–March 1751, BL, Add. MS 32865, f. 334.

89. 4 January 1743, Morton papers, NAS, GD150/3481/3; Rothes to Newcastle, 17 May 1742, BL Add. MS 32699, f. 232; 8 March 1744, Order Book of Lord Stair, May 1743–June 1744, Stair papers, BL, Add. MS 20005, f. 10.

90. 'Military Recommendations of the Marquis of Tweeddale', 6 June 1743, PRO, SP 41/14; the second Marquis was his maternal grandfather (Paul (ed.), *Scots Peerage*, vol. 7, pp. 303–4).

91. J. Thomson, *The History of Dundee*, rev. and ed. J. Maclaren (Dundee: John Durham & Son, 1874), p. 119; *Scots Magazine*, 8 (2 April 1746), pp. 170–1; City dignitaries attended Leslie's election in 1743, and contributed towards his expenses in 1747, DCA, Treasurer's Book of the Burgh of Dundee 1733–53 [unpaginated]; Perth Magistrates Loyal Address, *LG*, 8–12 June 1756; the relationship was reciprocal; see Leslie to [Treasury Secretary?] on behalf of Yeaman, Provost of Dundee, 7 June 1751, PRO, SP 54/41, f. 7.

92. 14 October 1747, BL, Add. MS 32713, f. 265; 'Joshua Guest', *ODNB*, vol. 24, pp. 177–8.

93. Bland to Leslie, 14 April 1748, Blaikie, NLS, MS 304, ff. 58–9; 'Orders to Officers Commanding Forts, Barracks & c.', 21 March 1752, Blaikie, NLS, MS 308, ff. 162–3.

94. Bland to Governor Collingwood, 3 May 1748, Blaikie, NLS, MS 304, f. 66; Dundas to Fawkener, June 1747, RA Cumberland, Box 59, f. 5; Dundas to Cumberland, June 1747, ibid., f. 6.

95. Lauderdale to Pelham, 11 August 1747, cited Sedgwick, *Commons*, vol. 1, p. 627; Argyll to Pelham, 15 August 1747, NeC 1953; Pelham to Argyll, 29 August 1747, Coxe papers, BL, Add. MS 9186, f. 152.

96. Pelham to Argyll, 1 August 1747, Coxe papers, BL, Add. MS 9186, f. 130; Argyll to Pelham, 11 August 1747, cited Sedgwick, *Commons*, vol. 1, p. 628.

97. 29 August 1747, Coxe papers, BL, Add. MS 9186, f. 152; Gardiner, as a councillor of Linlithgow, the burgh at the centre of Dundas's disputed election, did not support Dundas (Gardiner to Andrew Fletcher, 29 June and 8 July 1747, Saltoun, NLS, MS 16646, ff. 46–7; R. M. Sunter, *Patronage and Politics in Scotland 1707–1832* (Edinburgh: Donald, 1986), p. 176).

98. *GM*, 18 (1748), p. 140; Guy, *Oeconomy and Discipline*, p. 126.

99. Fox to Churchill, 3 January 1752, PRO, T 1/407, f. 102.

100. Bland to Leslie, 2 April 1748, Blaikie, NLS, MS 304, ff. 53–4.

101. Bland to Leslie, 8, 15 and 22 March 1748, ibid., ff. 44, 46–7, 49–50.

102. See below, p. 118; Leslie received an annual allowance per company for fire and candle, Leslie to Pitt (Paymaster General), n.d., Chatham papers, PRO 30/8/73, f. 80.

103. 5 March 1750, PRO, T 52/45, p. 317.

104. Bland to Fox, 13 August 1751, PRO, WO 4/48, pp. 167–9; Order to Royal Galley commander, Loch Ness, to take aboard provisions for Fort Augustus upon application from Leslie or his agent, 27 July 1748, Blaikie, NLS, MS 306, f. 9.
105. Churchill to Ordnance, 19 December 1751, Blaikie, NLS, MS 308, f. 99; 'Rules of Standing Orders, to be Observed by the Troops Quartered in North Britain', 2 December 1753, Yester, NLS, MS 14512, f. 5.
106. James Stewart to Leslie, 23 November & 21 December 1752, Blaikie, NLS, MS 309, ff. 52–3, 92–3.
107. Orders to Barrack Master General's Agent, 14 April 1752, Blaikie, NLS, MS 308, ff. 176–7; Fox to Churchill, 30 June 1752, PRO, WO 4/48, p. 556; Churchill to Leslie, 14 October 1752, Blaikie, NLS MS, 308, f. 343; James Stewart to Leslie, 10 January 1753, Blaikie, NLS, MS 309, f. 109; Fox to Bland, 16 May 1755, PRO, WO 4/50, p. 282.
108. Fox to Bland, 9 June 1755, PRO, WO 4/50, p. 317 [original underlined].
109. 'Memo to the King', 3 April 1760, BL, Add. MS 32904, f. 176; Leslie to Newcastle, 7 June 1760, BL, Add. MS 32907, f. 68; 4 April 1761, BL, Add. MS 32921, f. 321; Namier, *Structure of Politics*, pp. 427, 441, 465.
110. Houlding, *Fit for Service*, pp. 44, 97–8; Cumberland considered it unlikely more troops would be sent to Scotland, Barrington to Bland, 26 February 1756, PRO, WO 4/51, p. 220; Beauclerk to Bute, 2 April 1761, *Calendar of Home Office Papers in the Reign of George III, 25 October 1760–1765*, ed. J. Redington and R.A. Roberts, 4 vols (London: Longman & Co., 1878), vol. 1, p. 30; 'A List of Regiments Quartered in Scotland, 24 June 1751–1763', Saltoun, NLS, MS 17506, ff. 61–4; State of Troops in Britain (March 1756), Hardwicke papers, BL, Add. MS 35389, ff. 190–1; 13 November 1756, Chatham papers, PRO 30/8/75, f. 206; 27 July 1757, BL, Add. MS 33047, f. 99; 9 January 1760, BL, Add. MS 33048, f. 7.
111. 12 December 1757, *HCJ*, 28, pp. 19–20; 29 April 1755, PRO, WO 47/45, p. 408; 3 June 1755, ibid, pp. 523–4, 12 June 1755, ibid, pp. 560–1.
112. Declared account, 14 March 1753, PRO, T 1/354, f. 1; Leslie and Gardiner's income calculated from *HCJ*, 25, p. 779; *HCJ*, 26, pp. 72, 349, 592, 930; *HCJ*, 27, pp. 86, 393, 818; *HCJ*, 28, pp. 190–1, 666, 671–2, 980; *HCJ*, 29, pp. 76, 378, 862–3; *HCJ*, 30, pp. 42, 47, 556; *HCJ*, 31, pp. 126–7, 138, 521; 22 May 1762, PRO, AO 1/174, f. 513; 17 March 1762, PRO, T 54/38, pp. 314–16; 21 December 1765, PRO, AO 1/175, f. 514.
113. Beauclerk to Barrington, 31 March 1757, PRO, WO 1/613, f. 71; 7 April 1757, ibid., f. 75.
114. Beauclerk to Barrington, 21 April 1757, ibid., f. 95; 10 May 1757, ibid., ff. 111–13; 14 June 1757, ibid., f. 125; for the capture of two French privateers with approximately 178 men, see Beauclerk to Barrington, 28 April 1757, ibid., f. 103.
115. Beauclerk to Barrington, 27 June 1759, PRO, WO 1/614, f. 133; C. Nordmann, 'Choiseul and the Last Jacobite Attempt of 1759', in E. Cruickshanks (ed.), *Ideology and Conspiracy: Aspects of Jacobitism, 1689–1759* (Edinburgh: Donald, 1982), pp. 201–17; pp. 203–9.
116. Barrington to Beauclerk, 8 May 1759, PRO, WO 4/57, pp. 569–70; Beauclerk to Barrington, 26 May 1759, PRO, WO 1/614, f. 113; Barrington to Beauclerk, 9 June 1759, PRO, WO 4/58, p. 57.
117. Robert Napier to Thomas Bradshaw, 24 June 1759, PRO, WO 1/978, f. 425; Tyrwhitt to Beauclerk, 28 June 1759, PRO, WO 4/58, p. 150.
118. Fort George, 20 July–23 October; Musselburgh, 17 July–18 October; 21 December 1765, PRO, AO 1/175, f. 514.

119. Barrington to Beauclerk, 28 June 1759, PRO, WO 4/58, pp. 151–3; Beauclerk to Barrington, 21 August 1759, PRO, WO 1/614, f. 153.
120. Warrant for tents, 17 May 1756, Blaikie, NLS, MS 306, f. 18v; 20 January 1756, *HCJ*, 27, p. 393; 28 March 1757, ibid, p. 818; 13 April 1758, *HCJ*, 28, p. 190; Beauclerk to West, 24 July 1759, PRO, T 1/396, f. 219.
121. 'Memorial relating to the Office of Commissary General for Forces in North Britain', November 1763, Saltoun, NLS, MS 17506, f. 59; Beauclerk was directed to make contracts, 10 July 1759, PRO, T 29/33, p. 207; Barrington to Beauclerk, 21 July 1759, PRO, WO 4/58, p. 259.
122. 17 July 1759, PRO, T 29/33, p. 211; 31 July 1759, ibid, p. 216; Munro to Barrington, 31 July 1759, PRO, WO 1/979; Barrington to Beauclerk, 9 August 1759, PRO, WO 4/58, p. 337.
123. Memorial, November 1763, Saltoun, NLS, MS 17506, f. 59.
124. Gardiner's Memorial on office of Commissary General (North Britain), 5 June 1764, ibid., ff. 66–7; General and Staff Officers, North Britain 1763, ibid., f. 58; soliciting Newcastle, Munro indicated James Oswald at the Treasury would recommend him, 23 April 1759, BL, Add. MS 32890, f. 290.
125. West to Townshend, 23 October 1761, PRO, WO 1/679, f. 85; Townshend to Beauclerk, 27 February 1762, PRO, WO 4/67, p. 393; Deputy Auditors Report [Copy], n.d., ibid, pp. 394–5.
126. Beauclerk to Townshend, 8 March 1762, PRO, WO 1/615, f. 281; Memorial, PRO, T 1/407, f. 101.
127. Munro to West, 16 October 1759, PRO, T 1/396, f. 218; advances of £3,000 were issued on 17 September 1759 & 8 January 1760, 21 December 1765, PRO, AO 1/175, f. 514.
128. Articles of Agreement, 27 July 1759, PRO, T 54/37, pp. 251–5; 5 September 1759, ibid, pp. 271–4.
129. By 1800 there was still no coaching service north of the Tay (W. Ferguson, *Scotland 1689 to the Present* (Edinburgh and London: Oliver & Boyd, 1968), p. 193).
130. 21 December 1765, PRO, AO 1/175, f. 514; Barrington to Beauclerk, 4 September 1759, PRO, WO 4/58, p. 496; Beauclerk to Barrington, 21 August 1759, PRO, WO 1/614, f. 153.
131. 27 July 1759, PRO, T 1/396, f. 221; in 1747 heather was supplied as bedding, 19 June 1754, PRO, AO 1/485, f. 50.
132. 'Estimate of Charges for an encampment of two regiments of dragoons and four regiments of foot for ninety-one days in North Britain', (1759), PRO, T 1/391, f. 107; £7,092 paid for provisions lost at sea. 21 December 1765, PRO, AO 1/175, f. 514.
133. William Robertson to Charles Townshend, 25 October 1759, Townshend papers from Buccleuch Muniments, NAS, RH4/98/295/3/21; 'Memos for the King', 28 October 1759, BL, Add. MS 32897, f. 437.
134. Whitehaven report, 1 March 1760, BL, Add. MS 32903, f. 5, Rigby to Newcastle, 2 March 1760, ibid., f. 31; Western, *English Militia*, pp. 162–3.
135. *Scots Magazine*, 22 (23 February 1760), p. 99; 3 September 1761, PRO, T 29/34, p. 164; 21 December 1765, PRO, AO 1/175, f. 514.
136. J. Yorke to Hardwicke, 4 March 1760, BL, Add. MS 32903, f. 76; Alex Boswell to Newcastle, 20 March 1760, ibid., ff. 398–9; Western, *English Militia*, p. 165; Beauclerk to Barrington, 30 August 1759, relating applications from Aberdeen and Montrose magistrates for arms, complicated by the 1746 Disarming Act, PRO, WO 1/614, f. 165.

137. Newcastle to Devonshire, 8 April 1760, BL, Add. MS 32904, ff. 259–60, Chesterfield to Newcastle, 13 April 1760, ibid., f. 350; Western, *English Militia*, pp. 162–7.
138. 15 March 1760, BL, Add. MS 32903, ff. 296–9.
139. Beauclerk to Barrington, 25 March 1760, PRO, WO 1/614, f. 347; 29 March 1760, ibid., f. 351; Officers' certificates, 18 October 1759 and 21 January 1760, Saltoun, NLS, MS 17506, ff. 2–3.
140. 'State of Three Regiments encamped at Musselburgh', 25 March 1760, PRO, WO 1/614, f. 359.
141. War Office to Gardiner, September and 23 October 1759, enclosing lists of commissions and regiments disposed of, Saltoun, NLS, MS 17505, ff. 213–14.
142. Tyrwhitt to Clevland, 27 May 1760, PRO, WO 4/61, p. 154.
143. Munro to Barrington [Copy], 2 September 1760, PRO, WO 4/62, p. 59; Barrington to Beauclerk, 6 September 1760, ibid., p. 58.
144. Beauclerk to Barrington, 10 September 1760, PRO, WO 1/614, f. 539; Martin to Beauclerk, 30 December 1762, PRO, T 27/28, p. 353; Beauclerk to Martin, 1 June 1763, PRO, T 1/425, ff. 247–8.
145. Lenman, *Jacobite Risings*, pp. 221–3.
146. *Scots Magazine*, 8 (20 February 1746), p. 92; *LG*, 29 April 1746; Salmond, *Wade*, p. 46.
147. Treasury to Ordnance, 8 March 1750, PRO, T 27/26, p. 406; Ordnance to Lords Justices, 5 May 1750, PRO, SP 41/37; M. Lindsay, *The Castles of Scotland* (London: Constable, 1986), pp. 92–3, 152; Gardiner to Andrew Fletcher, 12 August 1747, Saltoun, NLS, MS 16646, f. 58.
148. Bland to Newcastle, 7 April 1748, PRO, SP 54/39, f. 6A; 'When it is finished one may venture to say (without saying much) that it will be the most considerable fortress and the best situated in Great Britain', Wolfe to father, 3 October 1751, cited J. T. Findlay, *Wolfe in Scotland in the '45 and from 1749 to 1753* (London: Longmans & Co., 1928), pp. 246–7.
149. Barrington to Marlborough, 1 July 1756, PRO, WO 4/51, p. 95; Beauclerk to Barrington, 24 September 1757, PRO, WO 1/613, f. 189; Tyrwhitt to Beauclerk, 6 October 1757, PRO, WO 4/54, p. 515; 8 October 1757, ibid., p. 526.
150. 2 and 26 March 1756, PRO, WO 47/47, pp. 229–30; Richard Coren to Bland, 27 February 1752, Edinburgh Castle Letter Book, NLS, MS 8027, f. 8.
151. Beauclerk to Ordnance, 8 October 1760, Skinner papers, BL, Add MS 17501, f. 44.
152. MacIvor, *Fort George*, pp. 8, 11, 13–14.
153. Gibson and Smout, *Prices, Food and Wages*, pp. 156–7.
154. Barrington to Beauclerk, 9 February 1757, PRO, WO 4/53, p. 197.
155. Beauclerk to Barrington, 25 February 1757, PRO, WO 1/613, f. 21; Barrington to Martin, 24 March 1757, PRO, WO 4/53, p. 399.
156. Beauclerk to Barrington, 12 May 1759, PRO, WO 1/614, ff. 105–7.
157. Barrington to Martin, 21 May 1759, PRO, WO 4/57, p. 630; Barrington to Beauclerk, 23 May 1759, ibid., p. 643.
158. 12 June 1759, PRO, T 29/33, p. 191; Articles of Agreement, 13 August 1759, PRO, T 54/37, pp. 246–50.
159. Memorial of Leslie, n.d. [*c.* May 1759], PRO, WO 4/57, pp. 626–9; Leslie to Beauclerk, 6 June 1759, PRO, WO 1/614, f. 119; Barrington to Beauclerk, 7 June 1759, PRO, WO 4/58, p. 36.
160. For opposition to Lowlands contracts, see above, p. 30.

161. 'Memorandum with respect to the present State of Stores and Provisions in the Several forts and Barracks in Scotland', 25 June 1759, Saltoun, NLS, MS 17505, ff. 208–9.
162. West, *Gunpowder*, p. 53.
163. 29 June 1759, PRO, T 29/33, p. 202; 10 and 17 July 1759, ibid, p. 207.
164. Articles of Agreement, 31 July 1759, PRO, T 54/37, pp. 240–1; 22 May 1762, PRO, AO 1/174, f. 513.
165. Dundas was Vice-President, Oswald, Haldane and Ross patrons ([Anon.], *A Short Account of the Institution, Progress, and Present State of the Scottish Corporation in London* (London: W. and A. Strahan, 1777), pp. 44, 48).
166. St George's Hanover Square, Poor rates 1751–4, WCA, C192, 195, 292–3: MF Reel 438; *Kent's Directory*, 13 (1755), p. 90; Probate, 6 April 1786, PRO, PROB 11/1141, f. 242; for Haldane, see above, p. 65.
167. 'Mr. Dundas is much out o' Temper at me about the Politicks', Gardiner to Andrew Fletcher, 9 July 1747, Saltoun, NLS, MS 16646, f. 56; Bond of Leslie and Dundas to Abraham Hume for £1,000, 22 March 1753, ZA, ZNK X1/11/9.
168. 12 June 1755, PRO, WO 47/45, pp. 560–1; 5 February 1760, PRO, WO 47/55, p. 100.
169. G. Menary, *The Life and Letters of Duncan Forbes, Lord President of the Court of Session 1685–1747* (London: A. Maclehose & Co., 1936), p. 222; *GM*, 31 (1761), p. 207.
170. T. Hunter (ed.), *Extracts from the Records of the Convention of Royal Burghs, Vol. 5 (1738–1759)* (Edinburgh: Scottish Burghs Record Society, 1915), p. 456.
171. Millar (ed.), *Forfeited Estates*, pp. 35–40; *Jacobite Trials: Proceedings in the House of Peers upon the Indictments against William, Earl of Kilmarnock, George, Earl of Cromartie, and Arthur, Lord Balmerino* (1746), p. 3; Memorial, 27 June 1753, Letters relating to forfeitures, NLS, Advocates MS 28.1.6 (I) 305–9.
172. Ross's recommendation of Archibald Fraser to Dundas, see above, p. 65; Ross solicited Newcastle for pensions for the sons of the Rebel Kilmarnock, 6 June 1748, BL, Add. MS 32715, f. 160; estates restored in 1751, Paul (ed.), *Scots Peerage*, vol. 5, p. 181.
173. 26 June 1746, PRO, T 29/28, p. 297; Maj. I. H. M. Scobie, 'The Highland Independent Companies of 1745–47', *JSAHR*, 20:77 (1941), pp. 34–5; *GM*, 32 (1762), p. 36.
174. Fox to Ross, 17 April 1755, PRO, WO 4/50, p. 245; Barrington to Ross, 16 August 1757, PRO, WO 4/54, p. 306; Regimental agents to Barrington, 26 January 1758, PRO, WO 1/975, f. 437; for his clothing contracts, Smith, 'Clothing Contractors', p. 156.
175. 9 April 1757, Calcraft papers, BL, Add. MS 17493, f. 58; Ross replaced Calcraft as Sackville's agent, Guy, 'Regimental Agency', p. 452.
176. 29 April 1755, PRO, WO 47/45, p. 408; 13 August 1759, PRO, T 54/37, pp. 246–50; Leslie to Newcastle, 14 March 1758, BL, Add. MS 32878, f. 212.
177. Dundas to Ross, 21 March 1759, ZA, ZNK X1/1/159, f. 15; Ross to Treasury regarding reimbursement for a bill drawn on him by Dundas, 22 May 1759, T 29/33, p. 184; Dundas to Ross, 19 September 1759, ZA, ZNK X1/1/159, f. 238.
178. 31 July 1756, Blaikie, NLS, MS 305, f. 226.
179. 20 February 1764, PRO, T 52/55, p. 403.
180. 'State of the Forts and Garrisons in North Britain', 6 November 1763, Saltoun, NLS, MS 17506, ff. 55–6; Townshend to Beauclerk, 6 March 1762, PRO, WO 4/67, p. 446.
181. Captain Wemyss to Townshend, 1 May 1762, PRO, WO 4/68, pp. 409–10.
182. Beauclerk to Townshend, 25 February 1762, PRO, WO 1/615, f. 265, 8 May 1762, PRO, WO 1/615, f. 339; Townshend to Beauclerk, 19 May 1762, PRO, WO 4/69, p. 24; Beauclerk to Townshend, 24 May 1762, PRO, WO 1/615, f. 351.

183. H. V. Jones to Newcastle, 12 June 1762, BL, Add. MS 32939, ff. 309–10; for Leslie's income, 'State of the Forts', 6 November 1763, Saltoun, NLS, MS 17506, ff. 55–6.
184. The post cost him £1600, 'Memo of Colonel Masterton of debts and obligations of Sir Lawrence Dundas', 25 March 1776, ZA, ZNK X1/11/66.
185. Expenditure of Public Money: Ordnance, 18 April 1763, *HCJ*, 29, p. 637.
186. Ibid.; *LG*, 13–17 January 1759; advertisements in the *London Gazette* were only placed in Edinburgh newspapers by particular order (Bland to Captain Smith, 10 February 1756, Blaikie, NLS, MS 305, f. 174).
187. Gardiner died in 1767, Leslie in 1772, and Dundas in 1781 (*Scots Magazine*, 29, p. 502; 34, p. 166; 43, p. 503).

8 Profit and Wealth

1. H. T. Dickinson (ed.), 'The Letters of Henry St. John to the Earl of Orrery', *Camden Miscellany*, 4th series, 14:26 (1975), p. 146 (letter of 9 July 1709); fears for aristocratic political authority underpinned the 1711 Property Qualifications Act for MPs (H. T. Dickinson, *Liberty and Property: Political Ideology in Eighteenth-Century Britain* (London: Weidenfeld and Nicolson, 1977), p. 52).
2. D. Defoe, *The Complete English Tradesman in Familiar letters*, 2nd edn, 2 vols (London: Charles Rivington, 1727), vol. 1, p. 307; Namier, *Structure of Politics*, pp. 45–58.
3. His observation of the 'stately Mansion-house' of Sir J. Eyles (Defoe, *Tour of Great Britain*, vol. 1, p. 19); in the early eighteenth-century, only elite merchants purchased estates (Jones, *War and Economy*, pp. 280–1).
4. Namier, *Structure of Politics*, p. 47.
5. The Portuguese contractors Pereira and Medina were amongst the 'cosmopolitan mercantile plutocracy' subscribing upwards of £5,000 to the 1707 loan (Dickson, *Financial Revolution*, pp. 113–17, 263); obituaries of descendants alluded to the wealth of contractor forebears (*London Evening Post*, 19–21 February 1760; 10 November 1784, *GM*, 54:2 (1784), p. 878).
6. Walpole, *Memoirs of George II*, vol. 3, p. 53.
7. L. Stone and J. C. F. Stone, *An Open Elite? England 1540–1880* (Oxford: Clarendon Press, 1984), p. 203.
8. That is, 'entrepreneurial *effort* is not as important as *place in the total economy* in determining entrepreneurial rewards' (W. D. Rubenstein, *Men of Property: The Very Wealthy in Britain since the Industrial Revolution* (London: Croon Helm, 1981), p. 163).
9. Regimental agents appear to have made considerable gains. John Calcraft's wealth was estimated at £250,000 (*GM*, 42 (1772), p. 392).
10. Obituaries with approximate valuations 'exist only on a hit-or-miss basis and are not comprehensive' (Rubinstein, *Men of Property*, p. 52 n. 11).
11. W. D. Rubinstein, 'The Structure of Wealth-Holding in Britain, 1809–39: A Preliminary Anatomy', *Historical Research*, 45:156 (1992), pp. 74–80; pp. 74, 83.
12. Based on London Aldermen and Court of Orphans records: R. Grassby, 'English Merchant Capitalism in the Late Seventeenth Century: The Composition of Business Fortunes', *Past & Present*, 46 (1970), pp. 87–107; R. Grassby, 'The Personal Wealth of the Business Community in Seventeenth-Century England', *Economic History Review*, 23:2 (1970), pp. 220–34; N. Rogers, 'Money, Land and Lineage: The Big Bourgeoisie of Hanoverian London', *Social History*, 4:3 (1979), pp. 437–54; W. D. Rubinstein, 'Vic-

torian Middle Classes: Wealth, Occupation, and Geography', *Economic History Review*, 30:4 (1977), pp. 65–89.
13. Brooke, suggesting further evidence of contracts held by MPs would probably be discovered in records of government departments, concluded 'the results would not be commensurate to the work involved' (Namier and Brooke, *Commons*, vol. 1, p. 135).
14. Grassby, 'Personal Wealth', p. 233.
15. Sir J. B. Burke, *A Genealogical and Heraldic History of the Landed Gentry of Great Britain and Ireland*, 2 vols, 6th edn (London: Harrison, 1879), vol. 1, p. 578; *GM*, 10 (1740), p. 203; *Ipswich Journal*, 19 April 1740.
16. 17 April 1721, Cobbett, *PHE*, vol. 7, c. 782; Sedgwick, *Commons*, vol. 2, pp. 70–1; Probate, 13 August 1763, PRO, PROB 11/891, f. 384; Anon., *A Particular or Inventory of Mr. John Gore Late One of the Directors of the South Sea Company* (London: Jacob Tonson, Bernard Lintot and William Taylor, 1721), pp. 3–5, 29; for another Director with an interest in contracts, see Anon., *A True and Exact Particular and Inventory of William Astell Esquire* (London: J. Tonson, 1721), p. 17.
17. Sedgwick, *Commons*, vol. 1, pp. 487–8.
18. Namier and Brooke, *Commons*, vol. 2, pp. 20–1; Probate, 22 August 1766, PRO, PROB 11/921, f. 290.
19. C. and A. Nesbitt, *History of the Family of Nesbitt or Nisbet in Scotland and Ireland* (Torquay: Privately published, 1898); Nesbitt provided security for Irish bankers distributing government lottery tickets in April 1757, PRO, T 1/375, f. 105; for Colebrooke, see above, p. 49.
20. Grassby, 'Business Fortunes', p. 102.
21. 19 January 1744, *Acts of the Privy Council*, Colonial Series (1720–45), vol. 3, pp. 721–2; Sutherland, *London Merchant*, p. 122.
22. Sir William Musgrave to Lord Carlisle, 10 November 1767, HMC, *Carlisle* (London, HMSO, 1897), pp. 219–20.
23. Sutherland, *London Merchant*, pp. 18–19, 26–9, 129–32; a partner in 'Fisher & Pearse' he obtained clothing contracts during the Seven Years' War (Accounts, 29 December 1759, PRO, AO 17/42, pp. 189–90); for links between contractors and East India Company merchants, see below, p. 159 (Table C.1); West, *Gunpowder*, pp. 138–9.
24. Namier, 'Brice Fisher', pp. 515–16, 519; Fisher's descendants, John and Brice Pearse, nineteenth-century Blackwell Hall factors and 'Army Clothiers' (*Pigot & Co's London & Provincial New Commercial Directory 1823–1824*, p. 30); Linwood's brother was a dealer in 'elephant's teeth' (*Lloyd's Evening Post, and British Chronicle*, 9–11 February 1763).
25. P.W. Kingsford, 'A London Merchant: Sir William Baker', *History Today*, 21 (1971), p. 339; Wadsworth and Mann, *Cotton trade*, p. 244.
26. Anon., *The Humours of the Town, A Dramatic Interlude in One Act* (Edinburgh: 1776), p. 11.
27. 'Sir Samuel Fludyer', *ODNB*, vol. 20, p. 194; *City Biography* (1800), p. 82; Rogers, 'Money, Land and Lineage', p. 440; Namier, *American Revolution*, p. 221 n. 2.
28. At Newcastle's request, Linwood sent wine to Hanover, 22 June 1749, BL, Add. MS 33066, f. 119; Lawrence Dundas remained a wine dealer after his contracting career began (Dundas to John Gourlay, 6 October 1748, ZA, ZNK X1/2/1).
29. Earle, *English Middle Class*, p. 38.

30. Lady E. and L. Cust (eds), *Records of the Cust family*, 3 vols (London: Mitchell and Hughes, 1894–1927), vol. 3, pp. 12–13; Peregrine Cust to Sir John Cust, 4 August 1747, ibid, p. 125.
31. Wilson, *Anglo-Dutch Commerce*, p. 115; Namier and Brooke, *Commons*, vol. 2, p. 235; vol. 3, pp. 129–30.
32. *GM*, 14 (1744), p. 225; Dickson, *Financial Revolution*, p. 289.
33. 29 December 1757, PRO, E 401/2598.
34. Dickson, *Financial Revolution*, pp. 288, 295.
35. 16 June 1758, PRO, T 1/380, f. 34; 2 August 1758, PRO, T 29/33, pp. 85–6.
36. For 1762 loan of £12 million, Fisher subscribed £40,000, Bacon £20,000. The financiers Sir James Colebrooke and Fonnereau subscribed £600,000 and £350,000 respectively, BL, Add. MS 33040, ff. 292–3.
37. L. Sutherland, 'The City of London in Eighteenth Century politics', in L. Sutherland, *Politics and Finance in the Eighteenth Century* (London: Hambledon Press, 1984) p. 53.
38. See below, p. 159 (Appendix C).
39. Grassby, 'Business Fortunes', p. 96; as exclusive supplier of bread, it was considered reasonable that Solomon de Medina made an annual payment to Marlborough (24 January 1712, Cobbett, *PHE*, vol. 6, cc. 1079–80).
40. Newcastle to Thomas Walpole, 17 December 1762, BL, Add. MS 32945, f. 301; Gore's application for Gibraltar remittances, 2 April 1756, BL, Add. MS 32864, f. 141.
41. Burrell & Bristow for Gibraltar and Minorca, 15 April 1740, PRO, T 29/28, p. 208; Gore's remittances, BL, Add. MS 33038, ff. 243–4.
42. Sedgwick, *Commons*, vol. 1, pp. 487–8, 509; vol. 2, pp. 70–1, 90.
43. Namier, 'Brice Fisher', pp. 523–6.
44. Amyand to Newcastle, 27 January 1762, BL, Add. MS 32934, f. 37.
45. Newcastle to Gore, 21 August 1762, BL, Add. MS 32941, f. 341; Gore to Newcastle, 23 August 1762, ibid., f. 366.
46. Newcastle to Walpole, 4 January 1763, BL, Add. MS 32964, f. 49.
47. Returning to office Newcastle planned to restore contractors 'turn'd out, from Resentment to me' ('Persons who should be immediately consider'd', 17 May 1765, BL, Add. MS 32966, f. 424).
48. *GM*, 9 (1739), p. 305; 26 February 1740, *CTBP* (1739–41), p. 223.
49. German remittances of 1758 estimated at £300,000 per year would yield a profit of only £1,500, but 'the honour & Credit of serving the Government is of the greatest Advantage to Men in Trade' (West to Newcastle, 29 July 1758, PRO, T 1/385, f. 75).
50. Thomas Walpole applied to Newcastle to exchange the victualling contract for a share of the remittance as better suited to his interest in a Lisbon financial house (14 September 1761, BL, Add. MS 32928, f. 162).
51. Victualling Office to Navy Commissioners, 3 September 1717, PRO, Adm. 110/7, p. 457; Baugh, *Naval Administration 1715–1750*, pp. 420–1; *GM*, 22 (1752), p. 44.
52. *GM*, 9 (1739), p. 307.
53. 28 July 1742, PRO, AO 1/184, f. 560.
54. Sir John Miller, soliciting Newcastle for the contract, mistakenly thought contractors excluded from Parliament by it (8 June 1747, BL, Add. MS 32712, f. 63).
55. Sir George Byng to Revell and Cooley, 13 July 1720, Chatham papers, PRO 30/8/92, f. 62; *Read's Weekly Journal*, 2 February 1734.
56. H. E. Malden (ed.), *The Victoria History: County of Surrey*, 5 vols (Oxford: Oxford University Press, 1902–14), vol. 3, pp. 287, 290; Sedgwick, *Commons*, vol. 2, p. 381; J.

Chamberlayne, *Magnae Brittanniae: Or, the Present State of Great Britain with Diverse Remarks upon the Ancient State thereof* (London: D. Midwinter, 1735), p. 211; *GM*, 2 (1732), p. 584.
57. Namier, 'Brice Fisher', pp. 524–7.
58. 26 June 1754, BL, Add. MS 32735, f. 573.
59. Memorial of Hume, n.d. [after 1752], BL, Add. MS 33054, ff. 372–3.
60. For price variation, 1776–82: Baker, *Government and Contractors*, pp. 242–7.
61. Comptrollers Report, 26 August 1745, PRO, AO 17/37, pp. 60–1; Woodford to Hans Stanley, 3 January 1760, BL, Add. MS 32901, f. 107.
62. Between 1754–8, Woodford received £13,149, PRO, T 54/37, pp. 289–91.
63. On 20/31 May, 4 July and 9 September 1709, Marlborough alluded to Medina's 'dismal complaints' and his 'running madd' [sic] claiming losses of £5,000 (H. L. Snyder (ed.), *The Marlborough-Godolphin Correspondence*, 3 vols (Oxford: Clarendon Press, 1975), vol. 3, pp. 1259, 1301, 1374); Medina later relinquished the contract (T. Harley to Comptrollers, 25 February 1712, PRO, T 27/20, p. 131); citing difficulties and obstructions to Newcastle, William Baker terminated his American contract after three years (21 September 1759, PRO, WO 34/69, f. 157).
64. Gore to Newcastle, 30 November 1755, BL, Add. MS 32861, f. 157.
65. Baker, *Government and Contractors*, pp. 190–7, 238.
66. Roseveare, *Treasury*, pp. 92–3.
67. 10 July 1856, Select Committee on Contracts, *PP* (1856) vii. [362], p. 210.
68. 8 May 1762, PRO, T 29/34, pp. 273–5; 16 August 1781, PRO, T 29/50, p. 362; Baker, *Government and Contractors*, p. 250.
69. Woodford to Hans Stanley, 3 January 1760, BL, Add. MS 32901, f. 107.
70. Woodford to West, 28 January 1760, PRO, T 1/393, f. 181; Woodford retained the contract until his death in 1767, having received it in 1734, Memorial of Mary Woodford, 22 October 1768, ibid., f. 191.
71. Hancock, *Citizens of the World*, p. 238.
72. *The Times*, 11 January 1785; *GM*, 51 (1781), p. 444; for Willan, see above, pp. 89–91.
73. Leaving a single legacy of £300 and one £10 annuity (Probate, 17 May 1783, PRO, PROB 11/1104, f. 264).
74. Leslie to Newcastle, 15 February 1756, BL, Add. MS 32852, f. 479; he received land in Fife from his brother, 1 February 1740 (Paul, *Scots Peerage*, vol. 7, p. 304).
75. Register of Seisins, Edinburgh, 1781–1801, NAS, 23 February 1782, 3 June, 12 and 22 July 1784, Nos. 350, 1044–5, 1100–1, 1109.
76. Hancock, *Citizens of the World*, p. 385; Hancock, '"Domestic Bubbling"', pp. 692, 696.
77. See above, pp. 94–5.
78. G. B. Hertz, 'England and the Ostend Company', *English Historical Review*, 22:86 (1907), p. 256.
79. Bryant, 'Scots in India', p. 32.
80. *The Directory*, (1736), p. 26; *Kent's Directory*, 2 (1736), p. 26; *Compleat Guide*, 4 (1740), p. 132; *Universal Pocket Companion*, 6 (1741), p. 101; Dickson, *Financial Revolution*, p. 412 n. 1.
81. 1 July 1742, BL, Add. MS 22542, f. 189, 28 July 1742, ibid., f. 196; for political links with Pelham, Alexander Hume to Newcastle, n.d., received 10 December 1748, BL, Add. MS 33034, ff. 265–7.
82. Shelburne to Fox, 19 August 1762, Ilchester (ed.), *Letters to Henry Fox*, p. 157.
83. See above, pp. 108–9.

84. Register of Deeds, January-June 1750, vol. 167, NAS, RDS 2/167, ff. 140–2.
85. 'The Crown in a General Account with Sir Lawrence Dundas 1759–1763', ZA, ZNK X 1/1/34.
86. Barrington to Newcastle, 11 October 1763, cited Barrington, *Eighteenth-Century Secretary at War*, pp. 144–5.
87. 'Subscription to government loans, January 1760–October 1762', ZA, ZNK X1/12/1.
88. 'State of Money in the Funds', February 1763, ZA, ZNK X1/11, f. 14; 'State of Property in the Funds', April 1763, ZA, ZNK X1/11, f. 15.
89. £50,000 stock sold in January 1764, Bank of England Archive, AC 27/1405; AC 27/1413, f. 2518.
90. Dundas to Duncan Clerk, 10 May 1769, ZA, ZNK X1/11, f. 35; L. S. Sutherland, *The East India Company in Eighteenth-Century Politics* (Oxford: Clarendon Press, 1952), p. 183; stockholding: 21 June 1769, ZA, ZNK X1/11, f. 41, 25 February 1771, ZA, ZNK X1/11, f. 46.
91. Newcastle to Devonshire, 23 December 1762, BL, Add. MS 32945, f. 345.
92. Anon., *A Letter to a Certain Baronet* (Edinburgh: 1777), pp. 2–3.
93. P. Fitzgerald, *Samuel Foote, a Biography* (London: Chatto & Windus, 1910), pp. 291–2; *Public Advertiser*, 24 May 1769; Review: *GM*, 35 (1765), pp. 253–4.
94. 'In the evening read Foote's farce of the Commissary, said to have been levelled at Sir Lawrence Dundas' (Sir W. Scott, *The Journal of Sir Walter Scott from the Original Manuscript at Abbotsford*, 2 vols (Edinburgh: D. Douglas, 1891), vol. 1, p. 335 (entry for 6 January 1827)).
95. Plate duty registers, (1757–62), PRO, T 47/5; (1764–6), PRO, T 47/4; Scotland, (1756–62), PRO, T 36/8.
96. Carriage duty registers (1764–6), PRO, T 47/4.
97. He died in Lisbon pursuing his debts, Probate, 23 April 1768, PRO, PROB 11/946, f. 77; Report, 31 August 1761, BL, Add. MS 33055, f. 334; Sedgwick, *Commons*, vol. 2, pp. 487–8.
98. Report from the Committee on the Petition of the Owners of Collieries in South Wales, *PP* (1810), iv [344], pp. 2–3; Namier, *American Revolution*, pp. 284–5; Namier and Brooke, *Commons*, vol. 2, pp. 235–7; *GM*, 79 (1809), pp. 787–8.
99. The 'combined skills of risk avoidance', experience, information and caution were as important as adventurous risk-taking (Hoppit, *Risk and Failure*, p. 181).
100. W. D. Rubinstein, 'New Men of Wealth and the Purchase of Land in Nineteenth-Century Britain', *Past & Present*, 92 (1981), pp. 125–6.
101. Hancock, *Citizens of the World*, pp. 43–4.
102. Before purchasing a small Essex estate in 1782 John Willan, aged seventy-one, was still supplying horses to the army. ERO, D/DTw/T43; WFA 1/3 (Box 1).
103. See his steward's letter implying Oswald should spend less time in London and more on improving his estate, Peter Malhench to Oswald, 21 July 1764, Oswald papers, Edinburgh University Library, Special Collections, Dk. 1.30, f. 1.
104. John Anderson to Oswald, 16 October 1784, Oswald papers, NAS, GD213/53, f. 112.
105. W. Page et al (eds), *The Victoria History of the County of Sussex*, 10 vols (Oxford: Oxford University Press, 1905–97), vol. 1, p. 306; vol. 2, p. 278; Namier, 'Brice Fisher', pp. 522–3.
106. See below, pp. 161–2 (Appendix D), includes estates held in each county successively by Sir James and Sir George Colebrooke (23 April 1762, *HCJ*, 29, p. 315); Middlesex, Sur-

Notes to pages 132–4 227

rey and Berkshire cited as most popular counties for merchants in Sutherland, *London Merchant*, pp. 5–6; cf. Hertfordshire, Surrey and Essex (Stone, *Open Elite?*, pp. 43–5).
107. Probate, June 1786, PRO, PROB 11/1155, f. 317.
108. Cust and Cust (eds), *Cust Family*, vol. 2, pp. 304–5; a study attempting to draw 'national' conclusions selected counties of varying socioeconomic complexion (Hertfordshire, Northumberland and Northamptonshire), thus effectively obscuring the close relationship between contractors and counties around London (Stone, *Open Elite?*, pp. 166–7, 203, 220).
109. Rogers, 'Money, Land and Lineage', p. 448; Malden (ed.), *Victoria History: Surrey*, vol. 3, pp. 196, 198.
110. W. Page (ed.), *Victoria History of the County of Hertford*, 5 vols (London: Constable, 1902–23), vol. 2, pp. 281, 283; Probate, 13 August 1763, PRO, PROB 11/891, f. 384.
111. Page (ed.), *Victoria History: Hertford*, vol. 3, p. 488; Probate, 28 September 1765, PRO, PROB 11/912, f. 334.
112. See below, pp. 161–2 (Appendix D).
113. 5 June 1764, *JCTP* (1764–7), p. 64; P. Marshall, 'Empire and Opportunity in Britain, 1763–75', *Transactions of the Royal Historical Society*, 6th ser., 5 (1995), pp. 111–28; p. 118.
114. Hancock, *Citizens of the World*, p. 385; Probate, 23 January 1790, PRO, PROB 10, f. 3152; L. R. Timperley (ed.), *A Directory of Landownership in Scotland c. 1770* (Edinburgh: Scottish Records Society, 1976), pp. 167–9, 171–3.
115. Minchison, 'Merchants in England', p. 294.
116. Probate, 17 April 1779, PRO, PROB 11/1052, f. 166; R. G. Thorne, *The House of Commons 1790–1820*, 5 vols (London: Secker & Warburg, 1986), vol. 4, pp. 655–6; Page et al (eds), *Victoria History: Sussex*, vol. 9, p. 187.
117. Probate, 18 May 1773, PRO, PROB 11/988, f. 211; H. A. Doubleday, G. H. Gotley, M. A. Hardy and W. Page (eds), *A History of Hampshire and the Isle of Wight*, 5 vols (London: Constable 1900–14), vol. 4, p. 8; Rogers, 'Money, Land and Lineage', p. 449; for sale of Fonnereau's copyhold Surrey villa, see *London Courant*, 1 April 1780.
118. *St James's Chronicle*, 8–10 July, 21–24 August 1784.
119. Sedgwick, *Commons*, vol. 2, p. 90; Namier and Brooke, *Commons*, vol. 2, pp. 560–2; ironically, Gulston senior stipulated in his will that his funeral should be frugal (Probate, 12 August 1766, PRO, PROB 11/921, ff. 303–4).
120. Malden (ed.), *Victoria History: Surrey*, vol. 3, pp. 198, 217, 224; Namier and Brooke, *Commons*, vol. 3, pp. 598–602.
121. Petition of Bristow, n.d., read 25 August 1767, PRO, T 1/412, ff. 5–6; sale of estates: 15 February & 10 May 1765, *House of Lords Journals*, 31, pp. 40, 197.
122. Probate, 21 February 1774, PRO, PROB 11/995, f. 75.
123. Probate, 21 October 1772, PRO, PROB 10, f. 2597.
124. Probate, 13 August 1763, PRO, PROB 11/891, f. 384; Probate, 9 December 1790, PRO, PROB 11/1199, f. 564.
125. Probate, 18 May 1773, PRO, PROB 11/988, f. 211; *Lloyd's Evening Post*, 14–16 March 1763; *GM*, 18 (1748), p. 185.
126. L. Stone, 'Social Mobility in England, 1500–1700', *Past & Present*, 33 (1966), p. 35.
127. Malden (ed.), *Victoria History: Surrey*, vol. 3, p. 288; Newcastle to Hardwicke, 16 October 1759, BL, Add. MS 32867, f. 148.
128. Probate, 13 February 1752, PRO, PROB 11/793, f. 47.

129. C. H. C. Baker and M. I. Baker, *The Life and Circumstances of James Brydges, First Duke of Chandos* (Oxford: Oxford University Press, 1949), p. 263 n. 3.
130. Probate, 23 April 1768, PRO, PROB 11/946, f. 77; Namier and Brooke, *Commons*, vol. 2, pp. 470–2, 627–8.
131. Namier and Brooke, *Commons*, vol. 2, pp. 394, 589–90.
132. Gibbs, *Complete Peerage*, vol. 1, pp. 272–3; 'Mrs. Crowley' retained an interest in Ordnance contracts (Newcastle to Ligonier [Copy], 17 May 1756, BL, Add. MS 32865, f. 39; Ashburnham to Newcastle, 30 June 1756, ibid., f. 472).
133. J. A. Venn, *Alumni Cantabrigienses 1752–1900*, 6 vols (Cambridge: Cambridge University Press, 1940–54), vol. 3, p. 484; *GM*, 9 (1838), p. 657.
134. Burke, *Landed Gentry*, vol. 1, p. 482; Namier, *American Revolution*, p. 280.
135. Rogers, 'Money, Land and Lineage', p. 437; as mercantile purchase of estates emanated mainly from reasons of security and status, Hoppit correctly criticizes Stone's critique as not always relevant (*Risk and Failure*, p. 102 n. 75).
136. 18 December 1764, HMC, *Stopford-Sackville*, vol. 1, p. 99.
137. See below, p. 137 (Appendix B); the Colebrookes are counted together as the honour was granted to James with remainder to his brother (J. Colebrooke to Newcastle, 20 September 1759, BL, Add. MS 32896, ff. 7–8).
138. P. Langford, *Public Life and the Propertied Englishman 1689–1798* (Oxford: Clarendon Press, 1991), pp. 529–30.
139. Namier, *Structure of Politics*, p. 47.
140. Thorne, *Commons*, vol. 3, pp. 330–1, 335–6, 652–3.
141. Gibbs, *Complete Peerage*, vol. 4, p. 523.
142. Foster, *Oxonienses*, vol. 1, p. 331; Namier and Brooke, *Commons*, vol. 2, p. 235.
143. J. and J. A. Venn, *Alumni Cantabrigienses, Part I: From the Earliest Times to 1751*, 4 vols (Cambridge: Cambridge University Press, 1922–7), vol. 1, p. 156; Foster, *Oxonienses*, vol. 1, p. 22; vol. 2, pp. 474, 541; vol. 3, p. 941.
144. Venn, *Cantabrigienses*, vol. 1, p. 435.
145. Descendants of Baker, Fludyer, Nesbitt and Mellish continued in business (Rogers, 'Money, Land and Lineage', p. 451; Thorne, *Commons*, vol. 4, pp. 578–80, 655–6; Namier and Brooke, *Commons*, vol. 2, p. 21; Baker, *Government and Contractors*, p. 62 n. 193).
146. Henniker's father was a timber merchant: *The Directory* (1736), p. 25; J. Henniker Major, *Some Account of the Families of Major and Henniker* (London; 1803), p. 6; For Gulston, see Sedgwick, *Commons*, vol. 2, p. 90; Namier and Brooke, *Commons*, vol. 2, pp. 560–1.
147. See below, p. 158 (Appendix B).
148. Foster, *Oxonienses*, vol. 2, p. 472; vol. 3, p. 904.
149. See above, p. 101.
150. Thorne, *Commons*, vol. 5, pp. 95–6; Hancock, *Citizens of the World*, pp. 11, 69–70.
151. Thorne, *Commons*, vol. 3, pp. 545–8; *City Biography*, p. 38; the business survived until at least 1823 (*Pigot & Co's London & Provincial New Commercial Directory 1823–1824*, p. 212).
152. 'Henry Thomas Colebrooke', *ODNB*, vol. 12, pp. 539–42; *GM*, 79 (1809), pp. 787–8.
153. Sutherland, 'City of London', p. 60 n. 3; Foster, *Oxonienses*, vol. 4, p. 1430; Venn, *Cantabrigienses 1752–1900*, vol. 6, p. 218; Probate, March 1770, PRO, PROB 11/958, f. 212.
154. *GM*, 94, (1824), p. 183; Thorne, *Commons*, vol. 3, pp. 114–17.
155. 'Sir Abraham Hume', *ODNB*, vol. 28, pp. 731–2.

156. 'James Hare', *ODNB*, vol. 25, pp. 251–2; Probate, 21 October 1772, PRO, PROB 10, f. 2597.
157. Sir I. Campbell, *Lawrence Dundas Estate: Information for Sir Thomas Dundas of Kerse* (1783), pp. 1–4, 49.
158. Marriage Articles (Copy), 23 May 1764, Campbell, *Dundas Estate*, pp. 35–6; Elizabeth Ingram to Viscountess Irwin, 5 June 1764, HMC, *Various Collections*, vol. 8, p. 182; for the Zetland estates, Gibbs, *Complete Peerage*, vol. 12 (ii), pp. 929–30.
159. House Duty to the year ending 5 April 1833, *PP* (1833), xxxii [Cd. 323], pp. 499–501.
160. In emphasizing the limits of social mobility Stone almost obscures that in some cases it did happen (*Open Elite?*, p. 403).

Conclusion

1. Baker, 'Changing Attitudes', p. 208.
2. By 1760, contractors were a 'much despised class' (Langford, *Public Life*, p. 295).
3. 'Norwich Citizens Instructions to Representatives', October 1768, *GM*, 39 (1769), p. 76.
4. On this theme, G. R. Searle, *Corruption in British Politics, 1895–1930* (Oxford: Clarendon Press, 1987), pp. 72–9.
5. Conversely, a government newspaper viewed the territorial gains of the Seven Years' War 'sufficient to compensate all the expence' (*Lloyd's Evening Post & British Chronicle*, 18–21 February 1763).
6. Baker, *Government and Contractors*, p. 254 n. 19; cf. Baker 'Changing Attitudes', pp. 211–12.
7. Shelburne 'did not blame any man for trying to get the most from government for his contracts ... It was the minister he blamed for making unwise contracts, not those with whom they were made'. 14 April 1780, Hansard, *PD*, vol. 21, c. 425; the controversy entered popular culture: see 'The Contractors' in J. Freech, *The Political Songster or, A Touch on the Times, on Various Subjects, and Adapted to Common Tunes*, 6th edn (Birmingham: J. Pearson, 1790), pp. 92–3.
8. *The Parliamentary Register; or, History of the Proceedings and Debates in the House of Commons*, 17 vols (London: J. Almon, 1775–80), vol. 7, p. 218 (22 May 1777); Baker, 'Changing Attitudes', p. 217.
9. H. Roseveare, *The Treasury 1660–1870: The Foundations of Control* (London: Allen Lane, 1973), p. 59.
10. D. C. M. Platt, 'The Commercial and Industrial Interests of the Crown', *Political Studies*, 9:3 (1961), p. 273.
11. E. Porritt and A. Porritt, *The Unreformed House of Commons: Parliamentary Representation before 1832*, 2 vols (Cambridge: Cambridge University Press, 1909), vol. 1, pp. 216–18.
12. Namier's classic exposition: 'The rise of 'interests' and classes can be traced through the personnel of the House of Commons' ('The Biography of Ordinary Men', in L. B. Namier, *Crossroads of Power: Essays on Eighteenth-century England* (London: H. Hamilton, 1962), p. 3.
13. Sedgwick, *Commons*, vol. 1, pp. 148–51; Ranft (ed.), *Vernon Papers*, p. 364.
14. See below, pp. 152–5 (Appendix A).
15. Sir William Baker was something of an exception. Newcastle sought his advice on raising money, but also respected his views on North America (18 April 1759, BL, Add. MS

32890, f. 133, West to Newcastle, 18 April 1759, ibid., ff. 162–3; 1761: BL, Add. MS 33039, f. 418; 1762: BL, Add. MS 33040, f. 288).
16. 23 November 1754, BL, Add. MS 32737, f. 385.
17. Sutherland, 'City of London', p. 53; Samuel Touchet helped draft the Townshend duties (Namier and Brooke, *Townshend*, pp. 106–7; Namier, 'Anthony Bacon', p. 64).
18. See below, p. 160 (Appendix C); a phenomenon noted by Namier (*Structure of Politics*, p. 51 n. 1).
19. See below, p. 160 (Appendix C); merchants as Commissioners of French Prizes: 31 July 1756, PRO, T 52/47, pp. 637–9; 3 May 1759, PRO, T 52/49, p. 470; 12 March 1761, PRO, T 52/52, p. 35; for patronage, Earl of Exeter to Newcastle, 19 May 1756, BL, Add. MS 32865, f. 57; as a Victualling Commissioner, Revell presented Victualling Office accounts to Parliament, 21 January 1740, *HCJ*, 23, p. 606.
20. Rockingham doubted Sir William Baker was a 'proper person' to head the Board of Trade (Namier and Brooke, *Commons*, vol. 2, p. 41; Baker, 'Changing Attitudes', p. 210).
21. Seven contractors of the Seven Years' War, supporting Wilkes, were feted as 'friends to liberty'. By this time, most, but not all, did not possess contracts (*St James's Chronicle*, 3–6 March 1764).
22. Peregrine Cust spoke against the German war in Parliament (Barrington's Report, 13 November 1761, BL, Add. MS 32931, f. 19); see Cust to Sir John Cust, 9 January 1762, Cust and Cust (eds), *Cust Family*, vol. 3, p. 218. Nevertheless, he happily accepted German remittances in 1762, and in twenty-four years in Parliament is not known to have voted against Government (Namier and Brooke, *Commons*, vol. 2, pp. 291–3).
23. See below (Appendix A), pp. 151–3.
24. Rogers, 'Money, Land and Lineage', p. 437.
25. Treasury Report on Memorial of Fonnereau et al, 8 February 1757, PRO, AO 17/42, p. 205; L. Sutherland, 'London and the Devonshire–Pitt Administration, 1756–7', in Sutherland, *Politics and Finance*, pp. 110–12; cf. 'by the mid-eighteenth century gentlemen-merchants were no longer a misnomer' (Rogers, 'Money, Land and Lineage', p. 446); cf. Richmond to Newcastle, 31 July 1745, BL, Add. MS 32704, f. 551.
26. Oswald to Lord Dartmouth, 9 February 1775, HMC, *Dartmouth*, vol. 2, p. 268; Benjamin Franklin to Caleb Whitefoord, 19 May 1785, W. A. S. Hewins (ed.), *The Whitefoord Papers: Being the Correspondence and Other Manuscripts of Charles Whitefoord and Caleb Whitefoord from 1739 to 1810* (Oxford: Clarendon Press, 1898), p. 197.
27. Shelburne disingenuously stated: 'Last war the contracts were not in parliament, and yet the army was as well served as it is now' (14 April 1780, Hansard, *PD*, vol. 21, c. 426); with only fifteen contractors in Parliament in 1781 compared to thirty-seven in 1761 there was far less justification for the legislation (Baker, 'Changing Attitudes', p. 214).
28. Ward, *Land Tax*, p. 81.
29. Hume was advised in 1748 not to insist on half-pay (Memorial, n.d. [after 1752], BL, Add. MS 33054, ff. 372–3).
30. Sutherland, *London Merchant*, p. 109.
31. Sir George Wombwell saw danger in 'little men buying the contracts, and the misfortunes that would arise from adventurers executing the business badly' (12 February 1779, Hansard, *PD*, vol. 20, c. 128); Lord Stormont argued 'contracts could not be made open on many occasions ... a very improper man might offer to contract at the lowest price' (14 April 1780, Hansard, *PD*, vol. 21, cc. 415–16).
32. 'Observations on the Nature of the Office making Contracts', n.d., Chatham papers, PRO 30/8/83, f. 222.

33. 1 May 1782, Hansard, *PD*, vol. 22, c. 1376.
34. 'Duty of a Comptrolling Commissary', 24 June 1761, Minto papers, NLS, MS 11039, ff. 23–4.
35. Paper on Contracts, n.d., Chatham papers, PRO 30/8/231, ff. 12–15; Baker, *Government and Contractors*, pp. 250–1.
36. West to Newcastle, 12 May 1762, BL, Add. MS 32938, f. 188.
37. Conway, *American Independence*, p. 3.
38. 'State of the Diminution that may be made in the expense of the Army, Navy & Ordnance', n.d. [*c.* 1763], Liverpool papers, BL, Add. MS 38331, ff. 218–20.
39. Memorial on Contracts, n.d., PRO, T 1/433, f. 67.
40. 9 March 1715, *CTB* (1714–15), p. 412.
41. 23 December 1762, PRO, T 29/35, p. 21; Treasury to Fonnereau, 23 December 1762, PRO, T 27/28, p. 351.
42. 29 April 1763, PRO, T 29/35, p. 75; Treasury to Colebrooke, 5 May 1763, PRO, T 27/28, pp. 390–1; 6 May 1763, PRO, T 29/35, p. 82; Treasury to Bacon, 9 May 1763, PRO, T 27/28, p. 392; 21 September 1763, PRO, T 29/35, p. 164; 9 January 1764, ibid, p. 251.
43. 22 January 1766, PRO, T 29/37, p. 311.
44. 'State of the Several Subsisting Contracts' (1764), Liverpool papers, BL, Add. MS 38338, ff. 109–11; East Florida, 13 June 1764, PRO, T 64/133; Namier, *Structure of Politics*, pp. 51–3.
45. P. Lawson, *George Grenville: A Political Life* (Oxford: Clarendon Press, 1984), p. 203.
46. Fox to Bute, 24 November 1762, Bute MS, BL, Add. MS 36796, f. 346; 24 August 1763, PRO, T 29/35, p. 153; 20 June 1764, ibid, p. 451; Thomas Walpole to Newcastle, 1 January 1763, BL, Add. MS 32946, f. 17; Walpole to Martin [Copy], 27 December 1762, ibid., f. 19; Newcastle to Walpole, 4 January 1763, ibid., ff. 49–51.
47. 'Loaves and Fishes, I find, carry great Weight with them', Newcastle to Devonshire, 20 November 1762, BL, Add. MS 32945, f. 90; contractors attending Bute's levees: H. V. Jones to Newcastle, 12 June 1762, BL, Add. MS 32939, ff. 309–10.
48. Douglas, *Seasonable Hints*, pp. 24–5; Namier, *American Revolution*, pp. 68, 72.
49. North permitted an element of bidding for Treasury contracts in 1780, Baker, 'Changing Attitudes', p. 213.
50. 28 April 1778, PRO, T 29/47, pp. 93–4.
51. Baker, *Government and Contractors*, p. 125.
52. Cf. British strategy of tying France down in Europe, Conway, *American Independence*, p. 53.
53. Select Committee Report on Contracts, *PP*, 1856, vii [362] pp. 212–13.
54. Horace Walpole mentioned these elements in Dundas's career, whilst considering him 'nobly generous', H. Walpole, *Memoirs of the Reign of King George III*, ed. D. Jarrett, 4 vols (New Haven, CT, and London: Yale University Press, 2000), vol. 4, p. 64. An anonymous correspondent was astonished that many country gentlemen considered Dundas made his fortune by competent performance of contracts: 'This may be very true; but still such a man fattens upon the spoils' ('Varro' for the *Morning Post*, 'Sir Lawrence Dundass' [*sic*], n.d., ZA, ZNK X1/21/21).
55. Hancock, '"Domestic Bubbling"', p. 681 n. 7.
56. Middleton, *Bells of Victory*, p. 215.
57. M. van Creveld, *Technology and War from 2000 B.C. to the Present* (New York: Free Press, 1989), p. 47.

58. The association between contracts and corruption continues. A recent authoritative dictionary illustrates the usage of venal by 'venal contract' (*Collins English Dictionary: 21st Century Edition* (London: Collins, 2000), p. 1689).

Appendix A: Sample of Army Contractors in Parliament

1. Sedgwick, *Commons*, vol. 1, pp. 487–8, 508, 509, 627–8; vol. 2, pp. 41–2, 70–1, 90, 157–8, 381; Namier and Brooke, *Commons*, vol. 2, pp. 21, 40–1, 235–7, 291–3, 340–2, 426–8, 607–9, 691–2; vol. 3, pp. 44–5, 99, 129–30, 194–5, 533–6, 536–7, 598–602; Namier, 'Anthony Bacon', pp. 20–70; Namier, *American Revolution*, p. 281; Bland to Governor Collingwood, 3 May 1748, Blaikie, NLS, MS 304, f. 66.
2. Namier, *Structure of Politics*, p. 51.
3. J. H. Philbin, *Parliamentary Representation 1832, England and Wales* (New Haven, CT: Yale University Press, 1965), pp. 9–10, 12, 34–8, 45–8, 53–4, 62–4, 82–3, 87, 98–9, 102, 121–2, 132–3, 155–6, 163–4, 169–70, 174–5, 180, 182–4, 187–8, 195–6, 198–200, 207–9, 211–12, 214–15, 218, 226, 228–9, 236–8.

Appendix B: The Legacy

1. 'Memos for the King', 15 October 1759, BL, Add. MS 32897, f. 85; *GM*, 32 (1762), p. 553; 20 March 1769, *Calendar of Home Office papers 1766–1769*, p. 564; Sedgwick, *Commons*, vol. 1, p. 508; Namier and Brooke, *Commons*, vol. 2, pp. 20–1, 40–1, 235–7; vol. 3, p. 99.
2. Namier and Brooke, *Commons*, vol. 2, pp. 21, 447, vol. 3, pp. 537–8; Namier, *American Revolution*, p. 257; Thorne, *Commons*, vol. 3, pp. 114–17, 335–6, 652–3, 780; vol. 4, pp. 179–80, 262, 578–80, 655–6; Venn, *Alumni Cantabrigienses 1752–1900*, vol. 1, p. 462.
3. Venn, *Cantabrigienses*, vol. 1, pp. 262–3; Foster, *Oxonienses*, vol. 1, p. 298; vol. 2, pp. 472, 576; vol. 4, p. 1430; Venn, *Cantabrigienses 1752–1900*, vol. 1, pp. 127, 130; vol. 3, p. 484; vol. 6, pp. 218, 332; Thorne, *Commons*, vol. 3, pp. 652–3.

Appendix C: The Business Life of Contractors

1. Based on Sedgwick, and Namier and Brooke (page numbers cited in Appendix A, note 1); additional information from *GM*, 2 (1732), p. 584; 25 (1755), p. 328; *Compleat Guide*, 4 (1740), p. 132; *Universal Pocket Companion*, 6 (1741), p. 99; *Compleat Guide*, 7 (1744), p. 138; *Universal Pocket Book*, 8 (1745), p. 101; 19 March 1752, *HCJ*, 26, p. 500.
2. 7 December 1742, *CTBP* (1742–5), p. 421; 25 December 1745, PRO, T 52/43 p. 449; Memorial, n.d. [after 1752], BL, Add. MS 33054, ff. 372–3, it is unclear when his commission ended; he is listed as Commissary General in the *Royal Kalendar* (1770), p. 189.
3. Namier and Brooke, *Commons*, vol. 2, p. 358.
4. *GM*, 18 (1748), p. 140.
5. 31 July 1756, PRO, T 52/47 pp. 637–9; 3 May 1759, PRO, T 52/49 p. 470; 12 March 1761, PRO, T 52/52 p. 35.
6. Namier and Brooke, *Commons*, vol. 2, pp. 340–2.
7. Baugh, *Naval Administration 1715–1750*, p. 498.

8. 31 July 1756, PRO, T 52/47, pp. 637–9; 3 May 1759, PRO, T 52/49, p. 470; 12 March 1761, PRO, T 52/52, p. 35.

Appendix D: Property-Holding

1. Namier and Brooke, *Commons*, vol. 2, p. 21; Probate, 22 August 1766, PRO, PROB 11/921 f. 290.
2. Namier and Brooke, *Commons*, vol. 2, pp. 35–6; Namier, 'Anthony Bacon', 20–70.
3. Namier and Brooke, *Commons*, vol. 2, pp. 40–1; Namier, 'Brice Fisher', pp. 518–19.
4. *House of Lords Journals*, 31, pp. 40, 197; Sedgwick, *Commons*, vol. 1, pp. 487–8.
5. Sedgwick, *Commons*, vol. 1, p. 508.
6. Probate, 28 April 1756, PRO, PROB 11/821, f. 97; Sedgwick, *Commons*, vol. 1, p. 509.
7. 29 April 1762, *HCJ*, 29, p. 315; Namier and Brooke, *Commons*, vol. 2, pp. 235–7; Marshall, 'Empire and Opportunity', p. 120.
8. 29 April 1762, *HCJ*, 29, p. 315; Namier and Brooke, *Commons*, vol. 2, p. 237.
9. Cust and Cust (eds), *Cust Family*, vol. 2, pp. 304–5; Namier and Brooke, *Commons*, vol. 2, pp. 291–3.
10. Probate, June 1786, PRO, PROB 11/1155, f. 317; Namier and Brooke, *Commons*, vol. 2, pp. 340–2.
11. Namier and Brooke, *Commons*, vol. 2, pp. 357–61; J. Harris, 'The Dundas Empire', *Apollo*, 86 (1967), pp. 170–9; Timperley, *Landownership*, pp. 95, 137, 144, 243–52, 324, 327.
12. Namier and Brooke, *Commons*, vol. 2, pp. 426–8; Namier, 'Brice Fisher', pp. 518–19.
13. Probate, 16 February 1768, PRO, PROB 11/936 f. 59.
14. Burke, *Landed Gentry*, vol. 1, p. 578; Sedgwick, *Commons*, vol. 2, pp. 41–2.
15. *London Courant, and Westminster Chronicle*, 1 April 1780.
16. Sedgwick, *Commons*, vol. 2, pp. 70–1.
17. Ibid., p. 90; Namier and Brooke, *Commons*, vol. 2, pp. 560–1.
18. Major Henniker, *Families of Major and Henniker*, 6; 11 May 1764, *JCTP* (1764–7), p. 51.
19. Probate, 21 October 1772, PRO, PROB 10 fo. 2597; Sedgwick, *Commons*, vol. 2, pp. 157–8.
20. Namier and Brooke, *Commons*, vol. 2, pp. 691–2.
21. Probate, 30 March 1772, PRO, PROB 10, f. 2582; Sedgwick, *Commons*, vol. 2, p. 210; Timperley, *Landownership*, p. 24.
22. Namier and Brooke, *Commons*, vol. 3, pp. 44–5; Namier, 'Brice Fisher', pp. 518–19.
23. Namier and Brooke, *Commons*, vol. 3, p. 99; 11 May 1764, *JCTP* (1764–7), p. 51.
24. Probate, 9 December 1790, PRO, PROB 11/1199, f. 564.
25. Nesbitt, *Family of Nesbitt*, p. 46; Namier and Brooke, *Commons*, vol. 3, pp. 194–5; 5 June 1764, *JCTP* (1764–7), p. 64.
26. Sedgwick, *Commons*, vol. 2, p. 381.
27. Namier and Brooke, *Commons*, vol. 3, pp. 533–6; B. Bailyn, *Voyagers to the West: Emigration from Britain to America on the Eve of the Revolution* (London: Tauris, 1987), p. 446.
28. Namier and Brooke, *Commons*, vol. 3, pp. 536–7.
29. Ibid., pp. 598–602.

WORKS CITED

Primary Sources

Manuscripts

Public Record Office, London
PRO 30/8/73, 75–8, 83, 92: Chatham papers (official).
PRO 30/8/18, 231: Chatham papers (correspondence).
Adm. 110/6–8: Admiralty (correspondence).
C103/32: Account book of John Warrington.
C171/48: Willan v. Willan.
WO 1: In-letters, Secretary at War.
WO 4: Out-letters, Secretary at War.
WO 26: Miscellaneous.
WO 30: Defence papers.
WO 34: Amherst papers.
WO 46: Out-letters, Ordnance Board.
WO 47: Minutes and reports, Surveyor General.
WO 55: Miscellaneous, Ordnance Board.
WO 71: Proceedings, Board of General Officers.
WO 72: Articles of War (1718–49).
WO 247: Royal Hospital Chelsea contracts.
T 1: Treasury Board papers (1710–70).
T 27: Out-letters, Treasury.
T 29: Treasury Board minute books.
T 36/8: Plate duty registers, Scotland.
T 47/3–4: Carriage duty registers, England and Wales.
T 47/5: Plate duty registers, England and Wales.
T 52: King's warrants.
T 54: Warrants not relating to money.
T 64/96: Correspondence between Baron Munchausen and T. O. Hunter.
T 64/132–3: Copies of contracts.
E 401/2598: Loan subscribers (1757).
AO 1: Audit Office, declared accounts.
AO 17: Minutes and reports, Comptrollers of Army Accounts.
PMG 60/1: Paymaster General's papers.
SP 8: King William's Chest (1693 and undated).

SP 36: Secretaries of State papers.
SP 37: Secretaries of State correspondence.
SP 41: State papers (domestic), military correspondence.
SP 42: State papers, naval correspondence.
SP 44: State papers, entry books.
SP 45: Lords Justices minutes.
SP 54: Secretaries of State, Scotland.
SP 55: Secretary of State for Scotland letter-book.
SP 87: State papers (foreign), military expeditions.
PROB 8: Probate act books.
PROB 10: Original wills and sentences.
PROB 11: Register of wills.
CRES 2/736: Papers concerning Marylebone Park.

British Library, London

Newcastle papers (correspondence): Add. MS 32687, 32693, 32699–701, 32704–6, 32712–13, 32715, 32726–8, 32735, 32737, 32852, 32861–2, 32864–6, 32870, 32873–4, 32877–8, 32881–2, 32883–4, 32889–32901, 32902–7, 32910–13, 32918, 32921–3, 32927–8, 32931–2, 32934, 32936, 32938–41, 32946, 32964, 32966
Newcastle papers (miscellaneous papers): Add. MS 33028, 33032, 33034, 33038–40, 33046–8, 33050, 33052, 33054, 33066.
Liverpool papers (correspondence): Add. MS 38204, 38304.
Liverpool papers (official): Add. MS 38330–1, 38338, 38343.
Liverpool papers (miscellaneous): Add MS 38379, 38383.
Register of correspondence of the Earl of Bute: Add. MS 36796.
Holland House papers: Add. MS 51398.
Fox papers: Add. MS 47589.
Private letter-books of John Calcraft: Add. MS 17493–6.
Barrington papers: Add. MS 73654.
Hardwicke papers (correspondence): Add. MS 35352, 35354.
Hardwicke papers (miscellaneous): Add. MS 35839, 36130, 36257.
Carteret papers (correspondence): Add. MS 22537–8.
Carteret papers (miscellaneous): Add. MS 22542.
Portland papers: Portland Loan 29/45f/44 (reclassified Add. MS 70171).
Coxe papers: Add. MS 9186.
West (Treasury) papers: Add. MS 30219, 34736.
Ligonier papers: Add. MS 57318.
Loudoun papers: Add. MS 44072.
Francis papers: Add. MS 40758–9.
Ordnance papers: Add. MS 33116.
Order Book of Lord Stair: Add. MS 20005.
Grant family papers: Add. MS 25409.
Skinner papers: Add. MS 174500–1.
Leeds (Holdernesse) papers: Egerton MS 3432.
Letter-book of David Mendes de Costa: Egerton MS 2227.

National Archives of Scotland, Edinburgh.

GD124: Mar & Kellie papers.

GD150: Morton papers.
GD158: Hume of Marchmont papers.
GD213/52: Letters of Mary Oswald to Richard Oswald (1761–3).
GD213/53: Miscellaneous letters to Richard Oswald (1764–84).
GD248: Grant of Seafield and Cullen House papers.
RD2: Register of deeds.
RH4/98/295–9: Townshend papers from Buccleuch Muniments, from originals at Clements Library, Michigan.
RH4/70: Sir Andrew Mitchell papers.

National Library of Scotland, Edinburgh

Acc. 8425: MSS Copybook of Lawrence Dundas.
MS 303: Blaikie papers, copy of the orderly-book of the Duke of Cumberland's army under Marshal Wade, 23 October 1745–14 August 1746.
MS 304–9: Blaikie papers, letter-books of Commanders-in-Chief (General Bland and General George Churchill) in Scotland, 1747–56.
MS 14512–13: Yester (Tweeddale) papers, Standing Orders (1756).
MS 17529: Saltoun papers (accounts connected with the Rebellion, 1745–1750).
MS 17505–6: Saltoun papers (military).
MS 16622 & 16646: Saltoun papers (correspondence).
MS 11039–40: Minto papers (Commissariat and Treasury).
MS 8027: Edinburgh Castle letter-book.
MSS 28.1.6 (I): Letters relating to forfeitures (Advocates MSS).

Royal Archive, Windsor

Boxes 3–48 (1748–56): Duke of Cumberland papers [microfilm copies from the British Library Lending Division, Boston Spa].

Willan Family Archive, Richmond: Private Papers of the Willan Family in the Possession of Mr. Peter Willan

WFA 1/1–3 (Box 1): Estate of John Willan (d. 1792).
WFA 2/1–4 (Boxes 1, 2 & 14): Estate of John Willan of Hatton Garden (d. 1822).
WFA 3 (Box 2): Papers of John Hemming Willan (d. 1826).
Gen 1: Transcript of will of John Willan of How Hatch and copy of Codicil D.

Essex County Record Office, Chelmsford

D/DTw/T41 & 43: Tower Family archive.

East Suffolk Record Office, Bury St Edmunds

E 18/853/5: Bunbury papers, Pay Office ledgers (1759–63).
E 18/853/18: Bunbury papers, accounts of Peter Taylor, Deputy Paymaster of the Forces in Germany.

North Yorkshire County Record Office, Northallerton

Sir Lawrence Dundas Papers, Zetland (Dundas) Archive
ZNK X1/1–2: Commissariat papers and correspondence.
ZNK X1/8, 11–12: Financial papers and bank accounts.
ZNK X1/21: Dundas family papers and miscellaneous.

Dundee City Archives
Montrose out-ports: customs correspondence: CE 53/1/4, CE 53/2/5.
Treasurer's Book of the Burgh of Dundee (1733–53).

Bank of England Archives, London
3% Consols ledgers (1752–98): AC 27/1390, 1422.

British Postal Museum and Archives, London
POST 10: Road transport.
POST 96: Private papers of John Palmer (1782–1813).

Manuscripts Department, Nottingham University Library
Henry Pelham papers: Newcastle (Clumber), part I (correspondence).
NeC 1614–19: Petitions and letters relating to the Earl of Rothes.
NeC 1620–51: Military correspondence (1745).
NeC 1707–48: Military correspondence.
NeC 1765–72: Pelham, Huske, and Albemarle correspondence.
NeC 1831–8: Petitions, patronage etc passed on via Cumberland.
NeC 1912–45: Elections (Scotland).
NeC 2203–9: Election papers (1753).

Edinburgh University Library (Special Collections)
Dk. 1.30 ff. 1–186: Letters to Richard Oswald (1764–84).

Guildhall Library, London
London Directories, 1736–95.
MS 5183/1–2: Bakers Company; wheat returns of London Corn Exchange (1756–66).
MS 7801: Bakers Company miscellaneous papers (1740–8).
MS 6651/1: Innholders Company Freedom Admissions (1673–1820).
MS 6656/2: Innholders Company Court livery and members lists (1706–76).
MS 25,745: St Paul's Cathedral register of prebendal leases, I (1721–96).

Westminster City Archives, London
D/Wh: White (Portland) Papers 1771–1833.
Acc. 449: Howard De Walden (formerly Portland) Estate archives (leases).
Acc. 921: Memorandum book of W. Anson, livery stable keeper, 1825–36, 1844–5 Grosvenor estate papers, Box 11.
St George's Hanover Square rate-books.
Parish of St Marylebone rate-books.

Historical Manuscripts Commission Collections

Earl of Egmont Diary, 3 vols (London: HMSO, 1920–3).
Laing MS, 2 vols (London: HMSO, 1914–25).
Mar and Kellie MS. (London: HMSO, 1904).
Mar and Kellie MS. supplementary report (London: HMSO, 1930).
Manuscripts of Lord Polwarth, 5 vols (London: HMSO, 1911–61).

Various Collections, vol. 5 (Hereford: HMSO, 1909).
Various Collections, vol. 8 (London: HMSO, 1913).
First and Second Reports (London: HMSO, 1870).
Third Report (London: HMSO, 1872).
Stopford-Sackville, 2 vols (London: HMSO, 1904–10).
Townshend and Dartmouth MS., 3 vols (London: HMSO, 1887–96).
Rutland MS, 3 vols (London: HMSO, 1888–94).
Fifteenth Report: Earl of Carlisle MS (London: HMSO, 1897).
Portland MSS., V: Harley papers, III (London: HMSO, 1899).
Hastings MSS., 3 vols (London: HMSO, 1928–34).

Official Documents

Calendar of Treasury Papers, 1557–1728, ed. J Redington, 6 vols (London: Longman & Co., 1868–89).

Calendar of Home Office Papers in the Reign of George III, 25 October 1760–1765, ed. J. Redington and R. A. Roberts, 4 vols (London: Longman & Co., 1878–99).

Calendar of Treasury Papers, 1714–19, ed. J. Redington (London: Longmans and Co., 1883).

Calendar of Treasury Books and Papers, 1729–1745, ed. W. A. Shaw, 5 vols (London: HMSO, 1897–1903).

Eighth Report of Commissioners appointed to inquire into fees in public offices, 17 April 1788, *PP*, 1806, vii [c.309].

Hay Contracts: Correspondence and Reports, *Parliamentary Papers*, 1854, xli.73 [260].

'History of the Earlier Years of the Funded Debt from 1694–1786', *Parliamentary Papers* (1898), lii.269 [Cm. 9010].

House of Commons Committee Reports, 1715–1803 (16 vols, 1803-6).

House of Commons Committees 1715–1803, Finance Reports (1797–8), xii–xxii.

Public Income and Expenditure, *Parliamentary Papers* (1868–9), xxxv.1 [366–1].

Report for the Select Committee on Contracts for Public Departments, Proceedings, Minutes of Evidence, Appendix & Index, *Parliamentary Papers*, 1856, vii.117 [362].

Report from the Committee appointed to consider The State of His Majesty's Land Forces and Marines, 6 June 1746, *House of Commons Committees 1715–1803: Reports*, vol. 2, pp. 73–212.

Report from the Committee on the Petition of the Owners of Collieries in South Wales, *Parliamentary Papers* (1810), iv.151 [344].

Report from the Select Committee on Mail Coach Exemption, *Parliamentary Papers* (1810–11), iii.705 [212].

Report into the Civil Administration of the Army, 13 December 1833, *PP* (1837), xxxiv. [78].

Second Report of Commissioners appointed to inquire into fees in public offices, *PP*, 1806, vii [c.309].

Seventh Report from the Committee on Public Expenditure, *Parliamentary Papers* (1810), ii.523 [370].

The Statutes at Large, from Magna Charta to 1869, ed. O. Ruffhead, rev. C. Runnington, 43 vols (London: 1786–1849).

Newspapers and Journals

Annual Register.
Cheltenham Chronicle.
Craftsman.
Daily Courant.
Flying Post.
Gentleman's Magazine.
Ipswich Journal.
House of Commons Journals (vols 17–21, 23–31, 38).
House of Lords Journals (vols 31, 47, 49)
Lloyd's Evening Post.
London Gazette.
London Evening Post.
London Courant.
North Briton.
Post-Boy.
Public Advertiser.
Read's Weekly Journal.
St James's Chronicle.
Scots Magazine.
The Times.
Whitehall Evening Post.

Printed Works

Allardyce, Col. J. (ed.), *Historical papers Relating to the Jacobite Period, 1699–1750* (Aberdeen: New Spalding Club, 1895–6).

[Anon.], *A Particular or Inventory of Mr. John Gore Late One of the Directors of the South Sea Company* (London: Jacob Tonson, Bernard Lintot and William Taylor, 1721).

—, *A True and Exact Particular and Inventory of William Astell Esquire* (London: J. Tonson, 1721).

—, *Jacobite Trials: Proceedings in the House of Peers upon the Indictments against William, Earl of Kilmarnock, George, Earl of Cromartie, and Arthur, Lord Balmerino* (London: S. Billingsley, 1746).

—, *Seasonable and Affecting Observations on the Mutiny-Bill, Articles of War, and Use and Abuse of a Standing Army: in a Letter from a Member of Parliament to a Noble Lord* (London: W. Owen, 1750).

—, *A Political and Satyrical History of the Years 1756, 1757, 1758 and 1759*, 3rd edn (London: E. Morris, 1760).

—, *The Humours of the Town, a Dramatic Interlude in One Act* (Edinburgh: 1776).

—, *A Letter to a Certain Baronet* (Edinburgh: 1777).

—, *A Short Account of the Institution, Progress, and Present State of the Scottish Corporation in London* (London: W. and A. Strahan, 1777).

Barnard, Sir J., 'Some Maxims Relating to the Funds', in M. Postlethwayt, *The Universal Dictionary of Trade and Commerce*, 3rd edn, 2 vols (London: H. Woodfall, A Millar, J. and R. Tonson et al, 1766).

Barrington, W., Viscount, *An Eighteenth-Century Secretary at War: The Papers of William, Viscount Barrington*, ed. T. Hayter (London: Bodley Head for Army Records Society 1988).

Bland, H., *A Treatise of Military Discipline*, rev. W. Faucitt, 9th edn (London: R. Baldwin, 1762).

[Burt, E.], *Letters from a Gentleman in the North of Scotland to his Friend in London*, 2 vols (London: S. Birt, 1754).

Campbell, Sir I., *Lawrence Dundas Estate: Information for Sir Thomas Dundas of Kerse* (1783).

Chamberlayne, J., *Magnae Brittanniae: Or, the Present State of Great Britain with Diverse Remarks upon the Ancient State thereof* (London: D. Midwinter, 1735).

Chapman, J. H. (ed.), *The Register Book of Marriages Belonging to the Parish of St George's Hanover Square, vol. 1, 1725–1787* (London: Harleian Society, 1886).

Cobbett, W., *Cobbett's Parliamentary History of England: From the Norman Conquest, in 1066, to the year 1803*, 12 vols (1806–12), continued as Hansard, *The Parliamentary Debates*, vols 13–36 (1812–20).

Coxe, W., *Memoirs of the Administration of the Right Honourable Henry Pelham*, 2 vols (London: Longman, Rees, Orme, Brown and Green, 1829).

Cust, Lady E. and L. (eds), *Records of the Cust family*, 3 vols (London: Mitchell and Hughes, 1894–1927).

Dalrymple, C., *A Military Essay, Containing Reflections on the Raising, Arming, Cloathing, and Discipline of the British Infantry and Cavalry: With Proposals for the Improvement of the Same* (London: D. Wilson, 1761).

Defoe, D., *A Tour thro' the Whole Island of Great Britain*, 3rd edn, 4 vols (London: J. Osborn, S. Birt et al, 1742).

—, *The Complete English Tradesman in Familiar Letters*, 2nd edn, 2 vols (London: Charles Rivington, 1727).

Dickinson, H. T. (ed.), 'The Letters of Henry St. John to the Earl of Orrery', *Camden Miscellany*, 4th series, 14:26 (1975), pp. 137–200.

Douglas, John, *A Letter Addressed to Two Great Men, on the Prospect of Peace; and on the Terms Necessary to be Insisted upon in the Negociation*, 2nd edn (London: A. Millar, 1760).

—, *Seasonable Hints from an Honest Man on the Present Important Crisis of a New Reign, and a New Parliament* (London: A. Millar, 1761).

Freech, John, *The Political Songster or, A Touch on the Times, on Various Subjects, and Adapted to Common Tunes*, 6th edn (Birmingham: J. Pearson, 1790).

Graham, J. M., *Annals and correspondence of the Viscount and the First and Second Earls of Stair*, 2 vols (Edinburgh and London: Blackwood, 1875).

Grose, F., *Military Antiquities Respecting a History of the English Army, from the Conquest to the Present Time*, 2 vols (London: S. Hooper, 1786–8).

Hewins, W. A. S. (ed.), *The Whitefoord Papers: Being the Correspondence and Other Manuscripts of Charles Whitefoord and Caleb Whitefoord from 1739 to 1810* (Oxford: Clarendon Press, 1898).

The History and Proceedings of the House of Commons from the Restoration to the Present Time, 14 vols (London: Chandler, 1741–4).

Hunter, T. (ed.), *Extracts from the Records of the Convention of Royal Burghs, Vol. 5 (1738–1759)* (Edinburgh: Scottish Burghs Record Society, 1915).

Ilchester, Lord (ed.), *Letters to Henry Fox, Lord Holland* (London: Roxburghe Club, 1915).

Kalm, P., *Kalm's Account of his Visit to England on his Way to America in 1748*, tr. J. Lucas (London: Macmillan & Co, 1892).

Keppel, W. A., *The Albemarle Papers: Being the Correspondence of William Anne, Second Earl of Albemarle Commander-in-Chief in Scotland 1746–1747*, ed. C. S. Terry, 2 vols. (Aberdeen: New Spalding Club, 1902).

Knatchbull, Sir E., *The Parliamentary Diary of Sir Edward Knatchbull (1722–1730*, ed. A. N. Newman, Camden Society, 3rd series, 94 (London: Royal Historical Society, 1963).

Maitland, William, *A History and Survey of London*, 2 vols (London: T. Osborne, J. Shipton and J. Hodges, 1756–7).

Memorials of the Public Life of the Right Hon. James Oswald of Dunnikier (Edinburgh: A. Constable, 1825).

Millar, A. H. (ed.), *A Selection of Scottish Forfeited Estates Papers 1715, 1745* (Edinburgh: Scottish History Society, 1909).

Nicolson, J., and Burn, R., *The History and Antiquities of the Counties of Westmoreland and Cumberland*, 2 vols (London: W. Strachan and T. Cadell, 1777).

Owen, W., *An Authentic Account Published by the King's Authority, of All the Fairs in England and Wales* (London: W. Owen, 1756).

The Parliamentary Register; or, History of the Proceedings and Debates in the House of Commons, 1775–1780, 17 vols (London: J. Almon, 1775–80).

Pitt, W., *Correspondence of William Pitt, Earl of Chatham*, ed. W. S. Taylor and J. H. Pringle, 4 vols (London: John Murray, 1838–40).

Postlethwayt, M., *Universal Dictionary of Trade and Commerce*, 3rd edn, 2 vols (London: H. Woodfall, A. Millar, J. and R. Tonson et al, 1766).

Ranft, B. McL (ed.), *The Vernon Papers* (London: Navy Records Society, 1958).

Russell, Lord John (ed.), *Correspondence of John, Fourth Duke of Bedford with an Introduction*, 3 vols (London: Longman, 1842–6).

Sausine, C. de, *A Foreign View of England in the Reigns of George I and George II: The Letters of Monsieur Cesar De Saussine to his Family*, tr. and ed. Madame van Muyden (London: John Murray, 1902).

Scott, Sir W., *The Journal of Sir Walter Scott from the Original Manuscript at Abbotsford*, 2 vols (Edinburgh: D. Douglas, 1891).

Smith, C., *Three Tracts on the Corn-trade and Corn-Laws*, 2nd edn (London: J. Brotherton, 1766).

Smollett, T., *The Expedition of Humphry Clinker* (1771), ed. L. M. Knapp, rev. P. Gabriel-Boucé (Oxford: Oxford University Press, 1984).

Snyder, H. L. (ed.), *The Marlborough–Godolphin Correspondence*, 3 vols (Oxford: Clarendon Press, 1975).

Swift, J., *The Conduct of the Allies, and of the Late Ministry, in the Beginning and Carrying on the Present War*, 4th edn (London: John Morphew, 1711).

Todd, W., *The Journal of Corporal William Todd 1745–1762* ed. A. Cormack and A. Jones (Stroud: Army Records Society, 2001).

Walpole, H., *The Yale Edition of Horace Walpole's Correspondence*, ed. H. Lewis, 34 vols (New Haven, CT: Yale University Press, 1937–83).

—, *Horace Walpole's Memoirs of the Reign of George II*, ed. J. Brooke, 3 vols (New Haven, CT and London: Yale University Press, 1985).

—, *Horace Walpole's Memoirs of the Reign of George III*, ed. D. Jarrett, 4 vols (New Haven, CT and London: Yale University Press, 2000).

Wolfe, J., *The Life and Letters of James Wolfe*, ed. B. Willson (London: William Heinemann, 1909).

Yorke, P., *The Life and Correspondence of Philip Yorke, Earl of Hardwicke, Lord High Chancellor of Great Britain*, ed. P. C. Yorke, 3 vols (Cambridge: Cambridge University Press, 1913).

Young, A., *General View of the Agriculture of the County of Essex*, 2 vols (London: B. McMillan, 1807).

Secondary Sources

Albion, R. G., *Forests and Sea Power: The Timber Problem of the Royal Navy* (Cambridge, MA: Harvard University Press, 1926).

Anderson, F., *Crucible of War: The Seven Years' War and the Fate of Empire in British North America, 1754–1766* (London: Faber, 2000).

Anderson, M. S., *The War of the Austrian Succession 1740–1748* (London: Longman, 1995).

Ashley, W., 'The Place of Rye in the History of English Food', *Economic Journal*, 31:123 (1921), pp. 285–308.

Atkinson, C. T., 'The Army under the Early Hanoverians', *Journal of the Society for Army Historical Research*, 21 (1942), pp. 138–47.

—, 'Some Letters about the 'Forty Five', *Journal of the Society for Army Historical Research*, 37 (1959), pp. 112–26.

Austen, B., *British Mail-Coaches 1784–1850* (New York: Garlands, 1986).

Bailyn, B., *Voyagers to the West: Emigration from Britain to America on the Eve of the Revolution* (London: Tauris, 1987).

Baker, C. H. C, and M. I. Baker, *The Life and Circumstances of James Brydges, First Duke of Chandos* (Oxford: Oxford University Press, 1949).

Baker, N., *Government and Contractors: The British Treasury and War Supplies 1775–1783* (London: Athlone Press, 1971).

—, 'The Treasury and Open Contracting, 1778–1782', *Historical Journal*, 15:3 (1972), pp. 433–54.

—, 'Changing Attitudes towards Government in Eighteenth-Century Britain', in A. Whiteman, J. S. Bromley and P. G. M. Dickson (eds), *Statesmen, Scholars and Merchants: Essays in Eighteenth-Century History Presented to Dame Lucy Sutherland* (Oxford: Clarendon Press, 1973), pp. 203–19.

Baldry, W. Y., 'Notes on the Early History of Billeting', *Journal of the Society for Army Historical Research*, 13:50 (1934), pp. 71–3.

Bannerman, W. B. and Captain R. R. B. Bannerman, *The Registers of Marriages of St. Marylebone, Middlesex, 1775–1783, Vol. 51* (London: Harleian Society, 1921).

Barnett, C., *Britain and her Army, 1509–1970* (London: Allen Lane, 1970).

Baugh, D. A., *Naval Administration in the Age of Walpole* (Princeton, NJ: Princeton University Press, 1965).

—, *Naval Administration 1715–1750* (London: Navy Records Society, 1977).

—, 'Maritime Strength and Atlantic Commerce: The Uses of a Grand Marine Empire', in L. Stone (ed.), *An Imperial State at War: Britain from 1689–1815* (London: Routledge, 1993), pp. 185–223.

Baxter, S. B., *The Development of the Treasury 1660–1702* (London: Longmans, Green and Co., 1957).

—, *William III* (London: Longmans, 1966).

Baynes, J., *The Jacobite Rising of 1715* (London: Cassell, 1970).

Beattie, D. J., 'The Adaptation of the British Army to Wilderness Warfare, 1755–1763', in M. Ultee (ed.), *Adapting to Conditions: War and Society in the Eighteenth Century* (Tuscaloosa: University of Alabama Press, 1986), pp. 56–83.

Beveridge, Sir W., *Prices and Wages in England from the Twelfth to the Nineteenth Century*, vol. 1 [no further volumes published] (London: Longmans and Co., 1939).

Binney, J. E. D., *British Public Finance 1774–1792* (Oxford: Clarendon Press, 1958).

Black, J., 'A Military Revolution? A 1660–1792 Perspective' in C. J. Rogers (ed.), *The Military Revolution Debate: Readings on the Military Transformation of Early Modern Europe* (Boulder, CO: Westview Press, 1995), pp. 95–114.

—, *Britain as a Military Power, 1688–1815* (London: University College London Press, 1999).

Blaikie, W. B. (ed.), *Origins of the 'Forty Five and Other Papers Relating to that Rising* (Edinburgh: Scottish History Society, 1916).

Braddick, M. J., 'An English Military Revolution?' *Historical Journal*, 36:4 (1993), pp. 965–75.

—, 'The Early Modern English State and the Question of Differentiation, from 1550 to 1700', *Comparative Studies in Society and History*, 38:1 (1996), pp. 92–111.

Brasz, H. A., 'The Sociology of Corruption' in A. J. Heidenheimer (ed.), *Political Corruption: Readings in Comparative Analysis* (New York and London: Holt, Rinehart, and Winston, 1970)

Brewer, J., *The Sinews of Power: War, Money, and the English State 1688-1783* (London: Unwin Hyman, 1989).

Brewer, J., and H. Eckhart (eds), *Rethinking Leviathan: The Eighteenth-Century State in Britain and Germany* (Oxford: Oxford University Press, 1999).

Brisco, N. A., *The Economic Policy of Robert Walpole* (New York: Columbia University Press, 1907).

Brown, M., '"The Fields of Cows by Willan's Farm": Thomas Willan of Marylebone (1755-1828)', *Westminster History Review*, 4 (2001), pp. 1-5.

Browning, R., 'The Duke of Newcastle and the Financial Management of the Seven Years War in Germany', *Journal of the Society for Army Historical Research*, 49 (1971), pp. 20-35.

—, 'The Duke of Newcastle and the Financing of the Seven Years' War', *Journal of Economic History*, 31:2 (1971), pp. 344-77.

Bryant, G. J., 'Scots in India in the Eighteenth Century', *Scottish Historical Review*, 64:177 (1998), pp. 22-41.

Burke, Sir J. B., *A Genealogical and Heraldic History of the Landed Gentry of Great Britain and Ireland*, 2 vols, 6th edn (London: Harrison, 1879).

Campbell-Maclachlan, A. N., *William Augustus Duke of Cumberland* (London: Henry S. King, 1876).

Chandler, D., *The Art of Warfare in the Age of Marlborough* (London: Batsford, 1976).

Childs, J., *The Army of Charles II* (London: Routledge and Kegan Paul, 1976).

—, *The Army, James II, and the Glorious Revolution* (Manchester: Manchester University Press, 1980).

—, *The British Army of William III, 1689-1702* (Manchester: Manchester University Press 1987).

—, *Armies and Warfare in Europe 1648-1789* (Manchester: Manchester University Press, 1982).

—, 'The Williamite War, 1689-1691' in T. Bartlett & Keith Jeffrey (eds), *A Military History of Ireland* (Cambridge: Cambridge University Press, 1996), pp. 188-210.

—, 'The Army and the State in Britain and Germany during the Eighteenth Century', in J. Brewer and E. Hellmuth (eds), *Rethinking Leviathan: The Eighteenth-Century State in Britain and Germany* (Oxford: Oxford University Press, 1999), pp. 53-70.

Christie, I. R., *The End of North's Ministry 1780-1782* (London: Macmillan & Co., 1958).

Churchill, W., *A History of the English Speaking Peoples*, 4 vols (London: Cassell & Co., 1956-8).

Clark, D. M., 'The Office of Secretary to the Treasury in the Eighteenth Century', *American Historical Review*, 42:1 (October 1936-July 1937), pp. 22-45.

Clausewitz, C. von, *On War* (1832), tr. J. J. Graham, Rev. F. N. Maude (Ware, Hertfordshire: Wordsworth, 1997).

Clode, C. M., *The Military Forces of the Crown: Their Administration and Government*, 2 vols (London: John Murray, 1869).

Colley, L., *Britons: Forging the Nation 1707–1837* (New Haven, CT: Yale University Press, 1992).

Collins English Dictionary: 21st Century Edition (London: Collins, 2000).

Conway, S., 'Britain and the Impact of the American War, 1775–1783', *War in History*, 2:2 (1995), pp. 127–50.

—, *The War of American Independence 1775–1783* (London: Edward Arnold, 1995).

—, *War, State, and Society in Mid-Eighteenth-Century Britain and Ireland* (Oxford: Oxford University Press, 2006).

Corsar, K. C., 'The Garrison of Scotland, 1719', *Journal of the Society for Army Historical Research*, 22:85 (1943), pp. 15–19.

Corvisier, A., *Armies and Societies in Europe, 1494–1789* (Bloomington and London: Indiana University Press, 1979).

Creveld, M. van, *Supplying War: Logistics from Wallenstein to Patton* (Cambridge: Cambridge University Press 1977).

—, *Technology and War from 2000 B.C. to the Present* (New York: Free Press, 1989).

Crewe, D., *Yellow Jack and the Worm: British Naval Administration in the West Indies 1739–1748* (Liverpool: Liverpool University Press, 1993).

Crowhurst, R. P., 'The Admiralty and the Convoy System in the Seven Years War', *Mariner's Mirror*, 57 (1971), pp. 163–73.

—, *The Defence of British Trade 1689–1815* (Folkestone: Dawson, 1977).

Cruikshank, C. G., *Elizabeth's Army* (Oxford: Oxford University Press, 1946).

Cruickshanks, E. (ed.), *Ideology and Conspiracy: Aspects of Jacobitism, 1689–1759* (Edinburgh: Donald, 1982).

Cubitt, G. (ed.), *Imagining Nations* (Manchester: Manchester University Press, 1998).

Cunnington, W. C., *The Military Encampments of James II on Hounslow Heath* (Hounslow: Hounslow and District History Society, 1964).

Dalton, C., *George the First's Army*, 2 vols (London: Eyre and Spottiswoode, 1910–12).

Davies, C. S. L., 'Provisions for Armies, 1509–1550; a Study in the Effectiveness of Early Tudor Government', *Economic History Review*, 17:2 (1964–5), pp. 234–48.

Davis, R., *The Rise of the English Shipping Industry in the Seventeenth and Eighteenth Centuries* (London: Macmillan & Co., 1962).

Dean, C. G. T., *The Royal Hospital Chelsea* (London: Hutchinson & Co., 1950).

Dickinson, H. T., *Liberty and Property: Political Ideology in Eighteenth-Century Britain* (London: Weidenfeld and Nicolson, 1977).

—, *The Financial Revolution in England: A Study in the Development of Public Credit 1688–1756* (London: Macmillan, 1967).

Doubleday, H. A, G. H. Gotley, M. A Hardy and W. Page (eds), *A History of Hampshire and the Isle of Wight*, 5 vols (London: Constable, 1900–14).

Dow, F., *Cromwellian Scotland* (Edinburgh: John Donald, 1979).

Duffy, C., *The Army of Maria Theresa: The Armed Forces of Imperial Austria, 1740–1780* (Vancouver and London: David and Charles, 1977).

Dundas, M. I., *Dundas of Fingask* (Edinburgh: D. Douglas, 1891).

Earle, P., *The Making of the English Middle Class: Business, Society and Family Life in London, 1660–1730* (London: Methuen London, 1989).

Eatwell, J. (ed), *The New Palgrave: A Dictionary of Economics*, 4 vols (London: Macmillan, 1987).

Edwards, P., *The Horse Trade of Tudor and Stuart England* (Cambridge: Cambridge University Press, 1988).

Ehrman, J., *The Navy in the War of William III: Its State and Direction, 1689–1697* (Cambridge: Cambridge University Press, 1953).

Elton, G. R. (ed.), *The Tudor Constitution: Documents and Commentary*, 2nd edn (Cambridge: Cambridge University Press, 1982).

Fayle, C. E., 'Economic Pressure in the War of 1739–1748', *Journal of the Royal United Services Institution*, 68 (1923), pp. 434–46.

Ferguson, W., *Scotland 1689 to the Present* (Edinburgh and London: Oliver & Boyd, 1968).

Fergusson, Sir J., *Argyll in the Forty-Five* (London: Faber & Faber, 1951).

Findlay, J. T., *Wolfe in Scotland in the '45 and from 1749 to 1753* (London: Longmans & Co., 1928).

Firth, C. H., *Cromwell's Army: A History of the English soldier during the Civil Wars, the Commonwealth and the Protectorate*, 2nd edn (London: Methuen, 1912).

Fitzgerald, P. H., *Samuel Foote, a Biography* (London: Chatto & Windus, 1910).

Forbes, Maj. Gen. A., *A History of the Army Ordnance Services*, 3 vols (London: Medici Society, 1929).

Fortescue, Sir J., *A History of the British Army*, 13 vols (London: Macmillan & Co., 1899–1930).

—, *The Royal Army Service Corps: A History of Transport and Supply in the British Army*, 2 vols (Cambridge: Cambridge University Press, 1930).

Foster, J. (ed.), *Alumni Oxonienses, 1715–1886*, 4 vols (Oxford and London: Parker and Co., 1888).

Fritz, P. S., *The English Ministers and Jacobitism between the Rebellions of 1715 and 1745* (Toronto, ON: University of Toronto, 1975).

Gentles, I., *The New Model Army in England, Ireland and Scotland, 1645–1653* (Oxford: Blackwell Publishing, 1991).

Gibbs, V. (ed.), *The Complete Peerage by G. E. C.*, 14 vols (London: St. Catherine Press, 1910–59).

Gibson, A. J. S., and T. C. Smout, *Prices, Food and Wages in Scotland 1550–1870* (Cambridge: Cambridge University Press, 1995).

Gillingham, J., *The Wars of the Roses: Peace and Conflict in Fifteenth Century England* (London: Weidenfeld and Nicolson, 1981).

Gordon, H., *The War Office* (London: Putnam, 1935).

Gordon, W. J., *The Horse World of London* (London: Leisure Hour Library, 1893).

Grassby, R., 'English Merchant Capitalism in the Late Seventeenth Century: The Composition of Business Fortunes', *Past and Present*, 46 (1970), pp. 87–107.

—, 'The Personal Wealth of the Business Community in Seventeenth-Century England', *Economic History Review*, 23:2 (1970), pp. 220–34.

Guy, A. J., 'Regimental Agency in the British Standing Army, 1715–1763: A Study of Georgian Military Administration', *Bulletin of the John Rylands University Library of Manchester*, 62:2 (1980), pp. 423–53; 63:1 (1980), pp. 31–57.

—, *Oeconomy and Discipline: Officership and Administration in the British Army 1714–1763* (Manchester: Manchester University Press, 1985).

—, 'The Irish Military Establishment, 1660–1776' in T. Bartlett and K. Jeffrey (eds), *A Military History of Ireland* (Cambridge: Cambridge University Press, 1996), pp. 211–30.

Haldane, Gen. Sir J. A. L., *The Haldanes of Gleneagles* (Edinburgh and London: W. Blackwood & Sons, 1929).

Hamilton, H., *The Industrial Revolution in Scotland* (Oxford: Clarendon Press, 1932).

Hancock, D., '"Domestic Bubbling": Eighteenth-Century London Merchants and Individual Investment in the Funds', *Economic History Review*, 47:4 (1994), pp. 679–702.

—, *Citizens of the World: London Merchants and the Integration of the British Atlantic Community 1735–1785* (Cambridge: Cambridge University Press, 1995).

Harling, P., and P. Mandler, 'From "Fiscal-Military" State to Laissez-faire State, 1760–1850', *Journal of British Studies*, 32:1 (1993), pp. 44–70.

Harris, J., 'The Dundas Empire', *Apollo*, 86 (1967), pp. 170–9.

Hart, H. W., 'Sherman and the Bull and Mouth', *Journal of Transport History*, 5:1 (1961), pp. 12–21.

Hay, D., P. Linebaugh, J. G. Rule, E. P. Thompson and C. Winslow (eds), *Albion's Fatal Tree: Crime and Society in Eighteenth-Century England* (New York: Pantheon, 1975).

Hayter, T., *The Army and the Crowd in Mid-Georgian England* (London: Macmillan, 1978).

Hazenkampf, Col. M., 'The Supply of an Army in Time of War', *Journal of the United Services Institution*, 21 (1877), pp. 1017–50.

Heidenheimer, A. J. (ed.), *Political Corruption, Readings in Comparative Analysis* (New York and London: Holt, Rinehart & Winston, 1970).

Henniker Major, J., *Some Account of the Families of Major and Henniker* (London: 1803).

Hertz, G. B., 'England and the Ostend Company', *English Historical Review*, 22:86 (1907), pp. 255–79.

Holmes, G., *British Politics in the Age of Anne* (New York: St Martin's Press, 1967).

Hoppit, J., *Risk and Failure in English Business 1700–1800* (Cambridge: Cambridge University Press, 1987).

—, Review of J. Brewer, *The Sinews of Power*, *Historical Journal*, 33:1 (1990), pp. 248–50.

—, 'Attitudes to Credit in Britain, 1680–1790', *Historical Journal*, 33:2 (1990), pp. 305–22.

Horwitz, H., *Parliament, Policy and Politics in the Reign of William III* (Manchester: Manchester University Press, 1977).

Hoskins, W. G., 'Harvest Fluctuations and English Economic History, 1620–1759', *Agricultural History Review*, 16 (1968), pp. 15–31.

Works Cited

Houlding, J. A., *Fit for Service: The Training of the British Army 1715–1795* (Oxford: Clarendon Press, 1981).

Hughes, E., *Studies in Administration and Finance 1558–1825: With Special Reference to the History of Salt Taxation in England* (Manchester: Manchester University Press, 1934).

Jarvis, R. C., *The Jacobite Risings of 1715 and 1745* (Carlisle: Cumberland County Council, 1954).

—, *Collected Papers on the Jacobite Risings*, 2 vols (Manchester: Manchester University Press, 1954).

—, 'Army transport and the English Constitution: With Special Reference to the Jacobite Risings', *Journal of Transport History*, 2:2 (1955–6), pp. 101–20.

Jones, D. W., *War and Economy in the Age of William III and Marlborough* (Oxford: Basil Blackwell, 1988).

Jones, E. L., *Seasons and Prices: The Role of the Weather in English Agricultural History* (London: George Allen & Unwin, 1964).

Jones, J. B., *Annals of Dover* (Dover: Express Works, 1916).

Kennedy, P., *The Rise and Fall of British Naval Mastery*, 3rd edn (London: Fontana, 1991).

Kennett, L., *The French Armies in the Seven Years' War* (Durham, NC: Duke University Press, 1967).

Kingsford, P. W., 'A London Merchant: Sir William Baker', *History Today*, 21 (1971), pp. 338–48.

Langford, P., *Public Life and the Propertied Englishman 1689–1798* (Oxford: Clarendon Press, 1991).

Lawson, P., *George Grenville: A Political Life* (Oxford: Clarendon Press, 1984).

Lenman, B., *The Jacobite Risings in Britain 1689–1746* (London: Eyre Methuen, 1980).

—, *Britain's Colonial Wars, 1688–1783* (Harlow: Longman, 2001).

Lillywhite, B., *London Coffee Houses* (London: George Allen & Unwin, 1963).

Little, H., 'The Treasury, the Commissariat, and the Supply of the Combined Army in Germany during the Seven Years War (1756–1763)' (Phd Dissertation, University of London, 1981).

Lindsay, M., *The Castles of Scotland* (London: Constable, 1986).

MacIvor, I., *Fort George* (Edinburgh: HMSO, 1970).

Malden, H. E. (ed.), *The Victoria History: County of Surrey*, 5 vols (Oxford: Oxford University Press, 1902–14).

Marshall, C. F. D., *The British Post Office from its Beginnings to the End of 1925* (Oxford: Oxford University Press, 1926).

Marshall, P., 'Empire and Opportunity in Britain, 1763–75', *Transactions of the Royal Historical Society*, 6th Series, 5 (1995), pp. 111–28.

Masse, C. H., *Predecessors of the Royal Army Service Corps* (Aldershot: Gale and Polden Ltd., 1948).

Matthew, H. C. G., and B. Harrison (eds), *Oxford Dictionary of National Biography*, 61 vols (Oxford: Oxford University Press, 2004).

Mattosian, M. K., *Poisons of the Past: Molds, Epidemics, and History* (New Haven, CT, and London: Yale University Press, 1989).

Menary, G., *The Life and Letters of Duncan Forbes, Lord President of the Court of Session 1685–1747* (London: A. Maclehose & Co., 1936).

Middleton, R., *The Bells of Victory: The Pitt-Newcastle Ministry and the Conduct of the Seven Years' War, 1757–1762* (Cambridge: Cambridge University Press 1985).

Minchison, W. E., 'The Merchants in England in the Eighteenth Century' in H. G. J. Aitken (ed.), *Explorations in Enterprise* (Cambridge, Mass: Harvard University Press, 1965), pp. 278–95.

Mitchell, B. R., *British Historical Statistics* (Cambridge: Cambridge University Press, 1988).

Morgan, G. W., 'The Impact of War on the Administration of the Army, Navy and Ordnance in Britain, 1739–1754' (Phd Dissertation, University of Leicester, 1977).

Namier, L. B., 'Brice Fisher MP: A Mid-Eighteenth-Century Merchant and his Connexions', *English Historical Review*, 42:168 (1927), pp. 514–32.

—, 'Anthony Bacon M.P., an Eighteenth Century Merchant', *Journal of Economic and Business History*, 2:1 (1929), pp. 20–70.

—, *England in the Age of the American Revolution* (London: Macmillan, 1930).

—, *The Structure of Politics at the Accession of George III*, 2nd edn (London: Macmillan and Co., 1957).

—, *Crossroads of Power: Essays on Eighteenth-Century England* (London: H. Hamilton, 1962).

Namier, L. B, and J. Brooke, *The House of Commons 1754–1790*, 3 vols (London: HMSO, 1964).

—, *Charles Townshend* (London: Macmillan & Co., 1964).

Nesbitt, C., and A. Nesbitt, *History of the Family of Nisbet or Nesbitt in Scotland and Ireland* (Torquay: Privately published, 1898).

Nordmann, C., 'Choiseul and the Last Jacobite Attempt of 1759', in E. Cruickshanks (ed.), *Ideology and Conspiracy: Aspects of Jacobitism, 1689–1759* (Edinburgh: Donald, 1982), pp. 201–17.

Norris, J., *Shelburne and Reform* (London: Macmillan & Co., 1963).

Nusbacher, A. J. S., 'Civil Supply in the Civil War: The Supply of Victuals to the New Model Army on the Naseby Campaign, 1–14 June 1645', *English Historical Review*, 115:460 (2000), pp. 145–60.

O'Brien, P., 'Agriculture and the Home Market for English Industry, 1660–1820', *English Historical Review*, 100:397 (1985), pp. 773–800.

—, 'The Political Economy of British Taxation, 1660–1815', *Economic History Review*, 41:1 (1998), pp. 1–32.

O'Brien, P. K., and P. A. Hunt, 'The Rise of a Fiscal State in England, 1485–1815', *Historical Research*, 66:160 (1993), pp. 129–76.

O'Donovan, J., *The Economic History of Livestock in Ireland* (Dublin and Cork: Cork University Press, 1940).

Orchard, V., *Tattersall's: Two Hundred Years of Sporting History* (London: Hutchinson, 1953).

Owen, J. B., *The Rise of the Pelhams* (London: Methuen & Co., 1957).

Page, W. (ed.), *Victoria History of the County of Hertford*, 5 vols (London: Constable, 1902–23).

Page, W. et al (eds), *The Victoria History of the County of Essex*, 10 vols (Oxford: Oxford University Press, 1903–2001).

—, *The Victoria History of the County of Sussex*, 10 vols (Oxford: Oxford University Press, 1905–97).

—, *The Victoria History of the County of York*, 3 vols (Oxford: Oxford University Press, 1907–13).

Pares, R., *War and Trade in the West Indies 1739–1763* (Oxford: Clarendon Press, 1936).

Parker, G., *The Military Revolution: Military Innovation and the Rise of the West, 1500–1800* (Cambridge: Cambridge University Press, 1988).

Parker, J. G., 'The Directors of the East India Company 1754–1790' (Phd Dissertation, University of Edinburgh, 1977).

Paul, Sir J. B. (ed.), *The Scots Peerage*, 9 vols (Edinburgh: David Douglas, 1904–14).

Perjes, G., 'Army Provisioning, Logistics and Strategy in the Second Half of the 17th Century', *Acta Historica Academiae Scientiarum Hungaricae*, 16 (1970), pp. 1–52.

Perkin, H., *The Origins of Modern English Society 1780–1880* (London: Routledge & Kegan Paul, 1969).

Peters, M., *Pitt and Popularity: The Patriot Minister and London Opinion during the Seven Years War* (Oxford: Clarendon Press, 1980).

Philbin, J. H., *Parliamentary Representation 1832, England and Wales* (New Haven, CT: Yale University Press, 1965).

Platt, D. C. M., 'The Commercial and Industrial Interests of Ministers of the Crown', *Political Studies*, 9:3 (1961), pp. 267–90.

Pool, B., *Navy Board Contracts 1660–1832: Contract Administration under the Navy Board* (London: Longmans, 1966).

Porritt, E, and A. Porrit, *The Unreformed House of Commons: Parliamentary Representation before 1832*, 2 vols (Cambridge: Cambridge University Press, 1909).

Price, F. G. H., *A Handbook of London Bankers* (London: Guildford, 1876).

Price, J. M., 'What Did Merchants Do? Reflections on British Overseas Trade, 1660–1790', *Journal of Economic History*, 49:2 (1989), pp. 267–84.

Quilley, G., '"All Ocean is her Own": The Image of the Sea and the Identity of the Maritime Nation in Eighteenth-Century British Art' in G. Cubitt (ed.), *Imagining Nations* (Manchester: Manchester University Press, 1998), pp. 132–52.

Redlich, F., 'Contributions in the Thirty Years War', *Economic History Review*, 12:2 (1959–60), pp. 247–54.

—, *The German Military Enterpriser and his Work Force: A Study in European Economic and Social History*, 2 vols (Wiesbaden: Franz Steiner Verlag, 1964–5).

Reed, J. W., and F. A. Pottle (eds), *Boswell, Laird of Auchinleck, 1778–1782* (New York and London: McGraw-Hill, 1977).

Richmond, H. W., *The Navy in the War of 1739–1748*, 3 vols (Cambridge: Cambridge University Press, 1920).

Robinson, M. (ed.), *The Concise Scots Dictionary* (Aberdeen: Aberdeen University Press, 1987).

Rodger, N. A. M., *The Wooden World: An Anatomy of the Royal Navy* (London: Collins, 1986).

Rogers, C. J. (ed.), *The Military Revolution Debate: Readings on the Military Transformation of Early Modern Europe* (Boulder, CO: Westview Press, 1995).

Rogers, N., 'Money, Land and Lineage: The Big Bourgeoisie of Hanoverian London', *Social History*, 4:3 (1979), pp. 437–54.

Roseveare, H., *The Treasury: The Evolution of a British Institution* (London: Allen Lane, 1969).

—, *The Treasury 1660–1870: The Foundations of Control* (London: Allen Lane, 1973).

Rubinstein, W. D., 'Victorian Middle Classes: Wealth, Occupation, and Geography', *Economic History Review*, 30:4 (1977), pp. 65–89.

—, *Men of Property: The Very Wealthy in Britain since the Industrial Revolution* (London: Croon Helm, 1981).

—, 'New Men of Wealth and the Purchase of Land in Nineteenth-Century Britain', *Past and Present*, 92 (1981), pp. 125–47.

—, 'The Structure of Wealth-Holding in Britain, 1809–39: A Preliminary Anatomy', *Historical Research*, 45:156 (1992), pp. 74–89.

Sainty, J. C., *A List of Representative Peers for Scotland, 1707 to 1963, and for Ireland, 1800 to 1961* (London: House of Lords Record Office, 1968).

—, *Office-Holders in Modern Britain: Treasury officials 1660–1870* (London: Athlone Press, 1972).

Salmond, J. B., *Wade in Scotland* (Edinburgh: Moray Press, 1934).

Saunders, A., *Regents Park: A Study of the Development of the area from 1086 to the Present Day* (Newton Abbot: David and Charles, 1969).

Schwoerer, L. G., *"No Standing Armies!": The Anti-Army Ideology in Seventeenth-Century England* (Baltimore, MD: John Hopkins University Press, 1974).

Scobie, Maj. I.H. M., 'The Highland Independent Companies of 1745–47', *Journal of the Society for Army Historical Research*, 20:77 (1941), pp. 5–37.

Scouller, R. E., *The Armies of Queen Anne* (Oxford: Clarendon Press, 1966).

Searle, G. R., *Corruption in British Politics, 1895–1930* (Oxford: Clarendon Press, 1987).

Sedgwick, R., *The House of Commons 1715–1754*, 2 vols (London: HMSO, 1970).

Sheppard, F. H. W., *Survey of London, Vol. 39: The Grosvenor Estate in Mayfair, Part I: General History* (London: Athlone Press, 1977).

—, *Survey of London, Vol. 40: The Grosvenor Estate, Part 2: The Buildings* (London: Athlone Press, 1980).

Smith, D. J., 'Army Clothing Contractors and the Textile Industries in the 18th Century', *Textile History*, 14:2 (1983), pp. 153–64.

Stevenson, J., *Popular Disturbances in England 1700–1870* (London: Longman, 1979).

Stocqueler, J. H., *The Military Encyclopaedia; a Technical, Biographical, and Historical Dictionary, Referring Exclusively to the Military Sciences, the Memoirs of Distinguished Soldiers, and the Narratives of Remarkable Battles* (London: William H. Allen, 1853).

Stone, L., 'Social Mobility in England, 1500–1700', *Past and Present*, 33 (1966), pp. 16–55.

— (ed.), *An Imperial State at War: Britain from 1689–1815* (London: Routledge, 1993).

Stone, L., and J. C. F. Stone, *An Open Elite? England 1540–1880* (Oxford: Clarendon Press, 1984).

Sunter, R. M., *Patronage and Politics in Scotland 1707–1832* (Edinburgh: Donald, 1986).

Sutherland, L., *A London Merchant 1695–1774* (London: Oxford University Press, 1933).

—, 'Samson Gideon and the Reduction of Interest, 1749–50', *Economic History Review*, 16:1 (1946), pp. 15–29.

—, *The East India Company in Eighteenth-Century Politics* (Oxford: Clarendon Press, 1952).

—, *Politics and Finance in the Eighteenth Century* (London: Hambledon Press, 1984).

Tabrahan, C. and D. Grove, *Fortress Scotland and the Jacobites* (London: Batsford, 1995).

Tallett, F., *War and Society in Early Modern Europe, 1495–1715* (London: Routledge, 1992).

Tayler, A., and H. Taylor, *1715: The Story of the Rising* (London: T. Nelson & Sons, 1936).

Thirsk, J., (ed.), *The Agrarian History of England and Wales*, 6 vols (Cambridge; Cambridge University Press, 1981–4).

Thompson, E. P., 'The Crime of Anonymity', in D. Hay, P. Linebaugh, J. G. Rule, E. P. Thompson, and C. Winslow (eds), *Albion's Fatal Tree: Crime and Society in Eighteenth-Century England* (New York: Pantheon, 1975), pp. 255–344.

—, 'Nineteenth-Century Horse Sense', *Economic History Review*, 29:1 (1976), pp. 60–81.

— (ed.), *Horses in European Economic History: A Preliminary Canter* (Reading: British Agricultural History Society, 1983).

Thomson, J., *The History of Dundee*, rev. and ed. James Maclaren (Dundee: John Durham & Son, 1874).

Thorne, R. G., *The House of Commons 1790–1820*, 5 vols (London: Secker & Warburg, 1986).

Timperley, L. R. (ed.), *A Directory of Landownership in Scotland c. 1770* (Edinburgh: Scottish Records Society, 1976).

Tylden, Maj. G., *Horses and Saddlery* (London: J. A. Allen & Co., 1965).

Ultee, M. (ed.), *Adapting to Conditions: War and Society in the Eighteenth Century* (Tuscaloosa: University of Alabama Press, 1986).

Venn, J. and J. A., *Alumni Cantabrigienses, Part I: From the Earliest Times to 1751*, 4 vols (Cambridge: Cambridge University Press, 1922–7).

Venn, J. A., *Alumni Cantabrigienses 1752–1900*, 6 vols (Cambridge: Cambridge University Press, 1940–54).

Wadsworth, A. P., and Mann, J. de Lacy, *The Cotton Trade and Industrial Lancashire 1600–1870* (Manchester: Manchester University Press, 1931).

Walton, Col. C., *History of the British Standing Army, 1660–1700* (London: Harrison & Sons, 1894).

Wanklyn, J. (ed.), *Guns at the Wood: A Record of St. John's Wood Barracks* (London: Privately Published, 1972).

Ward, G. A., *A History of South Weald and Brentwood* (Waddon: Spenser Press, 1961).

Ward, W. R., *The English Land Tax in the Eighteenth Century* (London: Oxford University Press, 1953).

Watson, C. B. B. (ed.), *Roll of Edinburgh Burgesses and Guild-Brethren, 1701–1760* (Edinburgh: Scottish Records Society, 1930).

Watteville, H. G. de, *The British Soldier* (London: J. M. Dent & Sons, 1954).

Webb, S., and B. Webb, 'The Assize of Bread', *Economic Journal*, 14:54 (1904), pp. 196–218.

West, J., *Gunpowder, Government and War in the Mid-Eighteenth Century* (London: Royal Historical Society, 1991).

Westerfield, R. B., *Middlemen in English Business* (New Haven, CT: Yale University Press, 1915).

Western, J. R., *The English Militia in the Eighteenth Century: The Story of a Political Issue, 1660–1802* (London: Routledge & Kegan Paul, 1965).

Whiteman, A., J. S. Bromley and P. G. M. Dickson (eds), *Statesmen, Scholars and Merchants: Essays in Eighteenth-Century History Presented to Dame Lucy Sutherland* (Oxford: Clarendon Press, 1973).

Whitworth, R., *Field Marshal Lord Ligonier: A Story of the British Army 1702–1770* (Oxford: Clarendon Press, 1958).

Wilkinson, F., *The Castles of England* (London: G. Philip, 1973).

Wilson, C., *Anglo-Dutch Commerce and Finance in the Eighteenth Century* (Cambridge: Cambridge University Press, 1941).

—, *England's Apprenticeship 1603–1763*, 2nd edn (London: Longman, 1984).

Wilson, K., *The Sense of the People: Politics, Culture and Imperialism in England, 1715–1785* (Cambridge: Cambridge University Press, 1995).

Winslow, C., 'Sussex Smugglers', in D. Hay, P. Linebaugh, J. G. Rule, E. P. Thompson, and C. Winslow (eds), *Albion's Fatal Tree: Crime and Society in Eighteenth-Century England* (New York: Pantheon, 1975), pp. 119–66.

Wrigley, C. H., 'A Simple Model of London's Importance in Changing English Society and Economy, 1650–1750', *Past and Present*, 37 (1967), pp. 44–70.

INDEX

African garrisons, 31, 37, 50, 77
Albany, 38
Albemarle, second Earl of, see Keppel, William Anne
Alloa, 106
America, North, 23, 32, 55, 115, 124, 128, 132, 161–2
    contractors to, 46–7, 48, 49, 50, 69
    garrison supply in, 24, 25, 36–7, 38
    growth in number of contracts to, 31
    remittances to, 36
American independence, war of, 140, 149
ammunition, 10, 15, 96
Amyand, George, 123, 134, 151, 153, 154, 157, 159, 161
Amyand, John, 157
Annapolis Royal garrison, 24, 25
Argyll, Dukes of, see Campbell, Archibald; Campbell, General Sir John
armies
    growth of by eighteenth century, 7, 8–9, 21, 75–6, 139, 143
Army of Observation, 15
Articles of War, 25, 81, 112
Ashburnham, John, second Earl Ashburnham, 134
Atholl, Duke of, see Murray, James
Austria, 8, 30
Austrian succession, war of, 25–30, 63–4, 105

Bacon, Anthony, 50, 128, 132, 151, 152, 153, 154, 161
Baker, Jacob, 158
Baker, John, 158

Baker, Sir William (1705–70), 46, 50, 124, 132, 133, 136, 151, 152, 153, 154, 157, 159, 161
Baker, Sir William (1743–1824), 157, 158
bakers, 60, 64, 77–8, 83
Baldwin, William, horse-dealer, 93, 96, 131
Balmerino, Lord, see Elphinstone, Arthur
barracks, 17, 73, 74–5, 82, 102, 104–5, 108, 112–13
    capacity, 74
    fewer in England than Ireland and Scotland, 73
    opposition to, 74–5
    poor condition of, 82, 115–16
    in Scotland, 104–5, 108, 112–13, 115–17
Barrack Master General (Scotland), 104–5; see also Leslie, Thomas
Barrington, William Wildman, second Viscount Barrington, 8–9, 32, 37, 62, 68, 69, 80, 82, 84, 113, 116
Beauclerk, Lord George, 113, 118
Beckford, William, 141
Benson, John, horse-dealer, 97
Bermuda garrison, 23
Bernera, 112
Bill of Rights (1689), 16
Blackness Castle, 116
Blakeney, William, first Baron Blakeney, 35
Bland, Humphrey, 27, 109, 110, 112, 117, 118
Boghurst, John, 66, 87, 131
Boyd, William, fourth Earl of Kilmarnock, 117
Boyle, Roger, first Earl of Orrery, 9
Braemar Castle, 112, 115

– 255 –

bread, 2, 3, 11, 12, 17, 18, 24, 26, 27–9, 31, 31, 46, 61–4, 66–7, 75, 77, 79, 80–3, 93, 107, 150
  adulteration, 83
  'ammunition' bread, 60
  prices, 67, 80, 85–6, 88, 95, 106, 108, 110, 114, 147
  rye bread, 78, 82, 83
bread wagons, 11, 18, 26, 30, 31, 36, 62, 63, 66–7, 76, 79, 81, 86, 88, 93, 94, 95, 96, 108, 114, 115, 121, 122
  capacity of, 29, 77
  expense of, 12, 28, 32, 110
  usage of, 29, 60, 61, 80
Bristow, Catherine, 134
Bristow, John, 36, 49, 123, 125, 126, 130, 131, 133, 134, 151, 153, 154, 159, 161
British army, 1, 2, 6, 11, 25–8, 31, 56, 74–6, 83, 104, 121, 139–40, 143–4
  accommodation of, 18–19
  augmentation of, 75–6
  constitutional restrictions and opposition to permanent force, 16, 21, 149
  experience of military officers in, 27, 71
  lack of central direction, 16
Brownlow, Baron, see Cust, John
Brunswick, Duke of, Prince Ferdinand, 148
Brydges, Sir Henry, second Earl of Carnarvon, 134
Bulkeley, Thomas James, Baron of Beaumaris, 134
Bull and Mouth Inn, London, 89–90, 100–1
Burke, Edmund, 140
Burrell, Merrick, 132, 151, 153, 154, 157, 159, 161
Burrell, Peter (1692–1756), 43, 44, 49, 125, 126, 142, 151, 153, 154, 159, 161
Burrell, Peter, junior (1724–75), 43
Burrell, Sir Peter, Baron Gwydir (1754–1820), 135, 157, 158
Burrell, William, 157, 158
Bute, Earl of, see Stuart, John

Calcraft, John, 50–1, 84, 93–4, 97, 98, 117
Campbell, Archibald, third Duke of Argyll, 111–12, 113, 117
Campbell, General Sir John, fourth Duke of Argyll, 65

Campbell, John, fourth Earl Loudoun, 47, 117
Canso garrison, 25
Cape Breton, 53
Carnarvon, Earl of, see Brydges, Sir Henry
Carpentier, Nicholas, 26, 28
Carteret, John, second Earl Granville, 27, 28, 129
castles, 73
Cavendish, William, fourth Duke of Devonshire, 71
Charles II, King of England, Scotland, and Ireland, 74
Chartered Companies, 43, 125, 142, 159
Chatham, Earl of, see Pitt, William
Chelsea Hospital, 50
Churchill, George, 110
Churchill, John, first Duke of Marlborough, 9, 51, 64, 126
Colchester, 75
Colebrooke, Sir George, 45, 49, 56, 123, 124, 130, 131, 133, 136, 151, 152, 153, 154, 157, 159, 161
Colebrooke, Sir James, financier, 49, 123, 125, 132, 151, 152, 153, 154, 157, 161
Commissariat, 6, 8, 11, 12, 56, 58
commissaries, 11–12, 24, 29–30, 38, 53, 105, 106, 108, 109–14, 129, 130, 145, 160
  employment of at encampments, 62, 63, 65, 66, 67–9, 71, 76, 84, 93, 95
Commissary General of Stores, Provisions, and Forage, 29–30, 62, 63, 66, 67, 68, 71, 105, 129, 145, 160; see also Hume, Sir Abraham, first baronet
competitive tendering, 43–4, 46–7, 59–62, 85, 86, 118, 145, 146–7
Comptrollers of army accounts, 38, 52, 53, 54, 56, 63
contracts for victualling garrisons, 23–5, 32, 33–5, 46–9, 36–8, 64, 103–4, 142
  advance payments, 36, 52–3
  advantages of, 28, 144–5
  competition for, 126, 127
  difficulties in performing, 34–7, 139
  failures, 33–4
  fees payable, 62

fraud and collusion in, 37–8, 56, 58, 140–1
growth of in eighteenth century, 21, 23–5, 141–3
procedures for awarding, 47–8
Parliamentary debate on North American contracts, 46–7
payments, 53
political patronage in awarding, 41–2, 47, 50–2, 125, 146–7, 152
politicians profiting from, 50–2
price movements, 56–7
profitability of, 122–3, 125, 126, 127–8, 144–5
sectors, 2–3, 41, 42
sureties, 52–3
terms and conditions, 52–6, 146
contracts, remittance, 19–20, 35–6, 42–5
controversies, 44–5
King's involvement in allocating, 43
patronage in, 44–5
organization of, 35–6
personnel, 43
procedures in allocating, 43–4
terms and conditions, 42–3
contractors, victualling and remittance, 19–20, 26, 32, 35–6, 42–50, 60, 63–4, 65, 123, 135, 146
as members of Parliament, 49, 141–2, 151–5
as office-holders, 142, 160
bankruptcy of, 36
diverse economic interests of, 49, 50, 128
foreign merchants as, 26–7, 31, 48, 62
geographical specialization of, 49–50
heightened employment of, 11, 12, 13, 20–1, 30, 38–9
historiography concerning, 1–2, 6, 21, 121–2, 142, 150
honours, 134–5, 157
Irish, 48
London merchants as, 47–8, 122–3
longevity of, 125–6, 127–8, 148
mercantile activities commensurate with contracts, 42, 50, 57, 146
multiple capacities of, 1–3, 49
purchase of rural property, 131–3, 161–2
Scottish, 48
sons of attending university, 135–6, 158
unpopularity of, 140–1
urban mentality of, 133
Contractors Act (1782), 141, 143
convoys, 34–5, 36, 37, 54–5
Cope, Sir John, 27, 105
Corgarff Castle, 112, 115
Cornewall, Sir George, 157
'Country' politics, 19, 20, 143
credit, importance of, 12–13, 30, 32–3
Cromwell, Oliver, Lord Protector of England, Ireland, and Scotland, 10
Crowley, Sir Ambrose, 134
Crowley, Elizabeth, 134
Crowley, John, 134
Culloden, battle of, 75, 107, 111
Cumberland, Duke of, see William Augustus
Curtis, Joseph (c. 1715–71), biscuit baker, 136
Curtis, Sir William, 136
Cust, John, second Baron Brownlow of Belton, 134
Cust, Peregrine, 124, 132, 135, 151, 153, 154, 159, 161
customs duties, 19, 20
exemption from, 54

Dalrmyple, John, second Earl of Stair, 27
Defoe, Daniel, 91, 111, 121
Devonshire, Duke of, see Cavendish, William
'Direct Supply', 26
Disbanding Act (1699), 16
Drummond, Adam, 48, 132, 134, 151, 153, 154, 160, 161
Duart Castle, 112
Dumbarton Castle, 116
Dundas, Sir Lawrence, 29, 30, 31, 67, 70, 98, 110, 117, 118, 136, 141, 151, 152, 153, 154, 160
contracts in Scotland, 106–7, 108, 113
dispute with Richard Oswald, 65
honours, 135, 157
investments, 130
partnership with Scottish merchants, 65
performance of contracts, 148
political alignment, 130
property, 132, 133, 136, 161

recommendations of, 106–7, 108
relationship with military commanders, 109
seeks appointment as Barrack Master General, 108, 111–12
suspected of fraudulent practices, 108–9
unpopularity of, 130
wealth of, 118–19, 124, 129–30, 134
Dundas, Lawrence, first Earl of Zetland, 135
Dundas, Thomas, 106
Dundas, Sir Thomas, first Baron Dundas of Aske, 135, 157, 158
Dundee, 111

East India Company, 65, 124, 129, 130, 159
Economical Reform, 140, 141
Edinburgh, 106, 107, 109, 113, 114, 124, 129
Edinburgh Castle, 114, 115, 116, 118
Elphinstone, Arthur, sixth Lord Balmerino, 117
encampments (England)
administrative organization, 67–71, 82–3
as defence against invasion, 73, 75, 76, 80, 86
German troops, ill-feeling caused by presence of, 76
location of, 67, 73–4, 76, 93
militia in, 79–80
novelty of, 77
number of troops in, 77, 79–80
sanitary condition of, 81–2
selection of, 76
during Seven Years' War, 76–7
seventeenth-century, 74
in 1740–1, 75
as solution to accommodating army, 73, 76
sutlers in, 81
symbol of British military power, 59
years when formed, 59, 77
encampment contracts (England)
advance payments, 62–3
competent performance of, 85, 87, 148
experience in performing, 62
fees payable, 62
method of awarding, 59–62, 86–7
nature of supplying, 64
patronage, 64
payments, 63, 64, 67, 87
prices, 79, 80, 85–6, 88
products supplied, 60–1, 77–9, 81, 83, 88
sureties, 62–3
terms and conditions, 66–7
encampment contractors (England)
personnel, 63–4, 74, 148
Scots as, 64–5
sectoral expertise of, 60, 65–6, 74, 129
wealth of, 129–30
ergot poisoning, 83
Excise, 19, 20, 21
extraordinary expenditure, 13–15, 28, 29, 31, 32, 33
Eyles, Sir Joseph, 44

Falkirk, 106, 109
Falkirk, battle of, 106, 109
Family Compact, 80
Farnborough, Baron, *see* Long, Charles
'fiscal-military state', 1–2, 8, 9–10, 20, 89
Fisher, Brice, 124, 130, 132, 133, 151, 152, 153, 154, 159, 161
Fisher, Cuthbert, 100
Fitzherbert, Thomas, 99–100
Fitzwilliam, Lady Charlotte, 136
Fletcher, Andrew, Lord Milton, 109
Fludyer, George, 157
Fludyer, Sir Samuel, 124, 131, 133, 135, 151, 153, 154, 157, 159, 161
Fonnereau, Martyn, 157
Fonnereau, Phillip, 157, 158
Fonnereau, Thomas, 123, 125, 131, 151, 153, 154, 161
Fonnereau, Zachary, 123, 125, 131, 151, 153, 154, 159, 161
Foote, Samuel, 130
forage, 2, 11, 18, 26, 67–8, 75, 86, 89, 95, 109–10, 150, 160; *see also* encampment contracts
contracts, 17, 26, 30, 61, 63, 70, 85, 106, 107, 108, 147
difficulties in supplying, 27, 28, 29, 105, 106
expense of, 12, 28, 29, 30, 32, 56–7

fraud allegations concerning supply of, 83–5, 94, 109
Government subsidy of, 67
money, 27, 61
poor quality, 67, 83
price of, 85, 88
rations, 61, 70, 77, 78, 80, 83–5, 88, 92, 93, 95, 106, 114
surplus, 70, 78–9
volume supplied, 77, 81, 88, 92, 114
Forage Masters, 9, 27
foraging, 9, 28, 29, 107
Forbes, Duncan, 117
Fort Augustus, 112, 115
Fort George, 108, 110, 112, 113–14, 115–16, 116–17
Fort William, 110, 112, 114, 115
Fox, Henry, first Baron Holland of Foxley, 45, 50–1, 98, 112, 130, 146
France, 19, 27, 96
military supply in, 8, 10–11
Revolutionary wars, 74, 149
threat of invasion by, 73, 75, 79, 93–4, 113, 114, 147
wars with Britain, 7, 8
Franco, Abraham, 106
Franco, Jacob, 106
Fraser, Archibald Campbell, of Lovat, 31, 65, 87, 132
Fraser, Simon, eleventh Lord Lovat (1667/8–1747), 65, 117
Fraser, Simon (1726–82), 65, 134
Frederick II, King of Prussia, 55
Frederick Lewis, Prince of Wales, 111
Furnese, Sir Henry, 43

Gardiner, Robert, 109–11, 112, 113–14, 115, 117–19
competence of, 110, 112, 118
as contractor, 113–14
during Jacobite Rebellion, 109–10
George II, King of Great Britain and Ireland, and elector of Hanover, 27, 75, 108
George III, King of the United Kingdom of Great Britain and Ireland, and King of Hanover, 80
Georgia, 25, 35, 47, 50

Germain, George Sackville, first Viscount Sackville, 32, 117, 134
Germany, 43, 62, 65, 69, 75, 79, 82, 83, 92, 93, 96, 98, 107, 117, 129, 148, 160
expense of campaign in, 31–2
fraud in, 56–7
supply organization during the Seven Years' War, 6, 11, 26, 31, 77–8, 139
Gibraltar garrison, 50–1, 52, 53, 54–5, 144, 152; *see also* Revell, Thomas
coal contract, 50–1
considered most lucrative garrison contract, 64, 126, 127
contractors for, 44, 46, 47, 48
expenditure at, 146
shortages at, 23–4, 33–4, 35, 37
storehouses at, 34, 36
Gibson, Joseph, 97, 98
Gibson, William, 97
Godfrey, William, 68–9, 93, 95, 148
Gore, John, 44, 123, 124, 125, 126, 132, 133, 151, 152, 153, 155, 159, 161
Goree, 37; *see also* African garrisons
Government loans, 15, 19–20, 32–3, 43, 45, 130; *see also* loan merchants
Granville, Earl, *see* Carteret, John
Grenville, George, 146
Grisewood, George, 96–7
Guadeloupe, 31
Guest, Joshua, 105, 108, 109, 111
Guernsey, 76
Gulston, Joseph (c. 1694–1766), 125–6, 133, 135, 151, 153, 155, 158, 159, 161
Gulston, Joseph (c. 1744–86), 133, 158

Haldane, Robert, 65, 67, 117
Halifax, 36, 38
Hanbury, John, 49
Hanoverian troops, 76, 77
Hardwicke, first Earl of, *see* Yorke, Philip
Hare, James, 136
Harrington, Earl of, *see* Stanhope, William
Harris, James, first Earl of Malmesbury, 134
Hawke, Edward, first Baron Hawke, 94
Hawley, Henry, 105, 106
Hay, John, second Marquess of Tweeddale, 111
Hemming, Bright, 99–100

Henniker, John (1724–1803), 49, 135, 151, 153, 155, 169, 161
Henniker, John (1752–1821), 157, 158
Hessian troops, 70, 76, 77
Hollamby, William, 97
Holland, first Baron, *see* Fox, Henry
Holles-Pelham, Thomas, Duke of Newcastle, 15, 28, 43, 50, 55, 71, 80, 81, 94, 115, 126, 142
　criticized over North American contracts, 46–7
　and employment of contractors, 126
　and expense of war, 32, 33, 56–7
　patronage of, 49, 101, 111, 113, 125
　removal from office, 45, 118, 130, 146
Holmes, Henry, 64
Honywood, Sir Philip, 27
horses, 8, 9, 10, 15, 17, 18, 27, 28, 32, 61, 62, 63, 67, 68, 69, 76, 77, 78, 83–4, 88, 89–90, 94, 101, 104, 107, 108, 129, 132; *see also* encampment contracts
　contracts for, 2, 3, 30, 93, 95–7, 99–100, 110, 113–15, 117–18, 130
　dealers in, 95–8, 133, 148
　demand for, 97–8
Hounslow Heath, 75
Hume, Sir Abraham, first baronet (*c.* 1703–72), 29, 30, 31, 80, 84, 127, 136, 148, 151, 152, 153, 157, 159, 160, 161; *see also* Commissary General of Stores, Provisions, and Forage
　on government attitude towards military supply officials, 70–1
　importance to supply system, 67–8, 82–3
　during Jacobite Rebellion of 1745/6, 105, 106–7
　mercantile experience of, 26, 129
　wealth of, 132, 133, 134
Hume, Sir Abraham, second baronet (1749–1838), 136, 157, 158
Hume, Alexander, 26
Hume, Amelia, 134
Hume, Sophia, 134
Huske, John, 27

Ingram, Charles, ninth Viscount Irwin, 134
Insurance, 43, 54–5, 146
Inversnaid, 112

Ireland, 6, 10, 11, 35, 58, 105, 132, 136
　military establishment of, 16
　market for provisions, 48
　invasion threat, 73
Irwin, Viscount, *see* Ingram, Charles
Isle of Man, 50
Isle of Wight, 64, 79, 92

Jacobite rebellion (1715), 11, 12, 15, 104, 105, 111
Jacobite rebellion (1745–6), 11, 75, 105–10
Jacobites, employment of, 108
Jacobitism, decline of, 104
Jamaica garrison, 23, 35, 44
James II and VII (1633–1701), King of England, Scotland, and Ireland, 74
Jenkinson, Charles, first Earl of Liverpool, 25, 87
Jersey, 76
Jervis, John, Earl of St Vincent, 92
Jones, Robert, 151, 152, 153, 155, 159, 161
Johnston, James, 25

Keppel, William Anne, second Earl of Albemarle, 107, 108, 109
Kilby, Christopher, 50
Kilmarnock, Earl of, *see* Boyd, William
Kynynmound, Gilbert Elliot Murray, first Earl of Minto, 134

Land Tax, 19
Lauderdale, Earl of, *see* Maitland, Charles
Legge, Henry Bilson, 45
Leith, 105, 106
Lennox, Charles, eighth Duke of Richmond, 75, 81, 84
Leslie, Thomas, 64, 116–17, 151, 152, 153, 160, 161
　barracks contracts, 112–13, 116, 118–19
　beneficiary of patronage, 111–13
　competition for position of Barrack Master, 111–12
　privileged position of, 112–13, 115–17, 118
　responsibilities of Barrack Master, 105
Leslie, John ninth Earl of Rothes (1679–1722), 111

Leslie, John, tenth Earl of Rothes (c. 1698–1767), 26, 111
Ligonier, John, Earl Ligonier, 18, 27, 61, 80, 83, 84, 92, 93, 96, 116–17
Linlithgow, 109–10
Linwood, Nicholas, 98, 124, 125, 133, 151, 153, 155, 159, 160, 161
Lisbon, 43, 126, 131
Liverpool, Earl of, *see* Jenkinson, Charles
Lloyd, Sir Richard, 134
loan merchants, *see also* City of London
   as contractors, 32–3, 125
   unpopularity of, 19
London, City of, 12, 32–3, 43, 44, 122–3, 125
London Gazette, 46
Long, Charles, Baron Farnborough, 134
Loudoun, Lord, *see* Campbell, John
Louisbourg garrison, 25, 31
Lovat, Lord, *see* Fraser, Simon
Low Countries, 25–7, 29, 43, 63–4, 75
Lumley-Saunderson, Thomas, Earl of Scarborough, 134

magazines, 10–11, 27–8, 61, 63, 66, 78, 92, 93, 95, 106, 107, 116, 121, 122
   inspectors of, 29–30, 68
   Superintendent and Keeper of, 69–70, 160
Maitland, Charles, sixth Earl of Lauderdale, 106
Major, John, 134, 135, 151, 152, 153, 155, 157, 159, 161
Malmesbury, Earl of, *see* Harris, James
Mann, Sir Horatio (Horace), 19
Marlborough, Dukes of, *see* Churchill, John; Spencer, Charles
Martyr, John, 61, 66, 87, 131
Masterton, James, 106, 118
Mellish, Joseph, 124, 133, 151, 153, 155, 161
Mellish, William, 137, 157
'merchant-attorneys', 26, 118
'military enterprisers', 8
military expenditure, 7–8, 12–16, 19, 20, 31–2, 143
'military revolution', 9–11

military supply
   historical background of, 9, 10
   organization of in Britain, 8, 17–18, 20–1, 139, 144
   relationship with logistics, 2, 9–11, 21, 31–2, 38, 77, 103–4, 143–4
Minorca garrison, 23–4, 25, 36, 37, 75, 101, 125
   contractors for, 44, 47, 48, 49, 126
   locally supplied, 24
   poor condition of buildings at, 36
Minto, Earl of, *see* Kynynmound, Gilbert Elliot Murray
Missing, Thomas, 47
Monck, George, first Duke of Albemarle, 10
Munro, George, 113–14
Murray, James, Duke of Atholl, 134
Mutiny Acts, 16, 18

Namier, Sir Lewis, 2, 98, 122, 142, 152
Naseby, battle of, 10
National Debt, 33, 139
Navigation Laws, 25
navy, *see also* Victualling Office
   method of awarding contracts, 46
   permanent establishment and organization of, 16–17
   as senior service of British military forces, 15–16
Nesbitt, Arnold, 48, 49, 123, 125, 128, 132, 133, 141, 151, 153, 155, 162
Nesbitt, John, politician, 157
Newbury, 75
Newcastle, Duke of, *see* Holles-Pelham, Thomas
Newfoundland garrison, 23, 30
New Model Army, 10
New Providence garrison, 25
New York garrison, 23, 38
North, Frederick (Lord North), second Earl of Guilford, 140
Nottet, Pierre, 26–7
Nova Scotia garrison, 23, 30, 35–6, 46, 50, 132

'off-reckonings', 18
Oglethorpe, James Edward, 50
O'Hara, James, second Baron Tyrawley, 84

'old corruption', 1–2, 4, 21, 42, 59, 89, 147
Ordnance, Board of, 15, 16, 20, 30, 34, 115
    contracts, 13, 17, 18, 48, 110, 129
    and competitive tendering, 145
Orford, Earls of, *see* Walpole, Sir Robert; Walpole, Horatio
Ostend Company, 129
Oswald, Richard, 67, 95, 98, 130, 131–2, 136, 142, 148
    as contractor, 62–3, 78, 86, 87, 92, 96
    dispute with Lawrence Dundas, 65
    part of Scottish mercantile network, 65
    wealth of, 129, 130, 131

Pardo, Convention of, 44
Parliament
    control of military finance, 9, 13–14, 16, 143
    enquiry into North American contracts, 46–7
    role in voting military estimates, 13–14, 16, 17
Paulet, Lady Katherine, 134
Pelham, Henry, 30, 44–5, 100, 108, 109, 111–12, 134
Perth, 105, 107, 115
Petty, William, second Earl of Shelburne, 140
Pitt, William, first Earl of Chatham, 71, 94, 145, 150
    threatens to impeach Duke of Newcastle, 56
Place Act (1742), 126
Placentia garrison, 24, 25
Poole, Sir Ferdinando, 100–1
Port Mahon, 126, 127
Portugal, 15, 43, 49
prostitutes, 82
Prussia, 30

Quebec, 36–7

Rattan, 25, 34, 53
regimental agents, 35, 50, 65, 69, 70, 84, 86, 117; *see also* Ross, George; Calcraft, John
Restoration, 9

Revell, Thomas, 47, 54, 126–7, 134, 151, 152, 153, 155, 159, 160, 162
Rich, Sir Robert, 111
Richelieu, Cardinal, 10
Richmond, Duke of, *see* Lennox, Charles
Rockingham, Marquess of, *see* Wentworth, Charles Watson-
Romilly Sir Samuel, 124
Ross, George, 65, 117–18
Rothes, Earls of, *see* Leslie, John (ninth Earl); Leslie, John (tenth Earl)
Royal Africa Company, 127, 159
Royal Exchange Assurance, 129, 159
Russia Company, 159

Sackville, Lord George, *see* Germain, George
St Vincent, Earl of, *see* Jervis, John
Sargent, John, 136
Scarborough, Earl of, *see* Lumley-Saunderson, Thomas
Scotland, 5, 10, 11, 30, 35, 61 64, 65, 74, 96, 129, 130, 136, 144, 147, 148, 149, 152, 160, 161; *see also* Jacobite rebellion (1715); Jacobite rebellion (1745)
    barracks in, 104–5, 115–16
    composition of contracting personnel in, 119
    encampments in, 108, 115–16
    loyalty to Hanoverian dynasty in, 104, 108, 111, 119
    number of troops in, 104, 107, 115
    patronage in allocating contracts in, 112–13, 118
    scarcity in, 106, 113
    supply organization in, 103–5, 106–7, 116–17
    threat of invasion of, 73, 113–14
Scotland, Royal Bank of, 35
Secretary at War, 17, 27, 62, 75; *see also* Barrington, William Wildman
Senegal, 37; *see also* African garrisons
Sephardic Jews, 11, 63–4, 107
Septennial Act (1716), 153
Serra, Jacob Gomez, 107
Seven Years' War, 3, 4, 6, 11, 18, 26, 31, 36, 55, 121, 128, 142, 148
    contracts for horses during, 95–8, 115, 118

encampment contracts during, 59–63, 64–71, 73–4, 75–88, 92–5
growth of contracting during, 31–2
military expenditure of, 15, 19–20, 31–2, 139–40
Scotland during the, 113–17
Shelburne, Earl of, *see* Petty, William
Sheriffmuir, battle of, 111
Sick and Wounded Office (Navy), 16, 46
siege warfare, 9
South Sea Company, 44, 123, 129, 142, 159
Spain, 7, 24, 25, 44, 124
Spanish succession, war of, 12, 23, 27, 75, 83
Spencer, Charles, third Duke of Marlborough, 26, 43
Stair, Earl of, *see* Dalrymple, John
Stanhope, William, first Earl of Harrington, 26
Stanley, Hans, 47
States General of the United Provinces, 28, 29
Stirling, 105, 106, 109
Stirling Castle, 115, 116
Stuart, John, third Earl of Bute, 56, 117, 125, 130
Sun Fire Office, 159
sutlers, 9–10, 20, 25, 60, 75, 81, 115; *see also* encampments (England)
Swift, Jonathan, 12

Tangier garrison, 46
taxation, 8, 19–20, 143
Tellier, François-Michel le, marquis of Louvois, 10
Tellier, Michel le, 10
Tewkesbury, Samuel, 66, 87, 129, 131
Thomlinson, John, 49
Touchet, Samuel, 50, 124, 125, 151, 152, 153, 155, 159, 160, 162
Townshend, Charles, 114–15
Townsend, Chauncy, 49, 50, 54, 127, 131, 132, 136, 151, 152, 153, 155, 162
Townsend, James, 157
Townsend, Joseph, 158
Treasury, 13, 16, 20, 25, 28, 50, 70, 78, 82, 85, 92, 100–1, 102, 103, 109, 113, 114, 116–17, 123, 126, 140, 146, 152

accused of mismanagement of Commissariat, 56
additional allowances made by, 54, 128
and allocation of contracts, 31, 52, 145
bargaining power of, 53–4
concern for economy, 42, 54–5, 66, 70–1, 79, 80, 128, 146, 147
contracts for 'non-military' supplies, 17, 26, 36, 37, 42
identifies potential contractors, 41, 57, 146
inexperience in awarding contracts, 23–4, 27, 33–4, 46
method of awarding encampment contracts, 59–63, 67–8, 87, 93, 94 95, 147
method of awarding remittance contracts, 42–4
method of awarding victualling contracts, 46–8, 49
warns against corrupt practices, 51–2, 55
warns against making improvident bargains, 26, 56–7
Trotter, John (d. 1790), 69, 86, 132
Trotter, John (1757–1833), 86, 137, 149
Tweeddale, Marquess of, *see* Hay, John
Tyrawley, Baron, *see* O'Hara, James

Utrecht, Treaty of (1713), 23, 46

venereal disease, 82
Vere, Beauclerk, Baron Vere of Hanworth, 134
Vernon, Edward, 30
Victualling Office (Navy), 16, 33–4, 47, 51, 59, 61, 126, 144
advises Treasury on making contracts, 46
as garrison supplier, 23–4, 34, 36–7
Votes of Credit, 15

Wade, George, 29, 75
Walpole, Horatio (Horace), fourth Earl of Orford, 19, 121–2
Walpole, Sir Robert, first Earl of Orford, 124
foreign policy of, 15
and irregular contracts, 51
patronage of, 44, 50, 51, 126

Walpole, Thomas (1727–1803), 124, 133, 151, 152, 153, 155, 159, 162
Walpole, Thomas (1755–1840), 158
War Office, 18, 20, 63, 76, 82, 84, 85, 93, 116
  as coordinating centre of army administration, 17, 36
  economy at the, 69
Warren, George, 134
Warrington, John, 83, 92, 93, 95–7, 98, 99, 131, 133
Watson, David, 76
wealth
  contracting as a means towards, 121–2, 131, 136–7, 149–50
  pre-existing, 123–4
  regional imbalance of, 122–3
  and social mobility, 133–4, 135–7
  usage of, 130–1
Wentworth, Charles Watson-, second Marquess of Rockingham, 136
West, James, 114, 127
West Kerse, Stirlingshire, 129–30
Willan, John (1711–92), 89–102
  business interests, 65–6, 89–92, 95–6, 98–100
  contract proposals (1757), 92
  disposal of property, 98–9
  dispute over estate, 99
  encampment contract (1759), 93–5
  fraud allegations, 83–5, 94
  influence on family, 90, 100, 102
  landholding, 91–2, 95
  wealth of, 90–1, 98, 101, 129
Willan, John (1746–1823), 99, 101
  as mail coach contractor, 90, 100
Willan, Thomas, 90, 99, 100, 101–2
Willan, William (d. 1780), inn-holder, 100
Willan, William, 99, 101
William III and II, King of England, Scotland, and Ireland, and Prince of Orange, 11–12, 43
William Augustus, Prince, Duke of Cumberland, 16, 18, 29, 67–8, 69, 78, 84, 89–90, 91, 105, 106–9, 112–13
Windsor, 75
Wolfe, James, 81–2
Woodford, Matthew, 47, 127, 128

Yorke, Philip, first Earl of Hardwicke, 15, 55, 94, 115, 142